Adjusting to Global Economic Volatility

Published by
ACADEMIC FOUNDATON
in association with

sanei
South Asia Network of Economic Research Institutes
www.saneinetwork.net

South Asia Network of
Economic Research Institutes
(SANEI), Bangladesh

Adjusting to Global Economic Volatility

The Case of South Asia

Edited by

MUSTAFA K. MUJERI

WAHIDUDDIN MAHMUD

ACADEMIC FOUNDATION

NEW DELHI

www.academicfoundation.com

First published in 2014
by

ACADEMIC FOUNDATION
4772-73 / 23 Bharat Ram Road, (23 Ansari Road),
Darya Ganj, New Delhi - 110 002 (India).
Phones : 23245001 / 02 / 03 / 04.
Fax : +91-11-23245005.
E-mail : books@academicfoundation.com
www.academicfoundation.com

in association with
South Asia Network of Economic Research Institutes (SANEI), Bangladesh.

Disclaimer:
The findings/views/opinions expressed in this book are solely those of the authors and do not necessarily reflect the views of the publisher.

Cataloging in Publication Data--DK
Courtesy: D.K. Agencies (P) Ltd. <docinfo@dkagencies.com>

Adjusting to global economic volatility : the case of South Asia / edited by Mustafa K. Mujeri, Wahiduddin Mahmud.
p. cm.
Contributed articles.
ISBN 9789332701649

1. Financial crisis--South Asia. 2. Recessions--South Asia. 3. South Asia--Economic integration. 4. South Asian cooperation. I. Mujeri, Mustafa K. II. Mahmud, Wahiduddin. III. South Asia Network of Economic Research Institutes (SANEI).

DDC 338.5420954 23

Typeset by Italics India, New Delhi.

Printed and bound by The Book Mint, New Delhi.
www.thebookmint.in

CONTENTS

LIST OF TABLES AND FIGURES

Tables

Figures

Editors/Contributors

Editors:

Mustafa K. Mujeri is the Director-General of the Bangladesh Institute of Development Studies (BIDS), and Coordinator of the SANEI, the South Asian regional arm of the Global Development Network (GDN). He obtained his PhD in Economics from McMaster University in Canada. Before joining BIDS, he served as the Chief Economist of the Bangladesh Bank (country's central bank), and United Nations Development Programme (UNDP) Advisor in Cambodia. Earlier, he served as Research Director at the Centre on Integrated Rural Development for Asia and the Pacific (CIRDAP), a regional inter-governmental organisation; national expert in the Bangladesh Planning Commission; and Professor of Economics at the University of Rajshahi. Dr Mujeri has extensive research experience in different areas of economics, especially in development economics, poverty and macro policy analysis, and application of modelling and quantitative techniques in development issues. He has to his credit a large number of publications in reputed journals at home and abroad.

Wahiduddin Mahmud (PhD in economics, Cambridge University, 1978) has recently retired as professor of economics at Dhaka University. He is currently a member of the UN Committee for Development Policy (UN CDP), and a Country Advisor to International Growth Centre at the London School of Economics. He has held visiting research appointments at, among other institutions, the World Bank, the UNDP,

Institute of Development Studies at Sussex University, and International Food Policy Research Institute. He is a founder and former Chairman of PKSF, the apex microfinance funding institution in Bangladesh. He was a member of the Caretaker Government of Bangladesh in 1996 in charge of the ministries of finance and planning. His books include *Adjustment and Beyond: the Reform Experience in South Asia* (Palgrave-Macmillan for International Economic Association), *Handbook on the South Asian Economies* (Edward Elgar), *Seasonality of Hunger and Public Policies* (World Bank publications) and *The Theory and Practice of Microcredit* (Routledge, forthcoming).

Contributors:

Nisha Arunatilake is a Research Fellow and Head of Labour, Employment and Human Resources Development research at Institute of Policy Studies (IPS), Sri Lanka. Her research and publications cover various dimensions of development, especially in areas of education, health, labour, employment and social protection. She has collaborated with, and been a consultant to the World Bank, Asian Development Bank Institute (ADBI), International Labour Organization (ILO), Save the Children, and the German Technical Cooperation (GTZ) in numerous research studies. She has served on national level committees on labour, employment, human resource development, health sector reform, and tobacco and alcohol policy formulation. At present, she is serving on the National Advisory Committee on Manpower Planning of the Ministry of Labour Relations and Manpower Planning. Nisha holds a BSc in Computer Science and Mathematics with *summa cum laude* from the University of the South, USA and an MA and PhD in Economics from Duke University, USA.

Bhuban B. Bajracharya, PhD from Delhi School of Economics, is an independent development economist. He served as a professor at the Center for Economic Development and Administration,

Tribhuban University. He has worked for several government agencies like the National Planning Commission and Ministry of Finance, and also for other development organisations like ADB, UNDP, International Center for Integrated Mountain Development (ICIMOD), Danish International Development Agency (DANIDA), Swiss Development Cooperation, World Bank, UN Economic and Social Commission for Asia and the Pacific (ESCAP). Having more than 30 years of experience in research and consultancy, his completed assignments are in the fields of national planning, poverty analysis, programme coordination and management, fiscal policy, monitoring and evaluation, and socioeconomic analysis.

Arindam Banik is presently Distinguished Professor and Dean (Research), International Management Institute (IMI), Bhubaneswar, India. He has been a consultant to a number of Indian companies, Government of India and multilateral institutions, including Associated Cement Companies, Ministry of Rural Development, World Bank, ILO South Asia Advisory Team (ILO-SAAT), International Development Research Centre (IDRC), Canadian International Research Agency (CIDA), and United Nations Industrial Development Organization (UNIDO). He has worked as consultant in St. Lucia, Trinidad and Tobago, Grenada, Bangladesh and Nepal. His current research includes global financial imbalances, international finance, poverty reduction strategies, technology transfer and skill development in developing economies. Author of more than 100 scientific articles on international economics, macroeconomics and economic development, his articles have appeared in journals of international repute. His latest book is "Foreign Capital Inflows to China, India and the Caribbean-Trends, Assessments and Determinants" (co-authored with Pradip K. Bhaumik).

Pradip K. Bhaumik, a Fellow of the Indian Institute of Management, Ahmedabad, India (equivalent to PhD), earned his BTech in Mechanical Engineering from the Indian Institute of Technology, Delhi, and pursued a post-graduate programme in Industrial Engineering at National Productivity Council (NPC), Delhi. He has more than 25 years of experience in teaching, research and consultancy at IMI. Prior to joining IMI, he was a senior consultant with the NPC. He has also been a consultant to many Indian companies including MNCs (multi-national corporations) and also to international organisations like UNDP, United States Agency for International Development (USAID), and GTZ. His research interests are varied and include issues like international trade, investment, innovation and R&D management, as well as topics like supply chain management, goal programming, game theory, regulation, management of projects and multivariate analysis applications in management. He has extensively published work in journals (both international and national), book chapters and conference proceedings. His latest book is "Foreign Capital Inflows to China, India and the Caribbean-Trends, Assessments and Determinants" (co-authored with Arindam Banik).

Nimai Das is currently TTI Fellow (Assistant Professor) at the Institute of Economic Growth, India. He is a doctorate in economics and involved in postdoctoral research on environmental resource economics and public economics. He has been a Fellow at the Centre for Studies in Social Sciences (CSSS), Calcutta and Centre for Economic Studies, Presidency College, Kolkata, India. His publications cover a wide range of international publishing houses like Elsevier, Routledge, Springer, Oxford, Sage, etc. He prepared an approach paper on climate change implications in tea economy for the 20th Food and Agriculture Organization's Intergovernmental Group (FAO IGG) on tea.

Namrata Ghosh is a Research Fellow at India Development Foundation (IDF), Gurgaon. At IDF, she is involved with research in areas of poverty, financial inclusion, cash transfers and market integration. She is also the managing editor of a peer-reviewed journal, *Review of Market Integration*, brought out by IDF thrice in a year. She is a post graduate in economics from Delhi School of Economics.

Naved Hamid is Director, Centre for Research in Economics and Business (CREB) and Professor at the Lahore School of Economics. He has served on various working groups and advisory panels of the government and boards of not-for-profit organisations. He has previously worked at the Asian Development Bank, Manila, Lahore University of Management Sciences (LUMS), and the Punjab University. He has a PhD in Economics from Stanford University, US, and BA (Hons) from University of Cambridge.

Noorulain Hanif has worked with a public policy think tank for the Ministry of Commerce, Pakistan. During her work experience, she has conducted various local and international research projects/studies with a high policy relevance. She has been part of the team that developed the Trade Policy of Pakistan (Strategic Trade Policy Framework 2009-2011). She has also worked with the team to review the progress and implementation status of the Trade Policy of Pakistan.

Monzur Hossain is currently Senior Research Fellow at BIDS. He obtained his Master's in public policy and PhD in international economics from the National Graduate Institute for Policy Studies (GRIPS), Japan. His primary research interests include: applied macroeconomics, international economics (trade and finance), and banking sector. He also has research interests in the ICT sector, the local government, and impact evaluation of development projects. He has published many scholarly articles in domestic and international journals.

Sheikh Md. Monzurul Huq, Professor (Full), Department of Geography and Environment, Jahangirnagar University, Bangladesh.

Yasin Janjua has been teaching core courses in Economics and Econometrics at University of New Brunswick at Saint John, Canada, and York University in Canada, since 2011. In 2010-11, he headed a public policy think tank, Centre for Poverty Reduction and Social Policy Development (CPRSPD), worked at the Planning Commission of Pakistan, and launched Pakistan MDG Report 2010. In the past, he has also worked as a Development Economist with the CIDA, and as a consultant at the World Bank. As an entrepreneur, he has established a policy research firm Centre for Research on Economic and Social Transformation (CREST) in Pakistan for advising governments and international development agencies. He holds an MA in Economics from Kansas State University, US.

Suwendrani Jayaratne is currently a Research Officer at the IPS, working in the International Economic Policy Unit. Since joining the IPS, in 2008, her research interests have been in the areas of international economics and trade, trade facilitation, regional integration and macroeconomic policy. She holds a BA (Hons) in Economics from the University of Peradeniya, Sri Lanka and an MA in International and Development Economics from the Australian National University (ANU), Australia.

Priyanka Jayawardena is a Research Officer at IPS, with research interests in education and skills development, labour market analysis, inequality analysis, health economics and child nutrition. She holds a BSc (Hons) in Statistics and an MA in Economics from the University of Colombo, Sri Lanka.

Roshini Jayaweera joined the IPS, Sri Lanka, in 2006, and is currently serving as a Research Officer. She has been involved in a number of projects and national level surveys. Her key research interests are: poverty impact assessment, development studies, social security, microfinance, micro-insurance, and migration. She holds a BA (Hons) in Economics from the University of Peradeniya, Sri Lanka and an MSc in Economics from the National University of Singapore.

Saibal Kar is Associate Professor of Economics at the CSSS, Calcutta, and a Research Fellow at the Institute for the Study of Labor, Germany. His research interests are mainly in labour and international economics, with publications in leading journals. A fellow of the Humboldt Foundation, he held visiting positions in Santa Fe Institute, Amsterdam School of Economics, United Nation University World Institute for Development Economics Research (UNU-WIDER), University of East Anglia, etc. He received the Canada Asia-Pacific Award in 2011.

Mahreen Mahmud is a doctoral student of Economics at University of Kent UK and did her Masters in Finance and Economics from the University of Warwick UK. Her PhD thesis is on small scale finance and behaviour of recipients. Previously, she worked on topics related to trade, remittances and Pakistani financial market during her time as a Research Fellow at CREB, Lahore School of Economics.

Minhaj Mahmud is currently Head of Research, BRAC Institute of Governance and Development (BIGD), BRAC University, Bangladesh. He completed his PhD in Economics from the University of Gothenburg, Sweden (2005) and MA in Economics from the University of Manitoba, Canada (1999). He has previously held academic and research positions at Queen's University of Belfast, UK; Keele University, UK; BRAC University, Bangladesh; Jahangirnagar University, Bangladesh; and BIDS, Bangladesh. He was visiting professor at the University of Tokyo, Japan and Jawaharlal Nehru University, India. He is also an adjunct faculty of Development Studies Department at the University of Dhaka.

Sadia Mariam Malik, PhD in Economics, is currently Assistant Professor at York University, Canada. She is also Vice-

President of CREST, Pakistan. In the past, she has held positions as Director, Mahbub ul Haq Human Development Centre (2006–2009), Pakistan, and Consultant, Pakistan Institute of Development Economics (PIDE). Her research interests include: human development, health inequality, conflict, poverty, institutions, and climate change.

D. Narayana, Director, Gulati Institute of Finance and Taxation, Thiruvathapuram, Kerala, India.

Krishna Prasad Pant, PhD in Agricultural Economics, is working as an Agricultural Policy Expert at FAO in Kathmandu. Earlier, he served in the Ministry of Agricultural Development in Nepal as an Economist, Senior Economist, and Joint Secretary. He also teaches Environmental Economics at Kathmandu University Nepal, and Cost Benefit Analysis at Tribhuvan University, Nepal. He was born in a remote hill area of Dhading district in Nepal.

Maliha Quddus, Research Associate, Pakistan Institute of Trade and Development, Pakistan.

Farhana Rafiq is currently Assistant Professor at the Department of Economics, American International University, Bangladesh. She has obtained her Bachelor and Master's degrees in Economics from Jahangirnagar University, Bangladesh, and Master's in Public Policy from GRIPS, Japan. She has academic and research interests in macroeconomics, public economics and labour economics.

S. Irudaya Rajan, is Chair Professor, Ministry of Overseas Indian Affairs (MOIA) Research Unit on International Migration, Centre for Development Studies (CDS), Thiruvananthapuram, Kerala. He has three decades of research experience and has coordinated seven major migration surveys in Kerala (with Prof K.C. Zachariah); has published books and articles on social, economic and demographic implications on international migration. He is editor of the annual series

India Migration Report and also a global journal, *Migration and Development*.

Partha Pratim Sahu is currently an Associate Professor with the Gujarat Institute of Development Research, Ahmedabad, India. He holds a PhD in Economics from the Jawaharlal Nehru University, India. His research interests include: issues related to industry, labour and employment. He has published papers in many peer reviewed journals, delivered lectures on quantitative and qualitative research methods, and also been associated with a number of research studies supported by international and national agencies.

Safdar Sohail, Director-General, Trade Policy, Ministry of Commerce, Government of Pakistan, Islamabad, Pakistan.

Syed Naimul Wadood is currently an Associate Professor at the Department of Economics, University of Dhaka. He obtained his PhD in Economics from North Carolina State University, US in 2004, and MSS and BSS (Hons) degrees in Economics from University of Dhaka in 1997 and 1995, respectively. He teaches advanced microeconomics courses. His principal research interests are empirical development microeconomics, micro market structure, remittances and migration issues.

Dushni Weerakoon is currently the Deputy Director and Head of Macroeconomic Policy Research at IPS. Since joining the institute in 1994, her research and publications have covered areas related to regional trade integration, macroeconomic policy, and international economics. She has extensive experience working in policy development committees and official delegations of the Government of Sri Lanka including as a member of the Macro and Trade Policy Steering Committee of the Ministry of Policy Development and Implementation and as an official delegate to the Committee of Experts to negotiate the South Asian Free Trade Agreement. She also served on the Trade and Tariff Committee of the

National Council for Economic Development (NCED) of the Ministry of Finance, Sri Lanka. She has worked as a consultant for international organisations such as the ADB, the World Bank, the ESCAP, and UNDP. Currently, she serves on the Board of Directors of the Nations Trust Bank (NTB) as well as the Centre for Poverty Analysis (CEPA) in Sri Lanka. Dushni holds a BSc in Economics from the Queen's University of Belfast, UK, and an MA and PhD in Economics from the University of Manchester, UK.

Preface

South Asia presents an interesting case study for development. While it is the second fastest growing region in the world, it is also the home to the largest concentration of people living in poverty. Even though the poverty rates in South Asian countries have declined with economic growth, poverty has not fallen fast enough to significantly reduce the number of poor people in the region. Moreover, despite variations across countries, social indicators such as human development, child and maternal health, and gender parities in general have not kept up with the pace of income growth. Thus, notwithstanding the fact that South Asia is fast becoming an emerging global economic powerhouse, it is yet to make a significant dent in poverty, human misery and deprivations, and gender disparities.

Although South Asia as a region has significant diversities in many respects and the performance of the countries differs, it is widely recognised that regional cooperation is vital for the region to prosper and fulfill the development objectives of individual countries. For widening such cooperation, cross-country findings especially in areas as complex as impact of financial crisis and regional trade can open up useful areas for win-win collaborations.

The present volume, which is an outcome of collaborative research of South Asian researchers under the guidance of well reputed South Asian professionals, contains selected studies covering two broad themes of current significance in South Asia—economic impact of recent global financial crisis and economic recession, and selected issues of economic cooperation among the countries in South Asia. These studies were conducted by young researchers under the 10th, 11th and 12th rounds of Regional Research Competition

(RRC) conducted by the South Asia Network of Economic Research Institutes (SANEI). It may be mentioned that SANEI is the South Asian arm of the Global Development Network (GDN) which works as a regional initiative to foster networking amongst economic research institutions in South Asia. The SANEI activities are aimed at developing the research and analytical capacities of South Asian research institutes by undertaking collaborative research and other activities on policy relevant issues in South Asia.

Chapter 1 of the volume, written by Sadia M. Malik and Yasin Janjua, examines the impact and the channels of transmission of recent financial crisis on growth, employment and poverty in three major South Asian countries—Bangladesh, India and Pakistan. The analysis shows that the degree of impact of financial crisis varies a lot across the countries depending a great deal on the strength of macroeconomic fundamentals and the policies implemented to preempt or minimise the impact of global financial crisis.

Chapter 2 by Mahreen Mahmud and Naved Hamid presents an analytical framework for understanding the impact of financial crisis on remittance flows at the macroeconomic level and examines the ramifications for growth and unemployment in Bangladesh, Pakistan and Sri Lanka. For the three countries, the final impact on the macro economy yields an impact multiplier of greater than one which makes intuitive sense and is consistent with the results in other developing countries.

In chapter 3, S. Irudaya Rajan and D. Narayana analyse the impact of the financial crisis in the Gulf on South Asian migrant workers through examining the effects on migrant workers in key industries of the Gulf Cooperation Council (GCC) economies and analysing the effects on return migrants in their countries of origin in South Asia covering Bangladesh, India, Nepal, Pakistan and Sri Lanka. The study reports that although the flow of workers from South Asia to the Gulf and the inflow of remittances have not fallen to any significant extent, the labour-sending countries of South Asia should work together to protect the legal and other rights of the migrant workers and ensure decent living conditions.

Chapter 4 by Partha Pratim Sahu, provides estimates of possible loss of employment in India resulting from the overall decline in growth and other changes due to financial crisis. It provides some insight about the magnitude of the problem to help formulate preventive and ameliorative policies that could avoid or lessen negative employment implications of financial crisis.

In chapter 5, Namrata Ghosh tests the market integration of agricultural commodity pieces in India with the rest of the world and estimates the welfare impact of a rise in price of principal traded agricultural commodities. The results show that there exists an integration between domestic and international prices for soybean, and that there is positive household welfare of an increase in international prices across all size classes.

Chapter 6 by Monzur Hossain and Farhana Rafiq, examines the pass-through elasticity of some selected commodities in Bangladesh and assesses the impact of inflation on the performance of the financial sector. The analysis suggests that increasing management and operational efficiency and prudent regulatory and institutional framework are necessary for the financial sector to overcome the negative effect of rising inflation on the performance of the sector.

Chapter 7 by Minhaj Mahmud and Syed Naimul Wadood explores the nature of competition at different stages of the domestic rice market in Bangladesh, and explains incentives and behaviours of different market agents. The study also examines price trends of local and international varieties of rice and observes long term cointegration relationship between prices of local varieties and several international varieties of rice.

In chapter 8, Saibal Kar and Nimai Das examine the tension between climate change, agricultural production and use of natural resources in India. The effects of climate change are felt most on the food production system as a whole, and the response to climate-induced supply shortfalls and consequent higher prices can have serious socioeconomic consequences. The study explores the effect of climate change on farmland value and provides a counter factual measure of the impact of farm revenue on rural consumption expenditure under alternative climate change scenarios.

In chapter 9, Arindam Banik, Pradip K. Bhaumik, Sheikh Md. Monzurul Huq and Bhuban B. Bajracharya examine the trade potential in health services in South Asia and estimate economic costs of barriers to trade in health services in Bangladesh, India and Nepal. Along with examining the structure and nature of health services, they also analyse the impact of liberalisation and regulatory reforms on economic welfare in the countries under study. The study concludes that the South Asian countries need to take cautious but forward looking steps in order to remove restrictions in services trade in general and in health services in particular.

Chapter 10 by Safdar Sohail, Noorulain Hanif and Maliha Quddus, examines the prospects and challenges of liberalisation of trade in services in Pakistan under South Asian Free Trade Agreement (SAFTA) covering several key sectors e.g., telecommunications, health, education and transport. Among others, the study calls for adoption of a systematic approach recognising both common and trade specific impediments to efficient trade and transport logistics in Pakistan.

In chapter 11, Krishna Prasad Pant assesses the health effects of using dung cake fuel in the rural areas of Nepal and estimates the household health costs of dung fuel use relative to the price of alternative cooking fuel, biogas. Along with exploring the factors affecting household decisions in favor of using dung cake as fuel, the study reports that the health cost is much higher than the price of the alternative fuel, biogas.

Chapter 12 by Nisha Arunatilake, Suwendrani Jayaratne, Priyanka Jayawardena, Roshini Jayaweera and Dushni Weerakoon, examines the impact of remittances on the Sri Lankan economy. It also assesses the effect of remittances on the households of the emigrants. The study maintains that it is important for Sri Lanka to strike a balance between maximising the development benefits of migration and protecting the migrant workers and their families from the adverse impacts of migration.

Overall, the volume underlines the fact that development does not take place in isolation. The countries in South Asia must work together to build a decent future for the millions of people who aspire to lead productive, innovative and prosperous lives commensurate with the potentials of the region for which informed policies and prudent actions can only emerge through credible and collaborative research.

It is our hope that the students, academicians, professionals and researchers including the policy research community will benefit from the studies contained in this volume and develop to a broader understanding of the challenges and prospects of regional cooperation and development in South Asia.

Needless to say, the volume would not have been published without the enthusiasm and encouragement of a number of people. While it is not possible to mention all their names, we express our deep gratitude to the members of the Research Advisory Panel (RAP) and the Steering Committee (SC) of SANEI for their untiring efforts in guiding and finalising the studies under RRCs. We are also thankful to Samiul Ahsan of SANEI for his all-out assistance and support in bringing out this volume. Finally, we gratefully acknowledge the help and assistance of the publisher of this volume, Academic Foundation, who readily agreed to publish the volume within a short time while ensuring a high professional standard.

—Mustafa K. Mujeri and Wahiduddin Mahmud

1

SADIA M. MALIK AND YASIN JANJUA

Growth, Employment and Poverty Implications of Recent Financial Crisis

A Comparative Study of India, Pakistan and Bangladesh

Introduction

The recent financial crisis that originated in the United States (US) from its subprime mortgage market in 2007 infiltrated rapidly into other financial markets particularly those in the industrialised economies that were well integrated with the US financial markets. The crisis—that was caused by a confluence of factors including unfettered liberalisation and deregulation of the financial sector as well as excessive financial innovation by the banking sector in the developed economies—resulted in a deep recession which was never witnessed in the global economic history since the Great Depression in the 1930s. Growth in world output plunged from 5.2 per cent in 2007 to -0.6 per cent in 2009 (Figure 1.1) with the advanced economies witnessing a much sharper reduction of 3.2 per cent in their output compared with the emerging and developing economies that still witnessed positive, yet an all-time low growth in their combined output.

The impact of financial crisis was not uniform across countries and varied according to: (i) the level of financial and trade integration of each country with the rest of the world particularly the advanced economies; (ii) macroeconomic fundamentals with which each country entered the period of financial crisis; and (iii) policies implemented by each country to stave off the negative repercussions of the crisis.

This chapter provides an in-depth analysis of the impact including the channels of transmission of the financial crisis on growth, employment and poverty in three major South Asian countries: India, Pakistan and Bangladesh. These are the three largest economies in South Asia that together represent around 97 per cent of the region's population and 96 per cent of total GDP (gross domestic product).[1]

Figure 1.1

Annual Percentage Change in Output during Financial Crisis

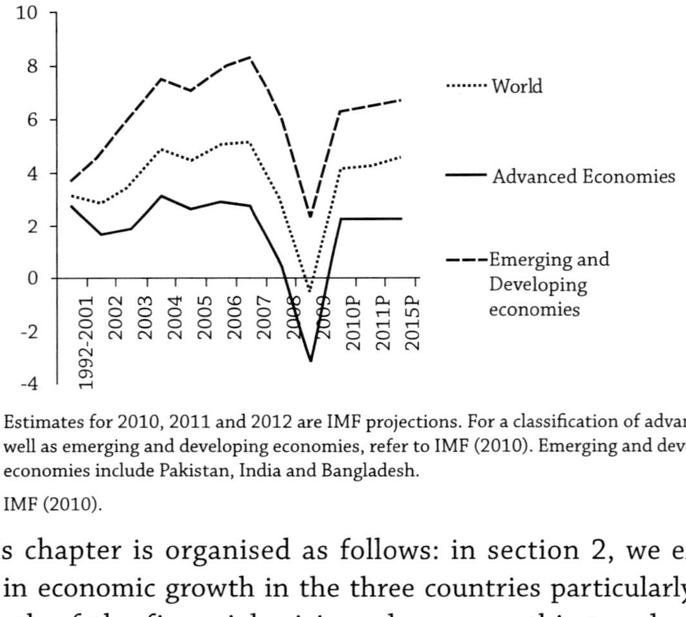

Note: Estimates for 2010, 2011 and 2012 are IMF projections. For a classification of advanced as well as emerging and developing economies, refer to IMF (2010). Emerging and developing economies include Pakistan, India and Bangladesh.

Source: IMF (2010).

This chapter is organised as follows: in section 2, we examine trends in economic growth in the three countries particularly in the aftermath of the financial crisis and compare this trend with the developing as well as the developed world. In section 3, we discuss the major channels of transmission of global financial crisis to South Asia. Two major channels, i.e. financial and international trade are identified in the context of South Asian countries and the level of impact through each of these channels is then compared. In section 4, we present the empirical results of the study along with the model and estimation strategy. In particular, we report the estimated impact of financial crisis on poverty and employment in the three countries. Section 5 summarises the key findings and concludes the chapter.

1. Mahbub ul Haq Human Development Centre, 2009.

Pre-Crisis and Post-Crisis Growth Trajectories in Selected South Asian Countries

In the aftermath of trade liberalisation policies adopted by the South Asian countries in late 1990s and early 2000s, growth in GDP per capita took off sharply. Figure 1.2 shows that GDP per capita increased sharply particularly from 2002 onwards in all the three countries. Growth of real GDP has been positive and is more or less on an upward trajectory since then. However, from 2005 onwards for Pakistan, and 2006 onwards for India and Bangladesh, we observe a descent in economic growth (see Figure 1.2).

Figure 1.2

Trends in Real GDP Growth

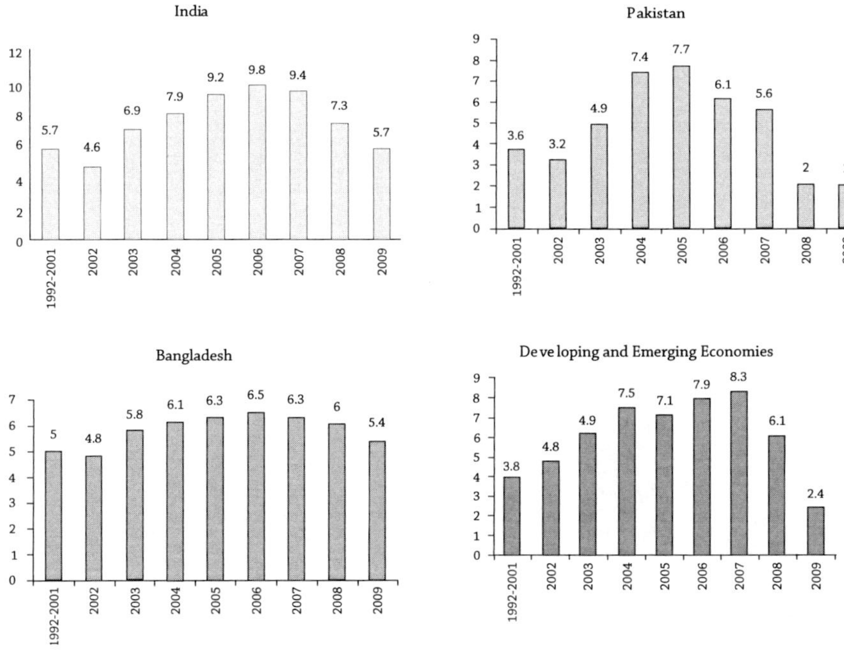

Source: IMF (2010).

It is important to note that financial crisis hit the advanced economies in 2007 and the developing economies in 2008 but the downward spiral in economic growth, particularly in Pakistan had already set in prior to 2007. Figure 1.3 shows that the decline in overall GDP also transpired in GDP per capita in Pakistan while it did not seem to impact GDP per capita in other leading regional economies of South Asia. This implies that a number of other factors, most prominent among them being the overall political and economic environment as well as the oil and the commodity price shock were in operation particularly in the case of Pakistan. Any analysis of the impact of global financial crisis on South Asia in isolation from these and other important shocks would therefore be incomplete. In Pakistan, growth had been depressed due to a number of factors that included the rising physical insecurity and war on terrorism. Global financial crisis had no doubt aggravated the situation but the onset of downfall in economic growth in Pakistan seemed to have preceded the financial crisis.

Figure 1.3

Trends in GDP Per Capita (Current Prices) Before and After the Crisis

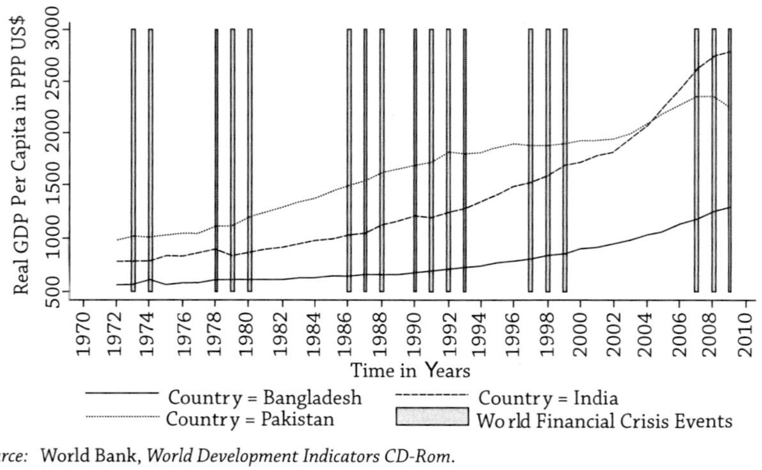

Source: World Bank, *World Development Indicators CD-Rom.*

Countries such as Bangladesh and India entered into the period of financial crisis with relatively strong economic fundamentals whereas Pakistan's economy was already drained prior to the crisis due to high costs of war on terrorism and deterioration in the investment climate due to rising physical insecurity. The current account balance, for instance, in Pakistan in 2006 was -4.0 per cent of its GDP compared with -1.2 per cent in India and 1.3 per cent in Bangladesh. Similarly, the budget deficit in Pakistan remained consistently high and ballooned to 7.4 per cent of GDP in 2008 compared with 2.2 per cent in India and 1.0 per cent in Bangladesh in the same year.[2] In fact, Pakistan had to resort to International Monetary Fund (IMF) for BoP (balance of payments) support. As a result of differences in these initial conditions, the downward spiral in economic growth was much sharper for Pakistan than for India and Bangladesh.

Figure 1.4

Current Account Balance as Per cent of GDP

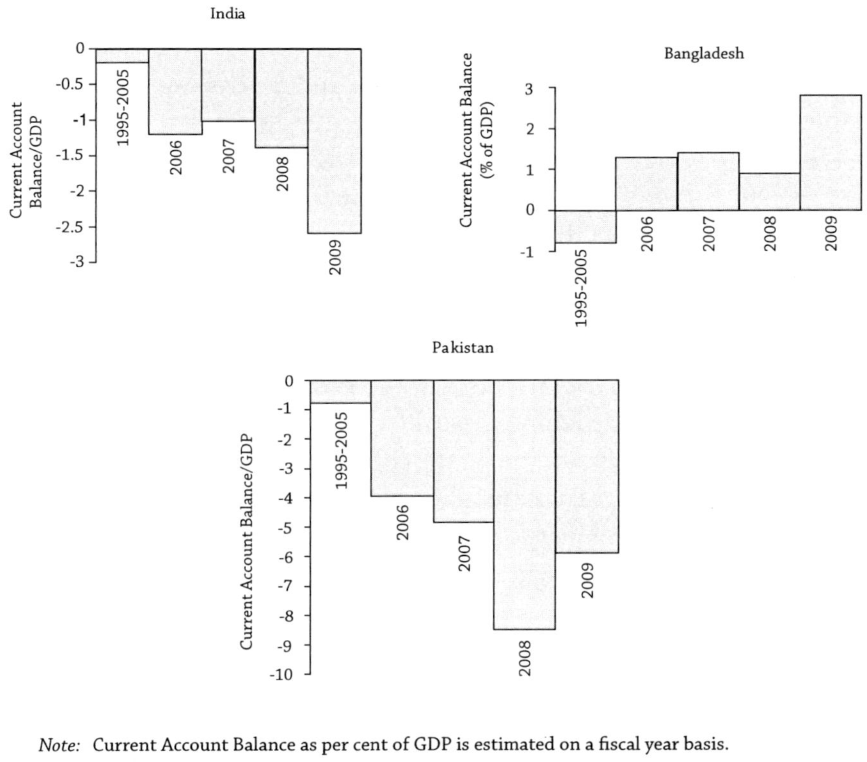

Note: Current Account Balance as per cent of GDP is estimated on a fiscal year basis.

Source: World Bank (2010b).

Empirical studies have shown that a higher current account balance in developing economies acts as a shield against transmitting the impact of global financial crisis to the real economies (see e.g., Balakrishnan *et al.*, 2009; Lane

2. World Bank (2010a).

and Ferretti, 2010). It is partly due to this reason that Bangladesh has been able to survive a number of negative shocks that included repeated natural disasters. The country's GDP growth has remained mostly stable, with a few exceptions, from 1990 till 2009 and grew in a predominantly upward trend. Its GDP per capita even reached an unprecedented USD (US Dollar) 621 in FY (financial year) 2009. In the crises years, it managed to remain stable, and economic growth was sustained in later years with success. This superior performance has largely been attributed to a higher current account balance and greater fiscal discipline; budget deficit consistently remained below 5 per cent of GDP from 1990 onwards to date. The Government of Bangladesh was able to contain the possibility of heightened levels of budget deficits successfully in the crises years by expanding its revenue base and controlling expenditures. Similarly India, despite having witnessed a downward trajectory in economic growth from 2008 onwards, was able to register a decent level of economic growth. Its GDP growth of 6.7 per cent in 2008 was the highest growth rate in the world during that particular year.

Financial Crisis: The Channels of Transmission in Selected South Asian Countries

The global financial crisis was transmitted from advanced economies to the developing world through two key channels: the financial channels and the real economy channels. In the initial phase, when the crisis was referred to as merely a 'liquidity crisis' or 'credit crunch' in the developed world, it was transmitted to the rest of the world through financial channels. Negative shocks to several financial variables such as the stock market index and portfolio equity investment were observed all over the world. Liquidity flows to several developing and emerging economies dried up. In the next phase, this credit crunch spilled over to the real economies in terms of overall economic slowdown and a significant contraction in aggregate demand. In the subsection that follows, we will examine the transmission of the crisis to South Asia through the financial channel. In the following subsection, we will take up the real economy spillover of financial crisis in the region.

South Asia and the Financial Contagion of the Crisis

South Asia remained relatively immune to the financial contagion of the crisis primarily because of two reasons. First, the level of financial integration remained quite low especially in Pakistan and Bangladesh. Apart from workers' remittances, most forms of foreign inflows and outflows did not contribute significantly in GDP of the three countries of our study. Financing through international capital markets for instance make up around 2.7 per cent of GDP in India compared with a paltry 0.1 per cent in Bangladesh and 0.4 per cent in Pakistan (see Table 1.1).

Table 1.1

Global Financial Integration in South Asia: International Finance as Per cent of GDP, 2008

	Financing through International Capital Markets (Gross Inflows)	*FDI-Net Inflows*	*FDI-Net Outflow*	*Workers' Remittances and Compensation of Employees Received*
Bangladesh	0.1	1.2	N.A.	11.3
India	2.7	3.6	1.6	4.3
Pakistan	0.4	3.3	0	4.3
South Asia	2.2	3.3	1.4	4.9
Memo items				
East Asia and Pacific	1.2	3.3	1.4	4.9
World	N.A.	3	3.5	0.8
Low income	2	5.1	N.A.	7.1
Middle income	2.2	3.5	1.3	1.9
High income	N.A.	2.8	4.4	0.3

Source: World Bank (2010b).

Second, the banking sector in the three countries also remained sound due to its lack of indulgence in the kind of financial innovations practised by the banking sector in the developed world. Bank deposits as percentage of GDP—an indicator of confidence in the banking system—remained stable with a slight reduction experienced in

Bangladesh and Pakistan after 2008. Commercial bank and other lending also remained more or less stable and the ratio of private sector credit to GDP continued to follow an upward trend.

Remittances, which have been the most important source of foreign exchange in all three countries of our analysis, held up well during the crisis year. In fact, quite contrary to general expectations, the flow of remittances continued to grow sharply in these countries particularly during the crisis years of 2007 and 2008. There could be a number of plausible explanations for this rather unexpected phenomenon. First, like employment, remittances tend to lag the downturn in economic activity. It is for this reason that the available data for 2009 and 2010 from national sources of all three countries reflected a downturn in the flow of remittances compared with 2008 and the previous years. Second, the sharp growth in the officially reported flow of remittances particularly after 2001 could be due to the fact that after September 2001 international laws governing the transfer of funds, through unofficial sources particularly from the US and Europe became stringent. This could have induced an increase of overseas remittances received through official sources. Third, the steep increase in the flow of remittances particularly in 2007 and 2008 could be attributed to migrants who returned to their home countries with their savings after losing employment in the US and Europe. Finally (and most importantly) for all the three countries, the leading source of the chunk of the remittances is received from the Middle East, Saudi Arabia and United Arab Emirates (UAE). In these countries, the impact of the crisis did not surface till the recent Dubai financial turmoil.

In terms of portfolio equity investment and FDI (foreign direct investment), however, all three countries witnessed a negative shock. Although the contribution of FDI in GDP is quite low (1.2% in Bangladesh, 3.3% in Pakistan and 3.6% in India), it is seen as an important source of employment generation as well as skill and technology transfer. The reduction in FDI, therefore, may have contributed to the slowdown in economic growth in these countries.

As a result of the reduction in foreign financial flows especially in the form of FDI and export revenue (as analysed in next section), the amount of foreign exchange reserves declined in both India and Pakistan (Figure 1.5). Bangladesh, on the other hand, did not witness a decline in its foreign exchange reserves during this period primarily because all major sources of foreign capital flows such as FDI, remittances and export revenue (see next section) remained stable in the same period. On the other hand, in both India and Pakistan, FDI declined significantly from 2008 onwards.

Figure 1.5

Gross International Reserves (US$ Million)

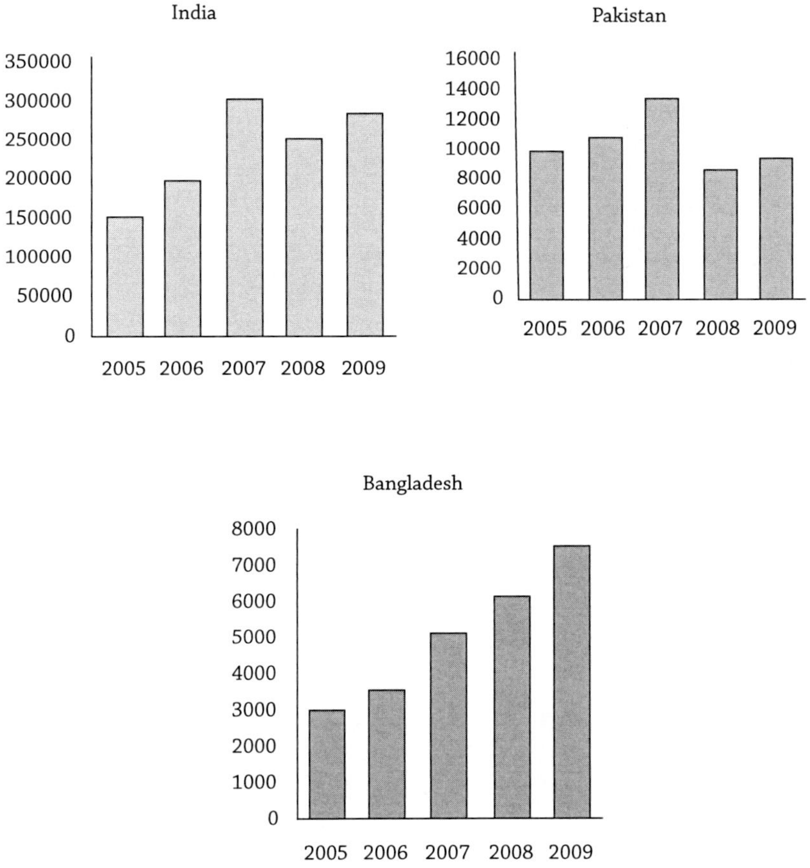

Source: Asian Development Bank (2010).

The reduction in international reserves—along with factors such as the current account deficit—exerted pressure on the exchange rates of domestic currencies. Figure 1.6 shows that between 2005 and 2009, all three countries witnessed depreciation of their domestic currencies.

Figure 1.6

Exchange Rates to the US Dollar (Annual Average)

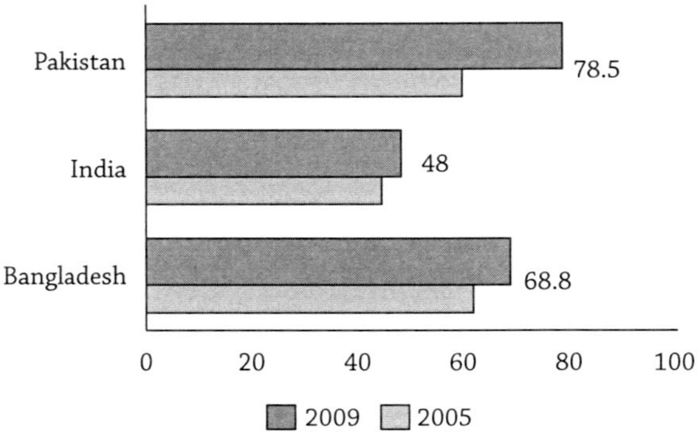

Source: Asian Development Bank (2010).

The reduction in gross international reserves and depreciation in domestic currencies, along with the collapse of the stock market exerted a strain on the financial sector in the region in 2008. The FSI (Financial Stress Index) constructed by IMF (2009) captures stress in three sectors: foreign exchange market, stock market, and the banking sector. The indexes computed for India and Pakistan show increased financial stress in 2008 (Figure 1.7).

Figure 1.7

Monthly Trends in IMF FSI

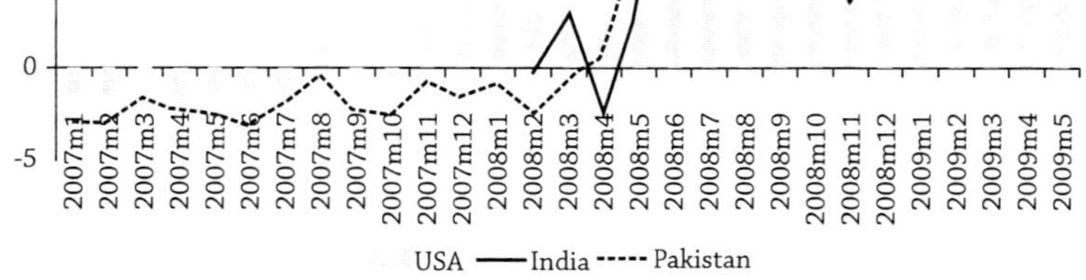

Note: Data for FSI corresponding to India prior to 2008 is not available. Data for Bangladesh is not available.

Source: International Monetary Fund (IMF) online data base.

Figure 1.7 indicates that financial stress in the US became prominent in the 11th month of 2007 when the FSI for the US turned from negative to positive. In India, the FSI turned positive in the 3rd month of 2008 suggesting a lag of around 4 months between the transmissions of stress from the US to India. The FSI for India started declining in the 2nd month of 2009 but remained positive. In Pakistan, the stress became evident in the 5th month of 2008. Notice that the values of FSI in Pakistan exceeded those of the US during 5th to 9th month of 2008, suggesting that the financial stress in Pakistan might have been aggravated due to domestic factors such as deteriorating security, war on terror, and the energy crisis.

Transmission of Global Financial Crisis through International Trade

Of all external channels, international trade has been one of the most important channels through which financial crisis hit South Asia and spilled over to the real economies of the region. This is primarily because global trade integration is much higher in South Asia compared with other forms of global integration such as international finance. At present, merchandise trade forms 49.3 per cent of GDP in Bangladesh, 40.6 per cent in India, and 38.1 per cent in Pakistan. The major chunk of exports of the three countries is directed towards high income economies. For instance, around 76 per cent of Bangladesh's exports, 65 per cent of India's exports, and 66.1 per cent of Pakistan's exports are directed towards high income economies including the US and European Union (EU).[3] As a result of slowdown in aggregate demand in developed economies, particularly in the US and EU, all three countries witnessed declining trends in growth of their merchandise exports. In Bangladesh, exports growth declined but still remained positive in contrast with India and Pakistan where the growth of exports turned negative in 2009. Growth in merchandise imports also declined; however trade deficit for all three countries continued to balloon.

3. ADB (2010).

Figure 1.8

Trends in Trade Balance (US$ Million)

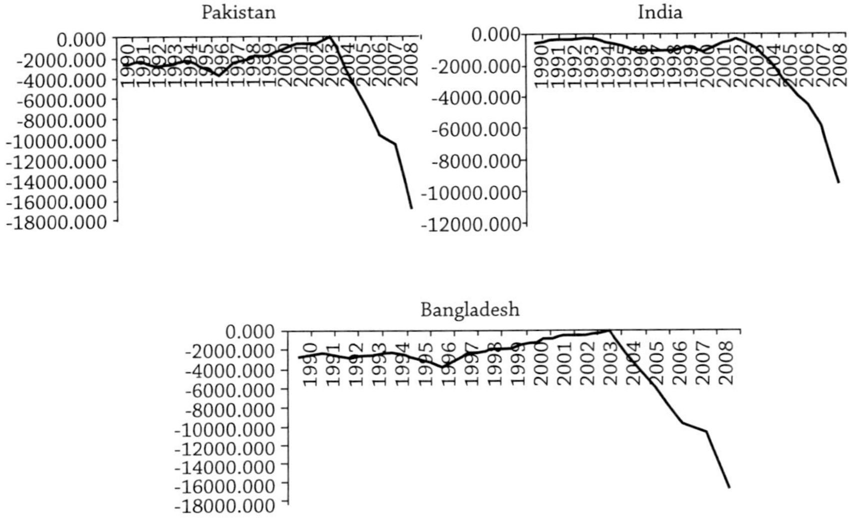

Source: International Finance Statistics, IMF.

A close observation of trade deficit in Figure 1.8 shows that in case of all the three countries, trade deficit started worsening from 2003 onwards pointing towards the role of other important factors such as oil and commodity price hike that increased sharply in the early 2000s. The slowdown in export demand as a result of global economic slowdown had a multiplier effect on export-led industries and overall industrial production.

A substantial proportion of exports of the export led industries in these countries originate in the SCIs (small and cottage industries). In India for instance, about 40 to 45 per cent of exports originates in SCIs and this sector is a source of employment to roughly 60 million Indians (Government of India, 2010). Sector wise analysis of specific industries indicates that a substantial loss of employment took place in some export led industries. In India, the Government of India (2009) indicates that around one million jobs were lost during September-December 2008.

Some sectors were hit more than others with the magnitude of the impact on each sector depending upon the export orientation of the specific sector and the income elasticity of demand for exports of the product. The cotton and textile industry in Pakistan and the gems and jewellery industry in India were among the worst hit by the global economic crisis. Analysts argue that many of these sectors such as the garments and jewellery sector in India, relied heavily on home based and piece-rate workers whose remuneration was already low. With a fall in export orders, many of these workers were affected through either a loss in their employment or downward pressure on their wage rates (see for example, Kumar *et al.*, 2009).

In Bangladesh, most of the exports remained quite resilient particularly in the US market that continues to be the top trading partner of Bangladesh after Germany and the UK. This trend can be explained by the "Walmart effect" according to which demand for low end products is sustained or continues to grow in times of economic slowdown.

Apart from exports, domestic investment in all three countries was also affected. In Pakistan, growth in total investment went down sharply from 36.1 per cent in 2005-06 to 15.7 per cent in 2006-07, and to a paltry 0.7 per cent in 2009-10.[4] Similarly, in India a declining trend was witnessed in gross fixed capital formation.[5] A close analysis of data shows that this declining trend in investment in India had set in 2004 before the financial crisis hit the developing countries including India—a fact also pointed out by Rakshit (2009). This implies that a number of factors other than the financial crisis such as a sharp hike in international commodity and oil prices that increased the cost of production might have contributed to the deceleration in overall investment. Financial crisis, however, could have very well strengthened the decelerating tendency in overall investment rates.

An Econometric Analysis of the Impact of Financial Crisis on Growth, Employment and Poverty

In this section, we present an econometric assessment of the impact of financial crisis on growth, employment and poverty using

4. Government of Pakistan (2010).

5. World Bank, *World Development Indicators*.

data from the three countries of our study. Existing studies on financial crisis and its impact on growth, employment and poverty have employed two types of methodological approach: (i) output elasticity of poverty approach; and (ii) micro-simulation approach. In the first approach, the elasticities of poverty and employment with respect to GDP are estimated which are then combined with macroeconomic projections to estimate the impact of financial crisis on employment and poverty (see for example, World Bank, 2010; Hasan *et al.*, 2009; Chen and Ravallion, 2009)

In the second approach which employs micro-simulation, macroeconomic projections are combined with the most recent household level data on income and consumption to determine the poverty and distributional impact of the financial crisis at the national and sub-national level. For a simulation exercise along these lines a World Bank simulation package called PovStat is often used (see for example, Habib *et al.*, 2010).

One major drawback of the existing studies is that most of these do not control for other factors such as the hike in food and commodity prices that coincided with the onset of the financial crisis and that may have led to the slowdown in economic growth. Similarly, each country had its own domestic vulnerabilities leading to a slowdown in economic growth. In Pakistan, for instance, the 'war on terror' related security and law and order problems and the energy crisis had put a strain on its growth prospects. In order to assess the impact of financial crisis on poverty and employment, it is important to isolate the slowdown in economic growth due to global financial crisis from that due to other external and domestic factors. In our study, we separate out other factors by controlling for country specific effects as well as global commodity and food price shocks.

The Model and Empirical Strategy

The following baseline model has been estimated in the study using panel data for India, Pakistan and Bangladesh spanning between 1973 and 2009:

$$G_{it} = \alpha + \beta FSI_{it} + \gamma EXP_{it} + \Sigma_k \delta X_{it} + u_i + e_{it} \quad (1)$$

where G_{it} is growth rate of real GDP, subscript i denotes country, and t denotes year. In our model, i=3 and t=37 (from 1972-2009). FSI_{it} is the FSI that captures financial stress in foreign exchange market, stock market and the banking sector. The components and the method of computation of this index are discussed in detail in a later section. This is a comprehensive index that is used to capture the impact of the crisis through financial channels as reflected in stress in stock markets, drying up of foreign exchange reserves, depreciation of domestic currencies, as well as reduced flow of foreign capital inflow in the form of foreign direct investment and remittances. EXP_{it} denotes the ratio of exports to GDP and is used to capture the impact of financial crisis through the trade channel. As discussed in detail in an earlier section, the two major channels through which global financial crisis affected growth in the three countries are the financial channel and the trade channel. We intend to capture the financial channel impact through the FSI and the trade channel impact through growth in exports. X_{it} is a vector of control variables. It includes growth in international oil and commodity prices. u_i denotes unobservable or uncontrolled country specific effects that do not vary over time.

Equation 1 is used to estimate the impact of financial crisis through the financial and trade channels on growth of real GDP per capita in the three countries. Panel data estimation techniques are used to estimate the long run impact of financial crisis on economic growth. The marginal impact of export growth and financial stress on growth of real GDP per capita derived from this equation is then used to estimate the respective elasticities of economic growth with respect to financial stress and with respect to export growth. These elasticities will tell us the percentage change in economic growth, on average, resulting from a one per cent change in financial stress or growth in exports. This will be a useful exercise in studying the relationship between economic growth and financial stress in the long run. Our ultimate objective, however, is to study the impact of the financial crisis of 2007-2009 on employment and poverty. For this purpose, we will first compute the growth elasticity of poverty and employment using real time data (the details related to the computation of these elasticities is contained later in this section) and then use these elasticities to predict the impact on poverty and employment resulting from the actual percentage change in financial stress and growth in exports between 2007 and 2009.

More specifically, this will be done in three steps. In the first step, we will compute the percentage change in FSI and exports growth between 2007 and 2009 in the individual countries as well as the overall average for the three countries.[6] In the next step, we will use the elasticities derived from the estimation of equation 1 to predict the impact of the given change in FSI and export growth on growth of real GDP per capita between 2007 and 2009. In the third step, the percentage reduction in economic growth estimated in the previous step will be combined with growth elasticity of poverty and employment to predict the impact of the given reduction in economic growth—via increase in financial stress and reduction in export growth—on poverty and employment between 2007 and 2009. Using the methodology, we shall be able to predict how much of the impact on poverty and employment is due to increase in financial stress and how much of it is due to the weakening of exports demand in the three countries.

Sample, Variables and Sources of Data

Our dependent variable is the growth of real GDP which is obtained from the World Bank. The export to GDP ratio is also taken from the same source. The oil and commodity price data is obtained from IMF. To measure financial stress, we have constructed an index (described in the next sub-section). All variables used in the construction of this index are obtained from IMF. Since we are using time-series data between 1972 and 2009, there is a possibility of unit root in the data. All time-series data that we use in our estimation is, therefore, checked for the presence of unit root. Since most of the variables that we use in the estimation of equation 1 are growth variables, they all turn out to be stationary.

---

6. For this purpose moving averages will be used to smooth out temporary fluctuations in FSI and export growth. The 2007 figure will therefore correspond to the average of 2005-2007 whereas 2009 figure will correspond to the average of 2007-2009.

The Measurement of Financial Stress

The FSI that we constructed for India, Pakistan and Bangladesh is primarily a modification of the FSI conducted by IMF (2009) for advanced and emerging economies. This index measures financial stress in the same three sectors that the IMF covers, namely: the foreign exchange market, the stock market, and the banking sector. These three sectors capture most of the financial and banking aspects relevant to financial stress in developing countries. The choice of variables to capture stress in each of these sectors is guided both by the scientific relevance of the variable as established in the literature as well as by the availability of time series data of the three countries. For the foreign exchange market, we used the EMPI (Exchange Market Pressure Index) which is the same as the one used by IMF (2009) but we compute a longer time series of this sub index. The stock market returns and stock market volatility component is also the same as the one used by IMF (2009). However, for the banking sector, data on the 'banking sector beta' (bank stock returns) used by IMF is not available prior to 1996 for the three countries. For this purpose, we selected three indicators that capture stress related to the banking sector in India, Pakistan and Bangladesh. These include: (i) the deposit lending spread that is an indicator of asymmetry of information between the borrowers and the lenders; (ii) year over year change in bank deposits as percentage of GDP which is an indicator of the confidence in the banking system; and (iii) spread between LIBOR (London Interbank Offered Rate) and the central bank discount rate which is an indicator of information asymmetry and increased uncertainty in financial markets.

More specifically, our FSI is given by the following identity:

FSI = EMPI + Stock Returns + Stock Returns Volatility + Banking Stability

where EMPI captures fluctuations in exchange rate and total reserves minus gold. This index is computed on a monthly basis first and then averaged over the year. The EMPI for country i and month t is computed using the following formula:

$$EMPI_{it} = \frac{\Delta e_t - \mu_{\Delta e}}{\sigma_{\Delta e}} - \frac{(\Delta RES_t - \mu_{\Delta RES})}{\sigma_{\Delta RES}}$$

where Δe_t is the month over month change in the nominal exchange rate relative to USD, ΔRES is the month over month change in total reserves minus gold, and σ and μ denote the mean and standard deviation of the relevant series. (The decline in international reserves (ΔRES) is expected to capture the impact of reduction in FDI and international remittances, if any, due to financial crisis.) For this reason, the correlation between FDI and remittances on the one hand and EMPI on the other hand is extremely high (over 0.7). Stock Returns is the year over year change in the stock market index multiplied by -1 so that falling stock prices depict increased market stress. Stock return volatility is derived from GARCH (1,1) specification using year over year returns modelled as an autoregressive process with 12 lags.

Banking stability includes three components each of which is expressed in the form of z scores (deviation from the respective mean and multiplied by the inverse of its standard deviation). These components include: (i) deposit lending spread which is the difference between the deposit rate and the lending rate of the banks. This indicator measures the extent of asymmetry in information between the borrowers and the lenders. This information asymmetry increases at times of financial stress when lenders lose confidence in determining borrowers' income (see Hakiko and Keeton, 2009); (ii) year over year change in bank deposits to GDP ratio. The bank deposits include both time and demand deposits and they reflect confidence in the banking system. Risk of a bank run is reflected in a sharp decline in the bank deposits ratio; (iii) difference between LIBOR and central bank discount rate. This measure is equivalent to TED spread used in studies related to the advanced economies. The LIBOR is a measure of international interbank lending cost. This rate may exceed the domestic central bank discount rate when international lending banks fear that the loan may not be repaid or in case banks worry that they may need unexpected liquid funds before the expiration of the loan period. In times of financial stress, therefore, the spread between the LIBOR and central bank discount rate increases.

All components of the FSI are normalised by taking deviations from their respective means and multiplied by the inverse of their standard deviation. These normalised components are then added together to construct the FSI.

Estimation Results

We use panel data estimation techniques to estimate equation 1. The advantage of using panel data is that it allows us to control for country specific factors that are either unobserved or not included in the regression such as culture, initial conditions or institutions. Panel data also allows us to control for unobservable variables that change over time but not across countries. There are two types of specification commonly used for panel data: fixed effects and random effects. The fixed effects model primarily explores the relationship between predictor and the outcome variable within countries. The model assumes that each country has its own specific characteristics that may influence the explanatory variables. This is a reasonable assumption in the context of our study since many country specific factors as explained above may influence financial stress and the growth of exports in each country.

For instance, initial conditions in the form of macroeconomic fundamentals were crucial in defining how countries responded to the financial stress. In Pakistan, macroeconomic fundamentals were weak at the outset due to its domestic security situation, the war on terror and energy crisis. The macroeconomic fundamentals in Bangladesh were strong in the form of low budget deficits and a stable foreign exchange reserves position, resulting in low financial stress and associated impact on GDP growth. The fixed effects model assumes that something within the country may bias the independent or the dependent variable and we need to control for this bias. The random effects model, on the other hand, assumes that differences across countries are random and uncorrelated with the independent variables. We report the results for both the models in Table 1.2.

Table 1.2

Panel Data Estimation Results

Dependent Variable: Real GDP Growth

GDPG	*(1)*	*(2)*	*(3)*	*(4)*	*(5)*	*(6)*
	FE	*RE*	*FE*	*RE*	*FE*	*RE*
FSI	-0.209	-0.217	-0.219*	-0.233*	-0.217*	-0.228*
	(-1.67)	(-1.68)	(-2.04)	(-2.11)	(-2.07)	(-2.11)
Export to GDP ratio	0.325***	0.223**	0.233**	0.142*	0.231**	0.142*
	(3.61)	(2.96)	(3)	(2.22)	(3)	(2.22)
International oil price (Y-O-Y change)			0.00977	0.0136		
			(0.69)	(0.94)		
Commodity Price Index (Y-O-Y change)					0.0157	0.0196
					(0.95)	(1.16)
Constant	1.984*	2.873***	2.982***	3.776***	2.991***	3.772***
	2.38	3.99	4.16	6.19	4.2	6.21
N	114	114	111	111	111	111
Hausman test						
chi2(2) = (b-B)' [(V_b-V_B)^(-1)] (b-B)		4.28		4.31		4.28
Prob>chi2		0.1174		0.2299		0.2329

Note: t statistics in parentheses. * p<0.05, ** p<0.01, *** p<0.001.

The results reported in Table 1.2 show that FSI has a negative and a statistically significant effect (columns 3, 4, 5 and 6) on growth of real GDP. The impact is robust in both the fixed effects and the random effects model. Exports also seem to exert a positive and statistically significant impact on real GDP growth. We have also controlled for growth in oil and commodity prices to net out the impact of financial crisis from that of oil and commodity price hike. Since oil and commodity prices are highly correlated with each other, we do not introduce them in the same regression. Both of them have positive signs which may appear counter intuitive but borne out by empirical studies on the relationship between growth and inflation particularly in the context of developing economies (see Rodriguez and Sanchez, 2004; Jinn, 2008).

The Hausman test in Table 1.2 does not favour simple fixed and random effects specifications. Since, we have time series data which tends to be persistent, it is important to include lag of GDP growth. However, when the lag of dependent variable is included in the model, the model becomes a dynamic panel data model and simple fixed effect panel regression does not give consistent estimators as the error term tends to be correlated with the lagged dependent variable (see Arellano and Bond, 1991). In this case, it is suggested that we use GMM (Generalised Method of Moments) where lags of regressors are used in the differenced equation as instruments. The results based on Panel GMM are presented in Table 1.3.

Table 1.3

Panel GMM Results for Dynamic Model

Dependent Variable: real GDP Growth

GDPG	*(1)*	*(2)*	*(3)*
FSI	-0.197	-0.220*	-0.216*
	(-1.92)	(-2.03)	(-2.04)
Export to GDP ratio	0.253**	0.241**	0.237**
	3.22	2.99	2.91
Real GDP growth (-1)	-0.025	-0.0313	-0.0195
	(-0.31)	(-0.39)	(-0.24)
International oil price (Y-O-Y change)		0.0104	
		(0.72)	
Commodity Price Index (Y-O-Y change)			0.0154
			(0.92)
Constant	2.959***	3.072***	3.051***
	4.04	4.04	4.05
N	108	108	108

Panel GMM results reported in Table 1.3 also suggest statistically significant impact of both financial stress as well as export to GDP ratio on real GDP growth. The size of the coefficients is not much different from the fixed and random effects models. The marginal effects of FSI and export to GDP ratio on growth of real GDP turn out to be -0.220 and 0.241 respectively. Using the mean values of FSI, export to GDP ratio, and real GDP, we compute the elasticity of GDP growth per capita with respect to FSI and exports to GDP ratio (Table 1.4).

Table 1.4

Elasticity of Per Capita GDP Growth With Respect to Financial Stress Index and Export Growth

	Marginal Impact	*Mean Value (FSI)*	*Mean Value (Growth of GDP)*	*Elasticities*
FSI (South Asia)	-0.220	0.03	4.82	-0.0014
		Mean Value (Export to GDP Ratio)		
Export to GDP Ratio	0.24	8.75	4.82	0.4357

The values of elasticity show the percentage change in per capita GDP growth with respect to a one per cent change in FSI or export to GDP ratio. Next, we compute the actual percentage change in average FSI and export to GDP ratio in the three countries between 2007 and 2009 to study its impact on economic growth, poverty and employment in the region. But before that, we need to compute the growth elasticity of poverty and employment.

The Computation of Growth Elasticity of Poverty and Employment

The growth elasticity of poverty and employment is used to measure the responsiveness of poverty and employment to economic growth. More precisely, it is the percentage change in poverty or employment brought about as a result of one per cent change in economic growth. Typically, it is computed by dividing the percentage change in employment or poverty over a specified time period by the observed growth rate of GDP per capita in that period. Using this method, we compute the growth elasticities of employment and poverty for India, Pakistan and Bangladesh. The reference period and the sources of data are presented below.

The Growth Elasticity of Poverty

For cross country consistency and comparison, we have used the international poverty line of US$ 1.25 and US$ 2.00 a day, data on which are obtained from World Development Indicators. Poverty data is mostly patchy and consistent series are not available for all years and all countries. The latest estimate available for headcount poverty for all countries is for 2005. Data on growth of real GDP per capita is obtained from Penn World Tables. The reference period that we have used on average to compute growth elasticity of poverty is 1992-2005.

Table 1.5

Elasticity of Headcount Poverty With Respect to GDP Growth

		Annual Rate of Reduction in Poverty			*Growth Elasticity of Poverty*	
Country	*Period*	*US$ 1.25 a day*	*US$ 2.00 a day*	*Average Growth of GDP*	*US$ 1.25 a day*	*US$ 2.00 a day*
Bangladesh	1992-2005	1.95	0.99	5.13	0.38	0.19
Pakistan	1993-2005	0.35	0.52	4	0.09	0.13
India	1994-2000	1.3	0.67	6.6	0.20	0.10
Average		1.2	0.73	5.24	0.22	0.14

Source: Authors' Computations.

The South Asian average for growth elasticity turns out to be 0.22 with a substantial amount of cross country variation; the elasticity estimate for Bangladesh (US$ 1 a day) is 0.38 as against 0.20 for India and 0.09 for Pakistan.

The Growth Elasticity of Employment

To compute the growth elasticity of employment, we use employment data from the International Labour Organization (ILO). The reference period for the computation of this elasticity is from 2000 to 2007.

Table 1.6

Elasticity of Employment With Respect to GDP Growth Per Capita, 2000-2007

Country	*Annual Rate of Growth in Total Employment*	*Average Annual Growth of Real GDP*	*Growth Elasticity of Employment*
Bangladesh	2.74	5.76	0.48
Pakistan	4.75	5.16	0.92
India	2.05	7.2	0.28
Regional average	2.37	6.05	0.39

Source: Authors' Computations.

The growth elasticity of employment in Pakistan turns out to be close to one which is an indication of low labour productivity (see SAARC, 2005). In Bangladesh and India, elasticity of employment with respect to GDP turns out to be 0.48 and 0.28 respectively. The high growth elasticity of employment in Pakistan and Bangladesh and low employment elasticity in India is also established in the literature (see SAARC, 2005). The overall growth elasticity of employment in the region turns out to be 0.39.

While interpreting the values of elasticities, a few caveats are in order. First, the absolute value of elasticity is sensitive to the period chosen. Second, the responsiveness of poverty and employment to changes in economic growth is not stationary and tends to vary over time. Therefore, while interpreting the results one needs to bear in mind the time period chosen. In our study, we have used the relationship between poverty and growth from 1992-2005[7] and between employment and growth from 2000-2007 and will make predictions for 2009 based on this relationship. Third, these estimates of elasticities do not capture important factors other than GDP growth which are likely to have an impact on poverty reduction and employment generation. With these caveats in mind, we use these elasticities to assess the impact of global financial crisis on economic growth, poverty, and employment between 2007 and 2009.

7. Post 2005, data on poverty is not available.

Estimating the Impact of Global Financial Crisis on Growth, Employment and Poverty

Next, we compute the percentage change in FSI and export growth in the entire region, on average, between 2007 and 2009 and use these elasticity numbers to estimate the percentage change in GDP growth per capita during this period. It is seen that the overall FSI for the three countries increased drastically by 308.6 per cent between 2007 and 2009. Using our estimate of elasticity of growth with respect to FSI, we find that this change in FSI would reduce GDP growth in the region by 0.43 per cent. Using our estimate of growth elasticity of poverty, we find that this reduction in growth would increase poverty rate by 0.1 per cent and the total number of poor living below US$ 1.25 a day in the three countries by 0.56 million (Table 1.7).

Table 1.7

The Impact of Financial Stress on Poverty in the Region

% increase in regional average of FSI between 2007 and 2009	308.16
Elasticity of GDP growth with respect to FSI	-0.0014
% reduction in GDP growth due to given change in FSI	0.431
Growth Elasticity of poverty in the region	-0.22
% increase in poverty due to predicted reduction in growth	0.1
Total number of poor (millions) in the region*	587
Addition in the number of poor (million)	0.56

Note: *Total number of poor in the region is estimated using the headcount poverty estimate of US$ 1.25 a day in each country in 2005 and their respective populations. The number of poor in each country is then added to derive the total number in three countries.

We have also computed the impact of the crisis on poverty through the trade channel. Between 2007 and 2009, exports to GDP ratio declined by 11.15 per cent (Table 1.8). Using our estimate of elasticity of GDP growth with respect to export growth, we find that the given reduction in exports to GDP ratio would reduce the regional average of GDP growth by 4.86 per cent. If growth elasticity of poverty is -0.22, then the given reduction in GDP would increase poverty by 1.07 per cent thereby adding around 6.27 million poor in the region.

Table 1.8

The Impact of Reduction in Exports to GDP Ratio on Poverty in the Region

% reduction in regional average of export to GDP ratio between 2007 and 2009	11.15
Elasticity of GDP growth with respect to export to GDP ratio	0.4357
% Reduction in GDP growth due to given reduction in exports to GDP ratio	4.86
Growth elasticity of poverty	-0.22
% increase in poverty due to estimated reduction in GDP growth	1.07
Total number of poor (millions)	587
Addition in the number of poor (million)	6.27

Notice that the size of the impact of financial crisis on overall poverty in the countries under study in the region is much higher through the trade channel than through the financial channel. The overall estimate of the additional number of poor as a result of financial crisis through both trade and financial channels turns out to be around 6.8 million in the three countries.

Similar computations for employment suggest that increase in financial stress in the region between 2007 and 2009 would reduce GDP growth per capita in the region as a whole by 0.43 per cent (Table 1.9). Using the estimated value of growth elasticity of employment, our calculations show that the estimated reduction in GDP growth led to a reduction in total employment by 0.96 million. This reduction in employment resulted exclusively from the financial stress occurring via financial channels.

Table 1.9

The Impact of Financial Stress on Employment in the Region

% Increase in FSI between 2007 and 2009	308.16
Elasticity of GDP growth with respect to FSI	-0.0014
% reduction in GDP growth due to given change in FSI	0.431
Growth elasticity of employment	0.39
% reduction in employment due to predicted reduction in growth	0.17
Total employment ('000)	570537.5
Reduction in the number of people employed ('000)	959.96
Reduction (in millions)	0.96

The calculated impact on employment occurring via the trade channel is much higher. Table 1.10 shows that the given percentage reduction in exports growth between 2007 and 2009 led to an estimated reduction in GDP growth by 4.86 per cent. Using our estimated value of growth elasticity of employment, we find that this reduction in economic growth reduced employment by 1.89 per cent. Using the given data on the total number of employed population in the three countries, we find that this amounted to a reduction in the total number of employed population by 10.8 million. Again, this is the reduction in employment occurring primarily through the trade channel. The aggregate reduction in employment resulting both from trade as well as financial channels between 2007 and 2009 in the three countries amounted to around 11.8 million people.

Table 1.10

The Impact of Reduction in Exports Growth on Employment in the Region

% reduction in export growth between 2007 and 2009	11.15
Elasticity of GDP growth with respect to export to GDP ratio	0.4357
Reduction in growth of GDP due to estimated reduction in exports to GDP ratio	4.86
Growth elasticity of employment	0.39
% reduction in employment due to estimated reduction in growth of GDP	1.89
Total number of employed population ('000)	570537.5
Reduction in the number of people employed ('000)	10807.29
Reduction (in millions)	10.81

The aggregate impact of financial crisis, both in percentage terms as well as in absolute numbers affected, is presented in Table 1.11. Overall, an addition of around 6.8 million poor living below US$ 1.25 a day resulted as a consequence of the financial crisis between 2007 and 2009 in the three countries of our study. The reduction in employment as a result of the financial crisis amounted to 11.8 million people.

Table 1.11

Estimated Overall Impact of Financial Crisis on Poverty and Employment

Channel	*Poverty*		*Employment*	
	% Increase	*Addition in the Total Number (million)*	*% reduction*	*Reduction in the Total Number (million)*
Financial channel	0.1	0.56	0.17	0.96
Trade channel	1.07	6.27	1.89	10.81
Overall impact (trade and financial channel)	--	6.83	--	11.77

While the results derived above are useful, they need to be interpreted with caution as they are based on certain assumptions that need to be kept in view. First, we have used the relationship between poverty and growth between 1992 and 2005. This relationship may have changed after 2005 but the lack of availability of comparable data on poverty during the post 2005 period limits us to use the time period quoted above. Second, we have used the headcount poverty rate of 2005 for our projections. National data, where available, does indicate a reduction in poverty in 2007. This suggests that using 2007 data might lead to reduced figures regarding the increase in the total number of poor between 2007 and 2009. Third, the impact on employment is based upon open unemployment rates. The effect might vary substantially if disguised employment is also included. For instance, it is possible that if open unemployment rates went up as a result of the crisis, disguised unemployment may have reduced. Fourth and most important, these projections regarding the impact of financial crisis on poverty and employment are made for the three countries in the region as a whole primarily because we pooled the data for the three countries spanning from 1972 to 2009. So the marginal impact that we derived from our regression corresponds to the region as a whole. But the possibility of cross country variation exists. Bangladesh, for instance, is relatively unaffected by the crisis. A close examination of the FSI shows that financial stress was low in

Bangladesh and it receded in 2009. Similarly in India, the stress has been reduced between 2008 and 2009. In Pakistan, on the other hand, the financial stress is still positive. Table 1.12 indicates the results of estimating equation 1 through OLS (Ordinary Least Squares) for each individual country using time series data. The results indicate that in India and Bangladesh, exports to GDP ratio were more important in affecting GDP growth compared to financial stress per se. In Pakistan, on the other hand, the impact of financial stress on GDP growth has a statistically significant impact on GDP growth.

Table 1.12

Country Specific OLS Regressions

Dependent Variable Real GDP Growth	*Bangladesh*	*India*	*Pakistan*
FSI_t	-0.193	-0.0944	-0.409*
	(-0.91)	(-0.54)	(-2.34)
X/GDP_t	0.320**	0.517**	-0.223
	3.39	3.17	(-1.17)
$\Delta OilPrice_t$	0.0272	-0.0514	0.0526*
	1.33	(-1.85)	2.23
$GDPGrowth_{t-1}$	-0.167	-0.161	0.171
	(-1.79)	(-0.97)	0.91
Constant	2.768***	2.960*	6.649*
	-3.82	-2.51	-2.4
Number of Observation	37	37	37

Note: t statistics in parentheses: * $p<0.05$, ** $p<0.01$, *** $p<0.001$

Summary and Conclusions

This section presents the major findings of the study that studied the impact as well as the channels of transmission of recent financial crisis on growth, employment and poverty in the three major South Asian countries—India, Pakistan and Bangladesh. These are the three largest countries in South Asia that together represent around 97 per cent of the region's population and 96 per cent of total regional GDP.

The methodology includes both an in-depth descriptive analysis of the three countries as well as econometric estimations using dynamic panel data and VAR estimations.

The study finds that due to relatively low levels of financial and trade integration with the developed world, the South Asian economies have remained less affected by the crisis compared with other economies particularly those in East Asia. The current level of trade integration, for instance, as measured by the trade to GDP ratio is 43.5 per cent for South Asia, which is way below the corresponding average of 86.2 per cent for East Asia and Pacific, and 65.3 per cent for low and middle income countries. The financial integration in particular, remains quite low especially in Pakistan and Bangladesh. Apart from workers' remittances, most forms of foreign inflows and outflows do not contribute significantly in the GDP of the three countries of our study.

The banking sector in the three countries is sound due to its lack of indulgence in the kind of financial innovation practised by the banking sector in the developed world. Bank deposits as percentage of GDP—an indicator of confidence in the banking system—remained stable with a slight reduction experienced in Bangladesh and Pakistan after 2008. Commercial bank and other lending also remained more or less stable. Remittances, which have been the most important source of foreign exchange in all the three countries of our analysis, held up well during the crisis year.

This however, does not imply that the region has not been affected at all by the crisis. Our study finds that growth in real GDP declined in all the three countries in the aftermath of the crisis and the corresponding effect on employment, and poverty was also non-negligible. Our descriptive analyses as well as econometric estimations indicate that the effect of the crisis was mostly transmitted through the trade channel. This is primarily because global trade integration is relatively higher in South Asia compared to other forms of global integration such as international finance. The major chunk of exports of the three countries of our analysis is directed towards high income economies. As a result of slowdown in aggregate demand in developed economies, particularly US and EU, all three countries witnessed declining trends in growth of their merchandise exports. Trade deficit for all three countries continued to balloon although it is hard to decipher whether this trend was due to financial crisis or due to other factors such as the hike in international prices of oil, food and commodities that began in 2003 and reached a peak around the last quarter of 2008. A close observation of trade deficit shows that in case of all the three countries, the deficit started worsening from 2003 onwards.

In order to estimate the precise effect of financial crisis on economic growth in the region, one needs to control for country-specific factors and isolate the impact of financial crisis from other shocks, the most important being the international oil and commodity price shocks. For the purpose, the present study conducted panel data regression by pooling historical data from 1972 to 2009 for the three countries. Panel data has the advantage of controlling for country specific factors. It also allows us to control for unobservable variables that change over time but not across countries.

The study uses a model in which growth of real GDP is used as the dependent variable. The explanatory variables include: (i) FSI that is computed to capture financial stress in the foreign exchange market, stock market, and the banking sector in the three countries of our study; (ii) exports to GDP ratio that is used to capture the impact of financial crisis through the trade channel; and (iii) international oil and commodity prices. Panel data estimation techniques are used to estimate the long run relationship between financial stress and economic growth in the region.

The results of our study indicate that both financial stress and trade to GDP ratio have a statistically significant impact on growth of real GDP in the region as a whole. The size of the effect as measured by the corresponding elasticities is however much higher for trade to GDP ratio than for the FSI. This confirms our descriptive analysis that indicates that much of the effect of financial crisis on economic growth in the region appears to have been transmitted through the trade channel.

The reduction in economic growth due to financial crisis is expected to affect employment and poverty in the region. Of course, the extent to which employment and poverty are affected by economic growth is determined by the relationship between the three variables. In order to estimate the precise relationship, we estimated growth elasticities of employment and poverty for India, Pakistan and Bangladesh. Using these elasticities, we estimated the precise impact of financial crisis (2007-2009) on employment and poverty in the region.

Our results show an overall addition of around 6.8 million poor living below US$ 1.25 a day in the three countries of our study between 2007 and 2009. The reduction in employment as a result of the financial crisis amounts to 11.8 million people. Much of this increase in the number of poor and unemployed has occurred via the trade channel.

A great deal of cross country variability exists. However, the level of the effect depends a great deal on the strength of macroeconomic fundamentals with which each country entered the period of financial crisis and the policies implemented by each country to pre-empt or minimise the impact of the global financial crisis. Bangladesh has remained least affected by the crisis due to its strong macroeconomic fundamentals that included greater fiscal discipline. Similarly India, despite having witnessed a downward trajectory in economic growth from 2008 onwards, was able to register a decent level of economic growth. Its GDP growth of 6.7 per cent in 2008 was the highest in the world during that particular year. Pakistan, on the other hand, was already experiencing a strain on its economy due to high costs of 'war on terrorism' and deterioration in investment climate due to rising physical insecurity. As a result of differences in these initial conditions, the downward spiral in economic growth was much sharper for Pakistan than for India and Bangladesh, both of which were able to survive through the financial shock in many respects.

References

Arellano, M. and S.R. Bond (1991). "Some Tests of Specification for Panel Data: Monte Carlo Evidence and an Application to Employment Equations", *Review of Economic Studies* 58: 277-97.

Asian Development Bank (ADB) (2010). *Asian Development Outlook 2010: Macroeconomic Management beyond the Crisis.*

Balakrishnan, Ravi, Stephan Danninger, Elekdag Selim and Irina Tytell (2009). "The Transmission of Financial Stress from Advanced to Emerging Economies", *IMF Working Paper* WP/09/133.

Chen, Shaohua and Martin Ravallion (2009). "The Impact of the Global Financial Crisis on the World's Poorest". Available at *http://www.voxeu.org/index.php?q=node/3520*. Retrieved on August, 16, 2010.

Government of India (2009). *Report on Effect of Economic Slowdown on Employment in India.* Ministry of Labour and Employment, Labour Bureau Chandigarh. April-June.

———. (2010) *Economic Survey of India: 2009-10.* Ministry of Finance.

Government of Pakistan (2010). *Pakistan Economic Survey 2009-10.* Islamabad: Finance Division, Economic Advisors wing.

Habib, B., A. Narayan, S. Olivieri and C. Sanchez-Paramo (2010) *Assessing Ex Ante the Poverty and Distributional Impact of the Global Crisis in a Developing Country: A Micro Simulation Approach with Application to Bangladesh.* Washington DC: The World Bank, Poverty Reduction and Economic Management Network, Poverty Reduction and Equity Group.

Hakikio, Kraig S. and William R. Keeton (2009). "Financial Stress: What is it, How Can it be Measured and Why Does it Matter?", *Economic Review: Second Quarter.* Federal Reserve Bank of Kansas City.

Hasan, Rana, Maria Rhoda Magsombol and J. Salcedo Cain (2009). "Poverty Impact of the Economic Slowdown in Developing Asia: Some Scenarios", *Asian Development Bank (ADB) Working Series* # 153, April.

International Monetary Fund (IMF) (2009). *World Economic Outlook: Crisis and Recovery.* April.

———. (2010). *World Economic Outlook: Rebalancing Growth.* April.

Jinn, Guo (2008). "The Impact of Oil Price Shock and Exchange Rate Volatility on Economic Growth: A Comparative Anlaysis of Russia, Japan and China", *Research Journal of Inetrnational Studies 8*, November.

Kumar, Rajiv, Bibek Debroy, Jayati Ghosh, Vijay Mahajan and K. Seeta Prabhu (2009). *Global Financial Crisis: Impact on India's Poor: Some Initial Perspectives.* India: United Nations Development Programme (UNDP).

Lane, Phillip and Gian Maria Milesi-Ferretti (2010). "The Cross Country Incidence of the Global Crisis", *International Monetary Fund Working Paper* 10/171.

Mahub ul Haq Human Development Centre (2009). *Human Development in South Asia 2009: Trade and Human Development.* Oxford University Press.

Rakshit, Mihir (2009). "India Amidst the Global Crisis", *Economic and Political Weekly* XLIV (13), March 28.

Rodriguez, Rebecca Jimenez and Marcello Sanchez (2004). "Oil Price Shocks and Real GDP Growth: Empirical Evidence for Some OECD Countries", *European Central Bank Working Paper No* 362, May.

South Asian Association for Regional Cooperation (SAARC) (2005). *SAARC Regional Poverty Profile 2005: Poverty Reduction in South Asia through Productive Employment.*

World Bank (2010a) *Global Economic Prospects: Crisis, Finance and Growth.*

———. (2010b) *World Development Indicators.*

2

MAHREEN MAHMUD AND NAVED HAMID

Migrant Remittances to South Asia

Determinants and Effect on Growth

Introduction

Remittance flows have registered remarkable growth in the past two decades, surpassing other inflows such as FDI (foreign direct investment) and ODA (official development assistance) for many developing countries. South Asia is the second largest remittance receiving region in the world after East Asia and the Pacific, accounting for around 20 per cent of the total remittances inflows in 2012. India is the largest remittance receiving country in the world after overtaking China in 2010,[1] and Bangladesh and Pakistan have consistently been in the top 10 remittance receiving countries in the developing world.

South Asian countries[2] are highly dependent on remittances, which are an important cushion against the trade deficit that these countries run (Table 2.1). Bangladesh's current account surplus is due to the large inflows of remittances that offset its trade deficit. These flows become especially important in the face of the relatively small contributions that ODA and FDI make to external financing. As many developing countries face a weakening balance of payments situation, remittances are becoming even more important. This is especially true for South Asia where Bangladesh, Pakistan and Sri Lanka receive remittances larger than their foreign exchange reserves.[3]

---

1. Ratha *et al.*, 2009 and Mohapatra *et al.*, 2010.
2. Because of lack of data on remittance flows to Nepal, the analysis in this chapter is restricted to four remittance-dependent economies in South Asia.
3. Ratha *et al.*, 2013.

Table 2.1

Importance of Remittances in South Asia (2008-2012 Average)

Per cent of GDP

	Bangladesh	*India*	*Pakistan*	*Sri Lanka*
Trade deficit	8.5	5.9	7.8	11.7
ODA*	1.7	0.2	1.5	1.7
FDI	1.2	1.1	1.3	0.8
Remittances	11.3	3.6	5.4	7.2
Current Account Surplus	1.9	-3.2	-2.9	-5.4

Note: * is a 2008-2011 period average.

Source: *World Development Indicators.*

Given the importance, it is critical to understand what determines the flow of remittances as well as the resultant impact on the economies of the four South Asian countries, namely Bangladesh, India, Pakistan and Sri Lanka. The remittances received by these countries have remained resilient during the financial crisis making them a reliable source of foreign flows and increasing their importance in times when FDI and ODA have sharply contracted.[4]

This chapter presents an analytical framework for identifying the determinants of remittance flows and their impact at the macroeconomic level in the South Asian economies. The existing literature on South Asia has mostly dealt with the earlier question. We augment the existing literature on the determinants of remittances and estimate the responsiveness of these flows to several factors at the country specific level;[5] and extend the dynamic Keynesian structural model developed in the seminal work by Glytsos (2005) to South Asian countries to understand the impact of changes in remittance flows on respective domestic economies. Finally, we use our estimates to understand the magnitude of the impact of change in remittances on the home country GDP (gross domestic product) after 2007.

4. There has been a 40 per cent decline in FDI between 2008 and 2009 and 80 per cent decline in private debt and portfolio equity flows from their peak in 2007 (Mohapatra *et al.*, 2010).

5. See Hagen-Zanker and Siegel (2007) for a review of the literature on determinants of remittances.

Methodological Issues

The analysis has been carried out in two parts: the first estimates a remittance-determinant equation for each country, identifying crucial macroeconomic factors that impact remittance flows historically. Then, the impact of a change in remittance flows on the home economy is analysed for each of the four countries.

Determinants of Remittances

Millions of the migrants determine the remittance flows to a country, i.e. their decision on what proportion of the income to remit which in turn depends on how much income they earn. Income earned is likely to be impacted by the economic conditions of the host country of the migrant. Thus, a change in host country's GDP is an important determinant of change in economic conditions and thereby, of remittance amounts.

The decision of how much to remit back to home country also depends on whether the migrant has moved with family or not. Migrants without families are likely to decide the amount to be remitted back first, and then adjust consumption and retained savings accordingly. In this case, the conditions in the migrant's home country will be an important determinant of the remittance flows. Hence, literature points to the possibility of the countercyclical nature of these remittance flows to the economic situation in the home country (see among others, Quartey and Blankson, 2004; Chami *et al.*, 2005). The state of the economy determines the local income levels and depending on them the migrants adjust the amount to be sent home. Therefore, the changes in the growth rates of real GDP of the home country are an important determinant which proxy for how the economy is performing. Where consumption is the driving motive for remittances, the sign on home country's GDP will be negative.

Next is the decision on where to invest savings, and several factors that capture the macroeconomic conditions in both home and host countries can be important determinants of this (see Schiopu and Siegfried, 2006). One such indicator is the real interest rate differential between the host and home country. This variable is included as a proxy for the relative returns to financial assets in the two countries. The expected sign is ambiguous as it will be determined by the motivation of the migrant. If s/he is making a decision to invest in financial assets, then the migrant will invest wherever the return in higher (positive sign on the interest differential variable). However, if the migrant is looking to invest in real assets, then high interest rates in a particular country might be reflective of the instability of the state of the economy thereby, deterring investment (negative sign). The relative risk perceptions of assets in the two countries will also play an important role in this decision.

Finally, the movements in exchange rates can impact the remittance amount in two opposing ways. If the migrant is targeting a certain consumption level in the home country, then a real exchange rate depreciation of home country's currency should decrease the amount sent home. On the other hand, it may make investments more attractive as the same amount will convert into a greater principal amount of domestic currency, thus increasing remittances on this account. However, this would not be the case if the migrant is planning to remit back the principal and the returns earned on the investment to the host country in future. Thus, the expected sign on this variable is again ambiguous, and will depend on which channel outweighs the other.

Modelling Determinants of Remittances

The two most important destination regions for migrants from South Asia are the Western Organisation for Economic Co-operation and Development (OECD) Countries and the Middle Eastern countries.[6] Owing to differences in labour demand and migration policies of these regions, the characteristics and nature of migrants to the two regions differ substantially (Mohapatara and Ozden, 2010). Migrants to the Middle East tend to be low skilled, mostly migrating

---

6. Between 2000-2010, nearly 75 per cent of all remittance flows to Pakistan and India and more than 85 per cent to Bangladesh are estimated to come from the US, UK, Kingdom of Saudi Arabia (KSA), Kuwait and UAE, while 66 per cent of all worker remittances flow to Sri Lanka have been from Middle Eastern countries.

alone while those to Western OECD countries are usually highly-educated, migrating with families and often permanently.

Migrants to the Middle East region are employed on a contractual basis (medium-term contracts), where remuneration is fixed for the period, while the pay of those living in Western OECD countries depends on the market. Contracts of the Middle East migrants are for a minimum of one to two years and so the impact of the economy is expected to be felt with a lag on the earnings and consequently on the remittances from the migrants. Furthermore, a majority of them are working in the construction, hospitality or domestic sector which is impacted by GDP growth with a lag. This is however, not the case for the Western OECD countries where the changes in growth rate of GDP are expected to be contemporaneously felt on the earnings of the workers there.

Owing to these underlying differences in migrants to the two regions, it is important to separately study the effects of these regions on remittance flows. Therefore, we employed weighted GDPs[7] for each region in the remittance determining equation to capture the impact of the state of the host economies. The weighted average GDP growth rate of the Western OECD economies enters in the same period in our remittance determining equation while that of the Middle East economies enters with a lag.

Also, aggregate remittance flows could be impacted by structural shifts in remittance flows which need to be accounted for. For example, 9/11 marks one such important global event which resulted in tighter control on international flow of money following the event (World Bank, 2006). This means that remittances flowing through the formal channel have increased and thus the reported increase in total remittance amounts may partly reflect a shift from informal to formal channels. Another contributory factor to the post-9/11 increase could be the uncertainty faced by migrants in the Western OECD economies prompting them to remit back most of their savings and also a larger amount of their incomes. Therefore, to account for

7. The real GDP of these countries were used instead of the nominal figures to 'difference out' inflation effects.

such structural changes in both volume and reasons for remittance flows to these countries, a dummy variable is included in the same spirit as in studies by Gupta (2005) and Barua *et al.* (2007). This acts as an indicator for the structural break, taking a value of 1 for the year 2002 onwards. Its statistical significance will indicate that there are important differences in the remittance flows before and after the event. The *a priori* expectation is that the coefficient of the dummy will have a positive value indicating that remittance flows through the formal channels have increased after 9/11.

Literature also explores the importance of additional factors like poverty levels in home country and the skill level composition of the migrants in different regions in determining remittance flows.[8] But due to lack of data for the period of analysis it is not possible to incorporate these factors in a country level analysis. Based on the discussion above, it is postulated that remittance flows to each country in our sample will be determined by a set of driving variables taking the following form:[9]

$$R_{it} = \alpha_0 + \beta_1 GDP^{ae}_{it} + \beta_2 GDP^{me}_{it-1} + \beta_3 GDP^{home}_{it} + \beta_4 intdiff_{it} + \beta_5 rer_{it} + \beta_6 d \quad (1)$$

where R_{it} is the aggregate remittance inflow to country i during year t. GDP^{ae}_{it} is the weighted GDP of Western OECD economies, GDP^{me}_{it} is the weighted GDP of Middle East economies which enters with a lag, d is a dummy variable included to account for structural break in the sample period discussed above. The difference between host and home country interest rates is captured by the $intdiff_{it}$ variable and rer_{it} is the real exchange rate of the home country relative to US dollar. All variables will be estimated in log-difference form as the resulting series is stationary while the series in levels is found to be non-stationary.

Modelling Impact of Remittances on Home Country GDP

As a next step, we estimate the impact of change in remittance flows on the home (remittance receiving) economy. This impact

8. See Adams (2008).
9. The variables in the specification are consistent with those employed in previous studies (see Zanker and Siegel, 2007, Singh *et al.*, 2009; Cali and Dell'Erba, 2009) but differ in how host country GDP enters the equation.

manifests through a complex interplay of factors involving the consumption and investment components of GDP as well as the balance of payments constraint faced by the country. Glytsos (2005) motivates our empirical estimation as the model outlined in his study is able to incorporate dynamic effects which allow estimation of not only the contemporaneous but also any subsequent impact on GDP of change in remittances. The model consists of the following three behavioural equations and the income identity:

Consumption function: $C_t = \alpha_0 + \alpha_1 Y_t + \alpha_2 C_{t-1}$ (2)

where current consumption (C_t) is explained by current income (Y_t) and previous period consumption (C_{t-1}) thereby incorporating both the adaptive expectations and partial adjustment.

Investment function: $I_t = \delta_0 + \delta_1 Y_t + \delta_2 K_{t-1}$ (3)

where investment (I) is assumed to be correlated with business profits, which in turn are positively related to national income; further it is assumed that businesses tend to converge towards some desired level of capital stock with a time lag. Consequently, investment is assumed to be positively related to national income and negatively related to lagged capital stock (K_{t-1}).

Import Function: $M_t = \gamma_0 + \gamma_1 Y_t + \gamma_2 Y_{t-1} + \gamma_3 M_{t-1}$ (4)

where Imports (M) are assumed to be a function of current and past period income as well as lagged imports; a relationship which is derived from the life-cycle hypothesis developed for consumption.

And finally,

National Income Identity: $Y_t = C_t + I_t + G_t + X_t - M_t + R_t$ (5)

Where Y, C, I, M enter as endogenous variables and X, R, G are exogenous variables.

Using the four equations above, we form a reduced form:

$X_{it} = \pi_0 + \pi_1 C_{t-1} + \pi_2 K_{t-1} + \pi_3 Y_{t-1} + \pi_4 M_{t-1} + \pi_5 G_t + \pi_6 X_t + \pi_7 R_t$ (6)

where X is any of the endogenous variables C, I, M, Y. Estimates of πs are the partial derivative of any endogenous variable X with respect to the variables entering equation (6) as explanatory variables. The coefficient of interest for our analysis is π_7 which gives the short term multiplier estimate of the contemporaneous impact of remittances on any of the endogenous variables X.

These πs can be estimated either directly through OLS (ordinary least squares) estimation of equation (6) or through the derivation of these reduced form estimates from the structural estimates obtained from TSLS (two stage least squares) estimation of equations 2-6. Glytsos (2005) finds consistent estimates for his sample of selected developing African countries when the latter approach is employed.

The dynamic nature of the model allows the long term impact on the macro economy of changes in remittances to be traced in addition to the short term impact. These interim multipliers can be estimated from the reduced form estimates:

$$N^{th} \text{ year multiplier} = \pi_r * \pi_v^{n-1} \quad (7)$$

where π_v is the multiplier of the dependant variable Y with respect to its own one year lagged value and π_r is the multiplier of current change in remittances.

Estimation Results

South Asia

The decision on how much to remit is the result of the interplay of a complex set of factors and several different motivations may exist simultaneously and migrants within the same regions may have different reasons to remit. Therefore, at the macro level we can at best approximate how migrants to a particular region respond on aggregate as a group. The remittance determining equation (1) defined above was estimated for all four countries and the consistent estimates are reported in Table 2.2.

The GDP coefficient of Western OECD countries is positive and significant for Pakistan and Bangladesh, negative for Sri Lanka while it is insignificant for India. Furthermore, while the home country GDP is insignificant for Pakistan and Bangladesh,[10] it is significant

10. The statistical insignificance of the coefficient is perhaps resulting from relatively small number of time series observations. Availability of monthly/quarterly data would have improved the robustness of results presented in the study.

for Sri Lanka and India but with opposite signs. Remittances to Sri Lanka with respect to its GDP turn out to be procyclical and seem to respond positively to home country conditions. These results might be indicative of the investment motivation dominating in Sri Lanka as compared with the more dominant consumption motivated migrant remittances in other three countries.

Table 2.2

OLS Estimates of Remittance Determination Equation

Dependant variable: Log of growth rate of remittances

	(1) Bangladesh	(2) India	(3) Pakistan	(4) Sri Lanka
Yearly dummy (=1 for after 2001)	0.0942	0.369**	0.172	-0.145*
	(1.62)	(2.48)	(1.38)	(-1.98)
Weighted GDP of Western OECD economies	4.021**	2.793	2.031***	-5.770*
	(2.55)	(1.23)	(3.45)	(-2.02)
Lagged Weighted GDP of Middle East^	0.833*	1.914**	1.399**	1.584**
	(1.93)	(2.80)	(2.34)	(2.41)
Lagged GDP of South Asia		-0.213***		
		(-3.65)		
Home GDP	-1.805	-3.452**	-0.387	3.447**
	(-0.90)	(-2.29)	(-0.17)	(2.14)
Interest rate differential (not in log)			2.394	1.004*
			(1.36)	(1.93)
Real exchange rate		1.277*	-0.567	
		(1.95)	(-0.60)	
Dummy (=1 for year>1992 and <2002)		0.266*		
		(2.74)		
Adjusted R-squared	0.28	0.36	0.31	0.38
observations	25	33	31	29

Note: All explanatory variables are in log difference unless stated otherwise. t-statistics reported in parentheses. *** $p<0.01$, ** $p<0.05$, * $p<0.10$ (two-tailed significant tests).

^ Lagged GDP of only KSA for the case of Bangladesh.

The results above are for the best specification for each country. In the country-wise discussion of the results in this section, it is explained why certain variables have been included and others dropped for that country.

The dummy for post-9/11 structural shift, while positive does not come out to be significant for Bangladesh and Pakistan.[11] It turns out to be significant but negative for Sri Lanka; possibly because the escalating civil war in the country during this period discouraged investment motivated remittances. India is the only country where remittances registered a significant increase in the post 2001 period as hypothesised.

Bangladesh

In their study, Barua *et al.* (2007) examine the macroeconomic determinants of workers' remittances using a panel data of host countries for the period 1993-2005 and conclude that in the case of Bangladesh interest rate differential, migrant stock and exchange rate positively impact remittance flows while inflation differential between host and home country, and home country GDP impacts the remittance flows negatively. They establish that a negative coefficient on the home country GDP is suggestive of the dominance of altruistic motive since deterioration in home country conditions leads to an increase in the remittances sent back.

Our study also points to the altruistic nature of the migrants from Bangladesh. However, we find that there is high correlation of both interest rate differential and real exchange rate with the host and the home country GDPs. Hence, they could not be included as explanatory variables resulting in the estimation of a simplified version of equation (1) using OLS for the 1980 to 2009 period[12] (see Table 2.2).

Employing weighted average of GDPs of Western OECD and Middle Eastern countries results in inconsistent estimates due to the high correlation between the two weighted host GDPs and the resulting collinearity induced by the inclusion of these variables. As an alternative, the GDP of Saudi Arabia is included as a proxy for the Middle Eastern region since it has consistently been the largest

11. Small sample size with low frequency annualised time series might not be allowing the change in relationship to be captured.

12. Due to the availability of country wise remittance flows only after 1980.

remittance source for Bangladesh. Consistent with the findings for other countries, lagged GDP growth rate of Saudi Arabia comes out as a significant determinant of changes in remittance flows to the country. A percentage point change in GDP growth rate yields a 0.83 percentage point change in remittance growth rate which is low compared with that for other countries. On the other hand, the elasticity number is very high (4.02) and statistically significant for the flows from Western OECD economies.

India

For India, the disaggregated data on actual remittances flows from each country are not available, therefore the data on migrant stocks to each country have been used. In terms of migrant stocks, the two South Asian countries Bangladesh and Nepal are also important migration destinations, in addition to the Western OECD and Middle East regions. India is the only country in South Asia for which the hypothesised link between performance of the home country and remittance flows holds. There is positive, significant and large responsiveness of remittances to slowdown of growth in the Indian economy.

Remittance flows from the Western OECD countries are not responsive to conditions in the host economies. As discussed earlier, bulk of the migrants to these countries are highly skilled who migrate with their families. As a result, a relatively smaller portion of income of these migrants is remitted and so the amounts might not be responsive to economic conditions in their host economies. On the other hand, migrants in the Middle East region are relatively low income earners who consistently remit a substantial portion of their income to their families in India and so the impact of downturn in those economies is more pronounced and significant (elasticity of 1.91). Furthermore, there is a negative relation between the performance of South Asian economies and remittance flows to India. Ratha and Shaw (2007) note that intra-regional remittance flows in the South region are constrained by restrictions making it difficult to explain the result.

We include a dummy variable to factor in the impact of financial reforms that were started in 1991. These reforms which liberalised the country's economic system boosted remittance flows through the formal channel. Earlier, the exchange rate was regulated by the authorities creating incentives for transfer of money through the informal *hawala*[13] system. The coefficient turns out to be positive and significant supporting the hypothesised relationship.

The events that folded during the post-9/11 period further boosted the shift towards formal channels as fears over terrorist financing resulted in greater regulation of these *hawala* networks.[14] This is why a second dummy variable is included to factor in the further shift away from informal channels during the post-2001 period. It is also possible that because of the impressive growth rate of the Indian economy in the past decade, more money is now flowing in for investment purposes. This dummy variable also yields a positive and significant coefficient.

Remittances do show sensitivity to the real exchange rate—a result which is unique to India. As expected, with appreciation of the Indian Rupee (INR), there is a positive change in remittance flows. This might be explained by the migrants aiming to maintain a specified consumption level for their households which in face of an appreciation of the INR can only be achieved by increased remittance flows.

Pakistan

Past studies on determinants of remittance flows to Pakistan have established the consumption needs of workers' families in the home country to be the dominant motive for the migrants to remit (see Nishat and Bilgrami, 1991). The estimation results for the 1976-2007 period indicate that remittance flows at the macro level are determined by the conditions in the host country with a strong statistically significant link between the growth rate of the host country's GDP and remittance growth rate (see Table 2.2). In line with the findings of the previous studies, investment channel is

---

13. Informal transfer of money through brokers from one geographic location to another.

14. Chisti (2007).

found to be less dominant. This is indicated by the insignificance of the interest rate differential as well as the signs on the host country GDPs (positive). Moreover, for the given sample period, changes in real exchange rate do not come out to be a significant determinant of remittances in the case of Pakistan.[15]

The remittances growth rate is elastic with respect to the weighted average of the growth rates of GDPs in the US and UK, the two regions from which 18 per cent of the remittance flows originated on average during the period from 1975 to 2009. A 1 percentage point increase in the growth rate of combined GDPs of the two countries leads to a 2 percentage point increase on average in the growth rate of remittances to Pakistan. While the coefficient indicates an elastic relationship between remittance and lagged GDP growth rates for the Middle Eastern countries (1.4), this is lower than the impact of GDP growth rates of Western OECD economies (2.04).

Sri Lanka

Consistent with the findings of Leuth and Arranz (2007) the coefficient on the domestic GDP is positive and significant indicating the procyclical nature of remittance flows in the case of Sri Lanka. A possible explanation presented by some researchers is the non-altruistic nature of the motives for remitting. Thus, remittances can be impacted by the investment climate of the home country which is reflected in the rates of growth of real GDP. The interest rate differential also comes out to be significant. *A priori* expectation is that the sign would be negative since a person making a portfolio allocation decision in financial assets would be inclined to invest where interest rates are higher. Hence, a high interest rate differential, which indicates high real interest rates in host country, would negatively impact remittances. However, we find that interest rate differential has positive impacts on remittance flows. This is in line with the findings of previous

15. There is a possibility that the relationship between remittances and changes in real exchange rate may be asymmetrical when consumption channel is dominant, i.e. in case of appreciation of the domestic currency migrants may feel compelled to increase the remittance amount (as in India) but are unable to reduce it in the case of a depreciation (as in Pakistan).

studies (Singh *et al.*, 2009) who argue that a higher interest rate in the home country reflects instability. This will in turn mean that returns on real assets are lower in such time periods and migrants will be sending lesser money home for such investment purposes. A positive sign in the case of Sri Lanka suggests that the latter argument dominates with investments in real assets driving the result. Historically, this impact has been large with 1 percentage point increase in the growth of domestic GDP resulting in a 3.56 percentage point increase in remittance growth.

Consistent with these findings, the remittances flowing in from the Western OECD economies have produced negative impacts on GDP growth rates of these regions. Positive GDP growth reflects the presence of lucrative investment opportunities and that the economy is thriving. Thus, migrants to these regions appear to be choosing to invest in their host countries as these economies perform well thereby cutting the amount remitted back home.

On the other hand, the relatively limited investment opportunities in the Middle East and the nature of migration (a huge number are females working as housemaids[16]) results in the positive elasticity figure for the region, which is consistent with the results for other South Asian countries.[17] The flows from the Middle East are elastic with respect to host countries' GDPs and are impacted with a lag as in the case of other three countries. Any increase in the growth rate of host countries' GDPs results in double the increase in the growth rate of remittances in the next period.

Remittances and the Financial Crisis

In spite of the contraction in 2009 due to the financial crisis, global remittances have seen tremendous growth in the last decade and have tripled from around US$ 125 billion in the mid 2000s to over US$ 380 billion by 2012.[18] The growth rate bounced back almost

16. Mohapatra and Ozden, 2010.
17. An in-depth micro study on the motivations of migrants to remit can give us a clearer picture of what appears to be a complex interplay of factors that motivate a migrant to remit.
18. *Migration and Development Brief* 11 and 21.

immediately after 2009 and though it remains lower than in the past, the impact has been nowhere as catastrophic as was feared at the outset of the financial crisis.[19]

Turning to South Asia, we find that India is the only country of the four to register a negative growth rate of remittances in 2009 in tandem with the world trend (Figure 2.1). The decline in the real effective exchange rate possibly contributed to this in addition to the slowdown in the host economies. Subsequently, the remittance growth bounced back in 2010 but still remained much lower than the pre-financial crisis growth rate (which was more than 30% for the 2006-2008 period). Bangladesh, which saw phenomenal growth in remittances leading up to the financial crisis, experienced a decline in growth rate in 2009.

Figure 2.1

Annual Growth Rate of Remittances (2006-2012)

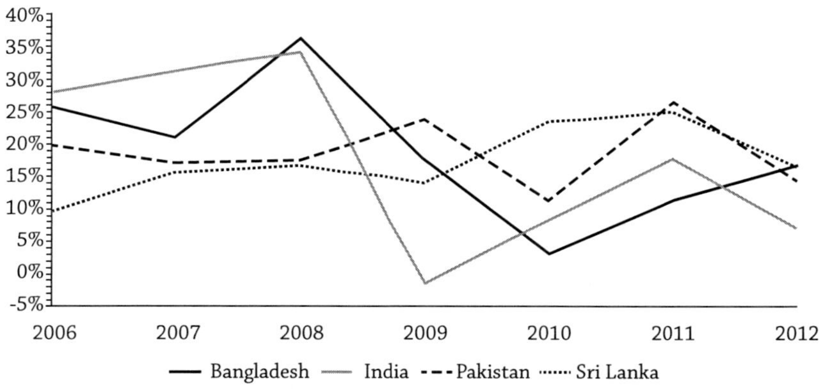

Source: World Bank.

This was followed by a larger fall in 2010 when the full impact of the Middle Eastern economies started to show, which like the other South Asian countries created impact on Bangladesh with a lag. Surprisingly, in Pakistan the growth rate of remittances increased in 2009 before declining sharply in 2010 due to the slowdown in

19. For a detailed analysis of the possible reasons, see introduction by Ratha *et al.* (2012) to the book *Migration and Remittances during the Global Financial Crisis and Beyond.*

the Middle Eastern economies in 2009 (UAE experienced a negative real growth rate in GDP during the year). Finally, the growth rate of remittances to Sri Lanka saw a slight decline in 2009 and a sharp increase in 2010, possibly because the impact of the recovery of the Sri Lankan GDP, to which we find remittances respond positively, outweighing the lagged impact of the slowdown in the Middle East.

Estimating Impact on Home Country GDP

The responsiveness of GDPs of the economies to changes in remittances is estimated by employing TSLS on equations 2-6 (Table 2.3). All data series employed are in levels and at constant prices covering the period 1975 to 2007. The signs on all coefficients are as hypothesised and the results are consistent with the findings of Glytsos (2005) for selected developing countries in Africa. Lagged consumption and this period's income are important determinants of consumption with the estimates of marginal propensity to consume for all four South Asian countries quite close to each other for the period under study. This might be attributable to the similar consumption oriented nature of the societies of the region.

The coefficient of interest is the derived reduced form estimate of the short run remittance multiplier (see Table 2.4). Its value gives the change in GDP as a result of a one unit change in remittances. In the short run, the impact of changes in remittances is more than one for a unit change in GDP for all countries. In addition, any change in remittances in one period will not just impact GDP contemporaneously but also affects the GDP in future. The estimates of equation (7) in Table 2.4 give the impact in the following years of any change in remittances during the current period. The highest impact is found to be in the same year with the impact on GDP dying down quickly in subsequent years for countries other than India where it persists strongly. Next we discuss for each country the estimated multipliers and the short run contribution of the change in remittances on the home country's GDP growth for the 2008-2012 period.

Table 2.3

TSLS Estimates of Structural Regression Coefficients

	C_t				I_t				M_t				
	Cons	Y_t	C_{t-1}	R_2	*Cons*	Y_t	K_{t-1}	R_2	*Cons*	Y_t	Y_{t-1}	M_{t-1}	R_2
Bangladesh	12734	0.349***	0.541***	99	-42343	0.111***	7.489***	98	-15268	0.0954*	-0.0875	1.066***	99
	(0.42)	(4.40)	(4.74)		(-1.45)	(4.08)	(6.84)		(-0.74)	(1.81)	(-1.69)	(11.07)	
India	225.3**	0.223***	0.677***	99	-1289.3***	0.129	0.116*	99	1433.7***	0.0155	0.0204	0.887***	99
	(3.35)	(6.44)	(9.80)		(-4.10)	(1.59)	(2.71)		(7.52)	(0.24)	(0.29)	(20.85)	
Pakistan	2265	0.283	0.650***	99	-38294***	0.414***	-0.068***	99	-1064	0.559	-0.541	0.831***	96
	(0.10)	(0.83)	(11.64)		(2.85)	(5.22)	(-2.35)		(-0.89)	(1.27)	(-1.00)	(7.61)	
Sri Lanka	36110**	0.232***	0.635***	99	39699***	0.386***	-0.0461***	98	9697	0.510***	-0.513***	0.962***	99
	(5.85)	(6.24)	(10.08)		(-4.84)	(12.89)	(-5.21)		(1.49)	(6.30)	(-5.76)	(8.68)	

Note: t-statistics reported in parentheses. *** $p<0.01$, ** $p<0.05$, * $p<0.10$ (two-tailed significant tests).

Table 2.4

Time Distribution of the Effects of a Unit Change in Remittances (ΔR=1) on GDP (Y)

	Short Run Effect	*Interim Dynamic Multipliers*			
Year	1	2	3	4	5
Bangladesh	1.57	0.22	0.03	0.004	0.001
India	1.53	1.37	1.23	1.10	0.98
Pakistan	1.16	0.73	0.46	0.29	0.18
Sri Lanka	1.12	0.64	0.37	0.21	0.12

Bangladesh

The second part of the analysis yields a high short run multiplier of 1.57, the highest for the South Asian countries in our study but interestingly the impact is the quickest to dissipate in subsequent periods. It drops to an almost negligible level within three years of any change in remittances indicating that effect on GDP of changes in remittances is a short run phenomenon in the case of Bangladesh.

Using the short run multiplier to estimate the impact of growth in remittances on the country's GDP for the 2008-2012 period, we find that remittances make a huge contribution to the growth of GDP in Bangladesh. The effect is much larger than in any other South Asian countries especially during the financial crisis years. This is likely to be due to the high remittance to GDP ratio for Bangladesh in comparison with the other three countries.

Table 2.5

Contribution of Change in Remittances to GDP Growth Rate (2008-2012)

(in Per cent)

	Bangladesh	*India*	*Pakistan*	*Sri Lanka*
2008	80	38	33	-12
2009	51	-1	44	46
2010	-16	-4	6	20
2011	24	8	30	20
2012	78	18	20	47
Overall average	43	12	27	24
2008-09 average	65	19	38	17

India

Not only is the contemporaneous impact on Indian GDP of any change in remittances quite strong but this impact also persists in subsequent years (Table 2.4). In fact, the impact barely drops below one till the fifth year after the change in remittance amount. The persistence in interim multiplier figures is much higher than found by Glytsos (2005) for any of the five African Mediterranean countries studied by him as well as the other three countries in our analysis. This is a result which could have important implications for the country, given the uncertainty regarding the growth prospects of the host economies, as it signals the huge aggregate impact that changes in remittances could have on the GDP over the years. This interesting result needs further investigation in future studies.

However, if we consider the short run impact of the growth in remittances on GDP growth alone, it averages at around 12 per cent for the 2008-2012 period, and is slightly higher during the financial crisis (Table 2.5). This is not as large as in other South Asian countries because of India's lower remittance to GDP ratio and higher growth in GDP during the financial crisis years.

Pakistan

The estimate of the impact on the economy of any change in remittances yields a short run multiplier of 1.16 (Table 2.4). This impact steadily declines but remains strong in the subsequent years indicating that the GDP of the country continues to be strongly influenced by past changes in the remittance amount. Thus, the aggregate impact of remittances is much larger than indicated by the initial estimated impact in the same period on GDP.

Again, considering the short run impact alone, according to our estimates, remittances growth contributes more than one-fourth of the growth in GDP for the 2008-2012 period (Table 2.5). This highlights the importance of remittances to the economy particularly in the period of slow growth.

Sri Lanka

The contemporaneous impact as well as the impact in the years following any change in remittance flows on the Sri Lankan economy mirrors the pattern seen for Pakistan (Table 2.4). The numbers are slightly lower but almost in line with those for Pakistan and the impact declines yet remains substantial till the last year of our analysis period, i.e. the impact is expected to be felt on the Sri Lankan economy not just in the period of change in remittance flows but also in years following the initial change.

The average short run impact on Sri Lankan GDP growth for the period 2008-2012 is about the same as for Pakistan, but the impact during the financial crisis was much lower. In fact, Sri Lanka is the only country for which this is lower as compared with the overall period average. This might be due to the recovery in Sri Lankan GDP growth since the end of the civil war in 2009 more than compensated for the negative impact of the financial crisis.

Conclusions

The present analysis brought to light both the important determinants of remittances and their resulting impact on the four countries of South Asia under study. Overall, the results indicate that consumption motive appears to be dominant for all countries except Sri Lanka, where investment considerations seem to outweigh purely altruistic motives of the migrants.

We found that conditions in the destination countries of the migrants do not uniformly impact remittance flows. Remittances from the Middle East region respond to changes in GDPs in these countries with a one period lag while those from the Western OECD countries are contemporaneously impacted. This result is driven by the relatively heterogeneous characteristics of migrants from South Asia going to the two regions due to differences in the labour market conditions in the destination countries.

For all countries, the impact on the output of the home economy of any change in remittances yields an impact multiplier greater than one pointing to the importance of these flows. However, the impact in subsequent years varied substantially across the countries in the South Asian region. It died down rapidly for Bangladesh while in the case of India it persists quite strongly. Finally, through the financial crisis, the impact on home country GDP of remittances varies depending on the resilience of GDP and the remittance to GDP ratios. It contributed only a little to a high growth country like India but much more in cases of Bangladesh and Pakistan which are highly dependent on remittances and/or experienced a slowdown in the home economy during the period.

References

Adams, R. H. (2008). "Determinants of International Remittances in Developing Countries", *Policy Research Working Paper* 4583. Development Economics Department, World Bank.

Asian Development Bank (2010). *Key Indicators for Asia and the Pacific*. 41st ed. Mandaluyong City.

Barua, S., M.A. Majumder and Md. Akhtaruzzaman (2007). "Determinants of Worker's Remittances in Bangladesh: An Empirical Study", *Working Paper* 0713. Policy Analysis Unit, Bangladesh Bank.

Brown, R.P.C and E. Jimenez (2008). "Estimating the Net Effects of Migration and Remittances on Poverty and Inequality: Comparison of Fiji and Tonga", *Journal of International Development* 20: 547-71.

Cali, M., and S. Dell'Erba (2009). "The Global Financial Crisis and Remittances: What Past Evidence Suggests", *Working Paper* 303." Overseas Development Institute.

Chami, R., C. Fullenkamp and M. Gapen (2008). *Measuring Workers' Remittances: What Should Be Kept in and What Should Be Left Out*? International Monetary Fund.

Chami, R., C. Fullenkamp and S. Jahjah (2005). "Are Immigrant Remittance Flows a Source of Capital for Development?", *IMF Staff Papers* 52(1). Washington DC.: IMF.

Chisti, M. (2007). *The Rise in Remittances to India: A Closer Look*. Migration Policy Institute.

Giuliano, P. and M. Ruiz-Arranz (2009). "Remittances, Financial Development, and Growth", *Journal of Development Economics* 90: 144-52.

Glytsos, N.P. (2005). "The Contribution of Remittances to Growth: A Dynamic Approach and Empirical Analysis", *Journal of Economic Studies* 32(6): 468-96.

Gupta, P. (2005). "Macroeconomic Determinants of Remittances: Evidence from India", *IMF Working Paper no*. WP/05/224. Washington DC.: European Department, IMF.

Hagen-Zanker, J. and M. Siegel (2007). "The Determinants of Remittances: A Review of the Literature", *Working Paper* WP003. Maastricht Graduate School of Governance, Maastricht University.

Lasagabaster, E., S. Maimbo and S. Hulugalle (2005). "Sri Lanka's Migrant Labor Remittance: Enhancing the Quality and Outreach of the Rural Remittance Infrastructure", *Working Paper No*. 0713. Policy Analysis Unit, Bangladesh Bank.

Lueth, E. and M. Ruiz-Arranz (2007). "Are Workers' Remittances a Hedge Against Macroeconomic Shocks? The Case of Sri Lanka", *IMF Working Paper* 22.

Nishat, M. and N. Bilgrami (1993). "The Determinants of Worker's Remittances in Pakistan", *The Pakistan Development Review* 32(3): 1235-45.

Quartey, P. and T. Blankson (2004). *Do Migrant Remittances Minimize the Impact of Macro-volatility on the Poor in Ghana?*. Global Development Network.

Ratha, D and W. Shaw (2007). "South-South Migration and Remittances", *Working Paper* 101. Washington DC: World Bank.

Ratha, D., S. Mohapatra and A. Silwal (2009). "Migration and Remittance Trends: A Better-Than-Expected Outcome for Migration and Remittance Flows So Far, But Significant Risks Ahead", *Migration and Development Brief* 11. Washington, DC: Migration and Remittances Unit, World Bank.

Ratha, D., J. H. Cohen and I. Sirkeci (2012). *Introduction: Remittance Flows and Practices during the Crisis in Migration and Remittances during the Global Financial Crisis and Beyond*. Washington DC: World Bank. pp.4-6.

Ratha, D., C. Eigen-Zucchi, S. Plaza, H. Wyss and S. Yi (2013). "Migration and Remittance Flows: Recent Trends and Outlook, 2013-2016", *Migration and Development Brief* 21. Development Prospects Group. World Bank.

Mohapatra, S. and C. Ozden (2010). "Migration and Remittances", in Ejaz Ghani (ed.), *The Service Revolution in South Asia*. New Delhi: Oxford University Press.

Mohapatra, S., D. Ratha and A. Silwal (2010). "Recovery after the Crisis, but Risks Lie Ahead", *Migration and Development Brief* 13. Migration and Remittances Unit, World Bank.

Schiopu, I. and N. Siegfried (2006). "Determinants of Workers' Remittances: Evidence from The European Neighbouring Region", *European Central Bank, Working Paper* No. 688.

Singh, R.J., M. Haacker and K. Lee (2009). "Determinants and Macroeconomic Impact of Remittances in Sub-Saharan Africa", *IMF Working Paper* WP/09/216. African Department, IMF.

World Bank (2006). *Global Economic Prospects (GEP)*. Washington, DC.

————. (2009). *Swimming against the Tide: How Developing Countries are Coping with the Global Crisis*. Washington DC.

3

S. IRUDAYA RAJAN AND D. NARAYANA

The Financial Crisis in the Gulf and its Impact on South Asian Migrant Workers[1]

Introduction

The financial crisis had its origins in the United States (US) in 2008, and spread to Europe, particularly the United Kingdom (UK), and then to Japan. It then engulfed most economies—developed, developing and emerging. However, the effect of the crisis has been slow to manifest in the six Gulf Co-operation Council (GCC) countries[2] than in the European and US economies. Their basic strengths—a public funded banking sector and huge trade surplus due to export of oil, the price of which saw unprecedented increase in a span of six months in 2008—shielded the GCC economies from the adverse impact during the initial period of the crisis. The large current account surpluses ranging from 6.1 per cent of GDP (gross domestic product) for Oman to 45 per cent for Kuwait also helped (IMF, 2009a; 2009b). This, coupled with significant inward FDIs (foreign direct investments) to all GCC countries, except Kuwait, also had a beneficial impact (ESCWA, 2008).

However, there were indications from various sources that the GCC economies began to feel the impact of global crisis since the last quarter of 2008. The most significant indicator was the slowdown

1. The study was funded by the Asian Development Bank (ADB), Ministry of Overseas Indian Affairs, Government of India and the Department of Non-Resident Keralite Affairs, Government of Kerala. The draft report was first presented in the conference organised by ADB in Singapore during 26-27 October 2009, followed by the final draft presentation organised by ADB in Dhaka during 3-4 December 2009. Another presentation was also made at the Centre for Development Studies (CDS) on 15 December 2009.

2. GCC countries are: United Arab Emirates (UAE), Saudi Arabia, Qatar, Bahrain, Kuwait and Oman.

in the GDP growth rate in 2008 and the predicted negative growth rate in 2009 in some of these economies (Gulftalent.com, 2009). The predicted decline in the growth rate in these economies was based on the first few months of 2009 during which period there was a continued decline in oil prices,[3] owing mainly to the decline in demand from the Organisation for Economic Co-operation and Development (OECD) countries. Moreover, given the link between the growth in hydrocarbon-based and non-hydrocarbon-based sectors in the economy, the decline in the price of oil reduced the growth of the latter. In the financial sector, the stock markets in all the GCC countries recorded a decline, owing mainly to the withdrawal of foreign institutional investors. A number of privately funded domestic and international projects in the Gulf region were cancelled or abandoned, leading to a large number of layoffs or retrenchment of the workforce. At the beginning of 2009, after observing the downturn in GCC economies, several international organisations showed interest in assessing the impact of the economic crisis on industry and trade (Nanto, 2009) and some in particular, on migration and remittances (Fix *et al.*, 2009; Awad, 2009; World Bank, 2009).

Nevertheless, these effects could not be generalised for all GCC countries given their diversity. Countries that were more exposed to global capital, investment and consumption demand faced a greater risk of being affected by the crisis than others. For instance, Dubai in the UAE, which depends heavily on international capital, tourism and real estate, was more adversely affected than other countries. On the other hand, Saudi Arabia, which has only 25 per cent foreign workers compared with much higher proportions in other GCC economies, was less affected than others (Zachariah and Rajan, 2009a). The crisis seemed to have visibly hit the GCC economies in the beginning of 2009. However, both the depth and intensity of crisis and the possibility of turnaround were not clear. Of course, the longer it took to reach a turnaround, the longer it took to overcome the crisis.

3. The price of crude oil had declined to average of US$ 50 per barrel, compared to the baseline price of US$ 75 in 2009.

Needless to say, the slowdown in the growth rates of GCC economies was of particular significance for the South Asian expatriates who were the main source of migrant labour in the GCC countries. This affected the flow of migration and caused unexpected large-scale return emigration and falling remittances (Kapiszewski, 2006).

Research Questions and Objectives

In the above context, for informed policy making in the countries of origin (South Asia) and countries of destination (GCC countries), the present study investigated the following research issues:

- How did the crisis affect the demand for South Asian migrant workers in the Gulf countries?
- What strategies could the emigrants adopt to cope with the situation at their place of work (countries of destination): what was the likely impact of the crisis on the home country in terms of decline in remittances, if any?
- Do countries in South Asia expect large-scale return emigration? Do they expect a decline in the outflow of emigrant labour to Gulf countries; and inward remittances from them?
- How do the strategies of the migrants to cope with the crisis in the countries of destination affect the coping mechanisms of their families in the home country, particularly those of the women left behind?
- What actions could the South Asian countries—collectively or independently—take to mitigate the hardships of the return emigrants and their families?

To seek answers for the above questions, the following objectives were pursued in the study:

- Assess the impact of the recession on key industries in the GCC economies which employ the majority of migrant workers from South Asia, and examine the migrants' strategies to cope with the crisis.
- Assess the impact of the crisis on the extent of repatriation of the migrants, decline in the flow of emigrants and fall in remittances.

- Analyse the effects of the return of the migrants to their respective households in their countries of origin.
- Study the changes in the characteristics of employment, savings and livelihood diversification of affected households, if any; and
- Identify the key measures to be carried out by various stakeholders, such as the South Asian Association for Regional Cooperation (SAARC) and the countries of origin and destination.

In the above context, the study makes a critical assessment of the emerging economic growth and employment trends in the context of the global financial crisis in the countries of destination, particularly in the six countries of the Gulf (UAE, Saudi Arabia, Oman, Qatar, Bahrain and Kuwait) and Malaysia. The scope also includes the impact of the global financial crisis on stocks and flows of migrant workers and inward remittances to the five countries of South Asia[4]—India, Pakistan, Bangladesh, Nepal and Sri Lanka.

The study is a collaborative effort of the CDS, Thiruvananthapuram and the social sciences research institutes within the South Asian region. Team members from the CDS and from social sciences research institutes within the South Asian region and the destinations where they worked are presented in Box 3.1.

A Brief Outline of Methodology

The initial approach of the study has been to assess the trends in relation to expatriate workers, imports, exports, investment, inflation, employment structure and other financial aspects and stimulus packages announced by the respective governments in the seven countries of destination.[5] These are based on the macro

---

4. The extension of the study to five South Asian Countries will lead us to provide policy framework at the SAARC level. With the senior author's experience in conducting studies on aging issues in South Asia, migration research at this juncture was extended to South Asian countries; see Irudaya Rajan, 2008; Irudaya Rajan *et al.*, 2008.

5. The senior author has conducted earlier research in the countries of destination (UAE, Qatar and Bahrain) both for the Department of Non-Resident Keralite Affairs, Government of Kerala and Ministry of Overseas Indian Affairs, Government of India; see details, Zachariah *et al.*, 2003; 2004; Irudaya Rajan *et al.*, 2009a.

picture from published national and international sources of data and discussions with respective ministries and other stakeholders in the Gulf. The researchers submitted a destination country report.[6] During their visit to the Gulf, the researchers also completed the emigrant survey questionnaires to assess the coping mechanisms of migrants in the Gulf.

BOX 3.1

Details of Team Members and Destinations Where They Worked

Country of destination	*Team members from the CDS*
Malaysia	S. Irudaya Rajan and Aparna Nair
UAE	D. Narayana, Vinoj Abraham, S. Irudaya Rajan and K.C. Zachariah
Saudi Arabia	A.V. Jose, D. Narayana and S. Irudaya Rajan
Qatar	Udaya Sankar Mishra, Hrushikesh Mallick and S. Irudaya Rajan
Bahrain	K Navaneetham, Arindam Banerjee and S. Irudaya Rajan
Oman	P. Mohanan Pillai, Arindam Banerjee and S. Irudaya Rajan
Kuwait	K. Pushpangadan, Parameswaran M. and S. Irudaya Rajan

Country of Origin	*Institute*	*Researcher(s)*
India	CDS, Thiruvananthapuram, Kerala	S Irudaya Rajan
Pakistan	Pakistan Institute of Development Economics, Islamabad, Pakistan	Nasir Iqbal and Saima Nawaz
Bangladesh	Bangladesh Institute of Development Studies, Dhaka, Bangladesh	Anwara Begum
Sri Lanka	Marga Institute, Colombo, Sri Lanka	Myrtle Perera
Nepal	Nepal Institute of Development Studies, Kathmandu, Nepal	Ganesh Gurung

6. The preparation of country report was undertaken by a two member team consisting of a professor and assistant professor from CDS, who made a one week trip to all the countries in the Gulf with the logistics support of the respective Indian Embassies in the Gulf. They were supported by the research assistants both in the Gulf and in India to prepare the country report and complete the emigrant survey. The senior author of the report visited most of the Gulf countries and Malaysia along with the team to gather the firsthand information on the crisis and its impact on migrant workers. The country reports are available for circulation at CDS, Kerala. With the growing interest on the destination country reports of the Gulf, the Ministry of Overseas Indian Affairs, Government of India, agreed to sponsor a one day seminar at CDS to present the country reports in January 2010 and to get the report published by a leading publisher in India.

This is followed by mapping of the trends and patterns of international migration, preferred countries of destination and trends in remittances over a longer period of time. The approach also attempted to assess the resilience of the outflow of migrant labour from South Asia and inflow of remittances from around the globe, especially from the Gulf region, in the context of the financial meltdown. These have been achieved by engaging with a research institute in the country of origin. The institutes involved[7] in the process are shown in Box 3.1.

In addition to the macro assessment of the situation in the five countries of origin and seven destination countries, three surveys have also been undertaken in the study. The purpose of these surveys is to obtain a micro level understanding of the coping strategies of: (i) emigrants in the countries of destination; (ii) emigrant households in the countries of origin; and (iii) return emigrants in the countries of origin who lost their jobs in the countries of destination due to the financial crisis.

Workers Survey[8]

A total of 350 workers in the seven countries of destination were surveyed with the sample size limited to 50 workers in each country. Logistic support of the Indian Embassies in the respective countries of destination and migrant associations[9] was obtained for the conduct of the survey. The survey was aimed at understanding the profile of migrant workers and their respective households; employment conditions; emoluments; working and living conditions; remittances, saving and investment at the time of the survey, six months before (at the time of the crisis) and a year ago (before the onset of the crisis); adaptation to and coping mechanisms by both

7. The report prepared by the five countries of origin—India, Pakistan, Bangladesh, Sri Lanka and Nepal—is available with CDS, Kerala. With a view to publicise the report, the Secretary, Ministry of Overseas Indian Affairs requested the senior author of this report to organise a one-day workshop on "Dynamics of Migration from South Asia in the Context of Global Financial Crisis" at Thiruvananthapuram, Kerala, in March 2010.

8. Separate report based on the survey was prepared by S. Irudaya Rajan and D. Narayana of CDS.

9. In Qatar, the survey was facilitated by Georgetown University School of Foreign Service in Qatar with the assistance of Dr Ganesh Seshan.

the migrant workers in the countries of destination and their families in the country of origin.

Emigrant Household Survey[10]

This survey was conducted among the households which had at least one emigrant currently in the Gulf, to examine their coping mechanism, if any, at the time of the crisis. The survey was canvassed among 50 households each in four countries of South Asia—Pakistan, Bangladesh, Nepal and Sri Lanka—with the support of a research partner in the respective countries. In India, CDS conducted the survey among 250 households in the five states of India selecting 50 each from the states of Andhra Pradesh, Tamil Nadu, Kerala, Maharashtra, and Punjab, from where large-scale migration to Gulf takes place. The total number of households that participated in the emigrant household survey in the five countries of origin in South Asia was 450. The survey elicited information on household details, profile of emigrants, household economic assets, remittances and their utilisation, current employment status of the emigrants and their coping mechanisms, economic impact of the crisis in terms of household expenditure, financial commitment and pattern of investment, change in the frequency of remittances, adapting and coping mechanisms, psychological impact—stress and anxiety, financial autonomy and health related issues.

Return Emigrant Survey[11]

This survey was conducted among the emigrants who lost their jobs and were forced to return home because of the financial crisis in the Gulf. It was aimed at examining their coping mechanism after their return to their home countries. The survey was canvassed among 50 return emigrants each in the four countries of South Asia—Pakistan, Bangladesh, Nepal and Sri Lanka—with support from research partner institutions. In India, the survey was canvassed

10. Separate report based on the survey was prepared by S. Irudaya Rajan and Arindam Banerjee of CDS.

11. Separate report based on the survey was prepared by S Irudaya Rajan and Vinoj Abraham of CDS.

among 250 return emigrants in five states of India, selecting 50 each in Andhra Pradesh, Tamil Nadu, Kerala, Maharashtra and Punjab. Thus, the total number of return emigrants surveyed among the five countries of origin in South Asia was 450. It should, however, be realised that it was difficult to locate the emigrants who lost their jobs in the countries of destination and returned to the countries of origin. In the beginning of 2009, most countries in South Asia expected that due to the crisis there would be large-scale return emigration to their countries. Our small scale survey of return emigrants conducted in South Asia proved those forecasts unsubstantiated, as we would see later in the chapter. The return emigrant survey collected information on household details, the profile of return emigrants, household economic assets, employment, remittances and their utilisation, household expenditure pattern, reasons for return, adaptation and coping mechanisms.

Return Migrant Resurvey 2009[12]

Return migration from the Gulf is a normal process of contract migration. Migrants from South Asia go on contract work to the destination countries; and in the normal course, they return to the countries of their origin once the contract ends. As of the time of this study, we had no estimate of return emigration from the Gulf to South Asia. However, the CDS has completed four large-scale migration surveys (1998, 2003, 2007 and 2008) over the last decade. One of the objectives of this study is to assess the flow of forced return emigration, or emigrants who return from the Gulf region to South Asia before the expiry of contract. To assess both regular return migrants and the crisis-led return emigrants from the Gulf, we revisited emigrant households from the 15,000 households of the 2008 Kerala migration survey. We estimated the extent of crisis-led return emigrants to Kerala after the revisit. In a later section of this chapter, we would apply the same methodology, and project the

12. This survey was financed by the Department of Non-Resident Keralite Affairs, Government of Kerala for the larger study on Impact on Global Recession on return emigrants in Kerala. This report has been prepared by K.C. Zachariah and S. Irudaya Rajan of CDS. The preliminary report was available by late December 2009.

figures to estimate the number of return emigrants from the Gulf to South Asia. In addition, the return migration resurvey in 2009 estimated the number of emigrants who lost their jobs in the Gulf, but had chosen to remain there without returning to their counties of origin. This is a new information ('lost job but have not returned') which would be generated for South Asia.

The Analytical Framework

The financial crisis had its own impact on the destination countries. It manifested differently on both employees and employers in the respective countries of origin and destination. For instance, some sectors in the destination countries were seriously affected, and both expatriates and nationals lost their jobs. Some expatriates chose to adjust to the situation and decided to work on lower wages under harsh living conditions, while the rest returned to their countries of origin; whereas the nationals of the destination countries declared themselves as 'unemployed'. The unemployment among nationals instigated respective governments to respond by implementing strong regulation in visa regimes and tightening the movement of labour from foreign countries (what the Gulf countries call "demographic imbalance"). Similarly, emigrant families in the countries of origin had to make several adjustments to cope with the crisis (see Figure 3.1). We shall briefly explain some of the aspects below.

Demand for Migrant Labour

For the countries of South Asia, such as India, Bangladesh, Sri Lanka, Nepal and Pakistan, which send their labour out, the repercussions of the financial crisis in Gulf economies are a set of specific issues relating to the flow of migrants to the Gulf, crisis led/forced return emigration from Gulf to the home country and the possibility of declining remittances to the home country. The demand for labour in a crisis-affected economy may be influenced by two kinds of effects. The first is the scale effect. The scale effect is a change in the total demand for labour in the economy owing to the change in total output of the economy. The second is the substitution

Figure 3.1

Analytical Framework for Impact of Financial Crisis on Migrant Workers

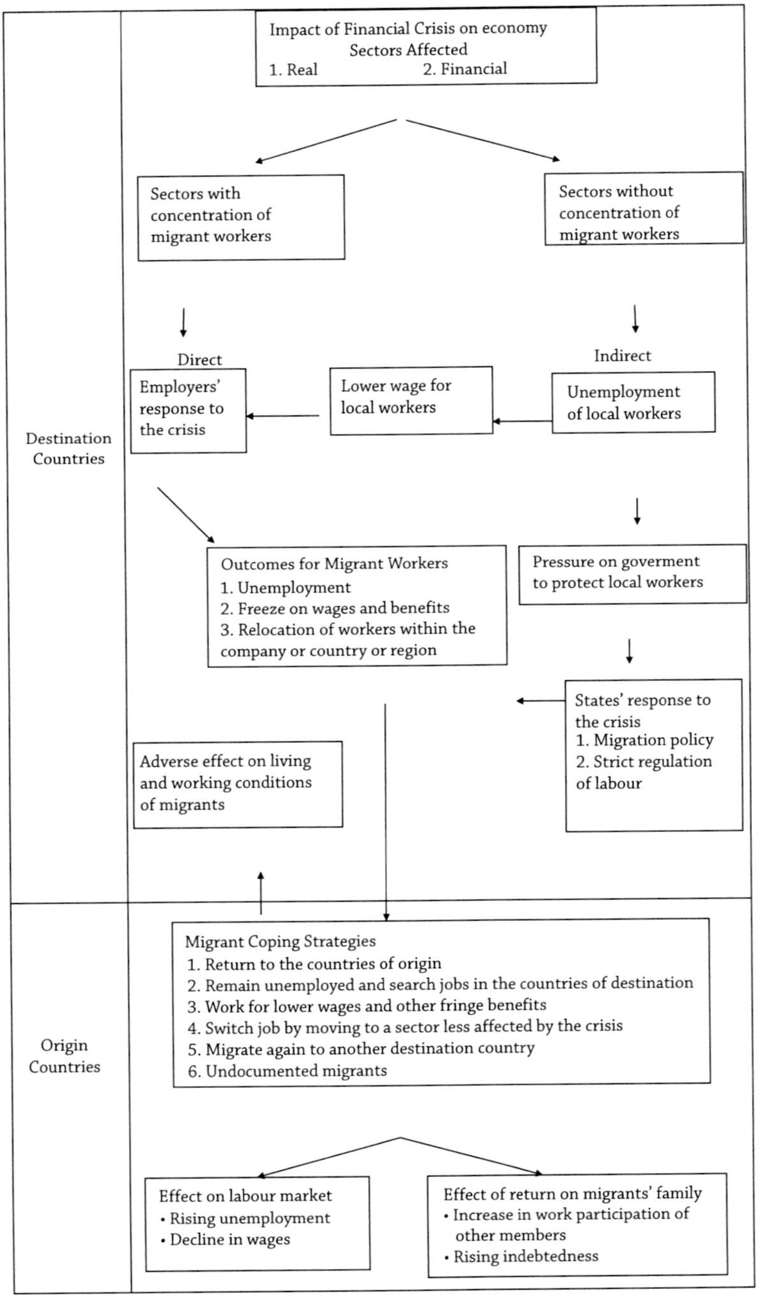

effect. It is the replacement of foreign labour with local labour or other factors of production. In the current scenario, the substitution effect may take place mainly in the form of local workers replacing the migrant workers. This could occur because the wage rates of the local workers might decline due to the slump in the economy. This could also occur because of the pressure from the political lobbies to employ local labour rather than migrant workers.

However, the scale and substitution effects may affect different industries differently. The scale effect may be industry specific: all industries may not face a decline in output, some may face a crisis. For instance, the scale effect of the crisis in UAE seems to be more concentrated within the real estate and tourism segments. Also, those industries which are in the value chains of affected industries, or which are intermediaries/final outputs of other affected industries, could also be affected depending on the strength of the linkages.

Migrant Workers' Strategies to Cope with the Crisis

In times of crisis, the migrant workers may adopt various strategies to tide over the situation or to mitigate the risks. The most common strategy adopted by the migrant workers would be to return to the home country and find alternate employment. Among the rest, some may decide to migrate to other destinations which are less affected by the crisis; some may remain in the same destination country but move/shift to new occupations/industries which are less affected by the crisis; and some may decide to work in the same industry/occupation in the countries of destination at a lower wage rate and under less favourable conditions of work.

Adding yet another dimension to the issue would be the reaction of the local workers and local governments in the face of increasing unemployment in the local economy it may take the forms of increasing stigma and persecution of foreign labour. Since the extent of return migration to the South Asian economies due to the crisis is often conjectural, an explicit understanding of the strategies adopted by the migrants to meet the crisis would allow one to draw correct conclusions about the size of return migration, re-migration, attrition, mobility, work and poorer earnings.

Impact of Migrant Workers' Strategies on Sending Country

In the countries which send migrant workers out, the strategies to cope with the crisis might get manifested mainly through three channels: (i) there could be an increase in the number of job seekers within the country; (ii) a reduction in remittances; and (iii) more importantly, changes in the spending habits of the return migrants/emigrant families.

The home countries are already overburdened with shrinking jobs due to the global crisis. Migrants returning home would mean that more workers would be added into the economy. Estimates show that GDP growth in South Asia decelerated in 2008, falling from 8.6 per cent in 2007 to below 7 per cent. It is projected to decline further to around 6 per cent or less in 2009, before recovering to around 7 per cent in 2010 (ADB, various issues). One issue in this context would be to find employment for the returning migrant workers when unemployment is on the increase (even though the overall effect of the global crisis on South Asian economies has been less compared with developed economies). However, given the fact that the inherent capacity of such economies is weak owing to their poor financial conditions and high level of poverty, any decline in the growth rates would greatly diminish their ability to cope with an influx of return migrants.

To assess the meaningful effect of the crisis on migrant workers, sectoral specificities of the destination countries should be understood as well. The manufacturing and construction sectors are likely to be among the severely affected sectors in these countries. Many of the return migrant workers might have been employed in these sectors in the destination countries, and hence, finding alternative employment would be a challenge for them in the countries of origin as those sectors are likely to be depressed there as well. Even if they are ready to switch roles as entrepreneurs/self-employed workers, as is the usual case with return migrants, in the present circumstances the possibilities of successful entrepreneurship require external support as well. For example, the Finance Minister of the Government of Kerala (Kerala has an estimated 2 million workers in the Gulf) announced a US$ 200 million entrepreneurship package for repatriates in the budget of 2009. Similarly, the Government of Nepal undertook measures to compensate Nepali migrant workers who had lost their jobs because of the global recession.

Another significant way in which the crisis might affect the home economy is through fall in remittances. Studies predict that remittance flows to South Asia would decline sharply from over 16 per cent growth in 2008 to zero per cent in 2009 (Ratha *et al.*, 2008). India is the largest recipient of remittances in the world today, and a significant share is contributed by the innumerable unskilled and semi-skilled Indian workers abroad. Remittances also play a vital role in the balance of payments in all South Asian economies. A fall in the number of migrants from the region, and the reduction in their wage rates and poorer work conditions of continuing migrant workers might reduce the flow of remittances to the home economy.

Effect of the Crisis on the Migrant's Family

As migrant workers are often the sole breadwinners of their families, any lay off in the destination countries is likely to push these families into poverty once again. The crisis may impose some changes in the spending and investment habits of the migrant workers. While repatriation would open the question of re-entry of the migrant in the home labour market, the stoppage or reduction in the remittances would necessitate changes in the spending and saving habits of their households. The sudden reduction in income might bring about employment and livelihood diversification within the household, trigger cutback in long gestation investments such as education and health expenditure and push the younger members of the households to prematurely enter the labour market.

Effects of the Crisis on Migrant Women Workers and Women Left Behind

In keeping with the Islamic tradition, the GCC countries, in general, do not encourage women to work. The presence of native women workers in the GCC workforce is marginal, and they constitute between 2-10 per cent of the national workforce. Because of the traditional policies regarding the place of women in the workforce, occupational segregation of women had been strong in the GCC countries. Most women workers in the GCC countries are poor expatriates from South Asian economies engaged as domestic help. According to some estimates, in the UAE over 80 per cent of the employed women were expatriates, while in Bahrain the proportion was 55 per cent. Expatriate women were between 10-25 per cent of the total expatriate workforce (Kapiszewski, 2006). Even during normal times, it is recognised that migrant women domestic workers face severe hardships including working for very low wages. Women migrant workers are also excluded from protection under labour laws because they are considered to be part of the employing family and are outside the reach of those laws. These difficulties may, in the context of the crisis, become more accentuated.

Similarly, women left behind in the home country face many difficulties in managing their families. According to our estimates, Kerala has one million married women whose husbands are emmigrants to the Gulf. They have to take steps to effectively reorient the use of remittances, if they expect that the remittances from their husbands are likely to decline due to the crisis.

Assessment of the Financial Crisis in the Gulf[13]

This section traces the transmission links of the global financial crisis to employment and remittances of the South Asian migrant workers to the GCC economies. The global crisis affected the gulf countries through its impact on export trade, finance and FDI. The sectors which were severely affected included manufacturing, trade and construction, which also were the sectors employing the bulk of the expatriate labour. The source for the number of expatriates affected and the extent to which the volume of remittances fell is the

13. This section is based on the six country reports prepared by the research team at CDS. Most of the members of the research team have already visited Gulf to assess the reality by talking to several stakeholders and additional research is done by the authors of this report.

size of the economy, and the policy of the GCC economies on migrant labour.

The Crisis and Growth

The US is at the epicenter of the global crisis, facing severe recession arising out of a squeeze on credit, sharp fall in housing and equity prices, and high level of uncertainty. These shocks depressed consumption and increased the saving rate. Equity prices were down and the exchange value of the dollar strengthened. Real GDP contracted since the fourth quarter of 2008, and employment fell rapidly since end 2007. Credit market remained unsettled despite the easing of policy rates. The economy was projected to contract by 2.8 per cent in 2009 and was expected to start recovering only by the middle of 2010.

The impact of the global crisis on the Asian economies has been severe despite their low exposure to US securitised assets, and better macroeconomic fundamentals. The group of advanced economies of Asia such as Korea, Taiwan, Hong Kong and Singapore were expected to contract by about 6 per cent in 2009. Given their extreme exposure to external demand, they would all suffer due to the contraction of the advanced western markets. The Association of Southeast Asian Nations (ASEAN) countries (e.g., Indonesia, Thailand, Malaysia, Philippines, and Vietnam) were also severely hit, especially Thailand and Malaysia which were expected to contract in 2009 by 3 per cent and 3.5 per cent respectively. The Chinese growth was expected to come down from 13 per cent in 2007 to about 6.5 per cent in 2009. Indian growth was expected to decline from over 9 per cent in 2007 to 4.5 per cent in 2009.

The global crisis affected the Middle East through a large fall in the price of oil, reversal of capital inflows, depression of property and equity markets, and losses in sovereign wealth funds. The effect of the global crisis was expected to vary across the countries depending upon country characteristics, such as high share of oil exports in total exports; large quantum of re-exports, sizeable share of services in GDP, especially transportation, trade, hotel and restaurants (Table 3.1). It was maintained that "in the region as a

Table 3.1

Real GDP Growth Rates (Annual Percentage Change)

	2001	2002	2003	2004	2005	2006	2007	2008	2009	2010	2011
Country of Destination											
Bahrain	4.62	5.19	7.25	5.64	7.85	6.65	8.07	6.12	2.64	3.47	3.94
Kuwait	0.22	3.01	17.33	10.24	10.62	5.14	2.51	6.33	-1.14	2.39	4.34
Oman	7.51	2.57	2.01	5.33	6.02	6.79	6.38	6.18	3.02	3.80	6.00
Qatar	6.32	3.20	6.32	17.72	9.24	15.03	15.35	16.40	17.99	16.37	8.90
Saudi Arabia	0.55	0.13	7.66	5.27	5.55	3.03	3.52	4.63	-0.91	2.90	4.40
UAE	1.70	2.65	11.89	9.69	8.19	9.39	6.34	7.41	-0.60	1.55	3.29
Country of Origin											
Bangladesh	4.83	4.85	5.78	6.11	6.30	6.53	6.32	5.59	5.00	5.38	6.01
India	3.89	4.56	6.85	7.90	9.21	9.82	9.30	7.29	4.52	5.61	6.89
Nepal	5.63	0.12	3.95	4.68	3.12	3.72	3.19	4.70	3.60	3.25	4.81
Pakistan	1.98	3.22	4.85	7.37	7.67	6.18	6.02	5.95	2.50	3.50	4.50
Sri Lanka	-1.55	3.96	5.94	5.45	6.24	7.67	6.80	5.95	2.20	3.59	4.98
Major Developed Countries											
Japan	0.184	0.262	1.414	2.744	1.934	2.039	2.392	-0.641	-6.197	0.515	2.168
US	0.751	1.599	2.51	3.637	2.939	2.779	2.028	1.111	-2.751	-0.491	3.53
UK	2.462	2.097	2.818	2.758	2.058	2.838	3.022	0.707	-4.086	-0.396	2.121

Note: Data for 2009-2011 are forecasts.

Source: *World Economic Outlook Database*, April 2009.

whole, growth is projected to decline from 6% in 2008 to 2½% in 2009... Among the oil producing countries, the sharpest slowdown is expected in the United Arab Emirates (UAE), where the exit of external funds... has contributed to a large contraction in liquidity, a sizeable fall in property and equity prices, and substantial pressure in the banking system... At the other end of the spectrum is Qatar, which is projected to grow by 18% in 2009 (up from 16½% in 2008), since its production of natural gas is expected to double this year" (IMF, 2009: 91).

The crisis affected expatriate labour through its adverse impact on GDP growth and employment opportunities in the Gulf.

Gulf Economies: Population and GDP Growth

The population of the GCC countries increased by 8.39 million between 2000 and 2008, an increase which is almost the size of GCC excluding Saudi Arabia, in 2000. Over half of this increase is contributed by Saudi Arabia, the country accounting for about 70 per cent of the population of GCC. However, the rate of increase has been low in Saudi Arabia and high in Qatar, UAE and Kuwait. Thus, two groups of countries may be identified in the Gulf, one with an increase in population of about 20 per cent between 2000 and 2009 and another with increases of three to four times (Table 3.2).

Table 3.2

Growth of Population and GDP in GCC Countries

	Population (million)				*GDP Growth*
Country	*2000*	*2009*	*Increase*	*Increase (%)*	*2000-2008 (%)*
Kuwait	2.217	3.443	1.226	55.30	6.68
Qatar	0.606	1.098	0.492	81.19	11.17
Saudi Arabia	20.474	24.897	4.423	21.60	3.91
UAE	2.995	4.764	1.769	59.07	7.74
Bahrain	0.670	0.779	0.109	16.27	6.29
Oman	2.402	2.769	0.367	15.28	5.36
Total	29.364	37.750	8.386	28.56	-

Source: World Economic Outlook Database, April 2009.

The large increase in populations of the Gulf countries is spawned by the high average growth of GDP between 2000 and 2009. Qatar's close to doubling of the population between 2000 and 2009 has come along with an average annual GDP percentage increase of over 11 per cent during this period. The UAE has grown at close to 8 per cent per annum. Only Kuwait has exhibited a large increase in population with a relatively low increase in GDP. Thus, the large increase in population and the large migration of labour has come about with a high GDP growth.

Short-run GDP growth in GCC countries should ideally be translated into population growth through migration as most of them are heavily dependent on expatriate labour. However, such translation is not simple and proportional as it is mediated through the government effort to employ nationals in different economic sectors. The high share of nationals in total employment in countries like Bahrain, Oman and Saudi Arabia despite smaller overall population increases in those countries indicates these trends.

Migration as a Component of Economic Growth

Countries like Oman and Bahrain, which have relatively less oil revenues, have begun to employ their nationals more and more in the work force. Between 2000 and 2004, 134,000 expatriates were laid off in Oman. The government had banned employment of expatriates in certain sectors, like selling and transporting fruits and vegetables. Bahrain also follows similar policies. For instance, in the construction sector, a mandatory 25 per cent Bahrainisation had been in effect for some years, which was brought down to 15 per cent later on. Saudi Arabia too is no exception. In 2003, the government decided to reduce its expatriate workforce by more than half within 10 years. It announced a 20 per cent ceiling on the number of expatriate workers and their dependents in the Kingdom; and issued a directive that workers from a single country should account for no more than 10 per cent of the workforce by 2013. Furthermore, about 54 job sectors have been reserved exclusively for nationals. The nationalisation drive is not so intense in Kuwait, Qatar and the UAE.

Reported figures by the respective Embassies in the Gulf and the following publications: (i) United Nations (2009), (ii) Kapiszewski (2006), (iii) Taattolo (2006) and (iv) Shah (2009).

As a result of migration policies, the rates of population increase and its composition in the countries of the Gulf vary showing distinct characteristics. In Qatar and UAE, expatriates constitute over 80 per cent, and in Kuwait they account for close to 70 per cent of the total population. While in Saudi Arabia and Oman, expatriates constitute slightly over a quarter of the population, Bahrain has over 40 per cent non-nationals in the total population. Over 60 per cent of the expatriates are from South Asia and in some countries, such as Oman and Bahrain, they account for over 90 per cent of the expatriates (Table 3.3).

Table 3.3

Profile of Expatriates in the Gulf, 2009

Country	*Population ('000)*	*% Expatriates to Total Population*	*% of South Asian Expatriates to Total Expatriates*	*% of Expatriates in the Labour Force*
Kuwait	3,443	68.8	52.8	83.9
Qatar	1,098	86.5	68.4	92.5
Saudi Arabia	24,897	27.8	54.9	55.8
UAE	4,764	81.0	68.7	89.8
Bahrain	779	43.0	95.1	58.3
Oman	2,769	28.4	89.0	64.3
GCC	37,750	40.3	61.8	...

Sources: Compiled from various sources such as 'Country Reports' prepared by CDS team.

Investment and Growth

GDP growth goes along with investment and the Gulf is no exception. While Qatar with 33 per cent investment rate reports a GDP growth of close to 12 per cent, UAE with investment rate of 22 per cent recorded a growth of close to 8 per cent. The rest of the countries invest between 16 per cent and 20 per cent of their GDP and show lower growth rates (Table 3.4).

Table 3.4

Growth of GDP, Investment and the Current Account Balance

Country	GDP Growth 2000-2008 (%)	Investment Rate, 2000-2008 Average (% of GDP)	Current Account Balance (% of GDP)	
			2000-03	2004-08
Kuwait	6.68	16	23.43	36.33
Qatar	11.17	33	24.44	30.01
Saudi Arabia	3.91	20	8.02	26.27
UAE	7.74	23	10.07	16.31
Bahrain	6.29	19	3.704	11.08
Oman	5.36	16	8.95	8.34

Source: World Economic Outlook Database, 2009.

When countries do not run a current account deficit and have resources to invest in the domestic economy, why do they not push up investment and growth rates? It seems to be a question of strategy given the fluctuating oil prices and the experience of the 1970s. The high oil prices of the 1970s and the investment of the surpluses in US Treasury Bills helped countries like Saudi Arabia to carry on through the difficult period of the 1980s and the 1990s when oil prices remained low.

The previous price spike also witnessed massive investment in physical and social infrastructure which yielded poor returns. The bloated, highly subsidised and inefficient public sector yielded poor growth. The US was the destination for most of the external investments. The steady increase of the price of oil since 2002 has enabled the Gulf states to reap an incredible windfall of at least US$ 1.5 trillion between 2002 and 2006 (Maloney, 2009: 129). Compared with the earlier price spikes, the recent windfalls display altogether different trends. Saudi Arabia and Kuwait reduced their external debt by more than half by 2005 (Smith, 2008: 37). They continued to base their budgets around revenue expectations of US$ 25 per barrel, raising it only after a considerable time lag when the price band had become obsolete. Many of the larger Gulf states have invested in large projects within their countries. For example, Saudi Arabia has invested about US$ 200 billion in new 'economic cities' to generate large scale employment. Together the GCC countries have approximately US$ 1 trillion in infrastructure investments in the pipeline, in power generation, water desalination, education, and housing (Maloney, 2009: 134).

The rising oil prices and booming investments in the oil and other sectors have seen an increased FDI (flow of foreign direct investment); a 10 fold increase in the region's proportion of global FDI is witnessed between 2001 and 2006. The region's share in total FDI flows into the developing world rose from a paltry 3 per cent in 2002 to 15 per cent in 2008. The flow is led by large increases in FDI into Saudi Arabia, Turkey and UAE. They accounted for 75 per cent of cumulated inflows during 2003-2007 (UNCTAD, 2009: 57). The increased flow of FDI into the Gulf boosted the investment rate in these economies as is evident from the share of FDI in gross capital formation (Table 3.5).

Table 3.5

FDI Flows and Stocks in Relation to Investment and GDP in GCC Economies

	FDI Inflow as a Percentage of Gross Capital Formation			*FDI Stock as a % of GDP*		
Country	*2006*	*2007*	*2008*	*1990*	*2000*	*2008*
Kuwait	0.8	0.5	0.2	0.2	1.6	0.6
Qatar	19.2	24.2	25.6	0.9	10.8	21.6
Saudi Arabia	29.4	31.8	46.1	18.8	9.3	24.4
UAE	38.9	37.2	24.9	2.2	1.5	26.7
Bahrain	74.4	40.1	35.6	12.8	73.6	69.9
Oman	18.9	24.6	17.7	14.7	13.2	22.8
West Asia	23.3	22.1	21.8	10.2	9.7	18.0

Source: UNCTAD, 2009.

FDI inflow into the Gulf had increased rapidly and the Gulf held foreign assets have more than doubled since 2003 to between US$ 1.8 trillion and US$ 2.4 trillion (Maloney,

2009: 135). Intra-Arab investments tripled between 2000 and 2005. About 11 per cent of Gulf foreign investment since 2002 remains within the region. Growing relationships with Asia have seen greater flow of Gulf FDI into Asia. Since 2002, 11 per cent of Gulf investment has gone to Asia, which is expected to double by 2020 (Maloney, 2009: 136).

FDI in services has become more prominent in recent years. While telecom, banking, power, water, and real estate have attracted a large amount of foreign investment, the ongoing crisis dried up credit in a number of infrastructure, residential-commercial and tourism-related real estate projects. The private sector played an important role in the emergence of West Asia as the world's largest market in project finance, surpassing Western Europe and North America. The first nine months of 2008 saw nearly US$ 40 billion in project debt raised for developments in West Asia and North Africa compared to US$ 32 billion in Western Europe and US$ 29 billion in North America (UNCTAD, 2009: 60). The deepening global financial crisis dried up this source of project finance which affected project prospects and forced governments to increase direct public funding of projects.

A further dimension of the financial crisis is the loss suffered by the Sovereign Wealth Funds (SWFs) of the GCC countries. The surplus oil revenues of the GCC countries flew into US Treasury Bills since the 1970s. These savings helped them fund expansions in the 1980s and 1990s when oil prices fell and deficits rose. In the late 1990s, SWFs started investing in riskier assets abroad, such as stocks and real estate. The rising oil prices in the 2000s saw this trend gain in strength. Recent years saw them investing in industries such as energy, automotives, aerospace, real estate and technology and helped reap the benefit in a rising market. The UAE had taken the lead in such investments. However, the recent collapse of the real estate and equity markets generated large losses for SWFs (Table 3.6).

Table 3.6

Estimated Gains and Losses of Gulf Sovereign Wealth Funds

(Billion Dollars)

Agency	*Value Dec. 2007*	*Changes in Value*		*Value Dec. 2008*	*Loss on Dec 2007 Portfolio (%)*
		Capital Gain/Loss	*Net Inflows*		
Abu Dhabi Investment Authority (ADID), Abu Dhabi Investment Council (ADIC)	453	-183	59	328	-40
Qatar Investment Authority (QIA)	65	-27	28	58	-41
Kuwait Investment Authority (KIA)	262	-94	57	228	-36
Saudi Arabian Monetary Agency (SAMA)	385	-46	162	501	-12
Other GCC	116	0	-33	84	0
GCC Total	1282	-350	273	1200	-27

Source: UNCTAD, 2009.

Employment Structure in the GCC Countries

In terms of value added by sectors, the structure of the GCC economies is loaded heavily in favour of the oil sector ever since the oil price spike in the mid-1970s. The evolving structure of employment reflects the growth trajectory followed by these countries. Early on, a sizable proportion of the oil revenues were set apart for building essential services such as health, education, transport, power, and water. The resulting gains in HDI (Human Development Index) of the GCC countries over the last three decades have been creditable. Infant mortality rates which ranged between 41 (for Kuwait) and 110 (for Oman) among the GCC countries in 1970-1974 have fallen to between 9 (for UAE) and 23 (for Saudi Arabia) in 2000-2004. Literacy rates have risen above 70 per cent by 2000 and HDIs ranged between 0.770 (Oman) and 0.843 (Bahrain) in 2002 (Tabutin and Schoumaker, 2005).

To start with, the workers in the service sectors were largely expatriates. Over a period of time, preferred employment of nationals in the workforce is changing in composition. For instance, in a country like Saudi Arabia, about 90 per cent of Saudi nationals work for the government sector as against 90 per cent of the expatriates who work in informal sectors as well as health sector.[14] The rapidly growing sectors like construction, trade and manufacturing, which employ the bulk of the workforce is largely dominated by the expatriates. And the pattern is not very different in other GCC countries.

In the GCC countries, over 50 per cent of the workforce is employed in manufacturing, trade, and construction. Kuwait and Saudi Arabia are the exceptions, where the share of public administration and defence is rather high (Table 3.7). The share of construction in total employment increased very fast during 2001-2008 in some of the GCC countries. For instance, in UAE the share of construction sector employment increased by five percentage points during the period. In Saudi Arabia, the increase in employment in the construction sector during the period was of the order of 300,000.

Inflation and Wages

As already indicated, the UAE, Qatar and Kuwait have high shares of expatriates; even in Oman and Saudi Arabia, they make up to 20 to 30 per cent of the total population. About 75 per cent of the UAE labour force is from Asia; and Indian workers constitute 42.5 per cent of the population. Indian embassy estimates that, "50 per cent of the 1.8 million Indian expatriates in the UAE are unskilled workers, 25 per cent semi-skilled and 25 per cent skilled professionals" (Woertz *et al.*, 2008: 20). As all the unskilled and a large proportion of the semi-skilled workers are housed in labour camps, and their rent, water and electricity charges are borne by their employers, the major outgo from their wages is towards the expenses on food. The food expense as a percentage of disposable income does not show much variation across the GCC economies. For over a quarter of the population, food expenses eats up over one fifth of their income, and only less than a quarter of the population spends less than 10 per cent of their income on food (Table 3.8). In the UAE, rent component for some

14. See country report.

Table 3.7

Share (in Per cent) of Employment Across Economic Activities in GCC Countries, 2007

Activity	*Bahrain*	*Oman*	*Kuwait*	*Qatar*	*Saudi Arabia*	*UAE*
Agriculture, Hunting & Forestry	0.47	9.09	2.60	1.92	4.69	5.0
Fishing	0.01	0.44	0.08	0.43	*	*
Mining & Quarrying	0.49	1.96	1.90	5.27	1.32	1.3
Manufacturing	17.54	10.77	4.43	8.69	7.28	13.0
Electricity, Gas & Water Supply	0.13	0.33	0.01	0.66	0.96	1.2
Construction	29.86	34.68	14.23	37.14	10.22	20.6
Wholesale, Retail Trade & Car Repairs	24.62	16.18	14.03	12.28	16.10	20.0
Hotels & Restaurants	6.55	5.97	2.89	1.96	3.20	4.2
Transport, Storage & Communication	4.20	1.30	3.85	4.33	4.42	6.2
Financial Intermediaries	3.46	0.29	1.21	1.09	1.08	1.4
Real Estate & Renting Services	7.54	1.77	5.59	3.43	3.22	3.3
Public Administration and Defence	0.01		14.75	6.35	18.03	10.8
Education	1.24	0.76	5.23	3.16	11.96	**
Health & Social Work	0.24	1.91	2.40	2.55	4.33	**
Community & Personal Services	2.11	1.08	4.18	1.54	2.26	4.5
Domestic Services	0.06	9.96	21.86	8.79	10.79	8.4
Extra-Territorial Org. & Bodies	0.21	2.59	0.11	0.21	0.13	-
Not Classified by Economic Activity	0.30	0.90	0.66	0.18	0.01	0.01
Total	100	100	100	100	100	100

Note: For Bahrain and UAE, figures show the paid employment by economic activity. For Oman, figures show expatriate workers in private sector. Kuwait figures show for year 2005.
*Fishing is included in Agriculture, Hunting and Forestry.
**Education and Health are included in Public Administration and Defence.

Source: International Labour Organization (ILO) Labour Statistics, ILO; *Statistical Year Book 2008*, Ministry of National Economy Oman; For Saudi Arabia and UAE the figures are taken from the country reports.

segments of the workers is also fairly large—21 to 50 per cent of the disposable income.

Table 3.8

Distribution of Population by Percentage of Disposable Income Spent on Food

	% of Population					
% Spent on Food	*Kuwait*	*Qatar*	*Saudi Arabia*	*UAE*	*Bahrain*	*Oman*
Less than 10%	14	24	22	24	22	13
10-20%	46	43	38	44	39	40
Above 20%	29	18	26	20	23	35
Don't know	11	15	13	13	16	10

Source: Woertz *et al.*, 2008.

Table 3.9

Inflation (in Per cent) in GCC Countries 2002-07

Country	*2002*	*2003*	*2004*	*2005*	*2006*	*2007*
Kuwait	0.5	1.2	1.3	4.3	3.3	6.6
Qatar	0.2	2.2	6.8	8.8	11.8	12.8
Saudi Arabia	0.2	0.6	0.3	0.7	2.2	6.5
UAE	2.9	3.1	5.1	7.1	11.3	11.6
Bahrain	-0.5	1.7	2.3	2.6	2.1	8.4
Oman	-0.7	-0.3	0.9	1.9	3.1	5.3
World	3.7	3.2	3.9	3.6	3.5	4.2

Source: Woertz *et al.*, 2008.

Food inflation which was non-existent in the GCC countries until 2002 has emerged as a serious problem in the Gulf during the post-2005 period. The UAE and Qatar were particularly affected. A major part of the inflation could be attributed to the global rise in food prices; the Food and Agriculture Organization (FAO) Food Price Index rose by 57 per cent between March 2007 and March

2008. This was on top of an increase of 23 per cent from 2006. The GCC countries responded to the unprecedented inflation by raising subsidies, allowances, public sector wage increases, and caps on rents. In the UAE, the Governments of Abu Dhabi, Dubai, and Sharjah announced a pay hike of 70 per cent to all public sector workers. However, it is not clear to what extent these measures had protected the expatriate workers. The crisis has only added to the afflictions of the expatriate workers.

Crude Oil Prices and Production Volumes

After the phenomenal increase in crude oil prices in the mid-1970s and early 1980s which touched almost US$ 30 per barrel in the early 1980s, nominal prices ruled below US$ 20 for over one and a half decades till 1999 (Table 3.10). Since 2000, crude oil prices began rising steadily and by 2004 they had crossed US$ 35 per barrel, reaching US$ 50 in 2005 and going above US$ 100 on average by mid-

Table 3.10

Crude Oil Price and Quantity

Year (5 Year Average Centered)	*Nominal Price (Dollar per Barrel)*	*Nominal Price Adjusted for Inflation*	*Nominal Price Adjusted for Inflation and Exchange Rate*
1976	11.63	8.30	8.65
1983	29.83	11.23	15.15
1990	18.17	4.79	5.38
1997	17.12	3.58	4.39
2000	27.60	5.42	7.93
2001	23.12	4.44	6.70
2002	24.36	4.58	6.65
2003	28.10	5.17	6.53
2004	36.05	6.49	7.57
2005	50.64	8.91	10.40
2006	61.08	10.50	12.20
2007	69.08	11.59	12.62
2008	94.45	15.33	15.99

Source: www.opec.org/library/AnnualStatisticalBulletin/PDF/ASB2008.pdf, accessed on 26 September 2009.

2008. "Oil prices have roller-coastered: starting 2008 at US$ 92/b, the OPEC Reference Basket rose to a record US$ 141/b in early July before falling to US$ 33/b by the end of the year, the lowest level since summer 2004" (*http://www.opec.org/library/worldoiloutlook/pdf/woo2009.pdf* accessed on 26 September, 2009).

The rise in price above US$ 70 was confined to about 15 months since June 2007 and the fall in price below US$ 50 for about four months since December 2008 (Figure 3.2).

Figure 3.2

Monthly Crude Oil Price, 2008-09

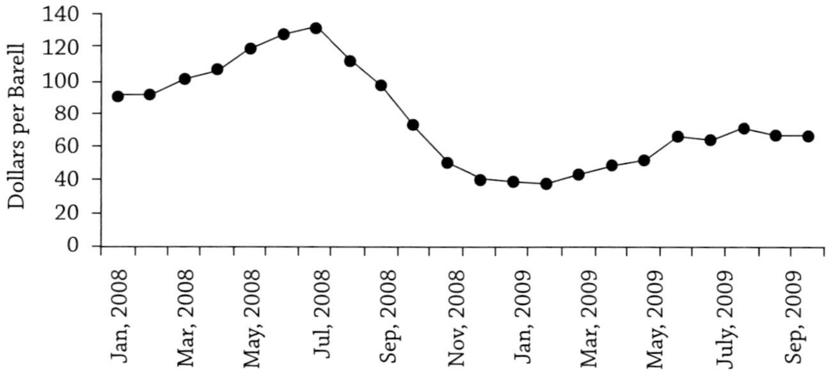

Source: *www.opec.org/library/AnnualStatisticalBulletin/PDF/ASB2008.pdf,* accessed on 20 November 2009.

The demand for oil is said to grow in the medium term despite a marginal fall in OECD demand: "OECD demand falls from 47.5 mb/d in 2008 to 45.5 mb/d by 2010, and remains at that level to 2013" (*World Oil Outlook*). Almost 80 per cent of the net growth in oil demand from 2008-2030 is in developing Asia, and as Asia is set to grow at moderate rates, the overall oil demand is not expected to be adversely affected to any great extent. The lower than expected growth in oil demand needs to be viewed in the context of the buoyant demand realised over the period 2003-2008.

Crude oil production in the Gulf countries has not shown any corresponding fluctuations to the variations in oil prices. Saudi Arabia has been producing about 8 million barrels/day since 1991 which has risen beyond 9 million barrels/day since 2005. The UAE has been producing over 2 million barrels a day since 1991 which has crossed 2.5 million barrels by 2006. Qatar has been producing about 400,000 barrels a day since 1990, 600,000 barrels per day by 1998, and 800,000 barrels by 2006.

Overall, oil revenues of the six nations under study are expected to remain high in the medium term. Prices are projected to remain at the levels reached by 2006, which are over twice the levels of 2003. While demand for oil may not grow at rates seen during the last three or four years, it is not expected to fall to any great extent either. The net result of the two processes is expected to generate moderately high levels of oil revenues for the oil exporting countries of the Gulf.

Growth Prospects

The immediate growth prospects in GCC countries may be viewed in the context of the fall in oil prices, a deepening of the global economic downturn, an increase in financial instability and a rise in protectionism. The fall in oil prices and worsening outlook for the world economy since the third quarter of 2008 have hit investments hard in development projects of GCC countries. The number of international banks willing to lend to projects in GCC countries has come down to 12 at the end of 2008 from 45 in 2006, hitting major oil & gas, industrial, and infrastructural projects that have substantial amount of FDI. The deepening global financial crisis has dried up project finance, led developers to reappraise projects in the light of falling demand and worsening outlook for credit markets. This has put pressure on governments to increase funding.

Domestic investments in the Gulf backed by larger FDI flows during 2003 and 2007 had surged. The global financial crisis had a dampening effect on FDI. Global inflows in 2008 fell by 14 per cent to $ 1,697 billion from a record high of US$ 1,979 billion in 2007 (UNCTAD, 2009: 1). The negative impact on FDI has been through access to finance affecting the capacity to invest and also through lower propensity to invest owing to gloomy economic and market prospects. The crisis has adversely affected mergers and acquisitions as equity and debt financing has become difficult in the face of falling stock market values and tightening credit conditions. Leveraged buyouts involving private equity funds or hedge funds have also dried up. This is further accentuated by the largest fall in FDI in finance (UNCTAD, 2009: Box I.3)

The export demand for the output from GCC would depend on the growth of demand in the rest of the world and the access to those markets. The growth of demand in the rest of the world is expected to be weak owing to rising unemployment, weak consumer and investor confidence, and unsettled financial sector. About a quarter of the total exports of the oil exporting countries[15] of the Middle East are to North America and the European Union (EU). This segment would not show much of a growth in 2010 and 2011. But the bulk of the trade to Asia (over 50 per cent of the total) would not suffer such serious fall as South Asian and Chinese growth is expected to be robust and ideally the GCC countries should be benefitting from it.

But what has come in the way of the GCC countries benefitting from it is the state measures by foreign countries increasing protectionism which would have an adverse impact on trade: "... while Middle Eastern countries are faced with 204 trade discriminatory measures implemented, or about to be implemented, by countries across the world, trade liberalizing measures affecting the region number only 36" (Pradhan, 2009: 191). The UAE faced the highest number of discriminatory trade measures followed by Saudi Arabia. Thus, the GCC countries are likely to face daunting challenges in their international trade activities during the current crisis.

Construction/Projects

As is evident, project finance and utilities have also taken a severe beating along with finance institutions in the current crisis. A recent survey of projects (worth at least US$ 10 million) reported 10 to 30 per cent cancellations or orders to put on hold in the GCC countries. Dubai, which has about 60 per cent of all projects in the GCC, has taken the largest hit, which in turn has affected the GCC as a whole.

15. GCC plus Algeria, Libya, and Sudan.

Table 3.11

Projects Affected by the Crisis in GCC Countries

Country	Projects and Finances Involved			
	Projects Under Construction (No.)	Projects Cancelled/On Hold (No.)	Total Project Worth (Billion $)*	% Cancellation
Kuwait	90	18	114	17
Qatar	124	7	42	-
Saudi Arabia	442	106	387	19
UAE	1372	566	900	29
Bahrain	148	54	36	27
Oman	95	8	38	8

Note: *All projects including those cancelled/on hold.

Source: Proleads.

Interestingly, the crisis has affected all subsectors—from commercial projects to residential properties—as the illustration from the UAE shows (Table 3.12).

Table 3.12

Projects Affected by Subsectors in UAE

Subsector	Projects under Construction (No.)	Total Number of Projects (No.)	% Cancellation
Commercial projects	340	487	147 (30)
Hospitality business	288	406	118 (29)
Residential properties	495	712	217 (30)
Retail projects	249	333	84 (25)
Total	1,372	1,938	566

Source: http://www.gulfbase.com/site/interface/NewsArchiveDetails.aspx?n=110724.

While new project starts have come down in the UAE, there is continuing high level activity in ongoing projects that would be "the envy of many" elsewhere in the world. There is evidence of increased construction activity in Abu Dhabi, Sharjah, and Ajman. Thus, while new starts have come down and those about to be started have been put on hold, lot of activity is continuing in ongoing projects.

Gulf Crisis and South Asian Labour: The Links

GCC countries are largely oil exporters and the quadrupling of oil prices during 2000-2008 brought windfall gains to them estimated to be over US$ 2 trillion. The rising oil prices, the large savings, and better credit ratings of the GCC countries attracted large FDI inflows into the Gulf, boosting investments and growth. Apart from the oil sector, other sectors such as tourism, trade, telecom, banking, power, and real estate have attracted massive private investments. Infrastructure development has been led by massive public investments in the Gulf. As a result of these investments, there is commensurate GDP growth in the GCC economies. This growth got translated into expatriate population increases subject to the policy on expatriate labour of the countries with the bulk of the labour flowing from South Asia.

Countries with few restrictions on the number and origin of migrant labourers, such as Kuwait, UAE, and Qatar, experienced 60 to 80 per cent increase in their populations during the first decade of 2000, and those with explicit policies of showing preference for nationals in employment, such as Saudi Arabia, Oman and Bahrain experienced about 20 per cent increase in their populations. Despite a restrictive migration policy, the number of migrants entering Saudi Arabia during 2000-2008 was more than those entering the rest of the five GCC countries put together. Except in Kuwait, in the rest of GCC countries, over 70 per cent of the expatriate labourers are employed in four sectors, namely agriculture, manufacturing, construction, and trade; whereas in Kuwait about a quarter of the total employment is in domestic services. The spike in global food price and the rapid rise in employment have led to rising inflation and a squeeze on real wages in the GCC economies.

The global crisis reached the Gulf with a time lag, as the oil prices reached record heights in early 2008 before falling precipitously. Commodity prices, real estate prices, and equity prices fell too. Along with the falling commodity and asset prices, FDI inflows into the Gulf began to be adversely affected, which in turn impacted investments in key sectors. The large losses incurred by the SWFs and mortgage defaults further eroded investor confidence. Growth of manufacturing, trade, tourism, and construction, which are all major sectors of employment growth, began to be adversely affected depressing expatriate employment. However, the impact of the crisis on GDP growth has varied across the GCC economies with Qatar, Oman, and Bahrain continuing to show positive growth; and the other three economies showing mild contraction, around one per cent in 2009; even these economies were expected to turn to positive growth in 2010.

The quick rebound of oil prices by mid-2009 and the not too depressing current account and budget balances have made the governments of the GCC countries bolder, and induced them to continue major infrastructure investments. The interventions in the banking sectors have also been decisive. A further boost has been the, albeit lower, but healthy GDP growth in the whole of South Asia in 2009, and the forecast of higher growth rates in 2010. South Asia and China have emerged as the major trading partners of GCC economies and the trade outlook does not look very depressing. However, the continuing adverse factors have been the depressed real estate and equity prices in the GCC countries.

Overall, large scale retrenchment of expatriate labour in the GCC economies did not take place due to the not too depressing GDP growth and encouraging economic outlook. Rather, the large infrastructure projects and public investments in some countries on the strength of rising oil prices have begun attracting new flow of labour, albeit at a slightly lower rate. The adjustment mechanisms of expatriate labourers to the layoffs caused by the crisis have been salary cuts, forced leave, and delayed renewal of work contracts. Hence, the expected large return flow of labour to South Asia has not happened.

Crisis, Employment and Wages

The crisis had affected a large number of workers in some way or the other. Some estimates indicate that nearly 40 per cent of the workers have been affected.[16] The effect varied across different industries, occupations, and skill levels and also depended on the

16. By a research consultant, Dr Janardhan, based in UAE.

number of years of experience of the expatriates. The strategies adopted by the workers to cope with the crisis were also varied. Contrary to the general expectation, the impression from the field visit was that expatriate workers did not leave the countries of their destination in large numbers. However, workers in some construction companies such as the 'Arabtec Construction Company' in Dubai had to leave the country because the company was severely affected by the crisis. In the normal course, in most cases the construction companies would provide the workers with the basic minimum facilities including food and accommodation. Hence, for the less skilled workers in the construction sector which retained the workforce, the effect of the crisis was not as severe. However, when the company faced sickness or closure, these workers had no choice of staying back in the country.

The most rampant effect of the crisis was the cut in salary, stoppage of increments, and stoppage of benefits and perks which the expatriates had to suffer. Almost all workers interviewed reported suffering in the recent past one of the above mentioned effects in their work life. The effect of this phenomenon was more severe in the case of middle income group workers engaged in semi-skilled and skilled jobs, since they have to make their own arrangements for accommodation and food. Salary cuts ranged from 10 to 30 per cent of the salary levels prevailing in 2007, just before the crisis. However, it is to be kept in mind that prior to the crisis there had been a large rise in the salaries and wages due to the boom in the sector. Hence, the decline in wages is a relative decline compared with the boom wage levels in 2007. Yet, the effect of this cut cannot be trivialised. This is so because the boom had also lifted the expectations of most workers leading to a high-spending lifestyle. Many workers stated that the rise in wages during the boom period induced them to borrow large loans for various purposes. The crisis alternatively led to a situation wherein most workers were in debt traps since their repayment capacity had fallen. And these traps acted precisely as a lock in for the workers, who could not leave the country even if they wanted to.

At the level of highly skilled workers and managerial class, the effect of the crisis had been curiously positive for the South Asian workers. Most positions at the senior managerial levels were held by European expatriates who claimed large salary packages. Many companies decided to lay off their European workers and replaced them with South Asian workers who needed to be paid much less. However, results from a survey among workers in UAE showed that almost all workers perceived the crisis as a potential threat to their jobs and so, the level of insecurity felt by them was very high.

Impact of the Crisis on South Asian Migrant Workers

This section provides an assessment of the impact of the crisis on the South Asian migrant workers in terms of return emigration, flows of labour emigration from Asia to the Gulf and inward remittances to South Asia. The assessment is based on the summary results of the emigrant household surveys and survey of return emigrants carried out to understand the coping mechanisms of individuals and families in times of crisis.

Return Migration to South Asia from the Gulf in 2009

All agencies working on migration and remittances in the South Asian countries and the Gulf region predicted an exodus of return emigrants from the Gulf to their countries of origin. But there do not exist firm estimates of the number of return emigrants due to the financial crisis from the Gulf to South Asia. Gulf migrants are basically workers who emigrated for work on a contractual basis and are supposed to return to the country of origin once the contract period is over. So, return migration[17] is not a new phenomenon among South Asian workers in the Gulf. Concerned officials in the countries of South Asia predicted possible increase in the number of return migrants to their respective places of origin following the impact of the crisis in the Gulf. For instance, Mr Vayalar Ravi, Minister of Overseas Indian Affairs, Government of India, informed the Parliament that accurate figures on the return of Indian workers are not available. However, he said, "it is estimated that about 50,000 to 150,000 workers have returned to India as a result of the delay in

17. The stock of return emigrants in Kerala was about 0.7 million in 1998, and increased to 0.9 million in 2003 and 1.2 million in 2008 (see Zachariah and Rajan, 2009).

execution of projects due to the economic slowdown and recession." Mr T.M. Thomas Isaac, Finance Minister of Kerala[18] State, India, informed the State Legislative Assembly that some 200,000 to 500,000 Keralites working in the Gulf could return home by mid 2009.

The CDS, Kerala, undertook four large-scale migration surveys in Kerala during the last 10 years to estimate the number of emigrants, return emigrants and remittances. The latest survey was conducted in 2008[19] and it was revisited in 2009[20] to arrive at reliable estimates of return emigrants due to the crisis. All those in the original sample who had returned were asked to cite the reasons for returning to Kerala. The questionnaire provided 10 possible reasons for return, among which the following three could be attributed to recession: job loss and return due to financial crisis, expiry of contract (renewal of contract did not take place as expected due to recession), and compulsory expatriation. The estimates of return migrants due to the crisis are provided in Table 3.13.

If we deduce that out of the stock of 2.19 million emigrants from Kerala, about 61,036 crisis-led migrants returned, then what could be the number of return emigrants from the Gulf to South Asia? According to the database available from various sources (both formal and informal), we arrived at a figure of 9.5 million South

---

18. According to the 2008 Kerala Migration Survey (KMS) conducted by the CDS, the emigrants from Kerala are estimated at 2.19 million (about 90% live in the Gulf) and the remittances are estimated at ₹ 43,288 crore. At present, Kerala leads the other states in India both in terms of outward emigration and inward remittances (Zachariah and Rajan, 2009).

19. The fourth Kerala Migration Survey (KMS, 2008) was conducted during August-December 2008, covering 15,000 sample households throughout the 63 *talukas* in Kerala. Out of 15,000 households, the survey enumerated 2,702 households with 3,981 emigrants. The KMS 2008 estimated the stock of emigrants from Kerala as 21.9 million based on the following method (more details, see Zachariah and Rajan, 2009)

    EMI (Emigrants) = [{sum of (Hi*ri/hi)}/Sum of Hi]*H

    ri = Number of Emigrants in the sample households in the ith locality

    hi= Number of sample HHs in the ith locality (50)

    Hi = Total number of HHs in the sample locality (from Census)

    H= Total number of HHs in the Taluk (from Census)

20. Return Emigrant Survey 2009 was conducted at CDS and sponsored by the Department of Non-Resident Keralite Affairs, Government of Kerala (for more details of the survey report, see Zachariah and Rajan, 2009). The field work was carried out during 16 June–7 September 2009.

Asian emigrants in the Gulf; and the projected return emigrants from the Gulf region to South Asia at about 263,660.[21] The country-wise estimates of return emigrants are provided in Table 3.14. India registered the highest number of return emigrants due to the crisis (140,000), followed by Pakistan (64,000), Bangladesh (25,000), Sri Lanka (27,000) and Nepal (7,000). One can also estimate the number of return emigrants from the countries of destination in the Gulf to countries in South Asia. For instance, India had a stock of 1.7 million migrants settled in UAE; and in the projected number of return emigrants from the UAE, there were 47,000 Indians.

Table 3.13

Number of Return Emigrants to Kerala in 2009 Due to Recession

	Sample	*Kerala*
Total emigrants in 2008 based on 2008 KMS	3,953	2,193,412
Return emigrants among emigrants of 2008 in Return Migration Survey in 2009	304	168,681
Return emigrants to Kerala due to financial crisis and recession	110	61,036

Source: Zachariah and Rajan, 2010b.

Table 3.14

Estimates of Return Emigrants to South Asia from the Gulf in 2009 Due to Financial Crisis

Country/State	*Stock of Emigrants*	*Return Emigrants Due to Crisis*
Kerala	2,193,412	61,036
India	5,050,000	140,526
Pakistan	2,300,000	64,002
Bangladesh	900,000	25,044
Nepal	250,000	6,957
Sri Lanka	975,000	27,131
South Asia	9,475,000	263,660

Source: Authors' estimates.

21. These could be underestimates as the composition of migrants from Kerala would have a lower proportion of unskilled workers.

Table 3.15

Average Cost of Emigration for Different Migration Corridors from Kerala to the Gulf, 2008

Countries	*Average Cost (₹)*
Kerala-Bahrain	57,172
Kerala-Kuwait	53,951
Kerala-Oman	56,840
Kerala-Qatar	66,316
Kerala-Saudi Arabia	74,606
Kerala-UAE	61,308

Source: Zachariah and Rajan, 2010a.

Table 3.16

Sources of Finances for Emigration, 2008

Source	*% of Emigrants*
From family members	26.8
Personal savings	40.1
Parents' savings	37.7
Borrowing from friends	42.1
Loans from money lender	12.6
Loans from banks	14.1
Sale/mortgage of land	4.9
Sale/mortgage of other assets	3.4
Sale/pledge ornaments	29.2
Government assistance	0.4
Others	7.0

Note: The total exceeds 100 as emigrants use more than one source.

Source: Zachariah and Rajan, 2010a.

The high cost of migration to the Gulf caused many emigrants to borrow money from various financial sources, including moneylenders and obtain cash from the sale of assets such as land and gold ornaments (for details, see Table 3.16). Under such conditions, even if the expatriates lose their jobs in the Gulf, they would prefer not to return home fearing inability to repay the debt already contracted there. They would rather accept any job at a lower wage and try to continue to send home remittances to repay their loans even during a crisis in the destination country.

Another characteristic of South Asian migration to the Gulf is the part played by the social network, which consists of friends and relatives, who perform a major role in the channel of migration flows by arranging visas and other requirements for the emigration process. For instance, an all-India survey conducted by CDS for the ILO and the Ministry of Overseas Indian Affairs reveals that close to 80 per cent of the Indian emigrants utilised their friends and relatives as an important channel for migration (Table 3.17). This also ensured that in the event of a job loss, they could rely on someone to provide them temporary support.

Table 3.17

Channels of Migration by Emigrants, 2007

Channel	*Male*	*Female*	*Total*	*Male (%)*	*Female (%)*	*Total (%)*
Friends and relatives	330	185	515	74.2	88.52	78.7
Government agency	3	0	3	0.7	0.00	0.5
Foreign employer	41	7	48	9.2	3.35	7.3
Private recruitment agencies	71	17	88	16.01	8.1	13.5
Total	445	209	654	100	100	100

Source: Rajan, Varghese and Jayakumar, 2009; 2010.

These features of South Asian migration (cost and social network) has minimised the extent of return emigration during the time of financial crisis.

Job Loss in Gulf but Not Returning to Origin Country

Thus there exists a category of migrants who have 'lost jobs in the Gulf but have not returned to the country of origin'. One of the strategies adopted by the emigrants who lost their jobs in the countries of destination due to the financial meltdown is to return to their countries of origin and look for employment. As we have seen in the earlier section, some of those who returned home after having lost their jobs in the Gulf are still unemployed and looking for jobs. The Nepal Government announced an incentive package to help such return emigrants. However, there is an equal number or more persons who lost their jobs and are still not able to return due to heavy investment they incurred in order to migrate.

This class of emigrants remains unemployed in the destination country and continues to look for jobs in the sectors which are less/not affected by the crisis, and are ready to work even for lower wages than what they were previously receiving and under hostile working conditions. The Return Emigrant Survey 2009 conducted in Kerala offered a unique opportunity to estimate the number of those who lost their jobs in the Gulf countries due to the crisis. According to the estimates, of the 2.2 million stock of emigrants from Kerala, about 39,396 persons lost their jobs between 2008 and 2009 but did not return to their country of origin (Zachariah and Rajan, 2010).

Table 3.18

Estimates of Emigrants Losing Jobs But Not Returning 2009

Country/State	*Stock of Emigrants*	*Number Losing Jobs but Not Returning*
Kerala	2,193,412	39,396
India	5,050,000	90,703
Pakistan	2,300,000	41,310
Bangladesh	900,000	16,165
Nepal	250,000	4,490
Sri Lanka	975,000	17,512
South Asia	9,475,000	170,181

Source: Authors' estimates.

Applying the same methodology to estimate the number of South Asian migrants who lost their jobs in the Gulf, but had not returned to the country of origin is placed at 170,181. This total comprise of Indians (90,000), followed by Pakistanis (41,000), Bangladeshis (16,000), Nepalese (5,000) and Sri Lankans (18,000). How these workers cope with their shattered livelihood in the destination countries requires a separate investigation.

Outflow of Workers from South Asia to the Gulf in 2009

As there were no official data to show the extent of the crisis-led return emigration from the Gulf to South Asia, we estimated the possible trends in the number of return emigrants. However, South Asian countries have reasonably well-managed database on the flow of workers from their respective countries to the country of destination. Evidence gathered from the five country reports prepared for this research clearly indicates a decline in the outflow of workers from South Asia to the Gulf in 2009. According to the projections made by the authors of the report based on the actual data available for the last seven to eights months of 2009, all countries in South Asia, except Sri Lanka, have reported decline in the flow of workers to the Gulf. The projected decline for India is huge—about 280,000—followed by Pakistan with 12,000 (See Table 3.19).

Table 3.19

Outflow of Migrant Workers from South Asia to the Gulf, 2005-2009

	India	*Pakistan*	*Bangladesh*	*Nepal*	*Sri Lanka*
2005	454.628	127,810	207,089	88,230	192,004
2006	618,286	172,837	307,620	128,306	170,049
2007	770,510	278,631	483,757	182,870	188,365
2008	818,315	419,842	643,424	169,510	215,793
2009*	538,090	407,077	N.A	152,272	226,299

Note: * Projected by the authors of this report based on the 2009 available data.

Source: This table is based on the country papers prepared by the respective country team at the countries of origin for this project.

India: Actual data available for January-September 2009; Pakistan: Actual data available for January-July 2009; Nepal: Actual data available for January to September 2009; Sri Lanka: Actual data available for January to August 2009.

Table 3.20

Outflow of Migrant Workers from South Asia, 2008-09

	India	*Pakistan* *	*Bangladesh*	*Nepal*	*Sri Lanka* #
2008	N.A	246,361	N.A	N.A	145,722
2009	N.A	237,462	N.A	N.A	150,866
Change	N.A	- 8,899	N.A	N.A	+ 5,144

Note: * January-July; # January-August.

Evidence available from all the countries in South Asia indicate that the number of workers going to the Gulf declined the most in the case of UAE, which was more severely affected by the crisis than the other countries in the Gulf. For instance, in 2008, 349,827 ECR (Emigration Clearance Required) passport holders left for the UAE from India for work; and their number had declined to just 75,000 in September 2009. On the other hand, Saudi Arabia attracted about 228,406 persons in 2008; and as of September 2009, 214,043 had already left for Saudi Arabia. This pattern holds true for Pakistan, Sri Lanka and Nepal as well. Thus, the recession has changed the migration and demographic dynamics of South Asian workers in the Gulf region.

Inward Remittances to South Asia in 2009

The money that migrants send home is important not only to their families, but also to their country's balance of payments. In many developing countries, remittances represent a significant proportion of the GDP as well as foreign exchange earnings. In 2009, the World Bank published the list of 10 developing countries (Table 3.21) with the volume of remittances and remittances as percentage of the GDP (World Bank, 2009). Among the South Asian countries, India was ranked number one in terms of the volume of remittances with US$ 52 billion in 2008 which is the equivalent of 4.2 per cent of GDP. Bangladesh ranked eighth among the first 10 countries with US$ 9 billion. Pakistan, another Asian country with US$ 7 billion ranked as 11th in terms of remittances. On the other hand, Nepal is being listed as one of the top 10 countries with the highest share of remittances to GDP at 22 per cent. Table 3.21 illustrates the importance of remittances in other South Asian countries such as Pakistan, Sri Lanka and the state of Kerala in India.

When the crisis hit in 2008, most of the people were more worried about the remittance flows rather than the migration flows. In November 11, 2008, the World Bank (2008) stated, "The outlook for remittances for the rest of 2008 and 2009-10 remains as uncertain as the outlook for global growth, oil and non-oil commodity prices, and currency exchange rates." After several years of strong growth, remittance flows to developing countries began to slowdown significantly in the third quarter of 2008 in response to a deepening global financial crisis. Based on the World Bank's economic projections for 2008-2010 and available monthly and quarterly data on remittances for January-August 2008, the present study estimated that remittance flows to developing countries would reach US$ 283 billion in 2008 compared with a revised US$ 265 billion in 2007. World Bank (2009) argued that "remittance growth was expected to be moderately significant, but that flow would remain resilient." This assessment was a relief to the policymakers, at least in the South Asian context.

Table 3.21

Top 10 Remittance-Receiving Countries, 2008

Rank	*Countries*	*(US$ billions)*	*% to GDP*
1	India	52	4.2
2	China	49	1.1
3	Mexico	26	2.4
4	Philippines	19	11.2
5	Poland	11	2.0
6	Nigeria	10	4.7
7	Romania	9	4.7
8	Bangladesh	9	11.4
9	Egypt	9	5.3
10	Vietnam	7	7.9
	Pakistan	7	4.2
	Nepal	3	21.6
	Sri Lanka	3	7.2
	Kerala State, India	10.4	30.7

Source: World Bank, 2009b; Zachariah and Rajan, 2010a.

Table 3.22

Inward Remittances to South Asian Countries from Migrant Workers, 2000-2009

	India	*Pakistan*	*Bangladesh*	*Nepal*	*Sri Lanka*
			Million US$		
2000	12890	1075	1968	111	1166
2001	14273	1461	2105	147	1185
2002	15736	3554	2858	678	1309
2003	20999	3964	3192	771	1438
2004	18750	3945	3584	823	1590
2005	22125	4280	4314	1212	1991
2006	28334	5121	5428	1453	2185
2007	37217	5998	6562	1734	2527
2008	51581	7039	8995	2727	2947
2009 *	47000	8619	10431	3010	2892
2009 +	53227	8856	10525	2812	3308
			% change		
2000-01	10.73	35.91	6.96	32.43	1.63
2001-02	10.25	143.26	35.77	361.22	10.46
2002-03	33.45	11.54	11.69	13.72	9.85
2003-04	-10.71	-0.48	12.28	6.74	10.57
2004-05	18.00	8.49	20.37	47.27	25.22
2005-06	28.06	19.65	25.82	19.88	9.74
2006-07	31.35	17.13	20.89	19.34	15.65
2007-08	38.60	17.36	37.08	57.27	16.62
2008-09 *	-8.88	22.45	15.96	10.38	-1.87
2008-09 +	3.19	25.81	17.01	3.12	12.25

Note: * World Bank Estimates + Our estimates

Source: World Bank and the country reports prepared by the research team for this project from five countries of South Asia.

Let us assess the trends in remittances to the South Asian countries since 2000 to examine the growth of remittances (Table 3.22). The remittance growth during 2007-08 was high for India, Bangladesh and Nepal, with Nepal registering the highest growth at 57.27 per cent. Based on the existing monthly data available for the South Asian countries, the World Bank (2009) predicted that remittances in Pakistan, Bangladesh and Nepal are expected to register growth, ranging from 22 per cent in Pakistan to 10 per cent in Nepal. Our estimates based on the simple average of remittances for the available months from the country reports prepared by the teams suggests that all the countries of South Asia are resilient to the crisis in terms of remittances. Our estimates put the growth in remittances in India at 3 per cent, from US$ 52 billion in 2008 to US$ 53 billion in 2009.

Table 3.23

Inflow of Worker's Remittances to South Asia, 2008-09

(Million US$)

	India	*Pakistan*	*Bangladesh*	*Nepal*	*Sri Lanka*
2008	26723	5731	6811	1654	2249
2009	23558	7380	7894	1875	2481
Change	- 3165	+1649	+1083	+221	+232

Note: Reference periods: Bangladesh: January-September; Pakistan: January-October; Nepal: January-August; Sri Lanka: January–September and India: January-June.

Source: Same as Table 3.22.

Remittance flows to South Asia grew strongly in 2008 despite the global economic crisis, but there are risks that these may slowdown due to a lagged response to the weak global economy. Why did remittances not decline in South Asia? From our study, the following six observations can be made: (i) debts contracted to meet the high cost incurred during their migration which remained unpaid kept the emigrants from returning to the countries of origin in spite the lay offs at the countries of destination; (ii) predictions of a large exodus of return emigrants from the Gulf did not come true; (iii) though the outflow declined in the first half of 2009, it has still not significantly affected the stock of South Asian migrants in the Gulf; (iv) appreciation of the US dollar *vis-à-vis* South Asian currencies; for instance, the current exchange rate of the Indian rupee to the US dollar is same as in 2001-02; (v) continuous rise in oil prices generating more income in the Gulf; and (vi) "reverse migration" of the crisis-led return emigrants back to the Gulf (as indicated by our quick field work in India).

Outward Remittances from the Gulf

Another way to assess the inflow of remittances to South Asia is to analyse the outflow of remittances from the Gulf countries. The World Bank (2009) provides data for 2008 for four countries in the Gulf—Bahrain, Kuwait, Oman and Saudi Arabia (Table 3.24). The World Bank could not obtain any information on outward remittances for the UAE and Qatar.

Table 3.24

Outflows of Remittances from the Gulf, 2001-2008

(Million US$)

	Saudi Arabia	*Oman*	*Bahrain*	*Kuwait*
2001	15120	1532	1287	1784
2002	15854	1602	872	1925
2003	14783	1672	1082	2144
2004	13555	1826	1120	2403
2005	13996	2257	1223	2648
2006	15611	2788	1531	3183
2007	16068	3670	1483	3824
2008	16068	5181	1483	3824

Source: World Bank, 2009. Information for the UAE and Qatar is not available.

Until 2008, the outflows of remittances from the Gulf were on the increase in all countries except Bahrain.

Emigrant Survey Results from South Asia

As discussed earlier in the methodology section, this survey was conducted in five countries of South Asia among the households which have an emigrant currently in the Gulf in order to examine their coping mechanisms at the time of the crisis. The survey was canvassed among 452 households in five countries of South Asia. We shall briefly discuss a few aspects of the analysis.[22] A few of the surveyed households have more than one emigrant, thus taking the total number of emigrants to 482 in 452 households. The

22. Separate report based on the survey was prepared by S. Irudaya Rajan and Arindam Banerjee of CDS.

average household size or emigrant support ratio is 3.8 persons per household. Only 5 per cent of the households have women emigrants. About 85 per cent of the emigrants went abroad on proper worker visas, while others went on visit visas, tourist visas, free visas and so on.

Families of poorer sections which have made huge investments to send one member abroad will not be able to make migration the path to their social mobility. Our survey indicates that about 75 per cent of the households with migrants own land, 85 per cent own houses, 50 per cent own refrigerators and 57 per cent own video recorders. Similarly, 25 per cent of the households have drinking water within their premises, 40 per cent use their own well or tube well and almost half of the households use LPG for cooking.

Table 3.25

Utilisation of Remittances among Emigrant Households in South Asia During the Time of Crisis, 2009

(in Per cent)

	Order of Importance		*Possible Uses of Remittances*	
Utilisation of Remittances	*2008*	*2009*	*2008*	*2009*
Day to day household expenses	55.1	60.4	84.7	90.9
Education	9.7	11.1	73.0	76.5
Medical expenses	10.0	11.9	67.5	69.9
Savings for constructing house, buying land	5.3	7.3	61.1	62.4
General savings, not earmarked any particular purpose	5.3	9.1	63.7	68.6
Business investment, share market venture, gold etc.	0.7	0.9	53.1	54.0
Repayment of debts incurred by the household	2.9	4.9	60.0	61.7
Repayment of debts related to the costs of migration	16.6	9.3	60.2	60.6
For important life course events (marriage, dowry)	2.2	2.2	54.4	55.8
Others	0.9	0.7	18.1	19.5

Source: Special survey conducted by the research team 2009.

Around 94 per cent of the households reported receiving regular remittances even during the crisis period; and about 30 per cent of the households also received gifts from emigrants. To assess the utilisation pattern of remittances, we asked the household members staying behind in the home country to list the uses to which remittances are expended in order of importance (Table 3.25). The results indicate that there is no major change in their expenditure pattern during 2008-09, and in fact, households were prudent in their use of remittances, devoting relatively larger sums of money to saving and investment. Table 3.25 also provides the general pattern of use of remittances in South Asia. About 90 per cent of households reported the use of remittances (in order of importance) as follows: day-to-day expenses, investment in human development (education and health), general savings, and saving for construction of house. About 61 per cent of the families reported the repayment debts related to the cost of the migration as one of the chief uses of remittances. It is found that the economic crisis had no impact on emigrant households' use of remittances.

To a query on their current job status in the host country, 13 per cent of the emigrant households reported that their breadwinners had lost their jobs due to the financial crisis since 2008. Among them, half had found another job and stayed on the countries of destination; one fourth had changed their sponsors; and another one fourth had continued to stay on illegally in the Gulf. Interestingly, about 40 per cent of the households reported that their emigrant members planned to return home soon.

When we enquired about the employment scenario in their work place at the time of the crisis, 25 per cent of the emigrants reported that there were large scale redundancies in their companies, 16 per cent reported that contracts were postponed/cancelled, 20 per cent reported that wages were reduced or not paid, 17 per cent reported that heavier workload was imposed with the same or lower wages, 8 per cent reported that they were forced to take annual leave, and another 10 per cent reported that there were shortfalls in provisions of food, shelter or health care by their employers.

Table 3.26

Changes in Household Expenditure During the Crisis in South Asia, 2009

Household Expenditure	*Not Much Change*	*Increase*	*Decrease*	*Decrease to Total (452) Emigrant Households (%)*
Food, clothing	25	119	34	7.52
Rent (room, house)	151	14	13	2.88
Basic utilities (water, electricity)	44	99	35	7.74
Transport and communication	24	111	43	9.51
Health (medications, hospitals visits, tests)	76	81	21	4.65
Education	71	85	22	4.87
Building construction	88	43	47	10.40
Life course rituals	124	16	38	8.41
Others	163	4	11	2.43

Source: Same as Table 3.25.

We were also keen on assessing the household expenditure on various items during the time of crisis as compared with pre-crisis situation among emigrant households. 6 out of 10 households reported no change in the pattern of household expenditure. Among those households who reported changes in the expenditure pattern (178 out of the 452 households) during the crisis, we asked them to provide feedback as follows: (i) increase (ii) decrease, and (iii) not much change (Table 3.26). Only 8 per cent of emigrant households reported decline in their household expenditure on food and clothing, 5 per cent each reported decline in expenditure on education and health respectively, and 10 per cent said that expenditure on construction of houses had to be cut down.

On the financial commitments and repayment status during 2008 and 2009, we found that among the surveyed households, there were only seven defaulters in 2008. And they continued to be defaulters in 2009 as well. There was no change in the financial commitment among the emigrant households during the time of the crisis (Table 3.27).

Table 3.27

Repayment Behaviour of Emigrant Households on Financial Commitments During the Financial Crisis in the Gulf, 2009

Financial Commitment	*Number of Households*	*Payment Status in 2008*			*Payment Status in 2009*		
		Regular	*Irregular*	*Default*	*Regular*	*Irregular*	*Default*
Mortgage	81	26	50	5	22	54	5
Car loan	2	0	2	0	0	2	0
Educational loan	1	1	0	0	1	0	0
Agricultural loan	2	2	0	0	2	0	0
Personal loan	25	16	7	2	18	6	1
Loan from private money lender	14	9	5	0	10	4	0
Credit card payment	16	10	6	0	13	3	0
Others	10	9	1	0	5	4	1
Total	151	73	71	7	71	73	7

Source: Same as Table 3.25.

Table 3.28

Postponement of Pattern of Investment among Emigrant Households in South Asia, 2009

Investment Pattern	*Number*	*%*
Land	54	11.9
Housing	48	10.6
Insurance	18	4.0
New/existing business ventures	17	3.8
Building/construction/renovation/maintenance	85	18.8
Private investment schemes	9	2.0
Bank deposits	74	16.4
Others	5	1.1

Source: Same as Table 3.25.

Looking at the patterns of investment, it was found that about 12 per cent of the households had postponed their investment in land or houses, about 19 per cent had put off construction activities on their houses and about 17 per cent had postponed depositing money in the bank. Following the crisis, 3 out of 4 households had taken some kind of loan to supplement the household income. 1 out of 10 households had borrowed money from their friends and relatives. On the use of borrowed funds, it was found that 42 per cent used them for routine household expenses, 23 per cent for human development (health and education) and another 18 per cent for meeting financial commitments (Table 3.29). In 1 out of 10 households, members left behind in the countries of origin had taken up new jobs/employment to supplement the income due to the crisis.

Table 3.29

Channels Used by Emigration Households to Supplement Their Household Income in South Asia, 2009

Source of Loan	*No.*	*% to Total Households*	*Purpose of Loan*	*No.*	*% to Borrowed Households*
Government	5	4.5	Routine HH expenses	47	42.0
Co-operatives	29	25.9	Education	14	12.5
Commercial bank	32	28.6	Medical expenses	11	9.8
Professional money lenders	18	16.1	Meeting financial commitments	20	17.9
Insurance/ Provident Fund	2	1.8	Life course expenses	13	11.6
Friends and relatives	48	41.1	Other purposes	39	34.8

Source: Same as Table 3.25.

The survey also enquired about a few selected events that had taken place in the households since the crisis and tried to find out how many of them were due to financial crisis. Only 19 households shifted the residence since the crisis and only five cited the reason for moving house as the financial crisis. Similarly, only 27 households reported that their children 'dropped out' or 'moved school or college' since the crisis and among them only 17 attributed this to the crisis. A number of households realistically postponed their life course events such as marriage (25) due to the crisis, 49 households postponed the medical treatment of one of the household members, and 22 households postponed medical checkup of a family member.

Did any of the households sell their existing assets to cope with the decline of remittances from their emigrant members abroad? It was found that during the crisis just 2 households closed their fixed deposits, 1 household sold land, 7 households sold jewelry, 2 households sold personal vehicles, and 35 households sold their livestock.

Table 3.30

Indicators of Psychological Assessment Among the Emigrant Household Members Left Behind in South Asia, 2009

Indicators	*Answer*	%
Did you feel confident that the household (emigrant and non-emigrant members inclusive) would be able to weather the financial crisis	No	64.8
Did you feel unsure whether you may be able to meet monthly financial commitments and or regular household expenditure	Yes	44.0
Do you worry that the emigrant members of the household are about to lose their jobs/would be forced to leave	Yes	47.8
If the emigrant members of the household did return to the household, do you think that it will be difficult for the household to manage its financial affairs	Yes	70.4
Do you know if there have been any changes in the status of the emigrants health in the country of destination since January 2009	Yes	24.8

When assessing the impact of the financial crisis, most researchers do not attempt to evaluate the psychological stress suffered by the emigrant members and by their household members left behind.[23] The research team at CDS assigned five questions to assess the psychological impact including anxiety and stress among emigrant households. The answers to these questions are presented in Table 3.30. About 70 per cent of the left

23. The CDS has undertaken major research on social and psychological impact of migration on left behind women, children and elderly (Zachariah *et al.*, 2003).

behind members of the emigrant households felt that it would be difficult for them to manage the financial affairs of the household, if their emigrant member did return due to the crisis. Similarly, one out of two households reported that they faced the imminent threat of their emigrant member losing his/her job. About one out of four emigrant members reported changes in their health status following the crisis.

Table 3.31

Reported Morbidity Patterns Among Emigrants and Women Members Left Behind in South Asia, 2009 (Out of 452 Emigrant Households)

Emigrant Member	*Descending Order (First 5)*	*Women Left Behind*	*Descending Order (First 5)*
Headache	45	Fevers	52
High blood pressure	27	High blood pressure	33
Anxiety/depression	3	Headache	31
Sleeplessness	4	Anxiety/depression	17
Weight loss	5	Gastrointestinal problems	10

Among the morbidity problems reported, headaches, anxiety/depression and high blood pressure have emerged as important ailments faced by emigrant members and women members left behind. Sleeplessness and weight loss are also problems reported among emigrant members.

Return Emigrant Survey Results

This survey was conducted among the return emigrants who lost their jobs because of the financial crisis in the Gulf and were forced to return home. The survey aimed at examining their coping mechanisms after return. The survey was canvassed on various issues connected to the crisis among 425 return emigrants in the five countries of origin. Among the emigrants, 22 were females. A few important findings from the survey[24] are discussed as follows.

24. Separate report based on the survey was prepared by S. Irudaya Rajan and Vinoj Abraham of CDS.

We were interested in assessing the livelihood options (employment patterns) of the return emigrants at various points of time: more than six months and less than one year prior to return; six months prior to return; two weeks prior to return; at the time of our survey; and one month after return. First, we assess the employment status and pattern of employment among return emigrants at the time of survey, and within one month after return. Among the return emigrants, 73 per cent remained unemployed even one month after their return, while the remaining 27 per cent managed to find employment as regular wage workers and as casual wage labourers or became self employed. However, at the time of the survey, the proportion of unemployed among the return emigrants declined from 73 per cent to 42 per cent. Among the employed, about 37 per cent managed to find regular employment, whereas casual and contract workers constituted 40 per cent and 8 per cent of the workers respectively at the time of the survey.

Table 3.32

Employment Status and Type of Employment Among Return Emigrants in South Asia, 2009

Employment Status	*Present Status*	*One Month After Return*	*Present Status (%)*	*One Month After Return (%)*
Self employed	86	39	20.24	9.18
Regular salary/wage employment	63	17	14.82	4.00
Casual wage labour	66	15	15.53	3.53
Unemployed	179	310	42.12	72.94
Others	31	44	7.29	10.35
		Employment Type		
Regular	80	26	36.70	35.62
On contract	18	2	8.26	2.74
Casual	86	27	39.45	36.99
Others	29	15	13.30	20.55

Source: Return Emigrant Survey, 2009.

The prevalence of unemployment among return emigrants immediately after return from the countries of destination and at the time of the survey indicates that such persons did not get any support from either the government or any banking institution. At the time of the survey, about half of the return emigrants lived by making use of their past savings, followed by borrowing and support from other members of the family.

Table 3.33

Coping with Unemployment by Return Migrants in South Asia, 2009

	Present Status	*One Month After Return*	*Present Status (%)*	*One Month After Return (%)*
Lived on past savings	73	126	48.67	62.07
Borrowed to stay on	52	40	34.67	19.70
Depended on other earning members of the household	25	37	16.67	18.23

Source: Return Emigrant Survey, 2009.

Table 3.34

Reasons for Return for Regular Salaried Workers from the Gulf to South Asia, 2009

Reasons for Return	*Number*	*%*
Contract period was over	38	17.19
Current employer terminated the contract	116	52.49
Employer enforced a leave	89	40.27
Employer reduced wages/salary	77	34.84
Employer changed the contracted nature of job (working and living conditions, perks, benefits, timing of work etc.)	82	37.10
Employer shifted job from one occupation/industry to another	45	20.36
Retired from job	19	8.60
Voluntarily resigned from job to take up another job at home country	16	7.24
Voluntarily resigned from job to take up job in another country other than the home country	7	3.17
Tried to migrate to another country but failed	7	3.17
None of the above have occurred till now, but any or all the above are expected to occur	12	5.43
Any other reason	1	0.45

Note: Multiple answers possible, hence percentages add up to over 100.

Source: Return Emigrant Survey 2009.

We also collected information on the reasons for return among the emigrants who were self-employed, in regular salary employment or unemployed in the destination countries two weeks prior to return. Out of the 425 return emigrants surveyed, 221 had jobs in the regular category and 144 were unemployed two weeks prior to return. About 52 per cent of them returned because their employer terminated the contract. Another 40 per cent were forced to leave the country on a long leave, while about 34-37 per cent left due to reduced wages and change of contract, followed by change of sponsor.

Table 3.35

Reasons for Returning of Unemployed Workers Two Weeks Prior to Return from the Gulf to South Asia, 2009

Reasons for Return	*Number*	*%*
Did not expect to get any job in near future	47	32.64
Expected to get some job in near future, but with a lesser salary than expected	78	54.17
Expected to get some job in near future, but not in the preferred occupation/industry	63	43.75
Expected to get some job in near future, but may not get preferred period of appointment/type of employment contract	67	46.53
Tried to migrate to another country but failed	12	8.33
Any other reason	2	1.39

Source: Return Emigrant Survey, 2009.

The survey also indicates that some of them were unemployed two weeks prior to return. Some probably lost jobs and became unemployed and were looking for a job but failed to get one and returned to the country of origin. There were also cases where a worker had arrived in the Gulf on a visit visa during the boom period, then acquired a job and converted his/her visit visa to an employment visa. However, due to the crisis, the opportunities to avail such jobs got limited in the Gulf so that those visitors had to return. About 54 per cent of the emigrants felt that they would get a job with a salary lower than expected; about 45 per cent left the countries of destination because they could not get the job in the preferred sector and another 33 per cent left because they felt that they would not get any job in near future.

Table 3.36

Channels Used by Return Emigrants to Supplement Household Income in South Asia, 2009

Source of Loan	*No.*	*Per cent of Total Households*	*Purpose of Loan*	*No.*	*% of Borrowed Households*
Government	4	0.94	Routine HH expenses	35	33.33
Co-operatives	13	3.06	Education	27	25.71
Commercial bank	4	0.94	Medical expenses	28	26.67
Professional money lenders	28	6.59	Meeting financial commitments	26	24.76
Insurance/PF	1	0.24	Life course expenses	16	15.24
Friends and relatives	55	12.94	Other purposes	8	7.62

Source: Return Emigrant Survey, 2009.

One out of four return emigrants took loans to supplement the family income; half of such borrowers depended on friends and relatives and seven per cent took loans from the professional money lenders. This again indicates that the emigrants were not from very poor families as they could mobilise the funds needed for the migration process. Half of the loans were used for human development (education and health), and the next most notable purpose of the loans was for routine household expenses.

The survey also made enquiries about the adaptation and coping mechanisms employed by the return emigrant households to cover the loss of remittances. About 2 per cent of the households shifted residence due to the crisis, 12 per cent postponed their life course events, 11 per cent postponed/cancelled vacation, 13 per cent postponed medical check-ups or treatment, and finally, about 3 per cent postponed the proposed emigration plan of another household member.

Table 3.37

Adaptation of Households After Return of the Emigrants, 2009

	Event Reported	*Due to Financial Crisis*	*% to Total Households*
Household has shifted residence	16	12	2.82
Children dropped out/moved school/college	32	24	5.65
Postponement/cancellation of life course event	59	51	12.00
Postponement/cancellation of trip/vacation by non-emigrant members	55	50	11.76
Postponement/cancellation of routine medical checkups for household member	15	12	2.82
Postponement/cancellation of medical treatment for household member	49	36	8.47
Postponement/cancellation of proposed emigration by household member	25	14	3.29

Source: Return Emigrant Survey, 2009.

Table 3.38

Assets of Return Emigrant Households, 2009

Asset	*Owned*	*% to Total Households*	*Assets Sold*	*% to Owned Households*
Savings	354	83.29	12	3.39
Land	364	85.65	10	2.75
House	383	90.12	3	0.78
Company/Business	298	70.12	2	0.67
Livestock	315	74.12	39	12.38
Consumer durables	384	90.35	9	2.34
Gold Jewellery	385	90.59	19	4.94
Vehicle	344	80.94	11	3.20
Other property	307	72.24	1	0.33

Source: Return Emigrant Survey, 2009.

Among the return emigrant households, 86 per cent owned lands, 90 per cent owned houses, 90 per cent owned gold jewelry and 81 per cent owned vehicles. Decline in income and prolonged unemployment in the countries of origin led 3 per cent of the return emigrants in South Asia to sell their lands, 5 per cent to sell their gold, and an overwhelming 12 per cent to sell their livestock.

Summing up: Impact of Crisis on Migrant Workers and Remittances

The unraveling of the impact of the crisis on output and employment in the US had generated an anticipation of large scale retrenchment of expatriate labourers in the Gulf region. The anticipated misery and the need for rehabilitation had got some governments in South Asia thinking about plans for the returning migrants. But our 'survey of emigrants and return emigrants' showed that the dimensions of the impact were not as large as was feared earlier. For a stock of approximately 9.5 million South Asian emigrants in the Gulf, the number who returned due to the crisis was about 264,000 (just around 2.8 per cent); and the number who lost jobs but was continuing to stay in the Gulf was about 170,000 (1.8%). Overall, less than 5 per cent of the South Asian emigrants had lost jobs owing to the crisis. But such an impact had not adversely affected the yearly flow of out-migrants from South Asia. Compared with the outflow of about 2.2 million workers in 2008, the number in 2009 was close to 2.0 million, which still was higher than the corresponding figure in 2007.

As regards remittances (in US$), the annual percentage increase since 2004-05 has been over 20 per cent for the South Asian countries, except for Sri Lanka. The magnitude of the increase has taken a hit all over South Asia, except Pakistan from where the outflow of migrants had been increasing at around 50 per cent every year since 2005. But remittances have not fallen following the crisis; either it has remained stagnant or has shown a mild rise depending upon the estimates. As most of the South Asian currencies have depreciated against the US$ (to which the GCC currencies are pegged) from late 2007, remittances in terms of domestic currencies would have shown an increase. The survey of migrant households in South Asia confirmed these estimates as 94 per cent of the households reported regular remittances during the crisis period also as in previous years and no significant change in the use of remittances was reported by these households.

Overall, less than five per cent of the stock of South Asian migrants in the Gulf had lost jobs and either returned back to home country or kept struggling to continue in the Gulf. The flow of workers from South Asia to the Gulf had also not been affected to any significant extent, but there were changes in the origin (in favour of Pakistan) and the destination (in favour of Saudi Arabia) of the flow. The volume of remittances into South Asia had also not fallen to any significant extent.

The crisis, however, had affected the workforce in some decisive ways. Those who returned home after losing jobs gave various reasons, such as termination of contract, forced to take long leave, and contract not renewed. A sizeable proportion reported reduced salary and benefits, shift to another job, and deteriorating working and living conditions. One out of four return emigrants had to take a loan to meet routine household expenses, education and medical expenses, and other life course expenses. Sale of assets, however, had not been a response to tide over the period of unemployment and lack of earnings.

Policy Recommendations

Labour is one of the critical factors of production and all economic activities are founded on labour inputs. As regards the GCC economies and to a large extent in Malaysia as well, labour is regarded as mobile as capital. Capital mobility requires sound general accounting procedures, but the burden of any form of accounting of labour mobility is put on the individual. The countries of origin too are to blame for it. That is why the database on migrant labour is weak and in the eventuality of a crisis, such as the global economic crisis, the policy makers are in the dark about the numbers, destinations, and skill base of the migrants to make any informed policy interventions. It is time that a sound database of migrants is built and regularly updated.

The countries of destination often have restrictive visa regimes. This does not allow enough time for migrants to plan their course of action when they become unemployed. Bearing the entire burden of adjustment on the part of the labourers is unjust. The countries of destination should allow a reasonable duration of stay for the labourers losing employment at normal times and a longer duration in periods of crisis.

The receiving countries should avoid forced expulsion of migrant workers. To ensure decent treatment of labour, they should extend the inspection to sectors and work places where migrant workers are concentrated. They should discourage the managerial tendencies to cut pay and resort to exploitative and discriminatory practices. Confiscation of passports and other documents and harassment of the workers by the employers should be prevented at all times. Adequate compensation should be paid to the workers who are forced to return due to economic crisis.

Despite rules prohibiting labour contractors from collecting the cost of migration from the migrants, the practice goes on unhindered. Especially high are the costs incurred by unskilled and poorly-paid labourers. It is important that labour receiving countries should introduce model labour contracts for various categories of workers, specifying the details of wages and non-wage benefits to be paid. They should take steps for their strict implementation. All the labour receiving countries in the Gulf should fix the minimum wages and regulate other working conditions like hours of work per day, paid holidays, accommodation facilities, provision for medical treatment and travel cost for return journeys.

Harassment, ill-treatment and sexual exploitation of female domestic workers by the employers should be treated as criminal acts; and the civil courts should treat these cases at par with those involving other citizens of the labour-receiving country. The labour redressal machinery should contain special labour laws for all categories of female workers such as domestic workers in the households, and skilled, semi-skilled, and unskilled female workers employed in establishments.

Some countries impose a tax on expatriate labourers. What they fail to recognise is that competitive migration helps to keep wages low in the destination countries which gives them competitive advantage in product markets. Instead of rewarding labour for such a gain, they seem to be penalising them by taxing them. Further, the burden of social security payments falls on the countries of origin, which do not reap the gains of any production by these workers. It may be made mandatory for the labour receiving countries to make payments for social security which should be distributed through the countries of origin.

The labour sending countries of South Asia and South East Asia should form a union like OPEC to ensure that the labour receiving countries implement minimum wages, zero cost of migration, decent working conditions, labour laws to protect the workers and special laws for female workers. The labour sending countries should collectively take a decision not to allow workers to go to those countries which are not prepared to fix a minimum wage and offer them decent working conditions.

References

Abed, George T. (2003). "Unfulfilled Promise: Why the Middle East and North Africa Region has Lagged in Growth and Globalization", *Finance and Development* 40(1): 1-11.

Al-Yousif, Yousif Khalifa (1997). "Exports and Economic Growth: Some Empirical Evidence from the Arab Gulf Countries", *Applied Economics* 29: 693-7.

Arayssi, Mahmoud (2008). "Pegging to the Dollar and the Feasibility of the Proposed Currency Area in the GCC", *International Review of Business Research Papers*, 4(5): 74-86.

Asian Development Bank (various issues). *Asian Economic Monitor.*

Awad, Ibrahim (2009). *The Global Economic Crisis and Migrant Workers: Impact and Response*. Geneva: International Labour Office.

Behrendt, Sven (2009). "Gulf Arab SWFs: Managing Wealth in Turbulent Times", *Policy Outlook*, Carnegie Endowment for International Peace.

Business Monitor International Ltd. (2009). *The UAE Business Forecast Report.*

Centre for Development Studies (2008). *Global Financial Crisis and Kerala Economy: Impact and Mitigation Measures*. Report submitted to the Government of Kerala.

Das, Dilip K. (2008). "Sovereign-Wealth Funds: Assuaging the Exaggerated Anguish about the New Global Financial Players", *Global Economy Journal* 8(4/5): 1-17.

Economic Intelligence Unit (2009). *Country Report: Bahrain*. United Kingdom. September.

———. (2009a). *Country Report: Saudi Arabia*. September. United Kingdom

———. (2009b). *Country Report: Sri Lanka*. October. United Kingdom

———. (2009c). *Country Report: Qatar*. October. United Kingdom

———. (2009d). *Country Report: India*. October. United Kingdom

———. (2009e). *Country Report: Nepal*. August. United Kingdom

———. (2009f). *Country Report: Pakistan*. October. United Kingdom.

———. (2009g). *Country Report: Bangladesh*. September. United Kingdom.

———. (2009h). *Country Report: Malaysia*. October. United Kingdom.

———. (2009i). *Country Report: Oman*. September. United Kingdom.

———. (2009j). *Country Report: United Arab Emirates*. September. United Kingdom.

Economic and Social Commission for Western Asia (ESCWA) (2008). *Foreign Direct Investment Report E/Escwa/Edgd/2008/Technical Paper*. 13 September. New York: UN.

Elekdag, Selim. (2009). "Financial Stress", *IMF Research*, 10(2): 1- 3.

Evenelt, Simon J. (ed.) (2009). *Broken Promises: A G-20 Summit Report by Global Trade Alert*. London: Centre for Economic Policy Research.

Fargues, Philippe (2008). "Emerging Demographic Patterns Across the Mediterranean and Their Implications for Migration through 2030", *Transatlantic Council on Migration: A Project of the Migration Policy Institute*. November.

Farrell, Diana and Susan Lund (2007). "The World's New Financial Power Brokers", *Economic Studies*. The McKinsey Quarterly. December.

Fix, Michael, Demetrios G. Papademetriou, Jeanne Batalova, Aaron Terrazas, Serena Yi-Ying Lin and Michelle Mittelstadt (2009). *Migration and the Global Recession—A Report Commissioned by the BBC World Service*. Migration Policy Institute. September.

Gaiy, A.H. and A.C. Worthington (2007). "A Primer on Islamic Finance: Definitions, Sources, Principles and Methods", *Faculty of Commerce Papers*. University of Wollongong.

Gulf Cooperation Council Credit Survey (2009). *How the Region is Weathering the Storm*. Standard & Poor's. June.

Gulftalent.com (2009). "Recession and Employment in the Gulf", Accessed on 15 November 2009.

Hasan, Maher and Hesham Alogeel (2008). "Understanding the Inflationary Process in the GCC Region: The Case of Saudi Arabia and Kuwait", *International Monetary Fund Working Paper* No. WP/08/193.

India: A Critical Assessment, 2009. Report submitted to the International Labour Organization, Thailand and Ministry of Overseas Indian Affairs, Government of India, New Delhi

International Monetary Fund (IMF) (2007). "United Arab Emirates: Financial System Stability Assessment", *International Monetary Fund Country Report No. 07/357*. October.

———. (2008). "Kuwait: Statistical Appendix", *International Monetary Fund Country Report* No. 08/192. June.

———. (2009). "Qatar: Statistical Appendix", *International Monetary Fund Country Report* No. 09/32. January.

———. (2009). *Country and Regional Perspectives*. Chapter 2. pp.63-96.

———. (2009a). *Regional Economic Outlook: Middle East and Central Asia*. Washington, DC.

———. (2009b). "World Economic Outlook: Crisis and Recovery", *World Economic and Financial Surveys*. Washington, DC.

Irudaya Rajan, S. (2003). "The Impact of Immigration Policy on Indian Contract Migrants: The Case of the United Arab Emirates", *International Migration* 41(4): 161-72.

———. (2004). "From Kerala to the Gulf: Impacts of Labour Migration", *Asia Pacific Migration Journal* 13(4): 497-509.

———. (2006). "Remittances", in Brij V. Lal (ed.), *The Encyclopedia of the Indian Diaspora*. Singapore/ Paris: Editions Didier Millet. pp.75-77.

———. (ed.) (2008). *Social Policies for the Elderly: Experiences from South Asia*. Routledge.

Irudaya Rajan, S. and Gopinathan P.R. Nair (2006). "Saudi Arabia, Oman and the Gulf States", in Brij V. Lal (ed.), *The Encyclopedia of the Indian Diaspora*. Singapore/Paris: Editions Didier Millet. pp.222-33.

Irudaya Rajan, S. and B.A. Prakash (2009). "Migration and Development Linkages Re-Examined in the Context of the Global Economic Crisis", Invited paper for the Civil Society Days of the *3rd Global Forum on Migration and Development*. November 2-3. Athens.

Irudaya Rajan, S. and Remya G. Prabha (2008). "India", *in Asia Pacific Migration Journal* 17(3/4): 277-86.

Irudaya Rajan, S., Carla Risseeuw and Myrtle Perera (eds.) (2008). *Institutional Provisions and Care for the Aged: Perspectives from Asia and Europe*. Anthem Press.

Irudaya Rajan, S., V.J. Varghese and M.S. Jayakumar (2009). "Overseas Recruitment in India: Structures, Practices and Remedies", *Working Paper* No. 421. Thiruvananthapuram: Centre for Development Studies.

———. (2009a). *Overseas Recruitment Practices in India: A Critical Assessment*. International Labour Organization and Ministry of Overseas Indian Affairs, Government of India.

———. (2010). *Dreaming Mobility and Buying Vulnerability: Overseas Recruitment Practices and its Discontents in India*. India: Routledge (forthcoming).

James, William E., Donghyun Park, Shikha Jha, Juthathip Jongwanich, Akiko Terada-Hagiwara and Lea Sumulong (2008). "The US Financial Crisis, Global Financial Turmoil, and Developing Asia: Is the Era of High Growth at an End?" *ADB Economics Working Paper Series* No. 139.

Jones, Stephany Griffith and Jose Antonio Ocampo (2008). *Sovereign Wealth Funds: A Developing Country Perspective*. Initiative for Policy Dialogue. Columbia University.

Kapiszewski, Andrzej (2006). *Arab versus Asian Migrant Workers in the GCC Countries*. UN Expert Group Meeting on International Migration and Development in the Arab region. UN/POP/EGM/2006/02.

Khadria, Binod (2006). *India: Skilled Migration to Developed Countries, Labour Migration to the Gulf*. Singapore: Asian Research Institute.

Lal, Brij V. (ed.) (2006). *The Encyclopedia of the Indian Diaspora*. Singapore/Paris: Editions Didier Millet.

Mahmood, Rafel (2009). "Islamic Governance, Capital Structure, and Equity Finance: Examining the Possibilities of American Financial Shari'ah Boards", *Working Paper*. Cornell Law School.

Maloney, Suzanne (2009). "The Gulf's Renewed Oil Wealth: Getting it Right This Time?" *Survival* 50(6): 129-50.

Martin, Philip (2009). "The Recession and Migration: Alternative Scenarios", *Working Paper* No. 13. International Migration Institute.

Milesi-Ferretti, Gian Maria (2009). "Challenging Fortunes", *Finance and Development*: 20-22, March.

Ministry of Overseas Indian Affairs (2009). *Annual Report 2008-09*. New Delhi: Government of India.

Nanto, Dick K. (2009). "The Global Financial Crisis: Analysis and Policy Implications", Congressional Research Service 7-5700, RL34742, *CRS Report for Congress*. July 10.

Organisation of Petroleum Exporting Countries (OPEC). (2009). *Monthly Oil Price Market Report*. September.

Papazian, Armen V. (2009). *Introducing Islamic Monetization*. Work in Progress. February 15.

Pradhan, S. (2009). "Economic Recession and the Middle East's World Trade: Recent Policy Trends and Implications", in Simon J. Evenelt (ed.), *Broken Promises: A G-20 Summit Report by Global Trade Alert*. London: Centre for Economic Policy Research.

Ratha, Dilip, Sanket Mohapatra and Zhimei Xu (2008). "Outlook for Remittance Flows 2008-2010: Growth Expected to Moderate Significantly, but Flows to Remain Resilient", *Migration and Development Brief*. Migration and Remittances Team. Development Prospects Group. World Bank. November 11.

Ratha, Dilip, Sanket Mohapatra and Ani Silwal (2009). "Outlook for Remittance Flows 2009-2011: Remittances Expected to Fall by 7-10 per cent in 2009", *Migration and Development Brief* 10. World Bank. July.

Rauch, James E. and Scott Kostyshak (2009). "The Three Arab Worlds", *Journal of Economic Perspectives* 23(3): 165-88.

Saudi Arabian Monetary Agency (2009). *Fifth Annual Report: The Latest Economic Developments*. 1430H (2009G).

Setser, Brad and Rachel Ziemba (2009). "GCC Sovereign Funds: Reversal of Fortune", *Working Paper*. Council on Foreign Relations—Centre for Geoeconomic Studies. January.

Shah, Nasra M. (2009). "Trends and Policies for Contract Worker Mobility of Asian to the Gulf Cooperation Council Countries", Paper for presentation at the 2009 IUSSP conference in Marrakech, Morocco, Session 603 on International Migration. September 27-October 2. Organised by Ayman Zohry.

Smith, Pamela Ann (2008). "GCC Foreign Wealth Rises to $2 Trillion", *Middle East* 388: 37, April.

Summit Report by Global Trade Alert. London: Centre for Economic Policy Research. pp.189-95.

Taattolo, Givonni (2006). *Arab Labor Migration to the GCC States*. Project on Arab Labour Migration.

Tabutin, Dominique and Bruno Schumaker (2005). "The Demography of the Arab World and the Middle East from the 1950s to the 2000s", *Population* 60(5/6): 505-91, 593-615.

Tong, Hui (2009). "The Real Effects of the 2007-08 Financial Crisis", *IMF Research* 10(2): 1, 4- 5, June.

United Arab Emirates–Dubai International Financial Centre: Financial Sector Assessment Program–Detailed Assessment of Observance of Iosco Objectives and Principles of Securities Regulation. (2007). *International Monetary Fund Country Report* No. 07/365. November.

United Arab Emirates Ministry of Economy (2006). *Preliminary Results of Population, Housing and Establishments Census* 2005: United Arab Emirates.

International Monetary Fund (2009). "United Arab Emirates: Statistical Appendix", *International Monetary Fund Country Report* No. 09/120. April.

United Nations (2009). *International Migration*, 2009. New York: Department of Economic and Social Affairs, Population Division.

United Nations Conference on Trade and Development (UNCTAD) (2009). *World Investment Report: Transnational Corporations, Agricultural Production and Development*.

United Nations Development Programme (2009). *Human Development Report 2009*. New York: UNDP.

Weiss, Martin A. (2008). "Sovereign Wealth Funds: Background and Policy Issues for Congress", *CRS Report for Congress*. Updated on September 3, 2008.

Woertz, Eckart (2008). "Impact of the US Financial Crisis on GCC Countries", *GRC Report*.

Woertz, Eckart, Samir Pradhan, Nermina Biberovic and Christian Koch (2008). "Food Inflation in the GCC Countries", *GRC Report*. May.

World Bank (2008). "Outlook for Remittance Flows 2008-2010: Growth Expected to Moderate Significantly, but Flows to Remain Resilient", *Migration and Development Brief* 8. Washington.

———. (2009). *Doing Business 2010: Overview*.

———. (2009a). "Revised Outlook for Remittance Flows 2009-2011: Remittances Expected to Fall by 5 to 8 Per cent in 2009", *Migration and Development Brief 9*. Washington.

———. (2009b). "Migration and Remittance Trends 2009: A Better-than-expected Outcome so far, but Significant Risks Ahead", *Migration and Development Brief 11*. Washington.

World Economic Outlook database.

Yatim, Mohd Nasir bin Mohd. (2009). "Sukuk (Islamic Bond): A Crucial Financial Instrument for Securitisation of Debt for the Debt-holders in Shari'ah-Complaint Capital Market", *International Journal of Business and Management* 4(10): 166-72.

Zachariah, K.C. and S. Irudaya Rajan (2007). "Migration, Remittances and Employment: Short-term Trends and Long-term Implications", *Working Paper* No. 395. Thiruvananthapuram: Centre for Development Studies.

———. (2009a). *Migration and Development: The Kerala Experience*. New Delhi: Daanish Publishers.

———. (2009b). "Migration as a New Demographic Transition in Kerala's Development", in Gopal K. Kadekodi and Brinda Viswanathan (eds.), *Agricultural Development, Rural Institutions and Economic Policy*. New Delhi: Oxford University Press. Chapter 12. pp.221-38.

———. (2010a). "Migration Monitoring Study, 2008: Emigration and Remittances in the Context of Surge in Oil Prices", *Working Paper* No. 424. Thiruvananthapuram: Centre for Development Studies.

———. (2010b). "Impact of the Global Recession on Migration and Remittances in Kerala: New Evidences from the Return Migration Survey (RMS) 2009", *Working Paper* No. 432. Thiruvananthapuram: Centre for Development Studies.

Zachariah, K.C., B.A. Prakash and S. Irudaya Rajan (2003). "The Impact of Immigration Policy on Indian Contract Migrants: The Case of the United Arab Emirates", *International Migration* 41(4): 161-72.

———. (2004). "Indian Workers in UAE: Employment, Wages and Working Conditions", *Economic and Political Weekly* XXXIX(22): 2227-34, May 29.

Zachariah, K.C., E.T. Mathew and S. Irudaya Rajan (2003). *Dynamics of Migration in Kerala: Dimensions, Determinants and Consequences*. Hyderabad: Orient Longman Pvt Limited.

Zachariah, K.C., Gopinathan P.R. Nair and S. Irudaya Rajan (2006). *Return Emigrants in Kerala: Welfare, Rehabilitation and Development*. New Delhi: Manohar Publishers and Distributors.

Zachariah, K.C., K.P. Kannan and S. Irudaya Rajan (2002). "Kerala's Gulf Connection: CDS Studies on International Labour Migration from Kerala State in India", *Monograph Series*. Thiruvananthapuram: Centre for Development Studies.

Websites

http://www.gulfbase.com/site/interface/NewsArchiveDetails.aspx?n=110724, accessed on 14 November, 2009.

http://www.opec.org/library/worldoiloutlook/pdf/woo2009.pdf, accessed on 26 September, 2009.

http://www.opec.org/library/AnnualStatisticalBulletin/PDF/ASB2008.pdf, accessed on 26 September 2009.

4

PARTHA PRATIM SAHU

The Employment Implications of Recent Economic Slowdown

Evidences from a Field Survey in India[1]

Introduction

The two fundamental goals of development, namely, provisioning of adequate employment opportunities and eradication of poverty got severely jeopardised in the wake of recent economic slowdown, especially in the developing economies. If one takes a long term view, economic growth in India accelerated significantly over the last two decades, but unfortunately there has hardly been any perceptible impact on generation of adequate employment at rising levels of productivity and poverty reduction. Higher levels and rates of economic growth are thus not sufficient for generation of employment and for poverty reduction. The pattern and sectoral composition of growth along with high rates of employment growth are equally important. Many studies have found that countries which attained high rates of employment growth alongside high rates of economic growth are also the ones succeeding in reducing poverty significantly (Islam, 2004). India, however, does not feature on that list and the weak impact of economic growth on employment generation and poverty reduction has therefore been characterised as

1. This chapter is an excerpt of a study titled "The Employment Implications of Current Financial Crisis: Challenges, Threats and Coping Strategies in India", completed at the Institute of Studies in Industrial Development (ISID), New Delhi, India, with research grant from the South Asia Network of Economic Research Institutes (SANEI). The author is grateful to SANEI, anonymous reviewers on the report, colleagues at ISID and workshop participants at New Delhi and Ahmedabad where the study was presented. The usual disclaimer applies for any errors, inaccuracy or omission.

the phenomenon of "jobless growth" and high incidence of "working poor."

The impact of the global economic slowdown of 2008 was felt in the developing world along with slowdowns in all emerging economies. The Indian economy also experienced a depressing economic growth. Furthermore, these growth declines had significant worsening effects on poverty. The World Bank estimates that a one per cent decline in developing country growth rate pushes an additional 20 million people into the poverty trap (World Bank, 2008). In addition, weaker growths are likely to cut into government's abilities to invest to meet education, health, and other social expenditure, hitting the poor the hardest. Several studies have identified possible channels or transmission mechanism of impacts of financial crisis on economic growth, such as decline in exports, foreign investment, exchange rates, interest rates, foreign aid and remittances (Iyanatul, 2009; ILO, 2009). Different sectors got affected differently through several channels requiring different set of policies. Major sectors in India which were hit by the financial crisis included construction, real estate, Information Technology (IT) and Information Technology Enabled Services (ITES), automobile, gems & jewellery, textiles, metal products, financial services, tourism and so on.

A series of reports and studies were brought out by bi-lateral and multi-lateral agencies (ILO, 2009; ADB, 2009; UN, 2010; IMF, 2009; UNCTAD, 2009a; World Bank, 2010) to understand the impacts of global economic slowdown on employment, output, exports, financial markets, real markets and other aspects. These reports suggested various measures including bail out plans, stimulus packages and country-specific measures. The Government of India also visualised the possible impacts of the global crisis on the Indian economy and undertook several measures including austerity measures, fiscal stimulus packages, lowering interest rates, cutting taxes and funding infrastructure programmes to leverage employment and income growth (Government of India, *Economic Survey 2008-09* and *Economic Survey 2009-10*).

However, the design, composition and implementation of the fiscal stimulus package are considered extremely important. Tax rebates, increased public spending targeted to sectors (like infrastructure) and groups (like social security measures for lower income people including retrenched workers) are expected to create multiplier effects and have greater expansionary potential. But it has also been argued that India, with a relatively insulated financial sector, is better positioned than many other developing economies for a quick recovery from the crisis. While at the national level, several measures were initiated, it would be interesting to know whether there were sector specific measures and coping strategies undertaken at the enterprise level to sustain the businesses. At the enterprise level, the entrepreneurs may restructure production organisations, increase subcontracting, undertake cost cutting measures and adopt improved marketing strategy, technological up-gradation, and enhanced focus on domestic market and so on.

There are, however, contrasting views on the impact of global financial crisis on the Indian economy. No doubt there are substantial evidences of decline in output, export and employment during 2008-09 and beyond, but it is difficult to segregate the impacts of slowdown from those of domestic changes. So far as the Indian economy is concerned, export has been the most crucial transmission channel to capture the effects of economic slowdown. Since the manufacturing sector accounts for more than 60 per cent of India's total exports, it seems to have been affected more by the economic slowdown than other broad sectors. It may be noted that the manufacturing sector has also emerged as an important sector with increasing employment potential in India. However, more than 90 per cent of the manufacturing enterprises and 80 per cent of employment comprise of micro and small/unorganised manufacturing activities. A significantly large proportion of these enterprises not only manufactures varieties of products for large domestic and exporting enterprises through subcontracting but exports the products directly. It is estimated that the small manufacturing enterprises account for nearly 40 per cent of the total manufacturing exports. So there are obvious reasons to believe that the small enterprises would also be affected by the economic slowdown. The study seeks to analyse the perception of the small exporting enterprises towards the financial crisis and examines the nature and magnitude of impact on their output, export and employment. It also analyses the mechanisms through which the small firms cope up with the difficult and uncertain times unleashed by the economic slowdown.

While there are cross country analyses and country specific studies on the impact of economic crisis, micro level or sector specific studies are very few in number. It needs to be recognised that the impact of the crisis was not limited to losses in jobs and income. The reduction in income forced workers in the unorganised sector of the gem polishing and construction industries in Rajasthan to cut down expenses on health and education and even on essentials like food, shelter, and clothing (Mohanakumar and Singh, 2011). Analysing the impact of economic slowdown on three labour intensive export sectors, *viz.*, textiles, diamonds and handicrafts, Sasikumar and Karan (2010) find that slowdown in production was more severe in the formal sector whereas the fall in employment was much higher in informal enterprises than in formal enterprises across all the sectors under the study. The total loss of employment in the three sectors of textiles, diamonds and handicrafts was about 7 per cent in informal enterprises as against only 0.28 per cent in formal enterprises. The laid off workers were mainly casual and unskilled workers. Thus, both formal and informal enterprises witnessed production and employment losses and wage cuts during the slowdown period. The forecast by United Nations Conference Trade and Development (UNCTAD) (2009b) mentions a total job loss in India of around 1.16 million due to negative export growth in sectors such as textiles, gems and jewellery, and ores and minerals.

To understand the impact of the global crisis on small producers and informal workers, United Nations Development Programme (UNDP) undertook a quick survey (2009) in some of the major affected sectors e.g. agriculture, auto parts, *chikan* craft, engineering industry, home based garments, and gems & jewellery. The survey mentions several effects such as loss of pay and jobs, increase in unemployment, move to less remunerative and low paid jobs and from skilled to unskilled jobs and so on with varying magnitudes. The gems & jewellery industry was among the worst affected sectors, as 30 per cent of the workers were unemployed, 49 per cent of workers moved to low-paid, petty services and trade. The Institute of Social Studies Trust (ISST) assessed the impact of the economic slowdown on handicraft industry in Sanganer, Rajsthan, India (2009). It found that the fall in employment was more severe on semi-skilled workers—a category largely dominated by women and migrant workers. There was no significant decline in wages, but the number of work days fell drastically. Since nearly 60 per cent of the workers engaged in the sector were migrants, some of them went back to their hometown and others were either unemployed or looked for jobs in other sectors. Most of these studies highlight features such as reduced employment creation, job losses particularly in export sectors, higher vulnerability of migrants, contract, unskilled, and women workers and deterioration of the quality of employment across different sectors in India in the wake of the crisis.

In this backdrop, based on a survey of 125 small exporting firms engaged in manufacturing of diverse products and exporting directly or through large enterprises and export houses, the present study seeks to answer following questions: (i) what did the sample enterprises feel about economic slowdown; (ii) how did these firms perceive the changes due to economic slowdown; and (iii) how did they respond to these changes. The chapter has been organised into four sections. Following the discussion carried out in this section, section 2 explains the performance of the Indian economy during the post-crisis period in terms of GDP, exports and employment. Section 3 summarises the experience of micro and small exporting firms during the post-crisis period. It also analyses the impact of global economic slowdown on employment, exports and general functioning of the surveyed firms. Section 4 summarises the main findings and policy implications of the study.

The Indian Economy during the Post-Crisis Period

The immediate negative impact of the economic slowdown was visible in the form of a decline in overall economic growth. The available data suggests that the growth rate declined in the first quarter of 2008-09 (April-June 2009) and the overall growth rate declined from 9.3 per cent in 2007-08 to 6.7 per cent in 2008-09 (Table 4.1). The overall growth rate of 6.7 per cent during 2008-09 was made possible primarily by the performance of the services sector, which had emerged as a fast growing sector over the last decade. Although the economy has shown signs of recovery, still the overall growth rate during 2009-10 (8.6 %) was still lower than that of 2007-08. This growth pattern raises concerns for the future growth prospects of the economy.

Table 4.1

Key Indicators of Indian Economy during Post-Global Slowdown Period

	2006-07	*2007-08*	*2008-09*	*2009-10*	*2010-11*	*2011-12*	*2012-13*
1. GDP growth rate (%) (at 2004-05 prices)	9.6	9.3	6.7	8.6	9.3	6.2	5.0
Annual % point change	-	-0.3	-2.6	1.9	0.7	-3.1	-1.2
2. Saving rate (% of GDP)	24.6	36.8	32.0	33.7	34.0	30.8	na
3. Capital formation (% of GDP)	35.7	38.1	34.3	36.5	36.8	35.0	na
4. Per capita income (₹) (at current prices)	31,206	35,825	40,775	46,249	54,151	61,564	68,747
Annual percentage change	-	14.8	13.8	13.4	17.1	13.7	11.7
5. Inflation rate (%) (CPI-IW: annual average)	6.7	6.2	9.1	12.4	10.4	8.4	10.0
6. Export growth (%)	22.6	29.0	13.6	-3.5	40.5	21.3	-4.9
7. Import growth (%)	24.5	35.5	20.7	-5.0	28.2	32.3	0.0
8. Foreign Exchange Reserves (in USD billion)	199.2	309.7	252.0	279.1	304.8	294.4	295.5
Annual percentage change	-	55.5	-18.6	10.8	9.2	-3.4	0.4

Source: Government of India, *Economic Survey*, various issues.

During the post-crisis period, India performed badly in terms of other macroeconomic indicators as well. Both savings and investment rate (as a proportion of GDP) declined during 2008-09 and 2009-10. The national per capita income which grew at a rate of 14.8 per cent during 2007-08, declined by 1 per cent in 2008-09. Inflation rate also picked up from 6.2 per cent to 9.1 per cent. Furthermore, both total import and export growth and the foreign exchange reserves declined significantly during 2008-09 (Table 4.1).

Almost all the broad sectors of the economy witnessed either slowdown or a decline in growth rates during 2008-09, except the community, social and personal services (Table 4.2). In particular, agriculture and manufacturing witnessed significant deceleration in their growth rates. The growth rate of agriculture declined from 4.7 per cent in 2007-08 to 1.6 per cent in 2008-09 and manufacturing exhibited even a sharper decline from 10.3 per cent to 3.2 per cent during the same period. Various sub-sectors of the services sector also showed signs of deceleration of varying magnitudes. For instance, in trade, hotels, transport & communications, the growth rate declined from 10.7 per cent in 2007-08 to 7.6 per cent in 2008-09. As discussed later, sectors with high employment potential such as agriculture, manufacturing, and construction witnessed large declines in growth rates which have significant implications for the employment situation and poverty reduction efforts.

The manufacturing sector, having the largest share in the export basket, was highly exposed to the export market and was severely affected by economic slowdown resulting in a growth rate of only 0.6 per cent during the last quarter of 2008-09. The performance of manufacturing sector was also affected by the decelerating growth performance of the construction sector.

Table 4.2

Quarterly Growth Rates of the Indian Economy during Pre-Global and Post-Global Economic Crisis (At 2004-05 Prices)

(in %)

Sector	*Period*	*Q1*	*Q2*	*Q3*	*Q4*	*AN*
Agriculture, Forestry & Fishing	2007-08	3.1	3.9	8.7	2.1	4.7
	2008-09	3.2	2.4	-1.4	3.3	1.6
	2009-10	1.9	0.9	-1.8	0.7	0.2
Mining & Quarrying	2007-08	1.1	4.6	4.5	5.1	3.9
	2008-09	2.6	1.6	2.8	-0.3	1.6
	2009-10	8.2	10.1	9.6	14.0	10.6
Manufacturing	2007-08	12.1	10.3	10.7	8.3	10.3
	2008-09	5.9	5.5	1.3	0.6	3.2
	2009-10	3.8	9.1	13.8	16.3	10.8
Utilities	2007-08	10.2	9.1	7.1	7.8	8.5
	2008-09	3.3	4.3	4.0	4.1	3.9
	2009-10	6.6	7.7	4.7	7.1	6.5
Construction	2007-08	10.7	13.1	9.6	7.1	10.0
	2008-09	7.1	8.0	3.0	5.6	5.9
	2009-10	4.6	4.7	8.1	8.7	6.5
Trade, Hotels, Transport & Communication	2007-08	11.9	9.5	10.7	10.9	10.7
	2008-09	10.8	10.0	4.4	5.7	7.6
	2009-10	5.5	8.5	10.2	12.4	9.3
Financing, Insurance & Real Estate	2007-08	14.0	13.8	13.3	11.9	13.2
	2008-09	9.1	8.5	10.2	12.3	10.1
	2009-10	11.8	11.5	7.9	7.9	9.7
Community, Social & Personal Services	2007-08	4.2	7.0	5.3	9.8	6.7
	2008-09	8.7	10.4	28.7	8.8	13.9
	2009-10	7.6	14.0	0.8	1.6	5.6
Overall GDP	2007-08	9.3	9.4	9.7	8.5	9.3
	2008-09	7.6	7.5	6.2	5.8	6.7
	2009-10	6.0	8.6	6.5	8.6	8.6

Note: Q1-(April-June); Q2-(July-September); Q3-(Oct-December); Q4-(Jan-March); AN-Annual

Source: CSO, *National Accounts Statistics*, various years.

As far as the impact of the financial crisis on India's real economy is concerned, the export sector was the first to get affected by it. Till 2007-08, India's exports were growing at fairly high rates (between 22 to 29%) and emerged as an engine of overall growth of the economy. But after such impressive growth, exports started declining during 2008-09 and afterwards. Overall export growth plummeted from 29 per cent in June 2007-July 2008 to 13.6 per cent in July 2008-August 2009. Many sectors witnessed either slowdown or negative growth rates. The sectors which carry significant weights in India's export basket such as gems and jewellery, textile products, chemical products, electrical and non-electrical machineries and so on, registered significant declines in exports growth (Table 4.3). Although the export sector started reviving and showing signs of recovery, it could not be treated as robust and sustainable, because the economic situation has not yet improved in many of India's export destination countries. Although India's export market is well diversified, the share of top 20 countries in India's total exports declined during 2008-09. India's export to most of its top partner countries witnessed declines of varying magnitudes. For few countries such as UK, Italy, Bangladesh, and Sri Lanka the decline and/or slowdown continued in 2009-10 as well. Of the top 20 countries, a total of 8 and 12 countries registered negative growth rates during 2008-09 and 2009-10 respectively. The share of India's export to the US was around 10 to 15 per cent and after 2007-08, both the share and the growth rate of export to US declined.

In addition to GDP and exports, employment growth also witnessed a significant decline. The available National Sample Survey Organisation (NSSO) surveys on employment and unemployment brought out disturbing signals on employment scenario in the country. Both the labour force and workforce participation rates declined during 2005-2008 and again during 2008-2010. However, the decline in labour force participation rate was steeper than decline in the workforce participation rate. Secondly, the decline was more marked for females compared to their male counterparts. Not only the quantity but also the quality of employment emerged as a

Table 4.3

Sectoral Share and Change in Major Exports Items

Sectors	*Sectoral Share (%)*					*Annual Change (%)*				
	2008-09	*2009-10*	*2010-11*	*2011-12*	*2012-13*	*2008-09*	*2009-10*	*2010-11*	*2011-12*	*2012-13*
Agriculture & allied	9.0	10.0	9.7	12.4	14.0	9.7	1.1	36.1	53.9	21.1
Ores & minerals	5.5	4.9	3.4	2.8	2.0	-12.5	9.9	-1.3	-0.4	-29.6
Crude petroleum products (incl. coal)	15.0	16.2	16.8	18.7	18.9	-5.2	4.6	46.8	34.9	-8.5
Others and unclassified products	3.3	1.5	0.9	0.5	0.7	-60.1	32.9	-12.9	-34.8	19.5
Manufactured products	67.2	67.4	69.0	66.1	64.5	23.1	-5.9	44.2	16.2	-10.4
Of which:										
Leather & manufacturers	2.4	1.2	1.0	1.0	1.1	1.5	-40.8	15.8	26.1	0.6
Leather footwear	0.8	0.7	0.6	0.6	0.6	6.0	0.8	17.2	16.8	-9.1
Gems & jewellery	12.6	16.3	16.1	14.7	15.4	42.1	3.7	39.6	10.8	-4.0
Drugs, pharmaceuticals & fine chemicals	4.7	5.0	4.3	4.4	5.0	15.0	1.8	19.7	23.8	12.3
Dyes/intmdts. & coltar chemicals	1.8	1.3	1.2	1.3	1.5	-15.6	-2.6	29.1	28.6	8.6
Manufactures of metals	4.0	3.1	3.4	3.1	3.6	7.1	-26.8	53.1	13.3	13.9
Machinery & instruments	5.3	5.4	4.7	4.7	5.2	19.9	-12.9	24.1	20.9	5.3
Transport equipments	3.9	5.5	6.4	6.9	6.3	58.8	-11.9	63.3	31.7	-20.2
Primary and semi-finished iron & steel	3.5	1.6	1.6	1.7	1.6	14.0	-39.0	38.6	29.1	-12.7
Electronic goods	2.3	3.1	3.3	3.1	3.0	104.2	-23.6	46.7	13.4	-9.0

contd...

...*contd*...

Sectors	*Sectoral Share (%)*					*Annual Change (%)*				
	2008-09	*2009-10*	*2010-11*	*2011-12*	*2012-13*	*2008-09*	*2009-10*	*2010-11*	*2011-12*	*2012-13*
Cotton yarn, fabrics, made-ups etc	3.3	2.1	2.3	2.2	2.5	-11.5	-10.5	57.0	17.6	2.2
Readymade garments	7.0	6.0	4.6	4.5	4.3	12.9	-2.1	8.4	18.0	-7.7
Handicrafts	0.3	0.1	0.1	0.1	0.1	-40.8	-25.3	14.3	8.2	-11.3
Total exports	100	100	100	100	100	13.6	40.5	21.3	32.7	-7.0

Note: Estimates are based on export figures in US dollar terms.

Source: Author's own estimates based on trade statistics from Government of India, Directorate General of Foreign Trade (*www.dgft.gov.in*).

major challenge during the post-crisis period. In particular, casual employment increased during post-crisis years.

Table 4.4

Employment-Unemployment Situation: 2004-05 to 2009-10

NSS Round/ Years	*(Number in million)* Labour Force	Work Force	Unemployed	Unemployment Rate (% as a Proportion of Labour Force)
61st_2004-05	475.7	464.4	11.9	2.5
64th_2007-08	485.0	473.8	11.4	2.3
66th_2009-10	468.8	459.1	10.1	2.2
Growth rate (%)			Change in employment (in million)	
04-05/07-08	0.65	0.67	9.4	
07-08/09-10	-1.68	-1.56	-14.7	
04-05/09-10	-0.29	-0.23	-5.3	

Source: Author's estimates based on NSS *Reports on Employment and Unemployment*, various years.

Employment growth declined from an annual rate of nearly 3 per cent in the period 2000-2005 to 0.67 per cent in the period 2005-2008 and registered a negative growth rate of 0.23 per cent during 2005-2010, resulting in consecutive loss of employment of nearly 15 million and 5.3 million during 2008-2010 and 2005-2010 respectively as compared with a creation of 10 million jobs during 2005-2008 (Table 4.4). A sectoral dis-aggregation of employment growth suggests that as compared with 2005-2008, sectoral employment growth rates during 2008-2010 either slowed down or became negative. Manufacturing experienced serious setback during the post 2005 period. The share of manufacturing sector employment declined from 12.2 per cent in 2004-2005 to 11.4 per cent in 2009-10 witnessing a growth rate of -1.64 per cent during 2005-2010. However, in mining & quarrying, construction and some segments of the services sector, employment did show some signs of expansion during 2005-2010. In the absence of up-to-date (post-crisis), systematic and matching dis-aggregated level of data on employment, output and exports, it is difficult to produce hard figures of employment losses due to the financial crisis.

Specifically to understand the employment implications of global economic slowdown, the Labour Bureau of the Ministry of Labour and Employment (MoLE) conducted quick surveys based on a limited sample of about 3,000 Annual Survey of Industries (ASI)-covered units in the manufacturing sector and in IT/Business Process Outsourcing (BPO) segment of the services sector which brought out some interesting results. Until September 2013, the Labour Bureau had conducted 18 quarterly surveys (Table 4.5).

According to these surveys, there was a loss of 4.77 lakh jobs in the quarter October-December 2008, a gain of 2.8 lakh jobs during the next quarter and again a loss of 1.3 lakh jobs during April-June 2009. It is significant to note that initially export-oriented sectors and units had a setback and those focussing on the domestic market, in fact, experienced positive growth in employment. The major part of the increase in employment is accounted for by only two sectors—textiles during the first quarter and the third quarter and IT/BPO during the last quarter of 2009. The subsequent surveys for quarters July-September 2009 and October 2009-December 2009 reveal significant increase, the estimates for the two periods being 4.97 lakh and 6.38 lakh respectively.

After the initial decline of 4.77 lakh in the first quarter during October-December 2008, employment is estimated to have increased at varying magnitude in the subsequent quarters. However, given the small sample size and thin coverage, the numbers do not provide conclusive evidence on the extent of recovery in the employment situation. The impacts of the crisis on different types of worker also seem to be mixed. But the decline in the number of contract workers has been more visible and seems to have continued in all quarters. The post-2008 period thus, exhibited a stubbornly high inflation, chronic joblessness and an economic growth rate of less than 5 per cent which together make the economic outlook rather gloomy.

Table 4.5

Changes in Estimated Employment based on Various Quarterly Survey Results

(in lakh)

			Type of Unit		*Type of Worker*	
Quarterly Report No.	*Survey Reference Period*	*Loss/Gain in Total Employment*	*Exporting Units*	*Non-Exporting Units*	*Direct Worker*	*Contract Worker*
1	October-December 2008	-4.77	na	na	na	na
2	January-March 2009	2.76	na	na	na	na
3	April-June 2009	-1.31	-1.66	0.35	-1.71	0.40
4	July-September 2009	4.97	2.04	2.93	3.92	1.05
5	October-December 2009	6.38	5.80	0.58	5.79	0.59
6	January-March 2010	0.61	1.87	-1.25	-0.13	0.74
7	April-June 2010	1.63	1.77	-0.15	1.22	0.40
8	July-September 2010	4.36	3.05	1.30	3.85	0.50
9	October-December 2010	2.07	1.41	0.66	1.61	0.46
10	Jan-March 2011	1.74	1.99	-0.25	1.80	-0.06
11	April-June 2011	2.15	0.67	1.48	1.90	0.25
12	July-September 2011	3.15	1.96	1.16	3.18	-0.03
13	October-December 2011	2.26	2.67	-0.41	1.94	0.32
14	Jan- March 2012	0.81	0.86	-0.05	0.84	-0.03
15	April-June 2012	0.73	0.33	0.39	0.97	-0.24
16	July-December 2012	1.68	0.80	0.88	1.09	0.59
17	January-March 2013	1.07	0.81	0.26	0.80	0.27
18	April-June 2013	0.86	1.21	-0.35	1.06	-0.20

Source: Author's estimates based on Government of India, Labour Bureau, *Report on Effects of Slowdown on Employment in India*, various quarterly reports.

Impact of Slowdown on Small Manufacturing Enterprises: Evidence from the Field Survey

The secondary data often fails to capture many practical difficulties faced by micro and small enterprises due to the economic slowdown. Therefore, besides using major secondary data sources, we also carried out a primary survey of 125 micro and small exporting firms during July-September 2010 with a set of structured questions pertaining to their functioning. The present section is based on first hand information gathered in the process of interviews during personal visits, telephonic interactions with the surveyed units. The analysis of the survey data provides information on the nature and magnitude of different constraints that these small firms face due to financial crisis. Moreover, we also enquired whether these firms are aware of and availing any assistances/policies initiated by the government especially to deal with the adverse impact of the economic slowdown. An attempt has also been made to analyse the coping strategies adopted by the individual firms in response to the financial crisis.

A total of 125 small sized exporting enterprises were surveyed in the National Capital Region (NCR) of Delhi, India. A more systematic, stratified random sampling could have been more appropriate but due to shortage of time and resources, a purposive random sampling was adopted to meet the specific requirements of our subject of enquiry. The quantitative data on output, employment, export of surveyed enterprises are less likely to be reliable as many of these enterprises did not maintain regular and systematic accounts. We also observed a slight exaggeration of figures as they were operating at a difficult time due to the global economic slowdown.

Most of the surveyed units employ less than 10 workers. The manufactured products of these units include fabricated metal products, furniture, wearing apparel, dressing and dyeing fur, rubber & plastic products, electrical machinery & appliances, paper & paper products, basic metal, and similar products. Surveyed enterprises are located both in urban and rural areas, and are mostly unregistered. More than 90 per cent of the surveyed entrepreneurs/owners have education up to class 10 and above, but 70 per cent of them do not possess any technical training such as in engineering, management or have any polytechnic education. These enterprises operate both in domestic and global markets, but very few export directly. They mainly produce for large exporting enterprises and export houses, and operate through subcontracting. In terms of exposure to information technology, 45 per cent of the enterprises use computers and 20 per cent have their own websites.

However, the biggest challenge during the survey has been to make the small firm owners/entrepreneurs understand about the predicaments of the global financial crisis. We observed that a large number of the surveyed firms, although realise the negative impacts of the slowdown, are not actually aware of the factors causing such outcomes. So before canvassing the real questionnaire, the research team had to a lot of time to apprise them of all the details of the event. Second, the small firms in India who operate in both export and non-export markets usually work under several size-related disadvantages like inadequate finance, low research & development (R&D), management constraints, and inadequate market information. Similarly, those small firms under subcontracting arrangements often reported to suffer from exploitative practices such as delayed payments, undue price-cutting, stringent quality control, undue rejection, sudden slash in order, and lack of continuity of work and so on from their respective buyer firms. Furthermore, the lower resource base and inadequate managerial capability of the subcontractors put them in a more disadvantageous position (Sahu, 2010). Therefore, many small firms in spite of having potential to export directly, operate through large firms, traders and export houses. The economic slowdown seems to have further exacerbated some of these problems.

It may also be noted that several questions remain largely unanswered from the analysis of available secondary data. For example, there are many pertinent issues such as: Is domestic crisis (if any) different from the global crisis? Is there a differential pattern of 'response' and 'coping strategy' for domestic and global crisis? Did India manage to escape from getting fully affected from the global economic slowdown? Were the employment impacts limited to quantity or quality or both? How effective were the stimulus packages/export sops and other incentives? Did small exporting firms get any benefit from the stimulus packages? Was there enough "social dialogue" in India, like in the US and other developed nations?

However, the primary data collected at the firm level show more or less a similar picture as reflected from the secondary data discussed in the foregoing sections. During 2007-08 and 2008-09, two sectors namely, food products and beverages and basic metals registered negative growth while, in other nine industry groups, the growth of exports slowed down as compared with 2006-07 and 2007-08. At the disaggregated level, few industry groups such as food & beverages, wood & wood products, chemical products, basic metals, and fabricated metal products registered higher export growth rates during 2008-09 and 2009-10 as compared with 2007-08 and 2008-09. But textiles & wearing apparel, paper & paper products, electrical & machinery continued to experience negative growth or slowdown in export growth rates. Thus, the negative impact of economic slowdown has been sector specific. Some industry groups managed to completely avoid the impact of economic slowdown while some were affected by it. So far as the employment situation of surveyed firms is concerned, overall employment remained almost unchanged. Even at the disaggregate level, employment figures did not show any significant change. Small enterprises mostly operate through casual/part time workers which they neither report nor keep any record. Therefore, during economic slowdown, it seems that they adjust their non-regular/casual/part time workers to deal with the changing size of output and exports. However, it is clear that the surveyed enterprises did not report hiring any new workers.

What did our sample units feel about the economic slowdown? About half of them reported of being affected by the global slowdown. Nearly 70 per cent of them reported that they witnessed varying degrees of decline in output, exports and employment due to the economic slowdown. Changes in domestic and export demands were the two important channels that the surveyed units perceived through which their units got affected by the economic slowdown since both, the world and domestic market witnessed immediate slump after the economic slowdown. Changes in both domestic and imported input prices were also reported to be crucial factors affecting their enterprises.

To mitigate the adverse impacts of the economic slowdown, various policies including stimulus packages were initiated by all multi-lateral and bi-lateral agencies and also by individual countries. The Government of India also initiated several measures not only to ease the liquidity situation and improve credit flow in the economy to restore the pre-crisis higher growth but also provided incentives to export oriented sectors and industries (see Box 4.1). Since manufacturing has been one of the worst hit sectors of the economic slowdown, particularly in India, these stimulus packages were designed to arrest the fall in industrial production and boost domestic demand in general. Several measures were also taken to expand infrastructure investment to achieve higher income and employment growth. However, many of the sample units were not even aware of these stimulus packages, policies or incentives. None of these small firms, who already operate in a very difficult and uncertain environment, had access to any such benefits announced after the economic slowdown. Though few of our respondents were aware of reduction in interest rate and excise duty, they maintained that these policies benefited mostly the larger firms and exporters. None of the surveyed units reported getting any kind of support from the industry associations or trade unions although they were members.

In the absence of any institutional support, individual firms undertook a variety of measures to cope with uncertain and difficult situations. We put before the sample units a number of coping strategies/responses relating to production organisation, marketing strategies, postponing plans of new investment, new recruitment and expansion. Nearly 67 per cent of the surveyed enterprises adjusted working hours and 72 per cent put more focus on efficiency and productivity by replacing labour with newer and improved technologies. A preponderant majority of them also undertook different strategies to tap new market for their products such as increased subcontracting activities, tapping new domestic and export markets and product diversification.

Box 4.1

Policy Measures Initiated by the Government of India in Response to Global Economic Slowdown

A. General

(i) Reduction in interest rates; (ii) Reduction in CENVAT; (iii) Reduction in excise duty by 4 per cent; (iv) Reduction in service tax; (v) Enhanced plan of expenditures on infrastructure, social security schemes etc.

B. Measures to support exports

(vi) Interest subvention of 2 per cent extended; (vii) Full refund of claims CST/Terminal Excise Duty/Duty Drawback on deemed exports; (viii) Increase in the limit of Credit Guarantee Scheme from existing ₹ 50 lakh to 1 crore; (ix) Enhanced funds (₹ 5,000 crore) to EXIM Bank for pre- and post-shipment credit; (x) Extension of Income Tax Exemption for 100 per cent export oriented units; (xi) Extension of Export Obligation period under EPCG scheme; (xii) Extension of DEPB scheme; (xiii) Reduction in custom duty under EPCG scheme; (xiv) Introduction of 'Focus Product' and 'Focus Market' incentive schemes.

C. Sector specific measures

(xv) Handicraft items included in Vishes Krishi and Gram Udyog Yojana (VKGUY) ; (xvi) Additional allocation of ₹ 14,000 crore for textiles sector; (xvii) Refinance facility of ₹ 7,000 crore for SIDBI.

Note: CENVAT = Central Value Added Tax ; CST = Central Sales Tax;
EXIM = Export Import Bank of India; EPCG = Export Promotion Capital Goods;
DEPB = Duty Entitlement Pass Book

Source: Compiled from Government of India, *Economic Survey*, various issues.

Even though we did not come across any significant downsizing or lay off, many of the sample units postponed their expansion plan (if any) and new recruitment and/or replacement of lay-off vacancies. We also observed cases of substituting permanent with contractual workers and filling work gaps with temporary trainees and apprentices. But a majority of the sample units reported operating at sub-optimal capacity utilisation levels. Some of them also found it difficult to repay loans, pay for utilities (e.g. electricity bills, telephone bills) and working capital. A few of them also cut down their expenses on occupational safety measures, and advertisements and promotional activities. Lack of relevant and timely availability marketing information was reported by all the sample units as one of the biggest difficulties during the post-crisis periods.

Major Findings and Policy Inferences

The analysis of both primary and secondary data suggests that output, exports and employment have witnessed varying degrees of slowdown during the post-crisis period. Even though there has been significant recovery in economic growth, the employment situation has worsened and thus the Indian economy is currently undergoing a phase of "jobless growth". There are large variations among the broad sectors of the economy in their deceleration experiences.

In order to improve the overall employment situation along with high economic growth, there is an urgent need to enhance employment-oriented investment especially in agriculture and infrastructure. During last two years, the government has taken a series of measures to address the problem of credit crunch in the economy, but its access to micro and small enterprises is still limited. Thus, there is a need for expanding the network of institutional banking especially for the micro and small enterprises. The impact of the fiscal stimulus package has been far from satisfactory so far as the small exporting firms are concerned. Most of the surveyed enterprises reported that they were neither aware of the policies and schemes initiated by the Government of India to tackle the problem of global economic slowdown, nor they received any benefit out of it. Although it is often claimed that small enterprises are given priority in credit disbursement, a large part of priority sector lending gets diverted to the real estate and construction sector.

It has also been observed that in case of any market fluctuation, as experienced during the economic slowdown, large industries easily shift the burden of market fluctuations to the small subcontracting units. In such situations, small firms with their low resource base and limited entrepreneurial abilities, usually operate under adverse and exploitative terms of contract. Therefore, administrative, legal and fiscal measures aimed at long-term development of the micro and small enterprises are of immense importance. It appears that the Small Industry Associations and the Micro and Small Enterprises Facilitation Council (MSEFC) did not play any noticeable role during the times of crisis.

To increase India's exports, there is a need to diversify the export market both in terms of the export basket and the export destinations. For the small exporting firms, in addition to ensuring adequate and low cost finance, availability of marketing information, regular awareness programmes on different government incentives and providing training on exporting strategy, procedures, and requirements of different overseas markets will also be crucial.

Needless to say, micro and small enterprises need better access to finance, training and skill development, marketing information and other crucial infrastructure to operate efficiently and ensure deliveries of quality products as per the schedule. Financial assistances—both from the large firms and formal financial institutions—will also be crucial for the small exporting firms given the growing investment demand for technological transformation and their internationalisation efforts.

While there is an urgent need to generate more employment opportunities, for the worker community in general and those engaged in micro and small enterprises and self-employed workers, a universal and inclusive livelihood system must be in place which can ensure them better health, education and training facilities. The Indian economy did show signs of recovery after 2009-10, but economic recovery will remain incomplete as long as the job crisis continues. Undoubtedly, India needs to push back its economy to a higher growth trajectory, but sector-specific concerns also need immediate policy attention for which comprehensive sector-specific micro studies could generate useful information for designing appropriate policies.

References

Asian Development Bank (ADB) (2009). *Enterprises in Asia: Fostering Dynamism in SMEs*. Manila: ADB.

Bhaskaran, Manu and Ritwick Ghosh (2010). "Impact and Policy Responses: India", *Report* 3, ADB Regional Forum on the *Impact of Global Economic and Financial Crisis*. Manila: Asian Development Bank.

Cazes, Sandrine, Sher Verick and Caroline Heuer (2009). "Labour Market Policies in Times of Crisis", *Employment Sector: Employment Working Paper* No. 35. Geneva: ILO.

Government of India (various quarters). *Report on Effect of Economic Slowdown on Employment in India*. Labour Bureau, Ministry of Labour and Employment.

Government of India (various years). *Economic Survey: 2008-09* and *2009-10*. Ministry of Finance.

ILO (2009). *World of Work Report 2009: The Global Jobs Crisis and Beyond*. Geneva: ILO-ILLS.

International Monetary Fund (IMF) (2009). *World Economic Outlook: Sustaining the Recovery*. Washington, DC.

Islam, Iyanatul (2009). "The Global Economic Crisis and Developing Countries: Transmission Channels, Fiscal and Policy Space and the Design of National Responses", *Employment Sector: Employment Working Paper* No. 36. Geneva: ILO.

Institute of Social Studies Trust (IIST) (2009). *Rapid Assessment Study of the Impact of the Economic Slowdown on the Handicrafts Industry in Sanganer, Rajasthan*. New Delhi.

Kannan, K.P. (2009). "A First Assessment of the Impact of the Global Economic Crisis in India: The Continuing Challenge of Employment", *The Indian Journal of Labour Economics* 53(3): 349-73.

Khatiwada, Sameer (2009). "Stimulus Packages to Counter Global Economic Crisis: A Review", *Discussion Paper* No. DP/196/2009. Geneva: IILS.

Mohanakumar, S. and Surjit Singh (2011). "Impact of the Economic Crisis on Workers in the Unorganised Sector in Rajasthan", *Economic and Political Weekly* 46(22): 66-71.

NSSO (2006). "Employment and Unemployment Situation in India: 2004–05 (Part – I & II)", *NSS 61st Round (July 2004–June 2005)*. National Sample Survey Organisation, Ministry of Statistics and Programme Implementation, Government of India.

———. (2010). "Employment and Unemployment Situation in India: 2007-08", *NSS 64th Round (July 2007–June 2008)*. National Sample Survey Organisation, Ministry of Statistics and Programme Implementation, Government of India.

———. (2011). "Key Indicators of Employment and Unemployment in India, 2009-10", *NSS 66th Round (July 2009–June 2010)*. National Sample Survey Organisation, Ministry of Statistics and Programme Implementation, Government of India.

OECD (2009). *Tackling the Jobs Crisis: The Labour Market and Social Policy Response*. Background Document. OECD Labour and Employment Ministerial Meeting.

Rizwanul, Islam (2004). "The Nexus of Economic Growth, Employment and Poverty Reduction: An Empirical Analysis", *Issues in Employment and Poverty Discussion Paper* 14. Geneva: ILO.

Sahu, P.P. (2010). "Subcontracting in India's Unorganised Manufacturing Sector: A Mode of Adoption or Exploitation?" *Journal of South Asian Development* 5(1): 53-83.

———. (2011). "The Employment Implications of Current Financial Crisis: Challenges, Threats and Coping Strategies in India", *SANEI Working Paper Series* No. 11-03. Dhaka: South Asia Network of Economic Research Institutes.

Sasikumar, S.K. and Anup K. Karan (2010). *Global Downturn and Export Sectors in India: Impact on Production, Export and Employment*. Noida: V. V. Giri National Labour Institute.

Singh, Sumanjeet (2009). "The Indian Response to the Global Financial Crisis", *International Journal of South Asian Studies* 2(2): 302-31.

United Nations (2010). *World Economic Situation and Prospects* 2010. New York: United Nations.

UNCTAD (2009a). "The Global Economic Crisis: Systemic Failures and Multilateral Remedies", Report by the *Secretariat Task Force on Systemic Issues and Economic Cooperation.*

———. (2009b). *Impact of Global Slowdown on India's Exports and Employment.* Prepared under UNCTAD-Govt. of India-DFID Project "Strategies and Preparedness for Trade and Globalization in India". UNCTAD-India.

UNDP (2009). *Global Economic Crisis Impact on the Poor in India: A Synthesis of Sector Studies.* New Delhi, India: UNDP.

Vandenberg, Paul (2009). *Micro, Small and Medium-sized Enterprises and the Global Economic Crisis: Impacts and Policy Responses.* Geneva: International Labour Organization.

World Bank (2008). G20: "Global Financial Crisis: Responding Today, Securing Tomorrow", *Background Paper.* Group 20 Summit on Financial Markets and the World Economy. Washington, DC.

———. (2010). *Global Economic Prospects: Crisis, Finance and Growth.* Washington, DC.

5

NAMRATA GHOSH

Market Integration in Agricultural Commodities in India

A Study on Impact of Movement in International Prices on Household Welfare

Introduction

Global commodity prices affect a country's domestic prices if these commodities form a major share of the country's trade. Studies on integration of markets, particularly commodity markets, have assumed greater significance in recent years. With increasing globalisation, markets that are otherwise spatially separated are being progressively linked through trade, be it financial or real. Different economies have reacted differently to global shocks depending on how integrated they are with the rest of the world.

For India, one would expect greater integration with the world economy as globalisation proceeds. However, while in some sectors India is highly integrated with world markets, in certain sectors (like agriculture) this may not be entirely true. This is not only because world trade in agriculture is more restricted than in manufacturing, but also because there are restrictions in agricultural trade among regions within the country. It is, therefore, possible for food price inflation to be different in different regions because it is not that easy to move such products from low price to high price areas. In a world of no transaction costs, the way to measure such integration is the difference in the prices of similar commodities in different regions/countries. The more integrated a market, the lesser the gap would be. If certain commodities in country A are more expensive than in the neighbouring country B, the free flow of goods will encourage B producers to sell in A and consumers from country A to buy from country B. This movement will continue till prices are equalised in the two regions. In the real world there are various transaction costs that prevent this from happening. Therefore, another way of measuring the degree of integration is to see how these prices have moved over time.

Agriculture contributes about 17 per cent to GDP in India and employs around 70 per cent of the workforce. Small farmers comprise 80 per cent of the holdings and own less than 2 hectares of land on average and marginal farmers, with less than 1 hectare, comprise 62 per cent of the holdings. Given this scenario, any change in prices of agricultural commodities can have varying impact on the producers or consumers. An increase in prices is known to hurt consumers as this leads to a lower purchasing power, given a fixed income. Ghosh and Sharma (2009) studied the impact of food price rise on the welfare of Indian households using changes in domestic prices. Obviously, the impact depends on whether they are net producers or consumers. Not immediately obvious, however, is the fact that the price rise also leads to increased nominal wages and this somewhat mitigates the adverse consequences of food price rise for the consumers.

Given the complexities, it is worthwhile to see whether the domestic agricultural prices move with international prices and check for the degree of price transmission from international to domestic market, if any. There are studies that analyse the impact of a change in domestic prices on household welfare. However, the impact of international prices, if remain integrated with domestic prices, on household welfare has not been widely studied in India. This chapter extends the analysis to measuring welfare impact using international prices, once the price of a commodity in the domestic market is cointegrated with the international market. The price elasticity of demand is used to calculate the welfare impact on households differentiated by states, depending on whether the state is a net consumer or producer of the commodity along with segregation by land size classes.

While there exists greater integration with the world economy, it is also important to note that India is a very small player in overall global trade. According to World Trade Organization (WTO) (2009), India's share in world total exports was 1.32 per cent while its share in total imports was 2.02 per cent in 2009. Agricultural products contributed 10.2 per cent to the economy's total exports while 5.6 per cent of agricultural products were imported.[1] Agriculture contributes much less than manufacturing and services. As such India does not provide a big enough market to create impact on world prices. However, with integrated markets, price transmission from the world to domestic markets is likely to take place, and we should expect some impact on domestic producers and consumers at least in the case of these commodities. In the absence of trade barriers, world food prices will establish upper and lower bounds for domestic food prices. One would expect price transmission to be higher when domestic price is near the import parity price or when it is near the export parity price. One would expect limited price transmission when there are policy barriers to international trade, lack of market information or uncompetitive markets (see Minot, 2010).

There are impediments to Indian trade (in the form of tariffs) especially in the agriculture sector that prevent the Indian markets from fully integrating with the world market. It is thus useful to study whether with increased globalisation we have achieved market integration in agricultural commodities, if not in the stricter sense of having "one price" then in a weaker sense where the price differentials move in the same direction.

The rest of the chapter is organised as follows: Section 2 provides a brief literature survey of market integration studies across the world and the transmission of world prices to domestic prices in terms of welfare impact on households. Section 3 provides the theoretical structure of market integration to be studied as well as the net benefit ratio model. Section 4 provides the econometric model for testing cointegration. Section 5 provides the data and methodology while section 6 gives the empirical results of cointegration tests and the net benefit ratios. Section 7 concludes the chapter.

---

1. For China, for example, the share in total world exports was 9.6 per cent while that in imports was 7.91 per cent in 2009. Agricultural products formed 3.4 per cent of the total exports while the share was 7.6 per cent in the case of total imports.

Literature Survey

Market integration studies have been carried out mainly by testing co-movement of prices that are indicative of competitive markets. Most studies utilise time series econometric techniques that test for co-movements in prices. Engle and Granger's co-integration and error correction mechanism techniques have become the standard tool for analysing spatial market relationships. Time series analysis, however, has been criticised as not entirely reliable. Recent research has therefore focused on models that incorporate data on prices, volume traded and transaction costs. Similarly, linear tests for market integration and price transmission are considered inappropriate. In theory, spatial price determination models suggest that if two markets are linked by trade in a free market regime, then excess demand or supply shocks in one market will have an equal impact on prices in both markets.

Barret (2005) mentions the concept of spatial market integration, where market aggregate demand and supply across actors are distributed in space. At the international level, monetary policy, exchange rate adjustment and the distribution of the gains from trade depend fundamentally on how well prices equilibrate across countries, as vast literatures on the law of one price and purchasing power parity emphasise (Froot and Rogoff, 1995; Anderson and van Wincoop, 2004). At the national level, well-functioning markets ensure that macro-level economic policies (for example, with respect to exchange rates, trade, and fiscal or monetary policy) change the incentives and constraints faced by micro-level decision-makers. Barret and Li (1999) introduce a new market analysis methodology based on maximum likelihood estimation of a mixture distribution of model incorporating price, transfer cost and trade flow data.

There has been a lot of debate on the welfare impact of inflation on rural households, both producers and consumers. It is maintained that net producers should benefit from a rise in price of their product. However, in developing countries, some of the rural farmer households are so poor that they are not able to sell their produce in the market at competitive prices and end up consuming their own produce. Hence, the positive impact of inflation on these households is suspect.

Deaton (1989) examines the effects of rice prices on the distribution of real incomes across different households, and finds that higher prices for rice are likely to benefit rural households at all levels of living. He finds that it is the households in the middle income group that stand to gain the largest percentage income gains from increase in the price of rice. Another similar study by Ravallion (1989), for Bangladesh, finds that in the short run, rural rich are likely to gain and rural poor are likely to lose from an increase in relative price of food staples in a food-producing economy. However, in the long run, the welfare of a typical rural household is more likely to be neutral, and the poorest households will benefit in some measure.

The responsiveness of wages to changes in prices of rice and wheat has been debated in a number of countries. However, there has been little agreement on how responsive agricultural wages are to food prices. While Sah and Stiglitz (1987) contend that the terms of trade against agriculture hurts everyone in the sector, whether rich or poor, de Jenvry and Subbarao (1984; 1987) highlight the adverse effects of higher food prices on the rural poor.

Theoretical Basis

Market Integration

An integrated market is defined as one in which geography or nationality does not have systematic effects on transaction prices for otherwise identical products (Goldberg and Knetter, 1997). The LOP (law of one price) holds that identical products sell for the same common currency price in different countries, assuming costless transportation and resale. If the price of good i is p_{i1} and p_{i2} in domestic and international markets respectively, then according to the LOP, the two will be equal when adjusted for the exchange rate.

However, the assumptions of costless transportation and resale (such as tariff barriers) do not hold in practice. Hence, these frictions should give rise to a stable price differential across the two markets. This is the weaker or relative version of the LOP. The two prices then differ by some constant, α.

Markets play an important role in reducing price variability faced by the producers and consumers. If two regions are integrated, then it is more profitable for the producers to sell in the region where goods are more expensive. The movement will continue till prices equate across regions. If price of good i in the international market is higher than that in the domestic market, then it is more profitable for the domestic producers to sell in the international market as they get higher returns for their product. The exports will take place till prices in the domestic market also rise and the gap between the two markets no longer exists. In such a situation, it is not more profitable to sell the commodity abroad. Conversely, if the price of good *i* in the international market is lower than that in the domestic market, imports of the commodity will be encouraged. They will take place till the domestic price comes down and it is no longer more profitable to import. The above situations take place when there are no trade restrictions. When either export or import restrictions are placed, then the prices in the national market might not move in line with those in the international markets.

Restrictions could be for imports but not for exports of the same commodity and vice versa. As mentioned earlier, if the domestic producers find it more profitable to sell in the international market as the price is higher there, exports will continue till the prices equalise. If the domestic market then faces shortage, with no import restrictions the commodity can be traded till the price differential is no longer there. However, if there are no export restrictions but some level of import restrictions, the shortage in the domestic market cannot be filled up, and the price differential among markets for the same commodity may not go away.

The ESTJ (Enke-Samuleson-Takayama-Judge) spatial equilibrium model (Barret, 2005) maintains that the dispersion of prices in two locations for an otherwise identical good is bounded from above by the cost of arbitrage between the markets when trade volumes are unrestricted, and bounded from below when trade volumes reach some ceiling value (for example, associated with a trade quota).

$$p_0 = p_1 + t_{10} \text{ if } q_{10} \in (0, q_{10^*})$$
$$\leq p_1 + t_{10} \text{ if } q_{10} = 0$$
$$\geq p_1 + t_{10} \text{ if } q_{10} = q_{10^*}$$

where p_0 is the price in market 0, p_1 is the price in market 1, t_{10} is the transportation cost of moving the good from market 1 to market 0, q_{10} is the physical volume of trade between the two markets and q_{10^*} is a maximal permitted trade volume between the two markets (for example, due to a trade quota). The strict equality is the situation where the LOP holds under competitive markets. The first inequality highlights a situation where no trade occurs. The latter weak inequality occurs with binding trade quotas that may yield positive returns through arbitrage. Spatial market integration occurs when the ESTJ equilibrium holds irrespective of whether trade occurs or not.

Net Benefit Ratio

If the domestic markets for certain agricultural commodities are integrated with world markets in terms of prices, we can estimate the effect of a rise in prices of these commodities on household welfare through the concept of net benefit ratio. In general, with inflation, the cost of purchasing food increases and hence, this adversely impacts food security of a poor household. However, the impact of price rise is not uniform across all households. It depends on whether the household is a net producer or a net consumer. In such a scenario, it is important for the policy makers to determine who is impacted the most during a food crisis.

To understand the net benefit of a rise in prices, we use Deaton's (1989; 1997) approach to estimate the short run welfare impact of price changes of agricultural commodities on household welfare. The welfare effect of food price change is proportional to the NBR (net benefit ratio). The NBR is calculated as the difference between the production share of the commodity and its consumption share in total household expenditures. The net benefit ratio can thus be interpreted as the elasticity of expenditures (or real income) to the commodity price change. We can capture the longer run effects arising from induced wage responses[2] to price changes, by combining Deaton's model with Ravallion's (1990) approach. The basic model is:

NBR_i (or ΔW) = $\Delta p\ [(PR_i - CR_i) + \Delta\ w\ L_i]$

where

NBR_i	=	Net benefit ratio or the welfare effect expressed as percentage of total expenditure of household *i*.
Δp	=	Percentage change in food price.
PR_i	=	Food production ratio or production of food item per household ÷ total household expenditure.
CR_i	=	Food expenditure ratio or consumption of food item per household total household expenditure.
Δw	=	Change in wages per household.
L_i	=	Labour share in household expenditure.

Econometric Model

The concept of cointegration (Granger, 1981) and the methods for estimating a cointegrated relation or system (Engle and Granger, 1987; Johansen, 1988; 1991; 1995) provide a framework for estimating and testing for long run equilibrium relationships between non-stationary integrated variables. If two prices in separated markets (or different levels in the supply chain) p_{1t} and p_{2t} contain stochastic trends and are integrated of the same order, say I(*d*), prices are said to be cointegrated if

$$p_{1t} - \beta\, p_{2t} = u_t \qquad (1)$$

is I(0). β is referred to as the cointegrating coefficient whilst equation (1) is said to be the cointegrating regression. The above relationship can be estimated utilising ordinary least squares (Engle and Granger, 1987) or a full information maximum likelihood method developed by Johansen (1988, 1991) that is most commonly encountered in the literature. More specifically, p_{1t} and p_{2t} are cointegrated, if there is a linear combination between them that does not have a stochastic trend even though the individual series contain stochastic trends.

2. In place of wage elasticity to commodity prices, we simply use nominal changes in wages. It is difficult to capture wage changes in response to a particular food item. Also, for estimating welfare impact of a household it is important to capture the changes in nominal wages and not changes in nominal wages arising out of the price change.

Cointegration implies that these prices move closely together in the long run, although in the short run they may drift apart, and thus is consistent with the concept of market integration. Engle and Granger test the null of no cointegration between two series by applying unit root tests on the estimate of the error term.

Economic theory often suggests that a certain subset of variables should be linked by their long term relationship. Although the variables under consideration may drift away from equilibrium for a while, economic forces might restore the equilibrium. According to the Engle Granger approach to testing for cointegration, if the two series p_{1t} and p_{2t} are I(d) or integrated of order d, and in general any linear combination of the two series is I(0), we can say that p_{1t} and p_{2t} are cointegrated. We estimate the long run relationship $p_{1t} = \beta p_{2t} + u_t$ and obtain the residuals of this equation.

A test for the order of integration is a test for the number of unit roots as provided in the steps below:

1. Test p_{1t} to see if it is stationary. If yes, then p_{1t}~I(0); if no, then p_{1t}~I(n); n>0.
2. Take first difference of p_{1t} as $\Delta p_{1t} = p_{1t} - p_{1t-1}$ and test to see if Δp_{1t} is stationary as in step 1.
3. Take second difference of p_{1t} as $\Delta^2 p_{1t} = \Delta p_{1t} - \Delta p_{1t-1}$ and test $\Delta^2 p_{1t}$ to see if it is stationary. We continue these steps till we find that the series is stationary and then we stop.

Dickey and Fuller (1979) devised a procedure to formally test for non-stationarity (testing for the existence of unit root).

$$p_{1t} = \phi p_{1t-1} + \varepsilon_t \qquad (2)$$

The null hypothesis is that the variable has unit root. ε_t is an independently and identically distributed zero mean error term and $p_0 = 0$, the OLS estimate. ϕ is the autocorrelation parameter.

The null hypothesis is $H_0 : \phi = 1$ against $H_1 : \phi < 1$.

A better and convenient version of the test can be obtained by subtracting p_{1t-1} from both sides of (2).

$$p_{1t} - p_{1t-1} = \phi p_{1t-1} - p_{1t-1} + \varepsilon_t \qquad (3)$$

$$\Delta p_{1t} = \gamma p_{1t-1} + \varepsilon_t \qquad (4)$$

where $\gamma = (\phi - 1)$

The null hypothesis is $H_0 : \gamma = 0$ against $H_1 : \gamma < 0$.

However, since the error term is unlikely to be white noise, Dickey and Fuller extend their test procedure to an augmented version that includes extra lagged terms of the dependent variable in order to eliminate autocorrelation. This is called the augmented Dickey Fuller (ADF) test. The three possible forms of the ADF test are given by the following equations with no constant, with constant, and with constant and trend respectively.

$$\Delta P_{1t} = \gamma p_{1t-1} + \sum_{i=1}^{n} \beta_i \Delta p_{1t-1} + \varepsilon_t \tag{5}$$

$$\Delta P_{1t} = \alpha_0 + \gamma p_{1t-1} + \sum_{i=1}^{n} \beta_i \Delta p_{1t-1} + \varepsilon_t \tag{6}$$

$$\Delta P_{1t} = \alpha_0 + \gamma p_{1t-1} + \alpha_2 t + \sum_{i=1}^{n} \beta_i \Delta p_{1t-1} + \varepsilon_t \tag{7}$$

Phillips Perron (PP) test is a more powerful test for checking stationarity. It is a modification of the ADF t statistics that take into account less restrictive nature of the error process. The Mackinnon (1991) critical values are applicable with both tests.

Once we have checked for the order of integration of the price series, we test for cointegration between the two series.

The Engle Granger cointegration test is carried out in two steps.

1. Run the OLS regression of $= p_{1t} = \beta\, p_{2t} + u_t$, t=1....T and obtain the residuals, as $p_{1t} - \beta\, p_{2t} = u_t$.
2. Apply a unit root test to u_t by constructing an AR(1) regression:

$$u_t = \Phi\, u_{t-1} + \varepsilon_t. \tag{8}$$

We test the null, $H_0 : \Phi = 1$ against $H_1 : \Phi < 1$.

If the series are found to be cointegrated, the residuals from the equilibrium regression can be used to estimate the ECM (error correction mechanism) and to analyse the long term and short term effects of the variables as well as to see the adjustment coefficient, which is the coefficient of the lagged residual terms of the long run relationship.

The error correction term is defined as

$p_{1t} -- \beta p_{2t} = u_t$ (9)

where β is the cointegrating coefficient.

The ECM can be derived as follows.

$p_{1t} = \beta p_{2t} + u_t$ (10)

$p_{1t-1} = \beta p_{2t-1} + u_{t-1}$ (11)

We know $u_t = \Phi u_{t-1} + \varepsilon_t$ (12)

Subtracting u_{t-1} from both sides in (12), we get

$u_t - u_{t-1} = (\Phi - 1) u_{t-1} + \varepsilon_t$ (13)

Subtracting (11) from (10), we get

$\Delta p_{1t} = \alpha u_{t-1} + \beta \Delta p_{2t} + \varepsilon_t$ (14)

Where, ε_t is identically and independently distributed (iid) and $\alpha = (\Phi - 1)$. Equation (14) says that Δp_{1t} can be explained by the lagged u_{t-1} and Δp_{2t}. u_{t-1} can be thought of as an equilibrium error. is the error correction coefficient and is called the adjustment coefficient. It tells us how much of the adjustment to equilibrium takes place each period, or how much of the equilibrium error is corrected.

Data and Methodology

We tested for cointegration of domestic prices with international prices of five agricultural commodities namely, rice, wheat, soybean, sugarcane, and groundnut oil. We used the Engle and Granger (1987) two-step method to test for cointegration between two variables, say prices p_{1t} and p_{2t}, which entails using OLS (ordinary least squares) to estimate the long-run equilibrium relation of the law of one price.

We have used monthly data on international producer food prices obtained from the Food and Agriculture Organisation's (FAO) website. Indian data on prices of commodities (*mandi* wise per state) were obtained from the Department of Agriculture and Cooperation, Government of India.

The NBR for the states in India is calculated primarily for the year 2004-05 for which the production and expenditure ratios are taken from the National Sample Survey (NSS) 61st round. We took the data on changes in prices from 2006-07 to 2007-08 as the year witnessed a big jump in food prices in the country. Wage data was also taken for the years 2006-07 and 2007-08. We also assume that the labour share in household expenditure (obtained from NSS 59th round 2003) has not changed significantly over the sample time.

The variables required for estimating household welfare are aggregated up from the household to the state level. While consumption expenditures at the household level can be aggregated to the state level using the NSS 61st round, the production data cannot be directly obtained from this dataset. We took those households that use their own produce of the commodity, confirming that these are producer households. Since, NSS 61st round does not provide the area under cultivation by commodity for a household, we multiplied the area cultivated of a household with the proportion of consumption of the commodity (say soybean) from home produce to the total consumption of all commodities from home produce for that household. This would give us at least the area that went into the production of the commodity for a household. The next step was to find the production of the food item. We estimated this by taking the total area cultivated per producer household (after adjusting for the home produce proportion of the commodity) and multiplying it with the total yield of the state (taken district wise). The value of production was obtained by multiplying it with the average price of the food item in the state in 2007-08.

For labour income as a share of total expenditure, we used NSS 59th round data from the Situation Assessment Survey of Farmers 2003 as NSS 61st round did not provide information on labour income. We imputed this data (income from wages to total consumption expenditure) to the NSS 61st round using land size classes as the common variable. The land size class is based on the Agricultural Census of India 2001 with categories starting from less than 0.01 hectare to greater than 10 hectares (for more details, refer to Ghosh and Sharma, 2009).

Empirical Results

The price series that were tested for cointegration in our study are the domestic prices (dependent variable p_{1t} of rice, wheat, soybean,

Table 5.1

ADF Test Results for Unit Roots

	World		*India*		*World*		*India*		
	ADF Test				*PP Test*				
Price Levels (Test Statistic)	*With Trend*	*Without Trend*	*With Trend*	*Without Trend*	*With Trend*	*Without Trend*	*With Trend*	*Without Trend*	*Lags*
log (rice)	-2.92	-1.72	-2.31	0.33	-2.71	-1.73	-5.82	-0.72	4
log (wheat)	-2.00	-1.47	-2.86	-1.46	-1.87	-1.33	-3.01	-1.40	2
log (soybean)	-2.70	-1.14	-2.62	-1.50	-2.85	-1.46	-2.48	-1.41	1
log (sugarcane)	-3.06	-1.16	-1.93	-0.77	-2.28	-0.95	-2.50	-1.04	2
log (groundnut oil)	-3.09	-2.02	-2.90	-0.91	-1.97	-1.07	-5.16	-1.65	4

	World		*India*		
	ADF Test				
Price - First Differences (Test Statistic)	*With Trend*	*Without Trend*	*With Trend*	*Without Trend*	*Lags*
log (rice)	-4.66*	-4.65*	-7.34*	-7.22*	3
log (wheat)	-5.01*	-5.05*	-4.27*	-4.28*	2
log (soybean)	-7.58*	-7.48*	-7.69*	-7.67*	1
log (sugarcane)	-5.25*	-5.26*	-8.44*	-8.47*	1
log (groundnut oil)	-3.25***	-3.27**	-6.09*	-6.11*	3

Note: * 1% significance level, ** 5% significance level, and *** 10% significance level.

sugarcane and groundnut oil) and international prices of those agricultural commodities (independent variable p_{2t}). The series were first tested for stationarity at levels and then at first differences (Table 5.1) and, if they were integrated of the same order, tested for stationarity of their residuals (Table 5.2).

Table 5.1 provides the standard ADF and PP test results (test statistics) when applied to the data in levels and first differences. For the data in levels, we cannot reject the null of a unit root while it can be rejected in first differences. Given that the ADF test suffers from poor size and power properties, we conducted another powerful test—the PP test. All unit root tests at first difference indicated that the price series are stationary or integrated of order 1.

The lag length was chosen according to Akaike's Final Prediction Error (FPE) criterion. Table 5.2 provides the results of the Engle Granger two-step methodology for testing cointegration between two series.

Table 5.2

Cointegration Test Results

	Cointegration Results					*Critical Values*		
ADF test of Residuals (Test Statistic)	*Rice*	*Wheat*	*Soybean*	*Sugar-cane*	*Ground-nut Oil*	*1%*	*5%*	*10%*
With lags	-2.21 (2)	- 1.82 (1)	-3.57** (2)	-2.69 (2)	- 2.50 (2)	-3.73	-3.17	-2.91
Without lags	-3.92**	-1.74	-4.51*	-3.56**	-3.66**	-4.07	-3.37	-3.3

Note: * 1% significance level, ** 5% significance level, and ***10% significance level.

The number in brackets is the lag length chosen according to Akaike's FPE criterion. The null hypothesis of no cointegration cannot be rejected for all commodities except soybean. Since soybean domestic prices showed integration with the world prices, we get the error correction model for the same.

The coefficient β in equation 14 provides us the price elasticity coefficient. This coefficient has been used in place of domestic prices in the NBR equation in section 3 while calculating the net benefit ratio. For soybean, the elasticity coefficient at all India level is 0.28 while the error correction coefficient is -0.41. The NBR for net producers and net consumers of soybean as a result of changes in international prices (price elasticity coefficient based on the error correction model) is provided in Tables 5.3-5.6.

We present results (NBR state wise) of a change in domestic prices with respect to international prices for the states of Maharashtra (price elasticity coefficient is 0.55) and Rajasthan (price elasticity coefficient is 0.54) for both net producers and net consumers of soybean and find positive welfare impact across all land size classes. For consumers, it is observed that the wage impact possibly overrides the impact of the higher price level. Tables 5.3 and 5.4 provide the NBR for net consumers and net producers of Maharashtra respectively. Note that for net consumers the net benefit declines as the land size class increases, that is, the lower land size classes gain more from the rise in prices than those in the higher land size classes. The rise in agricultural wages seems to have dominated the small land size holding of the small farmers. For net producers (in Maharashtra, producers of soybean are those who possess land between 2-4 hectares), the net benefit is positive for this land size class as well (Figures 5.1 and 5.2). Tables 5.5 and 5.6 provide the NBR without taking into account changes in wages in Maharashtra. Note that if we do not take into account changes in wages, the NBR is negative (even though marginally) for the land size classes for which the NBR with the wage change was positive earlier. For net consumers, this would mean that the wage impact is clearly benefitting them especially in rural areas and those with lower land size classes, below 2 hectares. For producers also the NBR is negative as the land size class is too low to give them a positive NBR with a rise in prices. It is possible that the producers are also working for wages to supplement their income.

Tables 5.7 and 5.8 provide NBR for net consumers and net producers respectively for the state of Rajasthan (with wage impact). For Rajasthan, as in the case of Maharashtra, the net benefit for consumers declines as one goes to the higher land size classes, and for producers who belong to the land size category 1-2 hectares, the NBR is positive (Figures 5.3 and 5.4). Again, the rise in agricultural wages seems to have dominated the small land size holding of the small farmers. Tables 5.9 and 5.10 provide the NBR for net consumers and net producers respectively for Rajasthan without the wage impact. As we observe, the NBR without taking into account the wage impact, is negative for both net producers and net consumers in their respective land size class. This shows that wage changes do mute the impact of price rise of a commodity to a large extent.

Table 5.3

NBR for Net Consumers of Soybean (Maharashtra)

Size Class	*Land Possessed (hectares)*	*NBR (%)*
1	Less than 0.01	3.28
2	Between .01 & .40	4.11
3	Between .40 & 1.00	3.55
4	Between 1.00 & 2.00	1.94
5	Between 2.00 & 4.00	1.48
6	Between 2.00 & 10.00	0.68
7	Greater than 10.00	0.49

Figure 5.1

NBR for Net Consumers (Maharashtra) of Soybean With Wage Impact

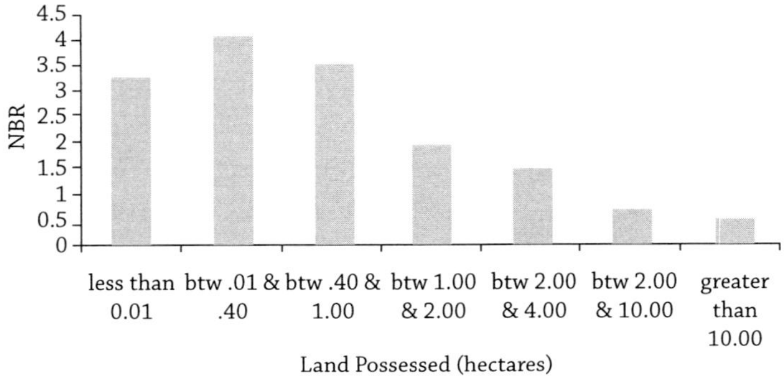

Table 5.4

NBR for Net Producers of Soybean (Maharashtra)

Size Class	*Land Possessed (hectares)*	*NBR (%)*
1	Less than 0.01	NA
2	Between .01 & .40	NA
3	Between .40 & 1.00	NA
4	Between 1.00 & 2.00	NA
5	Between 2.00 & 4.00	1.19
6	Between 2.00 & 10.00	NA
7	Greater than 10.00	NA

Figure 5.2

NBR for Net Producers (Maharashtra) of Soybean With Wage Impact

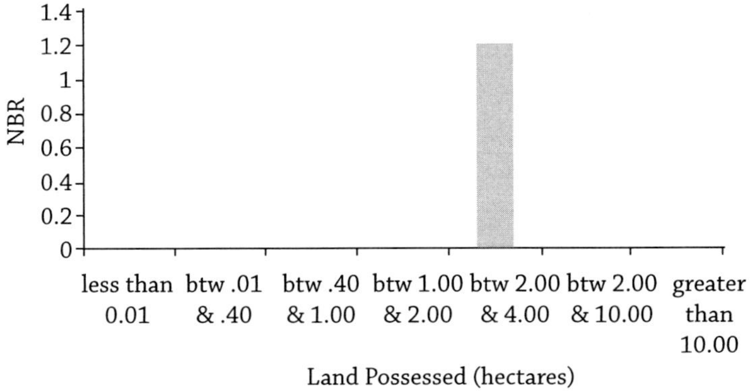

Table 5.5

NBR for Net Consumers of Soybean Without Wage Impact (Maharashtra)

Size Class	*Land Possessed (hectares)*	*NBR (%)*
1	Less than 0.01	-0.001
2	Between .01 & .40	-0.001
3	Between .40 & 1.00	0.00
4	Between 1.00 & 2.00	0.00
5	Between 2.00 & 4.00	0.00
6	Between 2.00 & 10.00	0.00
7	Greater than 10.00	0.00

Table 5.6

NBR for Net Producers of Soybean Without Wage Impact (Maharashtra)

Size Class	*Land Possessed (hectares)*	*NBR (%)*
1	Less than 0.01	NA
2	Between .01 & .40	NA
3	Between .40 & 1.00	NA
4	Between 1.00 & 2.00	NA
5	Between 2.00 & 4.00	-0.284
6	Between 2.00 & 10.00	NA
7	Greater than 10.00	NA

Table 5.7

NBR for Net Consumers of Soybean (Rajasthan)

Size Class	*Land Possessed (hectares)*	*NBR (%)*
1	Less than 0.01	7.27
2	Between .01 & .40	7.89
3	Between .40 & 1.00	8.23
4	Between 1.00 & 2.00	6.81
5	Between 2.00 & 4.00	4.68
6	Between 2.00 & 10.00	3.66
7	Greater than 10.00	2.65

Figure 5.3

NBR for Net Consumers (Rajasthan) of Soybean with Wage Impact

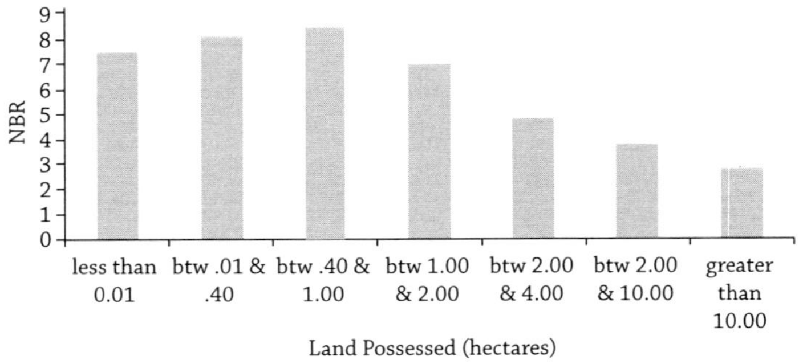

Figure 5.4

NBR for Net Producers (Rajasthan) of Soybean with Wage Impact

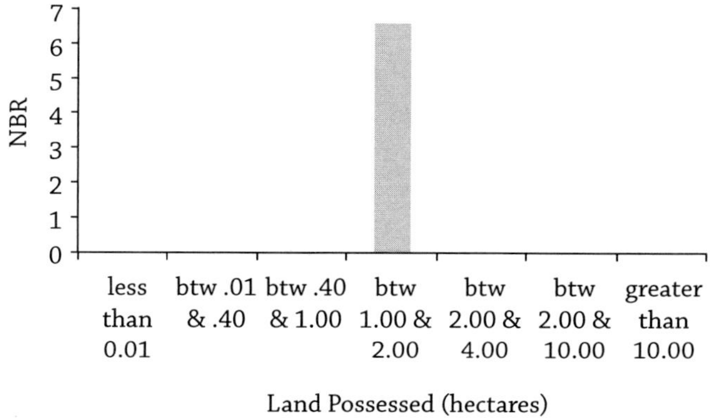

Table 5.8

NBR for Net Producers of Soybean (Rajasthan)

Size Class	*Land Possessed (hectares)*	*NBR (%)*
1	Less than 0.01	NA
2	Between .01 & .40	NA
3	Between .40 & 1.00	NA
4	Between 1.00 & 2.00	6.59
5	Between 2.00 & 4.00	NA
6	Between 2.00 & 10.00	NA
7	Greater than 10.00	NA

Table 5.9

NBR for Net Consumers of Soybean Without Wage Impact (Rajasthan)

Size Class	*Land Possessed (hectares)*	*NBR (%)*
1	Less than 0.01	0
2	Between .01 & .40	0
3	Between .40 & 1.00	0.00
4	Between 1.00 & 2.00	-0.0013
5	Between 2.00 & 4.00	0
6	Between 2.00 & 10.00	-0.00079
7	Greater than 10.00	0

Table 5.10

NBR for Net Producers of Soybean Without Wage Impact (Rajasthan)

Size Class	*Land Possessed (hectares)*	*NBR (%)*
1	Less than 0.01	NA
2	Between .01 & .40	NA
3	Between .40 & 1.00	NA
4	Between 1.00 & 2.00	-0.21
5	Between 2.00 & 4.00	NA
6	Between 2.00 & 10.00	NA
7	Greater than 10.00	NA

Note that even though prices of rice and wheat in India are not cointegrated with the rest of the world, since these are staple food items, it would be interesting to see how the rise in domestic prices would impact the net producers or consumers of rice and wheat.[3] Tables 5.11 and 5.12 show the NBR for net producers of rice and wheat for 17 major states of India. Our results show that the net benefits of a price rise in staple food items improves the impact on producer households in the states under study. However, an adjustment of wages over time can lessen the impact of a price rise. For rice, most of the states have a positive NBR across all land size classes, except Assam, Bihar, Orissa, Maharashtra and Uttar Pradesh. For Assam, the NBR is positive till the land size of 2 hectares and then it turns negative. For Bihar, for land size of 1 hectare onwards, the NBR turns negative, while for Maharashtra, it is negative for the largest land size category of greater than 10 hectares. For Uttar Pradesh, NBR is positive only for the bottom two categories and negative for the remaining ones. For Orissa, the NBR is negative only for the lowest land size category of less than 0.01 hectares. For wheat, the NBR is again positive for all states under study.

Assam has shown a fall in price of rice (1%), with an increase of 8 per cent in wages. The smaller land size category is compensated of

3. Ghosh and Sharma (2009).

a fall in prices by the wage increase while the bigger land size category clearly shows a fall in surplus as a result of the price fall.

For Bihar, for the period under study, prices of rice declined by four per cent while that of wheat rose by five per cent. Wages rose by seven per cent. The NBR for wheat is higher for the lowest land size category as compared with the medium land size classes, rising thereafter for the land size class of two hectares and above—implying a wage effect taking precedence over the price effect for the smaller land size classes.

Maharashtra consumes both rice and wheat per capita as a proportion of total expenditure in a similar manner (about 9 per cent). However, the state witnessed a -0.4 per cent decline in prices of rice, and a 9 per cent rise in prices of wheat. There was a 9 per cent increase in wages for the state over the same time period. As expected, a decline in prices affects household welfare adversely, which declines as one goes up the land size class. The net benefit even turns negative for the largest land size class category. The net benefit for wheat follows a U-shaped pattern with the lowest land size category benefitting more than the next two categories. The rise in agricultural wages seems to have dominated the small land size holding for the small farmers.

Orissa is predominantly a rice consuming state and is the fifth largest rice producing state in the country. Orissa has positive NBRs for all land size classes except the lowest land size category. It is important to note that Orissa is one of the poor states of the country, and it is clear that despite being one of the largest rice producing state, the smallest land size category does not benefit from a rise in prices of rice.

Uttar Pradesh is a predominantly wheat consuming state. It also happens to be the largest wheat producing state and the third largest producer of rice in the country. The NBR for wheat follows a U-shape as Uttar Pradesh witnessed a 3 per cent increase in prices of wheat and a 12 per cent rise in agricultural wages.

Table 5.11

Net Benefit Ratio (%) for Net Rice Producers

Land possessed (hectare)	*Andhra Pradesh*	*Assam*	*Bihar*	*Gujarat*	*Haryana*	*Himachal Pradesh*	*J&K*	*Karnataka*	*Kerala*
Less than 0.01	18.76	2.18	2.28	NA	NA	NA	NA	5.64	NA
Between .01 & .40	6.40	4.33	2.31	19.58	17.78	6.85	12.45	9.53	2.98
Between .40 & 1.00	6.57	1.13	0.31	39.22	18.53	9.52	25.26	8.63	13.07
Between 1.00 & 2.00	6.31	0.73	-0.76	69.24	35.95	14.42	43.81	9.53	24.68
Between 2.00 & 4.00	8.47	-0.2	-1.81	75.42	45.75	18.84	71.26	13.83	30.31
Between 2.00 & 10.00	11.17	-0.72	-4.98	164.33	83.39	17.23	117.98	23.83	91.45
Greater than 10.00	23.68	-2.07	-11.23	NA	104.84	NA	148.44	49.76	NA

Land possessed (hectare)	*Madhya Pradesh*	*Maharashtra*	*Orissa*	*Punjab*	*Rajasthan*	*Tamil Nadu*	*Uttar Pradesh*	*West Bengal*
Less than 0.01	NA	NA	-6.57	3.17	NA	NA	4.18	1.81
Between .01 & .40	7.40	4.05	3.82	8.83	10.79	13.28	2.45	4.12
Between .40 & 1.00	14.68	3.37	9.84	10.76	18.92	22.42	-0.31	8.26
Between 1.00 & 2.00	25.36	1.56	24.38	18.56	18.70	33.10	-1.24	12.05
Between 2.00 & 4.00	37.47	1.01	44.80	29.18	35.26	48.07	-3.32	18.97
Between 2.00 & 10.00	59.50	0.07	77.85	44.79	44.37	73.57	-6.68	36.14
Greater than 10.00	101.86	-0.12	147.74	77.23	NA	117.01	-12.10	73.07

Table 5.12

Net Benefit Ratio (%) for Net Wheat Producers

Land possessed (hectare)	*Andhra Pradesh*	*Assam*	*Bihar*	*Gujarat*	*Haryana*	*Himachal Pradesh*	*J&K*	*Karnataka*	*Kerala*
Less than 0.01	NA	NA	6.58	NA	11.19	8.12	NA	NA	NA
Between .01 & .40	NA	NA	2.8	6.64	10.00	4.73	4.54	NA	NA
Between .40 & 1.00	4.63	NA	2.55	14.71	10.11	4.12	5.67	10.58	NA
Between 1.00 & 2.00	3.88	NA	4.11	26.53	16.62	4.19	7.64	8.35	NA
Between 2.00 & 4.00	3.51	NA	6.98	42.53	23.24	3.57	11.70	13.13	NA
Between 2.00 & 10.00	8.43	NA	11.85	76.08	36.00	2.44	17.02	16.29	NA
Greater than 10.00	6.74	NA	24.64	155.38	66.60	0.11	20.25	37.69	NA

Land possessed (hectare)	*Madhya Pradesh*	*Maharashtra*	*Orissa*	*Punjab*	*Rajasthan*	*Tamil Nadu*	*Uttar Pradesh*	*West Bengal*
Less than 0.01	5.22	9.36	NA	1.36	NA	NA	5.39	NA
Between .01 & .40	4.44	5.02	2.04	3.82	8.34	NA	4.00	3.16
Between .40 & 1.00	7.11	7.20	NA	6.78	9.74	NA	3.25	4.43
Between 1.00 & 2.00	9.98	9.82	NA	12.53	9.11	NA	4.31	4.50
Between 2.00 & 4.00	16.47	13.49	13.61	22.78	8.99	NA	6.21	6.47
Between 2.00 & 10.00	24.59	21.18	NA	33.49	10.71	NA	8.97	11.02
Greater than 10.00	48.12	32.89	NA	56.00	21.09	NA	12.05	NA

Conclusions

We observe that out of the five agricultural commodities that we have considered in the present study, only one, that is, soybean shows integration between domestic and international prices. We calculate the household welfare of an increase in international prices of this commodity. The welfare is positive across all land size classes. In 2008-09, India produced 9.91 million tons of soybean as opposed to 99.18 million tonnes of rice and 80.68 million tonnes of wheat. Indian imports of soybean oil far outpace its exports. India is thus a net consumer of the commodity. The welfare impact on the consumers is positive for most of the states as the wage impact shields the consumers from higher international prices of soybean that get transmitted to India.

References

Anderson, James E. and Eric van Wincoop (2004). "Trade Costs", *Journal of Economic Literature* 42: 691-751.

Barrett, C.B. (2001). "Measuring Integration and Efficiency in International Agricultural Markets", *Review of Agricultural Economics* 23: 19-32.

Barrett, Christopher B. (2005). "Spatial Market Integration", in Lawrence E. Blume and Steven N. Durlauf (eds.), The New Palgrave Dictionary of Economics. 2nd Edition. August.

Barret, C.B. and J.Li (1999). "Distinguishing between Equilibrium and Integration in Markets Analysis", *Working Paper* #99-8. International Agricultural Trade Research Consortium.

Barrett, C.B. and J.R. Li (2002). "Distinguishing between Equilibrium and Integration in Spatial Price Analysis", *American Journal of Agricultural Economics* 84: 292-307.

Blauch, B. (1997). "Testing for Food Market Integration Revisited", *Journal of Development Studies* 33: 477-87.

Dasgupta, D., R.N. Dubey and R. Sathish (2011). "Domestic Wheat Price Formation and Food Inflation in India", *Working Paper Series*, Paper No. 2. Department of Economic Affairs, Ministry of Finance, Government of India.

Deaton, A. (1989). "Rice Prices and Income Distribution in Thailand: A Non-parametric Analysis", *Economic Journal* 99(395) (Supplement): 1-37.

————. (1997). *The Analysis of Household Surveys*. World Bank and John Hopkins University Press, Balitmore.

Debroy, Bibek and Amir Ullah Khan (eds.) (2003). *Enabling Agricultural Markets for the Small Indian Farmer*. Bookwell. pp.121-84, 235-76.

De Jenvry, A. and D. Subbarao (1984). "Agricultural Price Policy and Income Distribution in India", *Economic and Political Weekly* 19(51/52): A166-178.

————. (1987). *Agricultural Price Policy and Income Distribution in India*. Delhi: Oxford University Press.

Dickey, David A. and Wayne A. Fuller (1979). "Distribution of the Estimators for Autoregressive Time Series with a Unit Root", *Journal of the American Statistical Association* 74(366): 427-31.

Dimitrios, Asteriou and Stephen G. Hall (2007). *Applied Econometrics: A Modern Approach Using E-Views and Microfit*. Palgrave Macmillan.

Engle, R.F. and C.W.J. Granger (1987). "Co-integration and Error Correction: Representation, Estimation and Testing", *Econometrica* 49: 251-76.

Engle, R.F. and C.W.J. Granger (1987). "Cointegration and Error Correction Representation, Estimation, and Testing", *Econometrica* 55: 251-76, March.

FAO (Food and Agriculture Organization) (2009). *FAO International Commodity Prices Database*. Rome (*http://www.fao.org/es/esc/prices/PricesServlet.jsp?lang=en*).

Froot, K.A. and K. Rogoff (1995). "Perspectives on PPP and Long-Run Real Exchange Rates", in G. Grossman and K. Rogoff (eds.), *Handbook of International Economics*. Vol. 3.

Ghosh, N. and P. Sharma (2009). "Estimating Welfare Impact of a Rise in Prices of Rice and Wheat in India", *Working Paper Series*, SSRN. November 20.

Ghoshray, A. (2009). "On Price Dynamics for Different Qualities of Coffee", *Review of Market Integration* 1(1): 103-18.

Goldberg, P.K. and M.M. Knetter (1997). "Goods Prices and Exchange Rates: What have We Learned?", *Journal of Economic Literature* 35: 1243-72.

Goodwin, B. and P. Fackler (2001). "Spatial Price Analysis", in B. Gardner and G. Rausser (eds.), *Handbook of Agricultural Economics*. Vol. 1(1). Amsterdam: Elsevier.

Granger, C. and P. Newbold (1974). "Spurious Regression in Econometrics", *Journal of Econometrics* 60: 1045-66.

Granger, C.W.J. (1981). "Some Properties of Time Series Data and their Use in Econometric Specification", *Journal of Econometrics* 16: 121-30, May.

Imai, Katsushi, Raghav Gaiha and Ganesh Thapa (2008). "Transmission of World Commodity Prices to Domestic Commodity Prices in India and China", *Brooks World Poverty Institute (BWPI) Working Paper*.

IMF (International Monetary Fund) (2009). "IMF Primary Commodity Prices". *http://www.imf.org/external/np/res/commod/index.asp*

Janvry, Alain de and Elisabeth Sadoulet (2007). "Impact of Rising Food Prices on Household Welfare in India", *Working Paper Series*, University of California, Berkeley.

Johansen, S. (1988). "Statistical Analysis of Cointegration Vectors", *Journal of Economic Dynamics and Control* 12: 231-54, July.

———. (1991). "Estimation and Hypothesis Testing of Cointegration Vectors in Gaussian Vector Autoregressive Models", *Econometrica* 59(6): 1551-80, November.

———. (1995). "Identifying Restrictions of Linear Equations with Applications to Simultaneous Equations and Cointegration", *Journal of Econometrics* 69(1): 111-32, September.

Karmakar, Suparna, Rajiv Kumar and Bibek Debroy (eds.) (2007). *India's Liberalisation Experience Hostage to WTO?* New Delhi: SAGE Publications. pp.39-55, 78-124.

Kose, M.A., C. Otrok and C.H. Whiteman (2008). "Understanding the Evolution of World Business Cycles", *Journal of International Economics* 75(1): 110-30.

Kose, M.A., C. Otrok and E. Prasad (2008). "Global Business Cycles", *IMF Working Paper*.

Maddala, G.S. and I. Kim (1998). *Unit Roots, Co-integration and Structural Change*. Cambridge University Press.

Mackinnon, J.G. (1991). "Critical Values for Cointegration Tests", in R.F. Engle and C.W.J. Granger (eds.), *Long-run Economic Relationships: Readings in Cointegration*. New York: Oxford University Press.

Minot, Nicholas (2010). *Transmission of World Food Price Changes to African Markets and its Effect on Household Welfare*. IFPRI. January.

Ravallion, M. (1986). "Testing Market Integration", *American Journal of Agricultural Economics* 68(2): 292-307.

———. (1990). "Rural Welfare Effects of Food Price Changes Under Induced Wage Responses: Theory and Evidence for Bangladesh", *Oxford Economic Papers* 42: 574-85.

Reddy, Amarender A. (2006). "Commodity Market Integration: Case of Asian Rice Markets", Discussion Paper. Centre for Studies in International Relations and Development (CSIRD).

Rojko, A.S. (1961). "Time Series Analysis in Measurement of Demand", *American Economic Review* 13: 37-54.

Sah, R.K. and J.E. Stiglitz (1987). "Price Scissors and the Structure of the Economy", *Quarterly Journal of Economics* 102(1).

Vyas, V.S. (1999). "Agricultural Trade Policy and Export Strategy", *Economic and Political Weekly* XXXIV(13).

WTO (2009). *Statistics Database*. World Trade Organisation.

6

MONZUR HOSSAIN AND FARHANA RAFIQ

Global Commodity Price Volatility and Domestic Inflation

Impact on the Financial Sector in Bangladesh

Introduction

Inflation in the developing world has been rising in recent years, mainly due to rising trend in food prices in the international market. An 83 per cent increase in global food prices was observed in 2007-08 (World Bank, 2010). The price of rice in the international market rose by 165 per cent between April 2007 and April 2008. During the same period, global wheat price increased by more than 100 per cent. Afterwards, global food prices continued to increase, but to a lesser extent. It is widely argued that global food prices showed an extraordinary increase during the period for several reasons: (i) higher food demand in the emerging economies such as China and India that have led to reductions in food exports from these countries; (ii) rising oil prices; (iii) increased demand for biofuel raw materials such as wheat, soybean, maize, and palm oil; and (iv) reduction of cropland due to biofuel production. Price developments in the global commodity markets have brought to forefront the effects of external price changes on domestic inflation.

Bangladesh has been experiencing persistent price increases, especially of food items, in the backdrop of rising global commodity prices for the last few years. For example, during the period 2006-2008, the price of rice increased by 61 per cent to Tk 29.90 per kg (kilogram) from Tk 17.69 per kg (yearly average), while it increased by 30 per cent during 2009-10. A similar pattern of price increase can be observed for wheat during the same period. Adverse price developments in the international market coupled with increasing prices of production inputs contributed to the rising prices of food commodities in the domestic market. As a result, Bangladesh has been facing high inflationary spiral for the last few years, particularly from 2007.

Overall inflation in Bangladesh rose to 9.94 per cent (yearly average) in 2008 due to higher food inflation (12.28%). This rising trend of inflation persisted in subsequent years as well. It is widely believed that higher domestic food prices reduce income of the households, particularly poor households, in real terms as effective inflation is higher than average inflation for the poor due to higher share of total expenditure devoted to food by the poor households. Thus, higher commodity prices at the international market not only increase the domestic price level, but they also negatively affect the welfare of the poor consumers and farmers. It is usually held that the problem with inflation is not so much with price increases rather the inefficiencies and inequities that result from inflation-induced changes in relative prices. Relative price changes affect supply-demand relationships for both factor and product markets. Changes in these relationships in turn influence the level and distribution of income both at the household as well as firm levels by influencing asset values, cash flows, debt, net worth, and structural characteristics of firms.

Rising trend of inflation not only affects household welfare, it also affects the performance of the financial sector. Inflation affects financial sector through several channels. For example, high inflation rate reduces the rate of return (interest), and thus exacerbates credit market frictions, which lead to credit rationing. If inflation is high enough, it reduces returns on savings, which also limits the supply of loanable funds. Several cross-section studies suggest that high inflation hampers financial development. (Haslag and Koo, 1999; Boyd *et al.*, 2001) These issues are examined in this study to assess the inflation-finance relationships in Bangladesh.

Specifically, this study aims to examine: (i) the extent of global commodity price volatility and whether such volatility in world commodity prices contributes to volatility in domestic prices; and

(ii) the impact of inflation on the financial sector (banks and equity market) performance using both aggregate and bank specific panel data.

The analysis proceeds in two stages. First, the chapter examines the extent to which increase of international food prices during the past few years has been transmitted to domestic prices in Bangladesh. Price transmission for three important food commodities—namely rice, wheat, and edible oil is examined. The pass-through elasticity has been estimated for the above food items using the VECM (vector error correction models). Second, the chapter analyses the impact of inflation on the performance of the financial sector in Bangladesh, particularly on the banking sector and capital market. The effects are analysed by using both aggregate and panel data (only for banks). The threshold ARCH (auto-regressive conditional heteroschedasticity) model has been applied to the aggregate data as it is assumed that inflation-finance relationship is non-linear and a threshold effect of inflation might exist. On the other hand, for bank-specific panel data, the Arellano-Bover/Blundell-Bond dynamic panel GMM (Generalised Method of Moments) estimator has been applied to a panel of 43 banks to assess the impact of inflation on banking performance. The data spans over the period between 1990 and 2010.

The chapter is organised as follows. Following the introduction, section 2 provides a review of theories and empirical evidences on the impact of inflation on the financial sector. Section 3 provides the analytical basis of the present study, that is, it analyses how much domestic inflation is influenced by the international commodity price volatility. Section 4 discusses methodology and the data. Section 5 discusses the empirical results. Finally, Section 6 concludes the chapter.

Review of Literature

Inflation has not been studied seriously in Bangladesh until recently. A few studies tried to cast light on different aspects of inflation in Bangladesh. It is generally argued that inflation in Bangladesh is biased towards food items rather than the non-food items. Although Bangladesh has been able to maintain a low-to-moderate inflation, recent years saw a surge in inflation. Ahsan (2007) tried to explain the causes of inflation in Bangladesh. They find that there exists a statistically significant positive relationship between world food price and domestic inflation. They also report that monetary variables, such as M1, M2 and private sector credit, have long-run (positive and significant) equilibrium relationship with the CPI (consumer price index). Moreover, market capitalisation and remittances also have positive significant effects on inflation.

Mujeri *et al.* (2009) and Shahiduzzaman (2009) attempted to forecast inflation in Bangladesh. While Mujeri *et al.* show an application of the P-star model, Shahiduzzaman argues for core inflation estimation instead of headline inflation for policy purposes. However, none of the available studies examine the impact of inflation on the performance of the financial sector in Bangladesh.

A growing theoretical literature describes mechanisms on how predictable increases in the rate of inflation interfere with the ability of the financial sector to allocate resources effectively. Recent theories emphasise the importance of informational asymmetries in credit markets and demonstrate how increases in the rate of inflation adversely affect credit market frictions with negative repercussions for the financial sector (both banks and equity market) performance and therefore long-run real activity (Huybens and Smith, 1998; 1999). The common feature of these theories is that there is an informational friction whose severity is endogenous. Given this feature, an increase in the rate of inflation reduces the real rate of return. The implied reduction in real returns exacerbates credit market frictions. Since these market frictions lead to the rationing of credit, credit rationing becomes more severe as inflation rises. As a result, the financial sector makes fewer loans, resource allocation is less efficient, and intermediary activity diminishes with adverse implications for capital investment. The reduction in capital formation negatively influences both long-run economic performance and equity market activity (Huybens and Smith, 1999; Boyd and Smith, 1996).

Theoretical studies suggest that if inflation is high enough, returns on savings are reduced, which leads to a reduction in savings, the pool of borrowers is swamped, and therefore credit becomes scarce in such an economy (Moore, 1986; Choi *et al.*, 1996; and Azariadis and Smith, 1996). In a slightly different strand, Schreft and Smith (1997), Boyd and Smith (1998), Huybens and Smith (1998), and Huybens and Smith (1999) explore the idea that economies with higher rates of inflation do not approach or reach the steady state where their capital stocks would be high, i.e. there are bifurcations, and development traps arise in such economies. Furthermore, financial markets in these economies are likely to be less efficient because of the higher interest rates that follow high rates of inflation. That is, the Mundell-Tobin effect[1] is relevant in a high inflation environment.

Rajan and Zingales (2003) highlight a political-economy dimension of inflation in financial development. Vested interests or incumbents trying to curtail competition play an important role in keeping (financial) development relatively low. Moreover, Acemoglu *et al.* (2003) argue that distortionary macroeconomic policies that fail to contain high inflation indicate weak institutions.

On the empirical side, Haslag and Koo (1999), and Boyd *et al.* (2001), using cross-sectional and panel international data from the 1960s to early 1990s, show that moderate inflation has a negative impact on financial development. Moreover, both studies find evidence of nonlinearities. Boyd *et al.* find that after a particular threshold—15 per cent per year—inflation presents only smaller marginal negative effects on financial development. The intuition is that the damage on financial development is done at rates of inflation lower than the proposed threshold. Moreover, Dehesa *et al.* (2007) use a panel of 120 countries between 1997 and 2004 to report that lower inflation increases the amount of credit in their sample.

1. The Mundell–Tobin effect suggests that nominal interest rates would rise less than one-for-one with inflation because in response to inflation the public would hold less in money balances and more in other assets, which would drive interest rates down. In other words, an increase in the exogenous growth rate of money increases the nominal interest rate and velocity of money, but decreases the real interest rate. The importance of the Mundell–Tobin effect is that it appears as a deviation from the classical dichotomy.

Furthermore, Choi, *et al.* (1996) use historical data from different countries, such as United States (US), Chile, Korea and Taiwan to confirm that inflation presents a negative impact on stock-market development in each of these countries.

Boyd *et al.* (2001) summarise the impact of inflation on the performance of the financial sector as follows:

i) higher rates of inflation are associated with greater interest and stock return variability.
ii) higher inflation implies less long-run financial activity. In economies with high inflation, intermediaries will lend less and allocate capital less effectively, and equity markets will be smaller and less liquid.
iii) inflation threshold may characterise the relationship between inflation and financial sector conditions. Most prominently, once inflation exceeds a critical level, incremental increases in the (long-run) rate of inflation might have less impact on financial sector activity.

Global Commodity Price and Domestic Inflation

Inflation Trend

The Bangladesh economy experienced a moderate rate of inflation in the last two decades. However, sources of higher inflation were different. While non-food inflation dominated in the first half of the 1990s, food inflation dominated in the latter half of the 1990s. Bangladesh experienced a low rate of inflation, at an average rate of less than 2.5 per cent during 2001-02; when a relatively low price of food at that time played the key role in overall price developments (Table 6.1). However, in the following two years, the inflation rate jumped to 5.1 per cent, followed by an average of 7.0 per cent during 2005-2007. In 2008, the 12-month average inflation rate rose to 9.94 per cent. A similar rising pattern of inflation continued in the subsequent years with a dominant role of food inflation.

Table 6.1

Inflation in Bangladesh and Other Country Groupings, 2001-2010

Year	*Bangladesh*			*Global*		
	General	*Food*	*Non-food*	*World*	*Advanced Economies*	*Developing Economies*
2001	1.94	1.38	3.04	4.06	2.15	6.72
2002	2.76	1.63	4.61	3.36	1.47	6.01
2003	4.38	3.46	5.45	3.65	1.86	6.15
2004	5.83	6.93	5.91	3.57	2.03	5.70
2005	6.49	7.90	6.32	3.63	2.32	5.45
2006	7.16	7.76	5.90	3.52	2.30	5.20
2007	7.20	8.11	6.40	3.90	2.21	6.13
2008	9.94	12.28	4.33	3.90	3.40	9.70
2009	6.66	7.19	4.37	2.20	-0.10	5.50
2010	7.31	8.53	5.66	3.40	1.60	6.20

Note: * Until May 2010.

Source: Bangladesh Bureau of Statistics (BBS); International Financial Statistics (IFS), International Monetary Fund (IMF).

Figure 6.1

International Prices of Selected Food Commodities (US$/month)

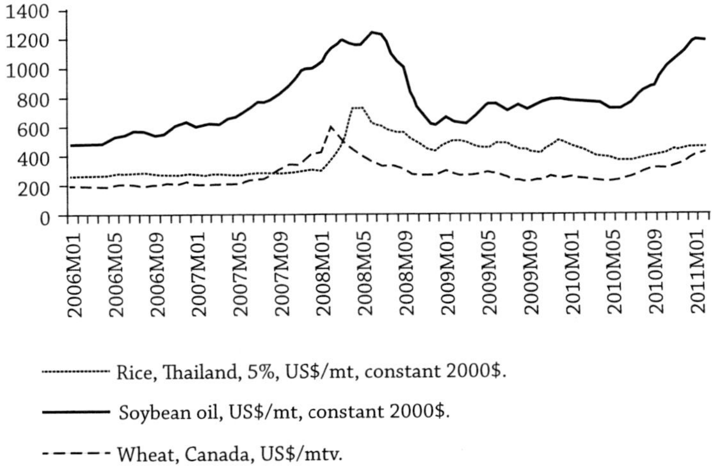

Source: Pink Data Set, the World Bank.

One general characteristic of recent inflation is that food inflation has been higher than non-food inflation along with increasing gap between the two. Though the role of food inflation in overall inflation was insignificant during 2001-2003, food inflation started to soar since 2004 which in turn, led to rising overall inflation (Table 6.1). Figure 6.1 shows that the price movements of some selected commodities in Bangladesh and global markets exhibit almost similar trend. As Figure 6.1 shows, the prices of some commodities, particularly rice, soybean oil, and wheat were exceptionally high in 2008.

Figure 6.2

Domestic Prices of Selected Food Commodities (Tk/kg)

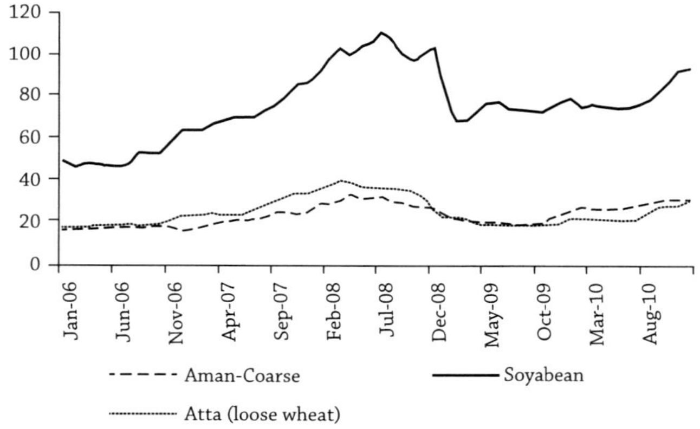

Source: Bangladesh Bureau of Statistics (BBS), Bangladesh Bank.

Commodity Price Volatility

We have provided commodity-specific price volatility for the period 2006-2010 in Table 6.2. Using monthly data, we estimated volatility of prices for *aman* rice (coarse and medium), soybean oil, palm oil, TSP and urea fertilisers for Bangladesh in Panel A and global price volatility in Panel B of Table 6.2. Commodity-specific price volatility was found to be higher in 2007-08 and again in 2010 in Bangladesh. For the year 2008, high price volatility is observed for rice, palm oil, Triple Superphosphate (TSP) and urea in Bangladesh as well as in international markets. While commodity price volatility reduced slightly in 2009, it again increased in 2010.

The volatility of commodity prices indicates that commodity price movements in Bangladesh largely follow the global commodity price trend. It calls for an analysis of the extent of pass-through effect on specific commodities so that policy makers can understand how much of global commodity price transmits to domestic prices.

Table 6.2

Commodity-Specific Price Volatility, 2006-2010

A. Commodity-specific price volatility in Bangladesh (monthly)

	Aman Medium	*Aman Coarse*	*Soybean Oil*	*Palm Oil*	*TSP*	*Urea*
2006	2.315	0.721	4.971	4.443	0.502	0.341
2007	2.183	2.809	7.498	12.082	9.617	0.175
2008	3.961	2.350	5.328	12.996	18.178	2.966
2009	2.893	1.846	3.400	5.111	7.443	0.113
2010	2.060	2.326	6.963	8.522	0.349	0.130

B. Global commodity-specific price volatility (monthly)

	Rice Thai 5%	*Rice Thai 25%*	*Soybean Oil*	*Palm Oil*	*TSP*	*Urea*
2006	8.15	6.23	26.58	19.00	1.39	18.8
2007	5.88	6.24	70.27	80.35	79.25	39.32
2008	127.06	158.85	161.49	134.49	248.13	197.12
2009	56.55	104.19	161.31	28.56	43.38	12.8
2010	36.42	32.21	51.74	20.65	60.17	48.81

Source: A. Department of Agricultural Marketing, Dhaka; B. Global Commodity Price, World Bank. Pink Data Set and United Nations Conference on Trade and Development (UNCTAD) Commodity Price Statistics.

Pass-through Effect: Error Correction Model Estimation

In this section, we estimate the pass-through elasticities for Bangladesh for the period 2000-2010 using a simple methodology applied for Australia by De Brouwer and Ericsson (1995), for Mexico by Garcé Diaz (1999) and for a cross-country analysis by Hausmann *et al.* (2001). The analysis is performed to assess the extent of pass-through effect of international commodity price volatility into domestic inflation.

We consider the model of domestic prices using a mark-up equation as follows:

$$P = \alpha W^{\theta} F^{\gamma} \qquad (1)$$

where P is domestic price, W wages, F international prices in domestic currency (obtained by multiplying the exchange rate with an index of international prices) and α, θ, and γ are three parameters representing mark up and the long run elasticities of wages and external prices. By taking the natural logarithm of the above equation it is possible to estimate the long run relationship among wages, international prices and local prices. Since we do not have the monthly data for wages, we estimate the following four long-run equations:

$$P = ln(\alpha) + \gamma f \qquad (2)$$

$$R_d = ln(\alpha) + \gamma_2 R_f \qquad (3)$$

$$W_d = ln(\alpha) + \gamma_3 W_f \qquad (4)$$

$$S_d = ln(\alpha) + \gamma_4 S_f \qquad (5)$$

In equation (2), p is the log of CPI of Bangladesh and f is obtained by adding the log of the US dollar exchange rate of Taka to the log of an index of international non-energy commodity price. In equation (3), R_d represents log of prices of rice (*aman* coarse) in the domestic market and R_f represents log of price of rice in the international market (Thai rice, 5%) expressed in domestic currency (Taka). Similarly, equations (4) and (5) are estimated for wheat and soybean oil. All the series we use are monthly and can be described as having a unit root process. Hence, we need to study the long-run relationship between internal and external prices using cointegration analysis as well as the speed of adjustment. For this reason, we apply the VECM.

Table 6.3

Estimates of Pass-through Elasticities, 2000-2010

	Changes in International Prices (Non-Energy)	*Rice (Thailand, 5%)*	*Soybean Oil*
Pass-through coeff. (γ)	0.47 (0.05)***	-0.21 (0.08)**	0.77 (.03)***
Constant	-0.52	-7.09	1.81
ECT (error correction term)	-0.01 (0.01)**	-0.06 (0.02)**	-0.23 (.10)**

Note: ***, ** indicate significance at 10 per cent and 5 per cent level respectively.

Table 6.3 shows that the long run pass-through coefficient is reasonably high and significant for Bangladesh. It is 0.47 for international commodity prices, -0.21 for the rice price and 0.77 for the soybean oil prices. This indicates that except for rice, any change in international commodity prices has a moderate positive effect on domestic prices. The reason of negative pass-through effect for rice could be that in recent times Bangladesh imports rice mainly from India and that is why Bangladeshi rice price could not follow the trend of Thai rice price. For soybean oil, which is completely an imported item, 77 per cent change of its international price translates to the domestic prices. The estimated error correction term is negative and significant indicating that the speed of adjustment to equilibrium is 1 per cent for international commodity prices, 6 per cent for rice prices and 23 per cent for soybean oil prices.

In summary, the analysis in this section suggests that commodity price volatility has been substantially high worldwide since 2007, and this has been the case for Bangladesh as well. Pass-through elasticity for non-energy commodities is estimated to be about 0.5, implying that almost 50 per cent change in global commodity prices translates into domestic prices. As we discussed earlier, high inflationary episodes might affect the performance of the financial sector. Since the Bangladesh economy has been facing a structural change in inflationary episodes, in the following sections we endeavour to analyse the impact of inflation on the performance of the financial sector of Bangladesh.

Data and Methodology

We use data on inflation, banking sector activity, equity market size, equity market liquidity, and the rates of return on stocks for Bangladesh for the period 1990–2009.[2] To assess the consequences of

2. The formal financial sector in Bangladesh, as in other regions of the developing world, essentially consists of banks. Although non-bank financial institutions and stock markets have been developing in Bangladesh, their influence generally remains marginal compared to the banking sector. The banking sector comprises of 48 banks including 4 state-owned banks (SCBs), 30 private commercial banks (PCBs), 5 specialised banks (SBs) and 9 foreign commercial banks (FCBs). Bangladeshi banks have been operating in a sound and stable macroeconomic environment for the last two decades. During this period, Bangladesh registered five to six per cent GDP (gross domestic product) growth with annual inflation rate ranges between two to nine per cent. The expectation is high on the banking sector as Bangladesh is envisioned to become a middle income country by 2021.

different long-run rates of inflation, we primarily use data averaged over the entire period. Next we examine the relationship between inflation and financial sector conditions using bank panel data for 48 banks, and particularly for different categories of banks. As the Bangladeshi banking sector is characterised by different types of banks, such as state-owned commercial banks, private commercial banks, specialised banks and foreign commercial banks with different level of efficiency, their performance might vary with the increase of inflation.

Analysing the aggregate data enables us to focus on the long-run relationship, as opposed to the cyclical relationship between inflation and financial sector activity. In addition, we conduct a panel estimation to exploit the time-series dimension of the data and control for possible endogeneity and omitted variable bias associated with the financial sector analysis.

We regress each of our measures of financial sector performance on inflation plus a conditioning information set of variables designed to control for economic development and other factors influencing financial sector performance. In particular, we examine the following aspects of inflation on the financial sector of Bangladesh:

(i) Applying the TARCH (Threshold ARCH) model to the time series aggregate data for the period 1990-2010, we assess the impact of inflation on the banking sector activities such as private credit, bank assets, liquid liabilities as well as on capital market indicators, such as market capitalisation, value traded, turnover after controlling for other factors, and

(ii) Applying the Arelano-Bover/Blundell-Bond GMM estimator to a panel of 43 commercial banks in Bangladesh for the same period, we examine whether there is any particular variations in the performance of specific types of banks in the context of rising trend of domestic inflation.

Data

As already mentioned, our dependent variables are assets, liquid liabilities (deposits only) and private credit for the banking sector analysis. For the capital market analysis, we use market capitalisation (MCAP), issued capital, value traded, turnover and equity return.

These variables are regressed on a set of explanatory variables including inflation. For the analysis of aggregate data, we consider only the per capita income as the control variable. For the bank panel data, some bank-specific variables such as ME (management efficiency), bank rate, interest rate spread are used as control variables.

Banking Data Set, 1990–2010

The 'banking data set' focuses on measures of banking development. Both aggregate and panel data cover the period 1990–2010.

Liquid liabilities is the ratio of liquid liabilities of the financial sector (currency plus demand and interest-bearing liabilities of banks and non-bank financial intermediaries) to GDP. Particularly, we consider different types of deposits held with banks in this category. This indicator measures the overall size of the formal financial intermediary sector, and has been found to be very strongly associated with both the level and rate of change of real per capita GDP (King and Levine, 1993a; 1993b).

An alternative measure is bank assets, which is the ratio of total assets of 'deposit money banks' (commercial banks and other deposit taking banks) to GDP. This variable measures the importance of deposit money banks, as reflected in their total assets, relative to the economy. Both liquid liabilities and bank assets are expressed as a per cent of GDP. Liquid liabilities and bank assets are size measures and do not consider the allocation of capital between the private and public sectors.

Therefore, private credit is used as a financial intermediary development measure. This measure equals banking institution credits to the private sector as a percentage of GDP. Thus, private Credit is not merely a measure of size. It isolates credits to the private sector and excludes credits issued to the government, government agencies, and public enterprises. This measure of financial development has been found to exert a causal impact on economic growth (Levine *et al.*, 2000).

For inflation, we use 12-month average inflation from the CPI data.

The sources of data are Economic Trends, Schedule Bank Statistics, Monetary Policy Review of the Bangladesh Bank (central bank). Bank-specific data are collected from commercial banks' annual reports.

Stock Market Data Set, 1990–2010

The 'stock market data set' consists of data from the Dhaka Stock Exchange and the Chittagong Stock Exchange and covers the period 1990–2010. We consider five financial performance measures, such as MCAP, issued capital, value traded, turnover and equity returns.

Market capitalisation (MCAP) equals the value of listed domestic company shares on major stock exchanges as a per cent of GDP. MCAP measures the overall size of markets. Analysts frequently use this as an indicator of stock market development, although of course MCAP does not measure stock market activity, but merely the value of listed shares. While positively associated with the level of economic development (Demirguc-Kunt and Levine, 1996), *MCAP* is not robustly linked to economic growth (Levine and Zervos, 1998).

Turnover equals the total value of shares traded (times 100) divided by the market capitalisation (that is, value traded*100/MCAP). Thus, turnover measures trading volume relative to the size of the market. Both value traded and turnover are frequently used as indicators of market liquidity—the ability to trade equities easily. The measures complement one another since Value Traded measures trading relative to the size of the economy and Turnover measures trading relative to the size of the market. Both Value Traded and Turnover are highly correlated with the level of real per capita GDP as well as its rate of growth (Demirguc-Kunt and Levine, 1996; Levine and Zervos, 1998). Here we consider only turnover for the analysis.

Finally, equity returns is the rate of growth of the nominal stock market price index. This measures the nominal rate of return (excluding dividends) from holding the index portfolio of major stock exchanges.

Stock market data is collected from stock exchange websites, publications of the Securities and Exchange Commission (SEC) and economic trends of the Bangladesh Bank. The summary statistics of the variables are reported in Table 6.4.

Table 6.4

Summary Statistics of Variables (Yearly Data)

A. Banks

Variable	*Obs.*	*Mean*	*Std. Dev.*	*Min.*	*Max.*
Private credit	18	24.02	6.25	15.01	34.83
Asset	18	115.34	41.78	40.59	159.09
Liability	18	31.13	7.53	19.36	42.76
Inflation	18	5.70	2.46	1.94	9.94

B. Capital Market

Variable	*Obs.*	*Mean*	*Std. Dev.*	*Min.*	*Max.*
Turnover	19	49.29	56.02	--	212.56
Equity return	13	11.84	54.26	-67.66	126.39
MCAP	19	4.34	3.05	0.86	11.17
Value traded	19	2.74	4.32	0.009	16.42
Inflation	18	5.69	2.46	1.94	9.94

Note: *Variables are expressed as per cent of GDP.

Methodology

A general regression model is specified as follows:

$$FSI_{i,t} = \alpha + \beta B_{i,t} + \gamma I_t + \delta M_t + \varepsilon_{i,t} \qquad (7)$$

where, FSI represents financial sector indicators, $B_{i,t}$ is a vector of bank-specific variables for bank *i* and time *t*; I_t contains time-varying market and ownership structure variables; M_t is a vector of time-varying macroeconomic variables.

Aggregate Time-series Data: Threshold ARCH Model

The aggregate data might have some time-series properties and they might depict long-term relationship. To examine the order of integration of the series, the Augmented Dickey-Fuller (ADF) test has been employed. The test suggests that the series under consideration have unit root properties.

As was discussed, variations in financial data depict non-linearity with inflation and thus a non-linear time-series model, namely the TARCH model is applied to aggregate time-series data. In the context of nonlinear time series, TAR (threshold autoregression) appears to be useful in a variety of financial applications mainly because TAR models are known to explain nonlinear features such as limit cycles and asymmetry (see Tong, 1990: Chapter 1). The simplest first-order TAR model was investigated by Petruccelli and Woolford (1984). It is defined by the equation

$$Xt = \theta_1 X^{+}_{t-1} + \theta_2 X^{-}_{t-1} + \varepsilon_t; \tag{8}$$

where $\{\varepsilon_t\}$ is a sequence of *iid* (independent and identically distributed) random variables. The notation X^{+}_{t} = max(Xt ; 0) and X^{-}_{t} = min(Xt ; 0) will be used throughout. They studied necessary and sufficient conditions of the ergodicity of equation (8) and discussed conditional least-squares estimation of the parameters. The random coefficient version of equation (8) in which θ_1 and θ_2 are permitted to be random was studied by Brockwell *et al.* (1992) and later by Hwang and Basawa (1994).

The present study deals with the case where the innovation $\{\varepsilon_t\}$ in equation (1) forms a variant of ARCH process where threshold concept is built into $\{\varepsilon_t\}$. Specifically $\{\varepsilon_t\}$ is assumed to be generated by the following equations:

$$\varepsilon_t = \sqrt{h_t}\, e_t \tag{9}$$

$$h_t = \alpha_0 + \alpha_1 (\varepsilon^{+}_{t-1})^2 + \alpha_2 (\varepsilon^{-}_{t-1})^2 \tag{10}$$

where $\{e_t\}$ is a *iid* sequence with arbitrary marginal pdf (probability density function) of zero mean and unit variance, and e_t is independent of ε_{t-s}; $s \geq 1$. Also α_0, α_1 and α_2 are parameters satisfying $\alpha_0 > 0$ and $0 \leq \alpha_j < 1$; j = 1; 2.

Consequently, the model specified by equations (8)–(10) allows a 'threshold' both in the conditional mean and in the conditional variance of the time series and thus we call this threshold ARCH(1) (TARCH(1), for short).

It may be noted that for $\theta_1 = \theta_2$ and $\theta_1 = \theta_2$, the TARCH (1) process reduces to the standard AR(1)-ARCH(1) model first introduced by Engle (1982).

Bank Panel Data: GMM Estimator

In the banking sector analysis, not all firm characteristics are captured in the available data. Information on managerial risk aversion, revealed preferences, governance structure, cash flow characteristics, and other relevant information may be difficult to measure. Ignoring the unobserved firm-level heterogeneity imposes the incorrect assumption of zero correlation between the observed variables and the unobserved effect. This leads to biased and inconsistent estimates (Wooldridge, 2002).

To address the biases, there are a number of choices. The first option is to use a traditional IV (instrumental variables) approach. If an appropriate IV is available, it can be used to instrument for the lagged dependent variable. However, in corporate finance, reliable instruments are difficult to find. Arellano and Bond (1991) suggest a GMM, or difference GMM estimator. They first-difference the panel data and then use the endogenous (or predetermined) lagged variables' levels to instrument for the transformed lagged dependent variable. The lagged levels provide little information about the first differences when the underlying series are relatively stationary and therefore, are weak instruments (Arellano and Bover, 1995; Blundell and Bond, 1998). The Arellano-Bover/Blundell-Bond GMM employs additional moment conditions based on the lagged variables' first differences (in addition to their levels) to increase the efficiency of estimation.

Therefore, to increase the efficiency of estimates as well as to capture some unobserved effects, the Arellano-Bover/Blundell-Bond GMM model is applied in the analysis following Boyd *et al.* (2001). We employ the GMM regressions for different sub-periods (pre- and post-liberalisation period—before 1999 and after 1999) as well as for different types of banks in Bangladesh.

Empirical Results

The empirical results are obtained by analysing aggregated banking and capital market data as well as bank panel data. For aggregate data, we analyse data for 18 years covering the period 1991-2010. Bank panel data, consisting of data from 48 banks also cover the same period.

Aggregate Analysis

Correlation between Variables

Pair-wise correlation between variables is estimated in Table 6.5. Since the literature review suggests that threshold effect of inflation may exist, we therefore examine if there is any such threshold effect in the case of financial performance in Bangladesh. We find that if annual inflation rate exceeds 4.6 per cent, it has some negative effects on financial development indicators (Panel A). Considering the inflation threshold at 4.6 per cent, we thus observe correlation between variables. While financial performance indicators and inflation depict positive and negligible correlation, they have negative correlation once inflation exceeds the threshold level. Particularly, higher inflation is negatively and significantly correlated with asset value of the banking sector, indicating existence of the threshold effect.

In Panel B (Table 6.5), we estimate the correlation coefficients between capital market indicators and inflation. While inflation has positive correlation with capital market indicators, higher inflation (threshold effect) is negatively correlated with MCAP and value traded.

All the financial variables are positively and significantly correlated with each other at high confidence levels.

Table 6.6 (Panel A) presents the average of indicators after sorting by inflation and creating percentile (quartile) groups. The first noteworthy feature is that the inflation rates in the second and third percentile groups remains very close to each other (about 6%

Table 6.5

Estimated Pair-wise Correlation between Variables

A. Banks

	Overall			*Inflation > 4.6*		
	Private Credit	*Asset*	*Liability*	*Private Credit*	*Asset*	*Liability*
Private Credit	1			1		
Asset	0.79 (0.0001)	1		0.63 (0.05)	1	
Liability	0.96 (0.00)	0.78 (0.0001)	1	0.9706 (0.00)	0.72 (0.01)	1
Inflation	0.26 (0.27)	0.02 (0.94)	0.11 (0.64)	-0.09 (0.79)	-0.52*** (0.11)	-0.24 (0.49)
N						

B. Capital Market

	Overall				*Inflation > 4.6*			
	Turnover	*Equity Return*	*MCAP*	*Value Traded*	*Turnover*	*Equity Ratio*	*MCAP*	*Value Traded*
Turnover	1				1			
Equity return	0.19 (0.51)	1			0.11 (0.78)	1		
MCAP	0.49 (0.03)	0.63 (0.02)	1		0.45 (0.16)	0.68 (0.06)	1	
Value traded	0.89 (0.00)	0.30 (0.30)	0.60 (0.01)	1	0.93 (0.00)	0.20 (0.62)	0.51 (0.10)	1
Inflation	0.22 (0.3791)	0.12 (0.70)	0.39*** (0.10)	0.46*** (0.05)	0.44** (0.19)	-0.38 (0.39)	-0.19 (0.58)	0.44** (0.19)

Note: *, **, *** indicate significance at 10%, 5% and 1% level.

versus 7%). However, inflation in the second and fourth percentile group dramatically exceeds the one in the first and third percentile group. The second noteworthy feature is that the three banking sector performance measures tend to increase albeit slightly, as inflation rises up to the third percentile group level, and decline very substantially if inflation exceeds third percentile group level, i.e. if annual average inflation rate exceeds 7.2 per cent. Note, however, that most of the 'action' occurs at the extremes—in the sense that the two middle quartile groupings differ substantially from the lowest and highest inflation quartiles. The second and third quartiles, however, do not exhibit much difference in banking development, suggesting that the finance-inflation relationship may be nonlinear.

Table 6.6

Financial Indicators (Average) Sorted by Inflation

A. Banks

	Asset	*Liability*	*Private Credit*	*Inflation*
p25	106.10	29.63	21.58	3.28
p50	118.59	30.58	23.33	6.15
p75	137.01	35.57	27.70	7.2
p99	96.55	28.02	23.18	9.94

B. Capital Market

Stats	*Turnover*	*Equity Return*	*MCAP*	*Value Traded*	*Inflation*
p25	40.79	1.19	2.40	0.99	3.28
p50	24.33	17.34	3.41	0.79	6.15
p75	36.88	23.50	6.77	2.74	7.20
p99	59.60	-17.12	3.78	3.46	9.94

Table 6.6 (Panel B) reports the results for the capital market indicators after the data have been sorted by inflation and broken into quartiles. For the lowest and highest inflation categories, turnover and value traded are found to be the highest while for the second and third inflation categories, all the indicators tend to increase. This implies that with the rise of inflation, value of stocks rises, thereby value traded increases. However, the rise in inflation

decreases equity returns and market capitalisation, as expected. Note that correlation analysis does not mean causality; therefore, we perform regression analysis in the following section.

Regression Analysis

Before running regression, we test the unit root properties of the variables. ADF test confirms that the financial sector indicators have a unit root. The results of the unit root tests are reported in Table 6.7. Since our preliminary analysis in the previous section suggests that threshold effect of inflation might exist in the financial sector performance, we therefore apply the TARCH model.

Table 6.7

ADF Test Statistics

Variables	*Test Statistic*	*Variables*	*Test Statistic*
Asset	1.488	MCAP	-2.209
Liquid liability	5.933	Value Traded	3.533
Inflation	-2.444	Turnover Ratio	-0.372
Per capita GDP	11.146	Equity Return	-2.65*

Note: *Significant at 10% level.

The TARCH model estimates for banks and the capital market are reported in Table 6.8 (Panel A and B respectively). For estimating the TARCH model, we consider only three indicators of capital market depending on the availability of monthly data.

The Threshold ARCH Model estimates suggest a long-run negative inflation-finance relationship. Inflation has negative effect on bank assets, private credit and deposits as well as capital market indicators, such as market capitalisation, total issued capital and turnover. The results are consistent with existing cross-country studies.

Panel Estimation

In this section, we present the results of a panel GMM estimator. The panel estimation: (i) exploits the time-series (as well as the cross-section) dimension of our data set; and (ii) accounts for the

Table 6.8

Threshold ARCH Estimates

A. For the Banking Sector

	Deposits			*Asset*			*Private Sector Credit*		
	Whole Period (1990-2009)	*Pre-liberalisation (Before 1999)*	*Post-liberalisation (After 1999)*	*Whole Period (1990-2009)*	*Pre-liberalisation (Before 1999)*	*Post-liberalisation (After 1999)*	*Whole Period (1990-2009)*	*Pre-liberalisation (Before 1999)*	*Post-liberalisation (after 1999)*
Inflation rate	- 0.009 (0.007)	- 0.02 (0.01)**	- 0.002 (0.001)**	-0.006 (0.008)	-0.004 (0.01)	-0.002 (0.01)	-0.006 (0.005)	-0.02 (0.01)**	0.0009 (0.001)
Per capita income (logarithm)	0.28 (0.11)***	0.43 (0.52)	0.29 (0.01)***	1.03 (0.08)***	3.69 (0.34)***	-0.73 (0.14)***	0.24 (0.08)***	0.33 (0.43)	0.28 (0.01)***
Constant	-2.41 (1.04)***	-3.82 (4.87)	-2.55 (0.10)***	-9.02 (0.84)***	-34.4 (3.25)***	8.66 (1.43)***	-2.12 (0.77)***	-2.91 (4.05)	-2.47 (0.14)***
N	212	112	117	212	111	118	212	112	117

B. For Capital Market

	Market Capitalisation			*Total Issued Capital+*	*Private Sector Credit+*
	Whole Period (1990-2009)	*Pre-liberalisation (Before 1999)*	*Post-liberalisation (After 1999)*	*Post-liberalisation (After 1999)*	*Post-liberalisation (After 1999)*
Inflation rate	- 0.00008 (0.002)	- 0.002 (0.0009)***	- 0.009 (0.002)***	-0.0006 (0.0002)	0.003*** (0.0006)
Per capita income (logarithm)	0.16 (0.02)***	0.15 (0.03)***	0.46 (0.02)***	0.04 (0.002)***	0.095 (0.009)***
Constant	-1.90 (0.20)***	-1.35 (0.28)***	-4.55 (0.23)***	-0.35 (0.02)***	-0.92 (0.09)***
N	230	113	117	90	110

Note: +Data are analysed only for the post-liberalisation period based on data availability.*, ** and *** represent significance at 10%, 5% and 1% level respectively.

possibility that financial market performance and inflation are simultaneously determined variables. We conduct the analysis for the banking performance measures. The panel consists of 43 banks over the period 1990–2010.

Blundell and Bond (1997) show that this estimator reduces the inefficiencies and inconsistencies of alternative panel estimators (e.g. Arellano and Bond, 1991). The consistency of the GMM estimator depends on: (i) the validity of the instruments; and (ii) the assumption that the differenced error terms do not exhibit second order serial correlation. We use two tests proposed by Arellano and Bond (1991) to test these assumptions. The first is the Sargan test of over-identifying restrictions, which tests the overall validity of the instruments by analysing the sample analog of the moment conditions used in the estimation procedure. The second test examines the assumption of no second-order serial correlation. Failure to reject the null hypotheses of both tests lends support to our estimation procedure.

Table 6.9 reports the results. While inflation has positive and significant impact on assets, relatively high inflation has negative and significant effect (as INFTH—inflation threshold is negative). Again, while there is some attenuation of the coefficient estimates relative to the pure cross-section estimates, the GMM panel estimates are consistent with our earlier finding that inflation exerts a positive impact on banking sector development, especially at low-to-moderate rates of inflation, but exerts a negative impact when it crosses a certain threshold. Furthermore, the diagnostic tests indicate that our econometric specification and the assumption of no serial correlation in the white-noise error terms cannot be rejected.

In Table 6.10 we assess the impact of inflation on the Bangladeshi banking sector for the pre-liberalisation (before 1999) and post-liberalisation (after 1999) period. With liberalisation toward a market oriented interest rate policy under the FSRP (Financial Sector Reform Programme) in the 1990s, the banks were allowed to set lending and deposit interest rates within bands set by the Bangladesh Bank; later the bands were removed allowing the banks to set interest rates along the lines of market conditions. In 1999, other restrictions were removed in order to enable banks to enjoy greater flexibility in setting interest rates and other banking operations. Thus, inflation might have a different impact on the banking activities in the liberalised period as banks were allowed to set interest rates based on market conditions. The results suggest that inflation has positive and significant effect on assets and deposits of banks in the liberalised period. We do not find any significant impact of inflation on the banking activities for the pre-liberalised period.

Table 6.9

GMM Estimator for Assessing the Impact of Inflation on Bank Activities

	Asset	*Deposits*	*Asset*	*Deposits*
L1.	0.64 (0.04)***	0.77 (.02)***	0.66 (.03)***	0.77 (.02)***
INF	0.02 (0.01)**	0.005 (0.005)	--	--
INFTH	--	--	-0.03 (.07)	0.02 (.04)
GDP	0.14 (0.04)***	0.11 (.02)***	0.15 (.04)***	0.11 (.02)***
INTSPREAD	-0.08 (0.03)**	-.04 (.01)***	-0.09 (.03)***	-0.04 (.01)***
ME	-0.39 (.63)	0.24 (.30)	-0.46 (.63)	0.22 (0.005)
BANKRATE	-0.01 (.01)	-0.02 (.005)***	-0.002 (.01)	-0.02 (.005)***
CONS	8.27 (0.89)	5.12 (0.45)***	7.90 (0.90)***	5.09 (0.45)***
N	350	348	350	348
Sargan Test	116.24	275.06***	116.64	274.25***

Notes: Standard errors are in parentheses. ***, ** and * indicate significance at 1%, 5% and 10% level. INF represents Inflation rate (annual average); INFTH represents inflation threshold at 4.6%; GDP represents GDP growth rate, INTSPREAD represents interest rate spread; ME represents management efficiency (interest expense/total loan); and BANKRATE represents central bank discount rate.

Table 6.10

Impact of Inflation on Bank Activities in the Liberalised Period

	Asset (Pre-liberalisation Period, Before 1999)	*Asset (Post-liberalisation, After 1999)*	*Deposits (Pre-liberalisation period, Before 1999)*	*Deposits (Post-liberalisation, After 1999)*
L1.	0.94 (0.05)***	0.58 (.05)***	0.82 (.07)***	0.72 (0.03)***
INF	0.01 (0.01)	0.05 (0.02)***	0.001 (0.01)	0.02 (0.01)**
GDP	- 0.06 (0.05)	0.16 (0.06)***	0.03 (0.06)***	0.12 (0.03)***
INTSPREAD	-0.02 (0.03)**	-0.08 (.03)***	0.01 (0.04)***	-0.04 (.01)***
ME	1.86 (1.08)*	-0.31 (0.73)	3.52 (1.38)***	0.23 (0.31)
BANKRATE	-0.10 (.07)	-0.02 (0.02)	-0.03 (0.10)***	-0.02 (.01)***
CONS	2.62 (0.91)***	9.60 (1.13)***	3.86 (1.27)***	6.22 (0.57)***
N	101	249	101	249
Sargan Test	71.63***	77.82	91.78***	190.16***

Note: Standard errors are in parentheses. ***, ** and * indicate significance at 1%, 5% and 10% level. Notes: Standard errors are in parentheses. ***, ** and * indicate significance at 1%, 5% and 10% level. INF represents inflation rate (annual average); INFTH represents inflation threshold; GDP represents GDP growth rate; INTSPREAD represents interest rate spread; ME represents management efficiency (interest expense/total loan); and BANKRATE represents central bank discount rate.

Next we analyse the impact of inflation on different types of banks. In Bangladesh, there are about 48 banks including four SCBs, 30 PCBs, 5 SBs, and 9 FCBs. Private banks were allowed to operate in Bangladesh from the early 1980s. Since the SCBs are highly controlled by the government, PCBs appear to lack proper competition and efficiency (Hossain, 2010). Therefore, behaviour of different banks in response to inflation may vary. In Table 6.11 we analyse the impact of inflation on assets and deposits of different types of banks.

The results in Table 6.11 suggest that the impact of inflation on Assets of SCBs and PCBs are positive and significant, while the impact is negative for Deposits of SCBs. For SCBs, none of the indicators are significantly associated with inflation—one of the reasons could be small sample size for SCBs.

Conclusions

This study, for the first time, analyses the impact of inflation on the financial sector in Bangladesh. Bangladesh has maintained a low-to-moderate inflation for the last two decades. However, in recent years, like in other developing countries, Bangladesh has also faced higher inflationary spiral. Our analysis suggests that inflation in Bangladesh follows the global trend of inflation. The estimated pass-through elasticities are found to be high for the commodities that are fully imported, for example, edible oil.

In the backdrop of rising inflationary spirals worldwide particularly after 2007, a pertinent issue is: what has happened to Bangladesh, particularly to its financial sector. It is important to analyse the impact of inflation on the financial sector as high inflation is likely to affect the credit market by shrinking the supply of loanable funds. Our descriptive analysis suggests that moderate inflation (6-7%) might have a positive impact on the financial development, while very low and high inflation has a detrimental effect on the financial sector. Also, it is evident from the analysis that threshold effect of inflation might exist, that is, inflation affects the financial activities if it crosses a critical level (threshold). Therefore, we apply the non-linear TARCH model to the aggregate time-series (monthly) data of banks and the capital market. The results suggest that there has been a long-run negative effect of inflation on financial development in Bangladesh. Though not significant for some cases, the negative sign of coefficients suggests a long-term negative impact of higher inflation on the financial sector.

We also analyse bank panel data to examine whether effect of inflation varies for different types of banks. We find positive effect of inflation on bank assets and deposits in the post-liberalisation period, particularly after 1999 when inflation was on a rising trend. However, when an inflation dummy with a threshold is included, the effect of inflation becomes negative on financial sector indicators.

Table 6.11

Impact of Inflation on Different Types of Banks

	SCBs		*PCBs*		*SBs*	
	Asset	*Deposits*	*Asset*	*Deposits*	*Asset*	*Deposits*
L1.	0.90 (0.03)***	0.96 (0.03)***	0.58 (0.04)***	0.73 (0.02)***	0.79 (0.34)**	0.69 (0.13)***
INF	0.01 (0.003)***	-0.004 (0.002)**	0.03 (0.01)***	0.01 (0.01)	- 0.02 (0.03)	0.0004 (0.01)
GDP	0.01(0.01)	-0.001 (0.01)	0.19 (0.05)***	0.15 (0.02)***	- 0.04 (0.13)	0.06 (0.05)
INTSPREAD	0.003 (0.01)	-0.02 (0.01)**	-0.09(0.03)***	-0.05 (0.01)***	0.04 (0.22)	-0.002 (0.06)
ME	-0.48 (0.73)	-0.41 (0.51)	-0.24 (0.69)	0.22 (0.33)	3.50 (9.12)	3.65 (2.79)
BANKRATE	-0.01 (0.004)***	0.004 (0.003)	-0.02 (0.01)**	-0.03 (0.01)***	- 0.01 (0.04)	-0.03 (0.01)***
CONS	2.47 (0.86)***	1.27 (0.70)	9.46 (1.01)***	5.83 (0.54)***	4.87 (7.64)	5.89 (2.42)***
N	58	58	279	277	13	13
Sargan Test	70.03	105.29***	89.38	203.58***	8.04	8.43

Notes: Standard errors are in parentheses. ***, ** and * indicate significance at 1%, 5% and 10% level.

INF represents inflation rate (annual average), INFTH represents inflation threshold, GDP represents GDP growth rate; INTSPREAD represents interest rate spread; ME represents management Efficiency (interest expense/total loan); and BANKRATE represents central bank discount rate.

This finding is consistent with our TARCH model estimates. Note that the results may be improved with the use of monthly bank panel instead of yearly bank panel data that we have used in this study.

Thus, in order to have a deeper and more active financial sector with all its attached benefits at the outset of rising inflation, the country should strive to increase institutional (financial) efficiency and strengthen legal and regulatory frameworks. Poor macroeconomic performance with high inflation only brings detrimental effects to the economy, i.e. high inequality, erratic growth, and most importantly, a restrictive financial sector. Therefore, it is also important that macroeconomic policies should be prudent and pragmatic so that inflation is kept at a tolerable level.

References

Acemoglu, D., S. Johnson, J. Robinson and Y. Thaicharoen (2003). "Institutional Causes, Macro-economic Symptoms: Volatility, Crises and Growth", *Journal of Monetary Economics* 50: 49-123.

ADB (2008). *Bangladesh Quarterly Economic Update*. Dhaka: Economics Unit of Bangladesh Resident Mission, Asian Development Bank.

Ahsan, Syed M. (2007). "Inflation in Bangladesh: The Evidence and the Policy Alternatives", *Mimeo*. Policy Analysis Unit, Bangladesh Bank.

Arellano, Manuel and Olympia Bover (1995). "Another Look at the Instrumental-Variable Estimation of Error-Components Models", *Journal of Econometrics* 68: 29-52.

Arellano, M. and S. Bond (1991). "Some Tests of Specification for Panel Data: Monte Carlo Evidence and an Aapplication to Employment Equations", *The Review of Economic Studies* 58: 277 – 97, April.

Azariadis, C. and B.D. Smith (1996). "Private Information, Money, and Growth: Indeterminacy, Fluctuations, and the Mundell-Tobin Effect", *Journal of Economic Growth* 1: 309-32.

Blundell, Richard and Stephen Bond (1998). "Initial Conditions and Moment Restrictions in Dynamic Panel Data Models", *Journal of Econometrics* 87: 115-43.

Boyd, J., R. Levinea and B.D. Smith (2001). "The Impact of Inflation on Financial Sector Performance", *Journal of Monetary Economics* 47: 221-48.

Boyd, John H. and Bruce D. Smith (1996). "The Co-Evolution of the Real and Financial Sectors in the Growth Process", *World Bank Economic Review* 10: 371-96.

———. (1998). "Capital Market Imperfections in a Monetary Growth Model", *Economic Theory* 11: 241-73.

Choi, S., B.D. Smith and J.H. Boyd (1996). "Inflation, Financial Markets, and Capital Formation." *Federal Reserve Bank* of St. Louis Review.

De Brouwer, Gordon and Neil Ericsson (1995). "Modelling Inflation in Australia," *Reserve Bank of Australia Research Discussion Paper* 9510.

Dehesa, M., P. Druck and A. Plekhanov (2007). "Relative Price Stability, Creditor Rights, and Financial Deepening", *IMF Working Paper*.

Demirguc-Kunt, Asli and Ross Levine (1996). "Stock Market Development and Financial Intermediaries: Stylized Facts, World Bank Economic Review", 10(May): 291-322.

Engle, R.F. (1982). "Autoregressive Conditional Heteroscedasticty with Estimates of the Variance of U.K. Infation", *Econometrica* 50: 987–1008.

Garcés Diáz, Daniel (1999). "Determinación del Nivel de Precios y la Dinámica Inflacionaria en México", Banco de México, Documento de Investigación Económica.

Greenwood, Jeremy and Bruce Smith (1997). "Financial Markets in Development, and the Development of Financial Markets", *Journal of Economic Dynamics and Control* 21: 145-81.

Haslag, J.H. and J. Koo (1999). "Financial Repression, Financial Development and Economic Growth", *Federal Reserve Bank of Dallas Working Paper.*

Hausmann, Ricardo, Ugo Panizza and Ernesto Stein (2001). "Why Do Countries Float the Way They Float?" *Journal of Development Economics* 66: 387-414.

Hossain, Monzur (2010). "Financial Reforms and Persistently High Interest Rate Spread in Bangladesh: Pitfalls in Institutional Development?", *Journal of Asian Economics* (Elsevier) 23(4).

Huybens, Elisabeth and Bruce Smith (1998). "Financial Market Frictions, Monetary Policy, and Capital Accumulation in a Small Open Economy", *Journal of Economic Theory* 81: 353-400.

———. (1999). "Inflation, Financial Markets, and Long-Run Real Activity", *Journal of Monetary Economics* 43: 283-315.

Hwang, S.Y. and I.V. Basawa (1994). "Large Sample Inference for Conditional Exponential Families with Applications to Nonlinear Time Series", *J. Statist. Plann. Inference* 38: 141–58.

King, Robert G. and Ross Levine (1993a). "Financial Intermediation and Economic Development", in Colin Mayer and Xavier Vives (eds.), *Financial Intermediation in the Construction of Europe.* London: Centre for Economic Policy Research.

———. (1993b). "Finance and Growth: Schumpeter Might be Right", *Quarterly Journal of Economics* 108 (August): 717-38.

Levine, Ross, Norman Loayza and Thorsten Beck (2000). "Financial Intermediation and Growth: Causality and Causes", *Journal of Monetary Economics* 46: 31-77.

Levine, Ross and Sara Zervos (1998). "Stock Markets, Banks, and Economic Growth", *American Economic Review* 88: 537-58.

Moore, B.J. (1986). "Inflation and Financial Deepening", *Journal of Development Economics* 20: 125-33.

Mujeri, M.K., Shahiduzzaman and Ezazul Isla (2009). "Application of the P-Star Model for Measuring Inflationary Pressure in Bangladesh", *Bangladesh Development Studies* XXXII (1).

Petruccelli, J.D. and S.W. Woolford (1984). "A Threshold AR(1) Model", *Journal of Applied Probability* 21: 270-86.

Rajan, R. and L. Zingales (2003). *Saving Capitalism from the Capitalists.* London: Random House.

Schreft, S.L. and B.D. Smith (1997). "Money, Banking, and Capital Formation", *Journal of Economic Theory* 73: 157-82.

Shahiduzzaman, Md. (2009). "Measuring Core Inflation in Bangladesh: The Choice of Alternative Methods", *Bangladesh Development Studies* XXXII(1).

Tong, H. (1990). *Nonlinear Time Series.* Oxford: Oxford University Press.

Wooldridge, J. (2002). *Econometric Analysis of Cross Section and Panel Data.* MIT Press.

Table A-6.1

List of Banks

State-owned Commercial Banks (SCBs)	*Specialised Banks (SBs)*	*Private Commercial Banks (PCBs)*	*Foreign Commercial Banks (FCBs)*
• Agrani Bank Limited	• BASIC Bank Limited	• AB Bank Limited	• Citibank N.A
• Janata Bank Limited	• Bangladesh Krishi Bank	• Al-Arafan Islami Bank Limited	• Commercial Bank of Ceylon
• Sonali Bank Limited	• Bangladesh Shilpa Bank	• BRAC Bank Limited	• Habib Bank Limited
• Rupali Bank Limited		• Bangladesh Commerce Bank	• Standard Chartered Bank
		• Bank Al-falah Limited	• State Bank of India
		• Bank Asia	• The Hong Kong and Shanghai Banking Corporation Limited
		• Dhaka Bank	• Woori Bank
		• Dutch-Bangla Bank Limited	
		• EXIM Bank Limited	
		• Eastern Bank Limited	
		• First Security Islami Bank Limited	
		• ICB Islamic Bank	
		• IFIC Bank Limited	
		• Islami Bank Bangladesh Limited	
		• Mercantile Bank Limited	
		• Mutual Trust Bank	
		• National Bank Limited	

contd...

...contd...

	• National Credit and Commerce Bank Limited • One Bank Limited • Premier Bank Limited • Prime Bank Limited • Pubali Bank Limited • Rupali Bank Ltd • Shahjalal Islami Bank • Southeast Bank Limited • Standard Bank Limited • The City Bank Limited • Trust Bank Limited • United Commercial Bank • Uttara Bank Limited

7

MINHAJ MAHMUD AND SYED NAIMUL WADOOD

Delinking of Local and International Prices[1]

Exploring Competition in the Bangladesh Rice Market

Introduction

In recent years, Bangladesh's rice market has often experienced price increases notwithstanding declining rice prices in the international market. For instance, rice prices increased by 27 per cent in Dhaka during late 2009 and early 2010 whereas rice prices in the international market fell by 6 per cent during the same period due to increased supply from Vietnam and Thailand (World Bank, 2010). This divergence of domestic and international prices is somewhat surprising given the presumption that prices of tradable goods of small open economies are supposed to be set at a level between respective export parity and import parity prices. This suggests that domestic prices should adjust close to their import parity price levels at least after a brief time period equivalent to the time required to transport the goods from abroad. Murshid *et al.* (2009), for example, conclude that the recent increase in rice prices was not related to domestic production per se and that such price increases might be explained by international prices, market forces, and other unobservable factors. By examining price trends of local and international varieties of rice, we observe that both nominal and real prices show upward and downward movements during 1997 to 2007 period with persistently upward trend in the last periods

---

1. This chapter is a substantially revised version of the study by Mahmud and Wadood (2012). The authors wish to thank Tawhid Ullah Al-Mahmood and Shafina Alam for excellent research assistance and Mustafa Mujeri, M. Ali Khan, Mohsin Khan, and Mohammed Helal Uddin as well an anonymous referee for helpful comments on an earlier draft of the paper. Financial support from South Asia Network of Economic Research Institutes (SANEI) is duly acknowledged. Usual disclaimer applies.

of investigation.[2] In case of international varieties, we also observe similar trends suggesting integration in an open economy context. Our time series analysis generally suggests the existence of long-term relationship between prices of local (Bangladesh) varieties of rice with several international varieties of rice. In particular, we find strong long-term relationship between the price of local varieties and the 'Indian 25 per cent variety', which is consistent with the fact that major rice imports were from India during the period of study. However, private import of rice is virtually not happening in recent years and hence, recent price divergences could only be explained through local market dynamics and agents behaviour. We make an exploratory attempt to understand this price divergence.

The query that follows is: what exactly is the nature of competition at different stages of the domestic rice market of Bangladesh? Existing literature concludes that rice markets in Bangladesh are generally competitive (Murshid *et al.*, 2009; Minten *et al.*, 2010), however, the conclusion is not based on rigorous assessment of the incentives and behaviours of the diverse groups of agents operating in the market. Unless the latter are closely examined, one cannot reach a convincing conclusion regarding the state of competitiveness of the market (see Timmer *et al.*, 1983). Moreover, it is entirely possible that the market operates quite competitively within one stage, whereas competition is greatly restricted in another stage. Therefore, this study focuses on aspects of market competitiveness by explaining incentives and behaviours of different agents in different segments of the rice market. The rest of the chapter is organised as follows: Section 2 briefly summarises the existing literature on rice market institutions in Bangladesh, Section 3 outlines the methodology of the current study and Section 4 discusses the state of competitiveness of different segments of the rice market, i.e. from growers to retailers. Section 5 summarises and concludes the chapter.

Rice Market Institutions in Bangladesh

Some of the early research (Ravallion, 1986; 1987; Chowdhury, 1992) suggests that the rice market in Bangladesh is highly competitive.

2. For detailed time-series analysis, see Mahmud and Wadood (2012).

Although a number of studies have systematically studied the rice market in Bangladesh, only a handful of past researches have specifically explored different agents operating in the paddy-rice trade circuit of Bangladesh (see Chowdhury, 1992; Crow and Murshid, 1994; Baulch *et al.*, 1998; Murshid, 2001; Murshid *et al.*, 2009). Studies on spatial integration of the rice market agree that some price transmission exists between Dhaka and other major rice markets indicating that markets are not totally segmented. Dorosh (1999) points out that there is little scope for a small group of traders to significantly affect market supply and prices. Contrary results are observed by Osmani and Quasem (1990), and Crow and Murshid (1994). Chowdhury and Haggblade (2000) mention intense competition among the traders and suggest that most market participants behave like competitive profit-makers. Due to increased use of high-yielding varieties, improved infrastructure, less tied credit, more information-efficient market structures and increasing number of market participants, the competitiveness increased. Murshid *et al.* (2009) discuss food insecurity, instability of food grain production and prices, nature of food markets, policies and, referring to previous studies (Ravallion, 1986; 1987; Dawson and Dey, 2002), conclude that the common perception is that the rice market in Bangladesh is sufficiently competitive and therefore there is little room for public interventions. The authors also find that the rice market in Bangladesh is well integrated except for some specific locations. Minten *et al.* (2010) discuss the issue of agricultural marketing, price stabilisation, value chain, and international trade. They conclude that the markets have become better integrated over time as a result of large investments in road infrastructure by the government and donor agencies, and wider availability of mobile phones. The authors suggest that information flows rapidly in the markets and food grains flow from surplus to deficit areas whenever the need arises. According to them, there also appears to be little collusion between traders to fix prices, except for short periods.

Methodology of the Study

We aim to assess market competitiveness by comprehensively surveying market segments in different parts of the country. The primary survey of rice market institutions was conducted during the months of March and April of 2011, covering the districts of Dinajpur, Naogaon, Bogra, Kushtia, Jessore, Chittagong and Dhaka. These locations were selected based on our objective to study major rice trading hubs of the country so that the overall state of the supply chain is captured. Hence, in addition to the major supply points (Dinajpur, Naogaon, Bogra, Kushtia and Jessore), major urban destinations (Chittagong and Dhaka) were also covered. The survey included structured and semi-structured interviews with growers (the very first node of the supply chain), millers, rice *aratdars* (brokers, also known as commission agents), rice wholesalers and retailers (the last point of the chain from whom consumers buy rice).[3] Moreover, key community persons of selected villages and key informants of surveyed markets were interviewed to gather details of rice trading in their respective areas/markets. The instruments that were used are described as follows:

(i) Enterprise questionnaire (for millers, wholesalers, aratdars and retailers) inquiring about firm-specific information on ownership, employees, assets, establishment, involvements in the business associations (*samiti*), business relations, financing, credit situation, suppliers and customers, costs and revenues, and details of pricing decisions and bargaining. In addition, market specific information, i.e. market shares, entry and exit, exports and imports and storage were also covered. Furthermore, the rice traders were asked to recall prices of different rice varieties sold during the last one year at an average monthly frequency.

(ii) KII (Key Informant Information) (for millers, wholesalers, *aratdars* and retailers) in each of the markets by interviewing knowledgeable paddy/rice traders who were active in the respective market for at least five years. The questions were designed to target market specific information such as market shares, entry and exit, exports and imports, storage, business financing and details of pricing decisions and bargaining.

3. See Murshid *et al.* (2009) for a detailed discussion on the agents in the supply chain.

(iii) Farmer questionnaire (for paddy growers) addressing information on agricultural land use, paddy/rice crops, business relations, financing, loan situation, customers, and details of pricing decisions and bargaining.

(iv) Community questionnaire (for key persons in the surveyed villages) focusing on general information of the village/locality, sources of credit in the area, production information, and distances to/from major destinations/locations.

(v) Price List (in each of the surveyed locations) exhibiting local retail and wholesale prices of various agricultural products, enterprise and agricultural inputs, cost of transporting goods and consumer goods.

The distribution of questionnaire in each location is summarised in Table 7.1.

Table 7.1

Sample Distribution of the Primary Survey

District	KII	Enterprise Questionnaire: Millers, Wholesalers and Aratdars	Enterprise Questionnaire: Retailers	Farmer Questionnaire	Community Questionnaire	Prices List
Bogra and Naogaon	7	16	-	6	2	3
Chittagong	10	20	10	-	-	5
Dhaka	9	24	11	-	-	4
Dinajpur	6	16	-	8	2	5
Jessore	10	20	-	-	-	5
Kushtia	10	20	-	-	-	5
Total	52	116	21	14	4	27

Competitiveness in the Rice Market

A starting point of discussion on market competitiveness can be the idealised textbook version of perfect competition. We can define perfect competition as a market outcome in which all firms produce homogenous (or identical) and perfectly divisible output, face no barriers (without incurring special expenses) to entry or exit, producers and consumers have full information about the market (including the price and quality of the product), incur no transaction costs, and are price takers (cannot individually influence the price at which the product is sold), and there are no externalities so that the firms bear the cost of its production process (see Carlton and Perloff, 2000). We can consider some industries as reasonably competitive if they have certain characteristics. Price-taking behaviour, many firms and free entry and exit are often used as criteria to judge the competitiveness of a market.

Market for Paddy Growers

In order to investigate the state of competitiveness in the primary grower's market, first we point out some basic features or testable implications that are expected to be present in this segment of the market if it were competitive. First, we expect a large number of buyers and sellers within this segment, and that no individual agent has control over market prices. This condition is fulfilled in the primary growers' market segment since there is a very large number of sellers (primary growers) and an arguably large number of millers, *farias* (middlemen), and paddy *aratdars* who function as buyers, and no single agent can dictate the market prices. Second, we expect free entry and exit. This condition is also met in this segment since we do not find any significant barriers for entry. Third, we expect bargains among the agents to settle the price, where no particular agent is constrained in any way to settle bargains. Constrained bargaining may lead to economic losses for the agent who faces this problem and thereby the opposite party in the transaction may gain out of this situation. A market cannot be considered sufficiently competitive where some agents are faced with restricted bargaining capacity due to problems that they face, for example, credit or cash constraints, lack of storage capacity and limited information. It is in the case of this third condition, that we find some problems related to competitiveness for the primary grower segment of the rice market.

Sample Villages for Paddy Growers

The primary survey covered a total of four villages in two districts. The villages are Harish Chandrapur in Bochaganj *upazilla* (sub-district) and Korimullahpur *mohalla* within Dinajpur Sadar area in Dinajpur district, and Kadowa and Debipur villages within Naogaon Sadar area in Naogaon district. Our survey team collected community information from selected key informants, verified those with a larger group of audience and completed face-to-face questionnaire interviews with 14 farmers. The selected villages are located within a five kilometer radius of some of the rice wholesaler markets that we have surveyed. These areas are well connected with important locations and establishments such as, roads and *bazaars* (market place). The number of households varied across villages—with the highest being 700 in Korimullahpur and lowest of 200 in Debipur, the remaining two consisted of around 350 households each. All four villages had access to electricity. Crop agriculture and daily agricultural wage labour were found to be the two most important economic activities of all of them whereas business/hotel/restaurant activities were ranked third. Mobile phones were seen as the principal means of information communication in all these places. Rickshaw vans, rickshaws and bicycles were considered the principal means of physical communication. All of the selected areas had some NGO (non-government organisation) programmes currently running. Agricultural credits were available from both NGOs and the Krishi Bank.

Profile of the Paddy Growers

In Dinajpur locations, the four surveyed farmers in the village Harishchandrapur had on an average 350 decimals of crop land, three of them are classified as 'medium' sized farmers and one as a 'small' farmer. The four farmers in the village Korimullahpur had an average of 120 decimals of crop land, three of them fell in the 'small' category and one in the 'landless, sharecropper' category. On the other hand, in the Naogaon locations, three Kadowa farmers had on an average 295 decimals (one 'medium' and two 'small') and three Debipur farmers had 110 decimals (one 'medium', one 'small' and one 'marginal'). Thus we surveyed five 'medium', seven 'small', one 'marginal' and one 'landless' category farmers. The median amount of crop land owned across the villages is 159 decimals—we understand a typical respondent is a 'small' farmer. The median amount of homestead land is only 10 decimals. Median age of the surveyed farmers is 53 years and median number of years of schooling is only 6 years, with a maximum value of 12 years. All the respondents are male. Farmers have reported to be intensely involved in crop agriculture in the months of April, May, and June, and again in November, December and January, while being involved in other activities during the rest of the year.

Paddy Growers' Pricing Decisions

The surveyed farmers have reported both, their crop returns and local harvest period price of paddy. We find that harvest prices varied across villages, for example, for the same BR-28 variety paddy, Harishchandrapur farmers reported harvest period prices to be Tk 12.50 per kg (cost of production is reported at Tk. 8.60 per kg) and Korimullahpur farmers reported Tk. 13.00 per kg (cost of production at Tk. 11.80). We find higher prices in Naogaon villages—both Kadowa and Debipur farmers report Tk. 15.00 (cost of production is Tk. 12.50 or less in both cases). Harvest period prices to be received by the farmers are settled in the local markets and this depends on local demand and supply conditions. We note that each individual grower bargains with *beparis* or *farias*, so the price they finally settle at depends largely on the individual-level bargaining. The surveyed farmers do not have any collective bargaining agency or co-operative associations in order to negotiate prices on a collective basis.

The paddy growers have contacts with *beparis* and *farias*, and sell paddy to them, mostly during the harvest period. On an average, a paddy grower has 13 business contacts (the maximum value found is 35 and the minimum is only 1); these contacts are with *bepari*, miller, paddy *aratdar*, and *farias*. All the business transactions with them are informal, with no legal documentation. The transactions are in both cash and credit. Taking credit from millers, *beparis* or *farias* is quite common among the paddy growers during the growing season, most commonly for purchase of inputs. We find that the number of business contacts a paddy grower has is statistically significantly positively associated with the amount of his landholdings at 10 per cent significance level (p-value = 0.068). This implies that a larger farmer tends to have larger number of business contacts (and therefore, larger set of options to choose from) whereas the situation tends to worsen for a small farmer with fewer number of business contacts. In addition, paddy growers do not have many reliable sources of credit; they have little access to formal banking sources.

A summary from the farmer questionnaire illustrates the pattern of transactions that take place. In Harishchandrapur, in 6 out of 12 cases, there was more than 80 per cent sale immediately after the harvest. In addition to that, in 6 cases there were tied transactions—advances were taken against production expenses. In Korimullahpur, in 7 out of 13 cases there were immediate sale of more than 80 per cent, and in 3 cases credit was taken in advance. The Naogaon farmers have reported better records of transactions, out of a total of 15 cases in two villages, there is only 1 case of immediate sale of more than 80 per cent and 7 cases of credit taken in advance implying tied transaction.

The surveyed farmers report that *beparis* and *farias* visit their places during the harvest time and collect samples. Most of these intermediaries are representatives of the millers. The intermediaries examine the quality of the paddy and then they offer the rate. There is often a maximum offer, beyond which *beparis* and *farias* rarely want to settle. Once the farmer agrees, the intermediaries arrange for transport and send it to the millers. The farmers admit that, even though both the parties come up with price quotations, the price quoted by the intermediaries normally matters. This happens because the farmers lack adequate storage facilities for paddy, and thus, keeping paddy is not a viable option. This implies that the surveyed farmers lack bargaining power and have to accept the price that is set by the millers or their representatives. We can summarise that even though the paddy growers' segment may look 'competitive', the very nature of competitiveness is cast in doubt due to the constrained pattern of bargaining on behalf of the primary growers in this segment.

Market for Wholesalers

We find that the rice wholesale market meets the first condition of competitiveness; that is it covers a large number of buyers (end-point wholesalers or retailers) and sellers (millers, commission agents or wholesalers). With regard to the issue of free entry, we find that entry into this market is not free in the sense that enterprises that operate in this market segment have long experience of operation, and they require solid business contacts with their counterparts. We also find that operation in a small rice wholesale market requires sufficient local knowledge and familiarity with the surrounding environment, which a non-local wholesaler enterprise most often may not be able to meet. With regard to price bargaining, we also find that larger size enterprises have advantages since their price quotations are often regarded as indicative market prices, and smaller enterprises do not have much choice but to follow prices quoted by the larger ones. Even though market prices are determined by interactions of large numbers of buyers and sellers, it is typically the prices quoted by the larger enterprises that dictate the direction of price movements—akin to the price-leadership model within the oligopolistic market structure. There are indications that the rice wholesale market segment operates to a large extent like a price-leadership oligopoly or a dominant firm oligopoly model.

Sample Enterprises

We have covered a total of 116 wholesale enterprises in our survey over a total of 12 rice wholesale markets across seven districts. More specifically, we covered five districts (Bogra, Dinajpur, Jessore, Kushtia and Naogaon) and two metropolitan city areas (Dhaka and Chittagong). A total of 52 key informant interviews were also undertaken to assess the state of competitiveness of these 12 markets which are basically small rice wholesale centres (see Table 7.2).

Profile of Enterprise Owners

A large majority of the sample enterprises (69%) are individually owned. The remaining ones are jointly owned, having 2.72 owners on average. Out of 179 owners recorded in the wholesale module, only 1 is female. Women are rarely found to be involved, even in the form of partnership. Average age of the owners is 44. The age of owners varies widely, from a low 24 years to a high 70 years. In terms of years

Table 7.2

Census Information of the Surveyed Rice Markets

District	*Market*	*Types of Trade Wholesale/Arat= 1 Import = 2 Retail = 3 Milling = 4*	*No. of Rice Trading Enterprises and Market Size*	*No. of Enterprises by Size*		
				Large	*Medium*	*Small*
Bogra	C.O. Office Road Bazaar	1	15 (Small)	5	4	6
Chittagong	Chaktai Bazaar	1, 3	275 (Large)	60	115	100
	Shah Amanat Bazaar (Bera Bazaar)	3	18 (Small)	5	7	6
	Bohoddarhat Bazaar	3	12 (Small)	3	4	5
Dhaka	Ray Shaheb Bazaar	3	10 (Small)	2	2	6
	Babubazaar (Badamtoli)	1, 3	280 (Large)	90	140	50
	Kochukhet Rajanigandha Market	1, 3	72 (Medium)	15	25	32
	Mohammadpur Krishi Market	1, 3	180 (Medium)	40	90	50
Dinajpur	Pulhat Bazaar	1	70 (Medium)	20	30	20
Jessore	Benapole Bazaar	1, 3	4 (Small)	2	2	0
	Jhikargacha Bazaar	1	9 (Small)	2	3	4
	Navaron Bazaar (Sharsha)	1, 3, 4	6 (Small)	2	2	2
	Nowapara Bazaar (Abhaynagar)	1, 4	24 (Small)	6	8	10
Kushtia	Khajanagar	1, 4	310 (Large)	10	30	270

of education, the average number of years of education of the owners has been found to be 10 years (Secondary School Certificate level).

Connectedness of the Wholesale Markets

In terms of operations of the rice market, the survey locations are intricately connected to each other. As an example, we consider the case of Dupchanchiya *upazilla* in Bogra district. The major suppliers to this market are Bogra (Sadar and other *upazillas*), Dinajpur, Gaibandha, Joypurhat, Naogaon, Netrokona, Porsha, Rangpur, Shapahar and Sirajganj. On the other hand, the major destinations are Comilla, Chittagong, Dhaka, Feni, Gazipur, Savar, Munshiganj and Narayanganj. Thus even a small rice centre like Dupchanchiya operates as a collection point in the northern region and it sends rice to all the major rice consuming locations in the country. Another point to note is that connections between rice centres are sometimes two-way, not always unidirectional. For example, rice is transported from Sylhet to Chittagong and, at the same time, rice is transported from Chittagong to Sylhet.

Size of the Wholesaler Markets

The survey locations clearly differ in terms of number of enterprises operating in the markets (Table 7.2). The rice wholesale markets studied in Dinajpur Sadar (Dinajpur) and Kushtia Sadar (Kushtia) are very large; around 250 enterprises or more in each of these locations. On the other hand, markets located at Dupchanchiya (Bogra), Jhikargacha (Jessore) and Sharsha (Jessore) are small, having number of enterprises of less than 20.

We categorise markets with more than 200 enterprises as 'large', between 40 to 200 enterprises as 'medium' and with less than 40 enterprises as 'small'. According to this categorisation, it turns out that we have covered four 'large' markets, three 'medium' markets as well as five 'small' markets. On the other hand, we have used indicators for the size of enterprises, such as 'large', 'medium' and 'small' (this is based on each respondent's self-reported assessment of the size of his respective enterprise as compared with other enterprises within the same market). Within the surveyed rice markets, on an average, around 20 per cent of the enterprises classify themselves as 'large', 35 per cent as 'medium' and the remaining 45 per cent as 'small' enterprises.

Entry and Exit of Enterprises in the Wholesale Markets

A number of rice wholesale markets are relatively old, with establishments dating back to the 1950s. Entry, however, continues in all locations even now. Some markets such as Chittagong City Corporation are quite active, with as many as 40 firms entering and another 35 firms exiting during the last five years. On the other hand, some locations such as Dupchanchiya have actually seen a reduction in the market size with five firms exiting during the last five years (Table 7.3).

Table 7.3

Oldest and Newest Wholesaler Enterprises' Entry and Exit

District/City	*Upazilla*	*Oldest Enterprise*	*Newest Enterprise*	*Entry: Last 5 yrs*	*Exit: Last 5 yrs*
Bogra	Dupchanchiya	1980	n.a.	0	5
Chittagong	Chittagong City Corporation	1970	2009	40	35
Dhaka	Babubazaaraka Badamtoli	1950	2011	35	32
	Kochukhet	1978	2009	4	2
	Mohammadpur Krishi Market	1984	2010	25	20
Dinajpur	Bochaganjaka Shetabganj	1950	2008	4	3
	DinajpurSadar	1965	2009	35	0
Jessore	Abhaynagar	1960	2010	4	2
	Jhikargacha	1961	2010	1	0
	Sharsha	1980	2010	1	1
Kushtia	KushtiaSadar	1978	2010	30	0
Naogaon	NaogaonSadar	1962	2008	7	4

With regards to the question of whether entry into the rice wholesale market is difficult or not, most key informants from different markets have mentioned moderate level of difficulty involved in the process. The difficulty on behalf of a potential entrant is that entry into this market requires a large amount of financial capital and sufficient knowledge as well as experience in the trade. In some large markets, particularly in major locations such as Chittagong and Dhaka, it is difficult to get suitable space for establishing the shop as some of these market locations are already crowded. An additional requirement for entry into this market is that the potential entrant enterprise needs to have contact with a large number of potential clients or business partners.

With regard to the question of whether there are cases of exit from the markets, most of the key informants of the respective rice trading centres cited cases of exit during the last five years. The frequency of exits differs in different surveyed locations. For example, Kushtia is a large sized market that did not register any cases of exit, while Dupchanchiya is a small sized market that registered five cases of exits along with zero cases of entry. This implies that markets themselves are evolving continuously at varying magnitudes of entry and exit.

Rice wholesalers often operate as commission agents who act as an intermediary between the rice millers and end-point wholesalers and/or retail wholesalers. As commission agents, the rice wholesaler often undertakes transactions on behalf of the millers on to the final-point wholesalers. Sometimes, on the basis of intermediary role played by the commission agent-cum-wholesaler, the miller sends the agreed upon rice stock to the final-point wholesaler, and obtains money from the commission agent within some specified period of time. Hence, the commission agent expects to receive payments from the final-point wholesaler. However, contracts between these two parties are often verbal or small note-based, not legally documented. Sometimes, the final-point wholesaler delays payment to the commission agent, and in extreme situations, he may fail to make the agreed upon payments. Thus, most of the cases of exit in the surveyed markets were due to default in transactions, as reported by the key informants.

Market Shares of Enterprises in the Wholesaler Market

The key informants of different rice wholesale centres collected information on market shares of enterprises in their respective local markets at different points in time during the last five years. Interestingly, the (perceived) market shares of the enterprises at different points in time, as mentioned by the key informants closely match with each other. This implies that in any market, there is a common perception of market leaders in terms of market shares and changes in the shares over time. We find that the names of top market shareholding enterprises do not change much and the market shares of these enterprises do not exhibit wide fluctuations either. These enterprises have been reported to have a broader client base and a larger long-term reputation in the market, and at the same time have huge financial resources that absorb most kinds of shocks, particularly in cases of default in transactions.

Pricing and Bargaining in the Wholesaler Markets

Wholesaler enterprises covered in the survey mostly function as 'commission agents' in the market, and in some cases they operate as 'wholesalers'. As commission agents, their role is to bridge millers to rice wholesalers and/or retailers at the end point. The basic steps involved within this bridge that lead to the price being set are described as follows.

The miller sends specifications of the rice and the reservation price to the wholesaler (commission agent). The price quotation is set on the basis of different costs such as paddy procuring costs, cost of transforming paddy into rice, storage and other additional costs, and agency fee of the commission agent. This agency fee in the rice markets is set by the market association based on a consensus among all the member enterprises. Hence, the fee is fixed for all the wholesalers within a particular market. Agency fees usually vary in different rice markets. Interestingly, the commission agent charges a fee on both suppliers (the millers) and buyers (wholesalers at the end point of the market).

As the commission agent is informed of the miller's quoted price (which already includes his fee from the miller), he adds his fee (to be taken from his buyers) and then bargains with the retail wholesalers, keeping in view the existing market prices. The commission agent tries to obtain a price which will be at least equal to the miller's quoted price and his fee. Meanwhile, representatives of the buyers would want to purchase rice at the lowest possible price given the quotations from the commission agent. Once the bargaining is done, the commission agent gives a handwritten invoice and informs the miller of the transaction. Accordingly, the miller arranges the transport and sends the quoted amount of goods to the destination.

An important point to note is that the commission agent gets his agency fees from both parties that he connects. In any case, if the price bargained minus the agency fee (charged on retail wholesalers) is higher or lower than the miller's quoted price, the miller receives the lower/extra revenue. Since the bargained price always depends on existing market prices, the commission agent eventually shifts the price burden on to the miller.

Once the goods have been supplied, the retail wholesaler is required to transfer money to the commission agent, and simultaneously, the commission agent is required to transfer money to the miller. Therefore, the miller holds the commission agent accountable, staying out of the transaction relation with the retail wholesalers. Herein lies the risky part of the commission agent's job. It normally takes quite a long time for the commission agent to acquire all outstanding sales. In a worst case scenario, the buyer can also become a defaulter in his payments.

Lastly, the retail wholesaler procures rice from the miller, stores it and sells it over time. Therefore, he requires storage space. The retail wholesaler bears all the price risk of the rice procured. The survey finds some enterprises operating both as commission agents and retail wholesalers.

Establishment of the Wholesale Enterprises

The sample wholesale enterprises have documented long years of stay in the rice trading business: the average number of years in business is 15.7 years. There is not much of a difference in terms of locations regarding the issue except for the northern location of Naogaon, where the average years of stay in business is around 24 years. Most of the sample enterprises had been newly started, whereas in some more prominent rice markets (such as Kushtia and

Naogaon), the tendency to inherit the business is slightly higher (Table 7.4). In terms of sources of financing, owners' own savings from non-agricultural activities have been cited as the major source of funds, and this is evident throughout the country. Remittances, sale of assets, borrowing from family and friends, loans from private and commercial banks are other sources of funds in several cases. The median value of costs of establishment in the whole sample is reported at Tk. 0.45 million (nominal values reported for the year of establishment, not converted into current values). The cost of entry into the rice wholesale market can thus be considered as reasonably high.

Table 7.4

Years of Stay in Business of the Sample Wholesaler Enterprises

District	*Number of Enterprises*	*How Established?*		*Average Years of Stay in Business*
		Newly Started	*Inherited*	
Bogra	9	5	4	15.22
Chittagong	20	16	4	13.2
Dhaka	24	19	5	15
Dinajpur	16	12	4	19.63
Jessore	20	18	2	15.85
Kushtia	20	12	8	12.7
Naogaon	7	3	4	23.86
Total	116	85	31	15.72

Business Contacts of the Wholesaler Enterprises

We find that the rice wholesale market is intricately interconnected and this has been facilitated by the widespread use of mobile phones. Rice wholesalers have business contacts with other businesses, and the contacts often cover the entire country. This is more prominent in the case of the northern wholesale markets. For example, an enterprise in Naogaon has on an average business contacts with 22.5 millers, 19.2 wholesalers and 14.3 paddy *aratdars*. These large number of business contacts indicate that there may be intense competition in terms of price offers and bargaining among wholesalers in different locations as well as within the same location. Another interesting feature is that all the contracts are informal, and nowhere is there any legal, written document in the entire rice market. Therefore, 'trust' and 'reputation' play important roles in day-to-day business transactions; default risk is always present in this environment. Transactions are done both in credit and cash, but credit transactions are more common.

Financing of the Wholesale Enterprises

In terms of sources of fund for working capital, all enterprises in Bogra area mentioned public commercial banks, and one enterprise mentioned taking loans from informal money lenders. Credit transactions with millers and other wholesalers are also reported to be widespread in the rice markets of Bogra. Chittagong rice market enterprises mention re-investments as the main source of fund for working capital. Dhaka rice market enterprises are evenly split in their responses. Nearly half of them mention re-investment from their own business, while most of the remaining ones mention private commercial banks and a few enterprises mention public commercial banks.

Rice Varieties Offered by Wholesale Enterprises

The sample wholesale enterprises have provided a list of rice or paddy varieties that they have sold during the last one year. The list presents an amazing array of rice varieties that are on offer, for example, on an average 7 rice varieties have been mentioned by each sample wholesaler. Taking into consideration common names across enterprises, we find that a total of 177 varieties of rice have been listed by 116 wholesalers. Out of the total of 177 varieties, 69 varieties have been listed as *aman* varieties, 97 as *boro* varieties, 3 as *aus* varieties and the remaining 8 as common for two crop seasons. Thus, the *boro* season offers more diversified varieties in the rice market as compared with the *aman* or *aus* season.

Rice varieties in the *aman* season includes BR-30, Chinigura, Govindabhog, Guti, Heera, Kataribhog, Sharna, Najirshail, Paijam, Ranjit and others. On the other hand, rice varieties in the *boro* season includes BR-11, BR-28, BR-32, Jirashail, Miniket, Pari, Chandina, Baashfuli, Hybrid Heera, and Parija, The varieties that have been listed as *aus* season varieties are Borshali Paijira, Sharna Thin, and Chinese. This incredible list of varieties implies that it is quite difficult for an economic agent in the rice market to be well informed about all the finer details, and be able to bargain with other agents on that basis. In a market like this, where quality and product characteristics vary significantly, bargaining of price within some range is expected since every agent may not have the same opinion about a particular variety and therefore their willingness to pay will differ. At the same time, it is also possible that agents may not have the same knowledge about the varieties in question. In an informal setting like Bangladeshi rice markets, we can expect widespread bargaining among the agents on the valuation of rice varieties.

Price Movements of Rice Varieties of Wholesale Enterprises

The sample enterprises were asked to recall the price movements of rice varieties that they had sold throughout the previous one year. We find some interesting features of the data. Firstly, prices of the same variety do not differ much across the entire country. Secondly, prices differ not only across markets but also within the same market. Even a small market like Dupchanchiya exhibits price differences across enterprises for the same variety of rice, and in some cases this difference is more marked compared with differences of average prices across the country.

We now examine price movements of the wholesale enterprises with respect to the size of enterprises, such as 'large', 'medium' and 'small' (this classification is based on the sample enterprises' assessment of their respective size compared with other rice enterprises within the same market). We find that within the same market there is some tendency for prices to move together across size of enterprises. One pattern that is found is that prices of 'large' and 'medium' enterprises in general slightly exceeds the prices settled by 'small' enterprises, for the same variety of rice and within the same rice wholesale market. In other words, generally the 'small' enterprises closely follow prices quoted by the 'large' and 'medium' enterprises, but they often settle for a slightly lower price compared with the 'large' and 'medium' ones. This can be interpreted as follows: the 'small' enterprises take into consideration the price being quoted by the larger enterprises, and yet settle for a lower price. This is plausible since 'small' enterprises do not have the same reputation and therefore do not possess similar bargaining power relative to the larger ones. Therefore, business enterprises face higher risks while doing business with 'small' enterprises than larger ones, especially in terms of the quality of rice supplied. Another disadvantage that 'small' enterprises have is that they may only be able to supply smaller quantities whereas larger ones can supply a much bigger amount. A third factor that may work against the 'small' enterprises is that they may have lesser number of contacts or references and thereby may have to take a discount in terms of price quotations. Thus, 'small' enterprises may have lower bargaining power in the market and this results in their accepting discounts for sale.

Profitability of Wholesale Enterprises

In the wholesaler enterprise module, we have collected enterprises' own reports of their respective monthly average profits. We estimate an OLS (ordinary least squares) regression (with heteroscedasticity-robust standard errors) of natural log of the monthly average profits as reported by the enterprises on enterprise size and area specifications as well as number of enterprises in the rice wholesale market. We find that the estimated regression coefficient of area dummy for Kushtia enterprises is statistically positively significant (p-value = 0.00). This implies that, controlling for size and number of enterprises, only Kushtia enterprises tend to have statistically significant higher amount of monthly profits compared with the Dhaka enterprises. We note that we have a mix of millers and wholesalers and also enterprises in dual roles of being millers and wholesalers as well as commission agents in Kushtia. A statistically significant result only for Kushtia may have the implication that within the rice wholesale market structure, enterprises that operate as a mix of millers and wholesalers/commission agents have a tendency to exhibit higher growth of profits. We find that both the estimated coefficients for size of enterprise dummies such as 'large' and 'medium' are statistically positively significant as compared with the base of 'small' enterprises, controlling for other variables in the model. A statistically significant result is also found in the joint significant tests for 'large' and 'medium' enterprises. This implies that controlling for other variables in our regression model, the growth of (self-reported) average monthly profits have a tendency to be higher for large and medium enterprises as compared with those of small enterprises. We can infer from this result that large and medium enterprises are more efficient and have a tendency to exhibit faster growth of profit as compared with the small ones. This indicates that there are some economies of scale in the wholesale sub-section of the rice market which is more prominent in cases where millers and wholesalers overlap in their operations.

Pricing Decisions in the Wholesale Enterprises

The wholesaler or commission agent is in between the miller on the one hand and the end-point wholesaler on the other hand. The commission agent bargains with the agents of the end-point wholesaler regarding pricing of some particular variety of rice; this bargain is set by the miller's minimum quotation and the maximum that the counterpart agent wants to offer for the requested supply. The commission agent's fee is fixed, thereby a good bargain brings in higher revenue for the miller while a bad bargain results in smaller revenues. A commission agent's reputation depends on how successfully he can make good bargains on behalf of the miller. Since this is not at all a one-time play, a business relationship between a miller and a commission agent is expected to last for many years, while the commission agents who make bad bargains may destroy this relationship (something a commission agent would want to avoid). A miller may have business relationships with many agents located in different places, therefore he may switch from one commission agent to another within the same market, or switch to some other agent in a different market, or may decide to wait and watch rather than agree to any agent. Since the rice wholesale market has become heavily interconnected, a miller has a large number of commission agents and rice market centres to choose from. Therefore, a miller in a North Bengal market such as Naogaon can compare prices offered by the Dhaka market wholesalers with that of Chittagong market or Sylhet market. Any difference in offers may result in rice supply being directed to Sylhet rather than Chittagong, or Barisal rather than Khulna. This is how the miller can exercise significant control over the price bargains because of his large number of business contacts. On the other hand, the situation for the miller can be unfavourable if he faces tough competition in the markets: say if some Dhaka retail wholesaler decides to bring supply from millers located in Naogaon market rather than those located in Kushtia market.

Market Structure of the Wholesale Market

Why Some Firms May Become Dominant?

As we investigate the rice wholesale markets in detail, we find that the small market centres are often dominated by a number of 'large' firms. In order to understand more about a market which is a mix of large firms and small firms, we refer to one particular type of oligopoly model described in Carlton and Perloff (2000), which suggests three main reasons for the creation of dominant firm-competitive-fringe market structure. First, dominant firms may have lower costs than fringe firms and that the firm may be more efficient than others. Second, a dominant firm may have a superior product in a market where each firm produces a differentiated product. Finally, a group of firms may collectively act as the dominant firm. The model shows that dominant firm cannot set a high price when entry is unlimited, compared to when entry is restricted and assuming that fringe firms are all identical in costs, the market price cannot go higher than a fringe firm's minimum average cost. In this model, a dominant firm provides a price umbrella for smaller firms and as long as competing firms set price at or below the level of the dominant firm, they will be able to find buyers. Thus, the price set by the dominant firm becomes an indicative price in the market. Carlton and Perloff (2000) show that even with unlimited entry of fringe firms, the dominant firm can gain and hold large share of the market for a long period due to cost or other advantages such as superior products, more business contracts, business goodwill, etc.

In the dominant firm model with competitive fringe model (see Carton and Perloff, 2000), two different equilibrium exists depending on the dominant firm's marginal cost structure. The amount to be produced by fringe firms depends on the dominant firm's cost structure. In the first case, with dominant firms having higher marginal costs fringe firms cannot set a price above minimum average cost of a fringe firm implying that the fringe firm could make zero economic profits and the dominant firm makes positive economic profits. A second equilibrium suggests that price is so low, with dominant firms having lower marginal costs, that no fringe firm stays in the industry and the dominant firm acts as a monopoly.

In our case, price and output determination in the rice wholesale market closely matches with the above model of a dominant firm with a competitive-fringe with free entry and exits, whereby dominant firm produces output alongside the competitive fringe firms (neither is able to drive the other out of the industry). The dominant firm provides an indicative price in the industry which we can associate with the phenomenon of price umbrella. The dominant firm (or a group of larger-size firms acting as a dominant firm) still holds on to a large share of the market, and this share does not change much over time. On the other hand, there are a number of cases of entry and exit in the market, more particularly among those firms which are on the fringe. Here also the cost advantage of the dominant firm (or firms) may arise from superior products (may be real or simply perceived), larger business networks, greater reputation and trust. Therefore, we can conclude that the rice wholesale market functions as a dominant firm oligopoly constrained by the presence of a competitive-fringe with free entry into and exit from the industry.

The Retailer Market

Examining the State of Competitiveness in the Market for Retailers

In order to investigate the state of competitiveness in the rice retail markets, we outline some basic features or testable implications that are expected to be present in this market. First we point out that a competitive market is one which contains a large number of buyers and sellers. The retail market covers a large number of buyers and sellers; thus we do not find problems with this condition. Second, we can expect free entry and exit of firms into this market. We find that even though it is not prohibitively expensive to enter the retail market, usually this requires long 'training' in the form of long (periods of) experiences of operations within the market. As was the case of enterprises in the rice wholesale market, enterprises in the rice retail markets also require business connections which takes a long time to build. Thus, we find that entry into this market to some extent is restricted in the form of entry barriers such as requirements for experiences and business connections.

Findings from the Selected Retailer Markets

The primary survey covered a total of 21 retailers in the two end-point retailer locations, Dhaka and Chittagong. Out of these, 10 retailers were interviewed in the Chittagong City Corporation area and 11 were interviewed in Dhaka City Corporation area (4 from Babubazaar and Badamtoli, 3 from Kochukhet and the remaining 4 from Mohammadpur Krishi Market).

Retailers are small in operation, most often there are only two full-time employees besides the owner-manager. Most of the surveyed retailers only have some office space, measuring around nine feet in length and seven feet in width. Very few retailers have storage spaces. We can infer that retailers mostly concentrate on delivering the output at the ongoing market prices, rather than keeping it for some time. Neither of the retail enterprises have any vehicle, nor do they have any branch offices. Most of the retailers have been established by the owners themselves, and some others have been inherited. On an average, the surveyed retailers are in operation for the last 10 years, while the oldest among them has been in operation for 30 years.

Retailers have lesser number of business contacts as compared with the wholesalers. On an average, the surveyed retailer has business contacts with 7 local wholesalers, 5 local retailers and 50 local customers. Almost all of these contacts are within the same locality, this implies retailers simply obtain the produce from the wholesalers and deliver those within the locality among the customers. They do not have long-distance networks as it is often the case with the wholesalers.

Pricing and Bargaining as Reported by the Retail Enterprises

The retail enterprises report that they simply pass the wholesale prices on to the customers with some pre-fixed amounts of profit margins. The common practice is that they obtain their supply from the wholesale market at the ongoing (wholesale) market price, and then add Tk. 25 or 30 per 50 kg bag of rice and sell it to the customers. How much to add to the wholesale market price is a common understanding reached among the retailers themselves prior to transactions. The retailers meet two categories of business counterparts in price bargaining. The first category is the rice wholesalers who would supply rice to them at the ongoing rice market wholesale price. The second category is the rice customers who would check with other enterprises and see if the price could be any lower anywhere for the same variety, quality, and specification. The prominent presence of the rice customers at the end of the rice market supply chain makes sure that the retail enterprises need to be watchful not to ask for 'too high' a price that would scare away the customers, and again not to ask for 'too low' a price which would reduce their own profit margin (the other group, the wholesalers, would want to have as high a wholesale price as possible). Since the retailers do not have any storage space, most often their role would be to just offload the rice produce on to the customers. In between two markets prices, one that of retail market and the other of the wholesale market—the retailers have their profit margins (and costs of value addition for the retailers). Because of the presence of the customer group on the one hand and the wholesaler group on the other, the retailers do not have much influence on the direction of the market prices.

Summary and Conclusions

We take a broader perspective on the issue of price divergence between international and domestic rice market in Bangladesh. In particular, we explore the nature of competition at different stages of the domestic rice market of Bangladesh by explaining incentives and behaviours of different agents in the market, particularly those of large firms operating in the middle of the rice market supply chain.

As observed, rice markets contain a large network of intermediaries from the beginning point of the farmers to the end point of the consumers. These intermediaries differ in terms of their respective sizes, roles, objectives, skill and expertise, technical support, constraints, and strategies. The intermediaries interact and often bargain with each other; each one striving to secure his self-interests. Almost all the contracts within this market are informal, in the form of verbal or mobile phone conversation or handwritten notes. Here, 'trust' and 'reputation' are important: values which firms invest in over time, to operate in this market in the long run. Often high default risk forces firms to exit from the market. Even though the entry cost is not prohibitively high, the issues of default risk, trust and reputation, skill and expertise, and correct knowledge of the business partners are very essential to survive. Hence, all of these seem to act as steep entry barriers.

The rice market has become heavily interconnected except for the case of the farmers, who may have limited number of contacts and limited options other than selling produce at the price offered by a miller. It has been observed that large and medium-sized enterprises enjoy greater economies of scale in their operations compared with the smaller ones. Within the rice market value chain, there are two points where major bargaining takes place: one is between the farmer and the *bepari* or *faria* (often working as agents of the miller) over the price and quantity of paddy, and the other is between the rice market wholesaler or commission agent (as agent of the miller) and the end-point wholesale or retail wholesaler over the price, quantity and quality combination of rice. The presence of rice miller in above bargaining processes potentially postpone sale. By taking advantage of storage capacity the miller is able to postpone sale for some period at least. This implies that millers or miller-cum-wholesalers have the potential to enjoy a large leverage over the entire rice market value chain and thus, potentially engage in opportunistic behaviour within the market. Price determination process within the rice market value chain depends on relative bargaining power of the concerned parties. Large and medium enterprises enjoy the advantage of setting prices in the market, and the small ones follow them. We therefore find prices of a variety of rice offered by all the enterprises to move together, whereas small enterprises sell the same at a slightly lower price. Additionally, within the rice wholesale market, the enterprises are free to sell any amount at any price they can obtain, making each of them concerned about prices of neighbouring enterprises.

With regards to the market structure, we observe that the rice wholesale market is characterised by a model of the dominant firm oligopoly with competitive-fringe firms with free, instantaneous entry and exit. The larger wholesale firms provide a price umbrella for the smaller firms whom we can consider as competitive, fringe firms. The status of dominance by one firm (or a group of firms acting as a single firm by way of an implicit cartel) may have arisen because of longer established reputation and trust in the market and real or perceived superior quality products and more business contacts.

It is obvious that agents in the market interacting with each other pursue different objectives and face different constraints in their operations. Hence, it is appropriate to examine different segments of the rice market separately to reach any conclusion regarding market competitiveness. The first segment of the rice market, one that involves primary growers, can to a large extent be considered competitive, although the benefits of competition do not reach the small and marginal farmers. The reason is that the small and marginal farmers often suffer from credit and cash constraints, and lack sufficient storage capacities, making them vulnerable to the opportunistic behaviour of rather powerful intermediaries. As we proceed to the second segment of the market, which is of the rice millers and the wholesalers, we find that the issue of competition is rather interesting. Given that an entrepreneur has to have large financial resources as well as business connections to be able to survive in the rice wholesale market, entry into this market (segment) is rather difficult. Also, default risks of financial transactions or delays in payments often serve as an entry deterrent for new potential entrants.

Usually, price bargaining depends on relative economic power and/or business connections of two agents whereby the more informed and connected agent can gain from the bargaining process. With regards to price movements of wholesale firms, the price quotations of large farms are often considered as the indicative price and small and medium sized firms often follow the price. This resembles the standard oligopolistic price-leadership phenomenon, where one dominant firm sets the price and the other firms (often smaller ones) act as followers. This shows that competition in the second segment of the market, i.e. wholesale market, is to a large extent restricted. Even though a large number of wholesale firms operate in the market, the ones with more economic resources and business connections dominate. In case of the third segment (of the retail firms), this mostly acts as a channel for prices set in the second segment (of the rice wholesalers).

These findings have implications for policy since the differential behaviour of different segment of the markets affects the consumers especially through creating burdens of the opportunistic behaviours of different agents. We cannot, however, conclude on how the competition (or lack of it) affects the end consumers since the present study concentrated mostly on the price bargaining and negotiations within the primary growers' segments, wholesalers' segment and retailers' segments. However, we did not follow the issue of burden of any opportunistic behaviour on the consumers directly.

References

Baulch, B., J. Das and N. Farid (1998). *The Spatial Integration and Pricing Efficiency of the Private Sector Grain Trade in Bangladesh: Phase II Report*. BIDS, Bangladesh Agricultural University and University of Sussex.

Carlton, D.W. and J. M. Perloff (2000). *Modern Industrial Organization*. New York: Addison-Wesley.

Chowdhury, N. (1992). *Rice Markets in Bangladesh: A Study in Structure, Conduct and Performance*. Bangladesh Food Policy Project Manuscript 40. Washington, DC: IFPRI.

Chowdhury, N. and S. Haggblade (2000). "Evolving Rice and Wheat Markets", in R. Ahmed, S. Haggblade and T. Chowdhury (eds.), *Out of the Shadow of Famine: Evolving Food Markets and Food Policy in Bangladesh*. Baltimore and London: Johns Hopkins University Press.

Crow, B. and K.A.S. Murshid (1994). "Economic Returns to Social Power: Merchants' Finance and Interlinkage in the Grain Markets of Bangladesh", *World Development* 22(7): 1011-30.

Dawson, P.J. and P.K. Dey (2003). "Testing for the Law of One Price: Rice Market Integration in Bangladesh", *Journal of International Development* 14: 473-84.

Dickey, D.A. and W.A. Fuller (1979). "Distribution of the Estimators for Autoregressive Time Series with a Unit Root", *Journal of the American Statistical Association* 74: 427-31.

Dorosh, P. (1999). "The Determination of Rice Prices in Bangladesh: Supply Shocks, Trade Liberalization and Cross Border Trade", FMRSP Draft Report. (*Mimeo*).

Dorosh, P. and K.A.S. Murshid (2004). "Trade Liberalization and National Food Security: Rice Trade Between Bangladesh and India", in P. Dorosh, C. delNinno and Q. Shahabuddin (eds.), *The 1998 Floods and Beyond: Towards Comprehensive Food Security in Bangladesh*. UPL and IFPRI.

Farid, N. and Rahman, M.S. (2002). "Market Structure and Price Determination of Foodgrains in Bangladesh", Paper prepared for the Early Warning and Food Information System Project, Ministry of Food, Government of Bangladesh, Dhaka.

Goletti, F. (1994). "The Changing Public Role in a Rice Economy Approaching Self-sufficiency: The Case of Bangladesh", *Research Report 98*. Washington, DC: IFPRI.

Mahmud, M. and S.N. Wadood (2012). "Delinking of Local and International Prices: Exploring Competition in the Bangladesh Rice Market", *SANEI Working Paper Series* No. 12-06. Dhaka: South Asia Network of Economic Research Institutes.

Minten, B., A.Z.M. Shafiqul Alam, Uttam K. Deb, Akhtaruz Zaman K. Kabir, David Laborde, Mohammed Hassanullah and K.A.S. Murshid (2010). *Agricultural Marketing, Price Stabilization, Value Chains and Global/Regional Trade*. Bangladesh Food Security Investment Forum. May.

Murshid, K.A.S. (2001). "A Market in Transition? The Case of the Bangladesh Rice Market", *FMRSP Working Paper* No. 28. IFPRI.

Murshid, K.A.S., Nazneen Ahmed, Md. Yunus and S.M. Zulfiqur Ali (2009). *Re-emergence of Food Insecurity in Bangladesh: Instability in Food Production and Prices, Nature of Food Markets, Import and Policy*. FAO-NFPCSP.

Osmani, S.R. and M.A. Quasem (1990). "Pricing and Subsidy Policies for Bangladesh Agriculture", *Research Monograph* No. 11. Dhaka: BIDS.

Ravallion, M. (1986). "Testing Market Integration", *American Journal of Agricultural Economics* 68(20).

———. (1987). *Markets and Famines*. Oxford: Clarendon Press.

Timmer, P.C., Falcon, W.P. and Pearson, S.R. (1983). *Food Policy Analysis*. Baltimore and London: Johns Hopkins University Press.

World Bank (2010). *Food Price Watch*. PREM Network, World Bank.

8

SAIBAL KAR AND NIMAI DAS

Exploring the Relations between Climate Change and Poverty in India

Introduction

Climate change and its implications for the economy and society is now an integral agenda for research in almost all international policy forums. The recognition of climate change as a significant global environmental challenge has its origin in the adoption of the United Nations Framework Convention on Climate Change (UNFCCC) in 1992. The Intergovernmental Panel on Climate Change (IPCC) in its fourth assessment observes that the earth's climate system, when compared with the pre-industrial era, has visibly changed at both global and regional levels. Global negotiations have paid greater attention to minimising the costs of mitigating GHG (greenhouse gas) emissions considered as the prime source of climate change. The IPCC also observes the importance of vulnerability of natural and human systems especially in weaker economies and their adaptation to such changes.

It is well known that climate change has several adverse effects on natural ecosystems and humankind; manifested through declining rainfall and rising temperatures. Consequently, the severity of drought and/or flooding that threatens food security and livelihood in the countryside, could be major fallouts of climate change. Crop production in developing and transition countries still relies heavily on the carrying capacity of the surrounding ecosystems for adequacy of water, soil quality, climate regulation, and other attributes associated with a cleaner atmosphere. Despite technological advances, such as improved crop varieties and irrigation systems, weather and climate continue to play critical roles in agricultural productivity. Loss of weather and climate benefits to the ecosystem seems to coincide with increasing biofuel production in several parts of the world. All of these could reduce the amount of land available for food crops (UNEP, 2010). In this context, an important issue is: what are the proximate links between climate change and poverty in developing countries, such as India? The present chapter is an exploration of the link via effects of climate change on food production in the country. First, we provide a general overview of the literature in the next few paragraphs. It is followed by a description of the data, methods and empirical specifications in section 2. Section 3 discusses the empirical results and section 4 concludes the chapter. Tables describing the extent of emission and biofuel use in India are provided in the Appendix A-8.1.

Global environmental problems like climate change affect various regions and sectors differently based on their sensitivity and adaptive capacity, and hence their vulnerability. Moreover, there is evidence that different groups of people are exposed to different degrees of vulnerability caused by the same degree of climate change (Forsyth, 2000). The IPCC report states that, "the ability of human system to adapt to and cope with climate change depends on such factors as wealth, technology, education, information, skills, infrastructures, access to resource, and management capabilities" (IPCC, 2001: 8). The report also states how vulnerability varies with geographical location, time, and social, economic and environmental conditions. This undoubtedly makes the problem endogenous and therefore, empirically vexing.

There is also considerable emphasis on the pragmatic investigation of the effects of climatic and environmental degradation on the issue of food security. Presently, more than 800 million people (about 80%) in tropical and sub-tropical countries are food insecure (UNDP, 2009). The situation is expected to worsen. The number of food insecure people is likely to increase as changes in extreme weather events and mean climate parameters negatively affect crop, animal yields and agro ecosystem resilience. The world food situation has deteriorated as the agriculture sector is unable to respond to climate-induced supply shortfalls. Higher commodity prices appear to be the direct consequences of these changes and resulting directly from increases in the price of factor inputs. Following the results of agricultural impact studies, summarised in the IPCC Working Group Report, Rosenzweig *et al.*, (1993) point out that the price increases ensuing from climate-induced loss in crop yield are estimated to lie between 25 per cent and 150 per cent. In particular, the responses on the part of the consumers and producers lead to about 24 per cent higher relative prices for cereals. The increase in prices clearly affects the number of people with insufficient resources for consuming adequate amounts of food. The estimated number of unfed people increases approximately 1 per cent for each 2 to 2.5 per cent rise in prices (based on climate change). The number of people at the risk of hunger may increase to almost 60 per cent, which in absolute terms implies an estimated increase between 60 million and 350 million people by 2060. If the rise in temperature is on the lower side (up to 2°C) cereal production is estimated to decrease by just over 1 per cent, while with the highest temperature increases (between 2 to 4°C) global production is estimated to decrease by more than 7 per cent. The greatest negative changes occur in the developing regions, which average 9 per cent to 11 per cent, though the extent of fall in production markedly varies between countries.

Countrywide Implications

Recently, Tirado *et al.* (2010) offered a vivid analysis of countrywide impact of climate change on food security and nutrition of the people. It addresses the three major challenges that threaten the current as well as future food security issues: (i) climate change and the consequent loss of ecosystems; (ii) growing use of biofuel crops that adversely affects land and soil fertility; and (iii) rising food prices and issues like malnutrition and morbidity. This becomes an even more serious issue, since according to the United Nations (UN) predictions in the next 25 years about 80 million people will be added to the world population every year (UN, 2006). Much of it would take place in developing countries where the urban share of population growth is expected to be the highest. As a result, the demand for food will increase, and meeting this incremental and changing food requirement would become seemingly the fundamental challenge facing the global order.

Agricultural Inputs, Natural Resources and Food Production

Agricultural inputs and natural resources are critical determinants of food supply. Degradation of natural resources (like soils, forests, and water) undermines the production capacity, while availability of and access to agricultural inputs (such as water, fertiliser, pesticides, and energy) determine agricultural productivity and thereby, food production as an endogenous outcome. Nevertheless, in most developing countries, there is a mounting inclination to use chemical fertilisers and pesticides to enhance crop productivity and attain food security in the current period, which subsequently results in depletion of soil nutrients in the foreseeable future. The trade off is directly measurable. In the medium to long run, the food supply is certainly going to fall and create pressure on prices, and hence on food security for millions of poor people in the developing countries.

Correcting depletion of soil quality and re-injecting appropriate nutrients is both costly and time dependent. At the same time, it is argued that while developing countries in general do not use excessive fertilisers, the share of inorganic fertilisers is disproportionately high in these countries. A balanced and efficient use of fertilisers of both organic and inorganic varieties could be of consequence for the longer run. Increasing use of pesticides affecting soil quality is also an added concern. The magnanimity of the problem is clearly beyond the purview of public or private sector alone. There should be incentive-compatible measures and policies that help both these sectors to promote sustainable use of existing natural resources and enhance productivity and food security. The Indian government, for instance, has promoted the concept of INSS (integrated nutrient supply system) that combines the use of mineral fertilisers, organic manures and bio-fertilisers (see Appendix Table A-8.1).

Agricultural Productivity and GHG

On a related context, it should be remembered that, intensive agricultural productivity is closely linked with high GHG emissions namely N_2O (nitrous oxide) and CH_4 (methane). The GHG emissions from developing countries have increased rapidly and presumably will exceed the GHG emission level of the developed countries by 2016. In 2007, developing and least-developed countries accounted for 73 per cent of the growth in global GHG emissions. The majority of the increase in GHG emission is linked to fossil fuel consumption as well as use of inorganic fertilisers (see Appendix Table A-8.2). In general, these emissions in turn affect the climate by creating extreme heat as well as contributing towards tremendous rainfall, which leads to loss in crop productivity and decrease in food supply (Beek *et al.*, 2010).

Climate Change and Implications for Urban and Rural Areas

A country's vulnerability to climate change depends on the presence of appropriate mitigation and adaptation options. The most adverse impacts are predicted in the developing world because of geographic exposure, reliance on climate sensitive sectors, low incomes and weak adaptive capacity. Socioeconomic impacts, though generally not well understood, are likely to be profound and will impact humans through a variety of direct and indirect pathways (IPCC, 2007). It is noteworthy that although climate related conditions affect everyone in villages and cities, the urban poor are likely to be the most vulnerable. This group has limited assets and is completely exposed to weather impacts. The social impacts of climate change include both physical as well as emotional well being of the people living in the urban areas. A major aspect of climate variability is the disproportional impact on residents resulting in disruption in the flow of goods and services within an area. This could arise from destruction of industrial infrastructures and loss of commercial activity. The economic and social challenges facing urban cities around the world due to climate change include: energy shortages, damaged infrastructure, and the general losses to the industry. Note that, extensive variability associated with climate related conditions generates substantial risk and uncertainty for residents anywhere. In order to mitigate the pervasiveness of the relation between poverty and natural resource degradation in agricultural productivity, certain policies may need to be taken up. These include: increase in poor people's access to natural resources, enhancement of productivity of natural resource-based assets of the poor, involvement of local people in resource management through various incentives, and development of cheap and reliable eco-friendly technology for the poor (Scherr, 2000).

Fuel Consumption, Emissions and Food Production

In the last two decades, growing use of fossil fuel has led to increasing emission of green house gases, energy dependency and supply insecurity. The UNFCCC database for the Annex-I Parties (covering 41 advanced economies) depicts the fact that the emissions from energy industries increased by 5.6 per cent from 1990 to 2007. The greatest increase occurred in transport sector (about 18%). Intensive cultivation of fuel- and food-crops to meet competing demand for energy and food of the growing population may lead to excessive use or poor management of water and farm chemicals, causing deterioration in environmental and climatic health. According to Rathmann *et al.* (2010) a shift to biofuel production from food in these lands takes place only in the short run.

Another route through which biofuel production affects agriculture is through water resources. Biofuel crops require significant amount of water that results in 'water wars' between the two varieties. This causes shifting of resources to fuel-crops. Appropriate policies for solving the problem of biofuels are to consider a more pro-poor approach to development. For example, this includes a drive towards enabling farmers to grow bio-energy crops on degraded or marginal lands not suitable for food production. Organising groups of small landholders through contract farming schemes to grow and market biomass is considered to be more pro-poor. In addition, a code of conduct has been developed that constrains excessive thrust on cultivating biofuels with fair trade guidelines to ensure that cultivation occurs in a sustainable manner.

Hypotheses, Data and Empirical Specifications

Recent literature on climate change concludes that growing atmospheric concentration of GHGs owing to LULUCF (land use, land use change and forestry) will have significant impacts on the surface climate in the coming decades. The IPCC projects that the global surface temperatures on an average will increase by 2.8°C during this century.

Global warming would alter natural climate and environmental systems in many ways, leading to an increased frequency of extreme weather events as well as changes in precipitation patterns. We closely follow these suggestions to measure the impact of higher surface temperature and high unusual rainfall on crop production and consumption losses for each quarter during 1998-2009 for 17 major states in India. These changes are expected to affect social and economic activities manifesting into greater income poverty in India. These constitute the main hypotheses of this study.

Due to a 2 to 3.5°C rise in temperature accompanied by a 7 to 25 per cent change in precipitation, the farmers may lose net revenues between 9-25 per cent which may adversely affect GDP by 1.8-3.4 per cent (Kumar and Parikh, 2001; Sanghi and Mendelsohn, 2008). Likewise, natural resources like forestland on which many people depend for their livelihoods in the countryside are most vulnerable to climate change. Some estimates show that nearly 55 million people in India depend on minor forest products, a critical component for their subsistence. The forestry sector contributes about 2.4 per cent to the country's GDP (GoI, 2003). But change in land use pattern and unsustainable exploitation of natural resources in conjunction with climate-induced effects is expected to affect the boundaries of natural resources and areas, primary productivity, and resource regeneration. The subsequent analysis, therefore, looks at the effect of climate change variations by degree on the income groups that we expect to be non-uniform.

We employ the Ricardian model, essentially as a restructured functional relationship between net revenue from agriculture and climate variables across space and over time for India, while controlling for various geographic and economic variables. Pooled data weighted by area under crop in each of the 19 major states over 12 years are used for estimating the annual revenue per hectare of farmland as functions of seasonal temperature and precipitation in linear and quadratic terms. To this end, we use control variables like the intensity of irrigation, intensity of high yielding variety seeds, interaction between high yielding and irrigated areas, value of human development index, soil type dummies and time (year) dummies. The regression results are presented in Table 8.1.

In the empirical literature, the standard Ricardian model relies on a nonlinear relationship between net revenue and climate variables. The quadratic term of climate variables, say temperature square, in our model exhibits this nonlinearity (Schlenker and Roberts, 2009). Our model specification is given by:

$$R = \alpha + \beta_{1J}NT_j + \beta_{2j}NT_j^2 + \beta_{3j}NT_j^3 + \beta_{4j}NR_j + \beta_{5j}NR_j^2 + \beta_{6j}NR_j^3 + \beta_{7j}NT_jNR_j + \lambda_1 IRR + \lambda_2 HYV + \lambda_3 IRRxHYV + \lambda_4 HDI + \gamma_m SD_m + \theta_n YD_n + u \quad (1)$$

where NT = normal temperature (j = January, April, July and October; or *kharif*, *rabi* and *zaid*), NR = normal rainfall, IRR = irrigation intensity, HYV = intensity of high yielding seeds, IRRxHYV = interaction between HYV and irrigated areas to reorganise their collective effect for green revolution, HDI = value of Human Development Index, SD = soil type dummy (m = 1 to 6 for 7 soil types), YD = year dummy (n = 1997 to 2008 for 12 years) and u = error term.

Prior to interpreting the regression results of climate coefficients, let us discuss the coefficients of the control variables. The net revenue from land is sensitive to differences in the types of soil as measured by soil fertility levels. The dummy variables for all the years turn out to be significantly positive. The time dummies suggest fluctuations in annual values because of un-weighted climate and economic effects. This might even lead to 'no trend' in the coefficients of year dummies. The irrigation intensity has a positive impact on net revenue, since more irrigation facility is indeed associated with the enhanced productivity and therefore revenue. The coefficient for HYV areas is positive, reflecting the desirable positive effect of net revenues in the course of higher productivity that followed the Green Revolution in India. Moreover, the coefficient of collective effect for HYV and irrigated areas is positive and significant but fairly low compared with their individual effects.

Results and Interpretations

The regression results clearly indicate that most of the climatic factors are statistically significant embodying a distinct impact of the climate variables on net revenue (Table 8.1). In addition, the quadratic and interaction terms for the climate variables reveal the underlying nonlinear effects. Looking at the marginal climate effects by seasons:

January, April and July temperatures have negative influence, while the effect of October temperature is positive.[1] Moreover, there are three successive stages for agricultural crop cultivation, sowing, growing and harvesting. These are accomplished for each of the cropping season by a specified period, which also varies slightly across the regions based on the arrival of the monsoon (south-west and north-east monsoons). In accordance with the national crop calendar, the consequence of temperature change on growing period of crop production during all the three cropping seasons is detrimental as shown by the negative sign of their coefficients. The positive effect appearing for October alone may be judged by the fact that a rising temperature during the harvesting period of *kharif* crops could possibly be favorable for the ripening process. In other seasons however the rising temperature might lead to heat stress on crop cultivation systems. For instance, incremental warmth for growing of *rabi* crops in January could cause strain on ripening of these heat-sensitive winter crops such as wheat.

The regression results show that the rainfall coefficients move in the expected direction, though not as intensive as one expects with temperature, offering *a priori* agronomic explanations. For example, the positive January precipitation seems to indicate the potential advantage in the growing period of *rabi* crops in consequence of additional moisture. Furthermore, the October precipitation (sowing period for *rabi* crops) turns out to be of strictly positive influence. However, an additional bit of precipitation in pre-monsoon and monsoon seasons adversely affect crop production. But, the comparative detrimental effect of supplementary monsoon rainfall is especially marginal as it usually harmonises with the monsoon. Note that, the adverse effect of higher rainfall for summer crops (during April) may cause harm to the growth of plants. Among the control variable, we have used the poverty rates (BPL: below poverty line) and HDI in separate regressions in order to eliminate the problems of multicollinearity, that may also exist in case of quadratic and cubic

1. Notably, cropping during monsoon (*kharif*), winter (*rabi*) and summer (*zaid*) (the first two are typically the predominant agricultural seasons) when most of the crops are cultivated in India, are also quite climate sensitive months.

transformation of the same variable. Most of the other coefficients are self-explanatory.

Table 8.1

Ricardian Regression Results for Net Land Revenue in India

Variable	*Regression 1 Coefficient*	*Regression 2 Coefficient*	*t-Statistic-reg1 (reg 2)*
Constant	198.15	200.03	18.68398(19.34)
January temperature	-172.84	-181.09	-3.41(-4.02)
April temperature	-360.23	-367.43	-5.98(-6.32)
July temperature	-205.58	-211.32	-4.57(-5.01)
October temperature	157.77	159.34	16.00(17.01)
January precipitation	11.51	11.51	3.01(4.23)
April precipitation	-5.68	-5.68	-6.53(-7.22)
July precipitation	-0.61	-0.61	-8.94(-8.99)
October precipitation	8.67	8.67	6.05(7.11)
January temperature square	-59.88		-17.11
April temperature square	110.51		3.44
July temperature square	-88.01		-2.93
October temperature square	-63.51		-8.84
January precipitation square	-2.32		-7.09
April precipitation square	2.36		2.72
July precipitation square	0.61		5.48
October precipitation square	1.17		2.23
January temperature cube	-8.75		-1.23
April temperature cube	2.09		4.15
July temperature cube	-7.95		-12.33
October temperature cube	-14.92		-2.71
January precipitation cube	-0.37		-1.18
April precipitation cube	0.06		1.79
July precipitation cube	0.01		0.52
October precipitation cube	0.02		3.39
January temperature x precipitation	-9.67		-5.19
April temperature x precipitation	3.65		2.62
July temperature x precipitation	-1.07		-1.44

contd...

...*contd*...

October temperature x precipitation	-0.76		-0.83
Irrigation	34.00	35.71	5.53(6.02)
HYV	28.18	29.22	11.63(12.90)
HDI	-	4.21	3.22
BPL	-1.48		-3.11
Soil dummy 1	7.05	7.61	8.19(8.76)
Soil dummy 2	8.14	8.80	6.47(6.78)
Soil dummy 3	3.56	4.06	2.57(3.01)
Soil dummy 4	1.18		1.00
Soil dummy 5	6.60		5.76
Soil dummy 6	-3.66		-2.33
Soil dummy 7	-6.08		-0.63
Year dummy 1997	76.59		3.05
Year dummy 1998	37.16		2.13
Year dummy 1999	-73.25	-75.41	-0.95(-0.99)
Year dummy 2000	-30.53	-31.03	-1.10(-2.21)
Year dummy 2001	-26.75	-28.33	-9.10 (-9.89)
Year dummy 2002	34.13	35.14	7.41(7.70)
Year dummy 2003	57.45	57. 19	7.06(7.99)
Year dummy 2004	-45.61	-46.60	-0.67(-0.72)
Year dummy 2005	29.38		-0.53
Year dummy 2006	4.89		0.07
Year dummy 2007	52.11		2.33
Year dummy 2008	70.00		0.80
Constant	34.00		5.53
R-squared	0.88	0.76	
Sample period	1996:2008		
Total panel (unbalanced) observations	229.00		
Dependent Variable	Net revenue		

Note: For explanation of Regressions 1 and 2, see text.

Source: Authors' own calculations.

Furthermore, observing that there may be any climatic fluctuation over an agricultural season in the countryside, our second Ricardian regression considers the average value of climate variables over the individual cropping seasons, namely *kharif*, *rabi* and *zaid*, keeping the control variables unchanged. Table 8.2 depicts the results of this regression. In line with the primary regression portrayed in Table 8.1, the results in Table 8.2 point to the fact that most climatic factors negatively and significantly affect the net revenue. We find that the temperature effect on net revenue is negative and statistically significant in every season. Of course, the intensity differs by seasons such that a rising temperature may lead to higher heat stress on *zaid* crops followed by that on the *kharif* crops. On the other hand, the precipitation effect is less intensive for the net revenue. Moreover, while the summer and monsoon crops are negatively affected by rising precipitation, the same is helpful to the winter crops.

Table 8.2

Ricardian Regression Results for Net Land Revenue by Cropping Season in India

Variable	*Coefficient*	*t-Statistic*
Constant	101.20101	27.25488
Monsoon (*kharif*) temperature	-116.04532	-8.12129
Winter (*rabi*) temperature	-67.22308	-4.08403
Summer (*zaid*) temperature	-278.26587	-4.60203
Monsoon precipitation	-1.25684	-5.30311
Winter precipitation	9.53641	6.04664
Summer precipitation	-6.07030	-6.12547
Monsoon temperature square	-48.65423	-11.20627
Winter temperature square	-7.05302	-9.04322
Summer temperature square	-92.17234	-3.01543
Monsoon precipitation square	2.03516	2.82192
Winter precipitation square	-0.76052	-6.14817
Summer precipitation square	2.10605	1.92302
Monsoon temperature cube	-14.02557	-2.58756
Winter temperature cube	1.0919	4.21548
Summer temperature cube	7.15096	6.25462
Monsoon precipitation cube	0.10525	2.57201
Winter precipitation cube	0.01035	1.11521

contd...

...contd...

Summer precipitation cube	0.07107	2.09014
Monsoon temperature x precipitation	-17.06248	-7.02010
Winter temperature x precipitation	0.80675	3.54362
Summer temperature x precipitation	-12.17562	-0.78229
Irrigation	29.05685	8.05257
HYV	21.24681	7.05688
HYV x Irrigation	8.11022	3.50811
HDI	7.06325	4.02173
Soil dummy 1	9.25041	5.22181
Soil dummy 2	7.11333	5.01721
Soil dummy 3	4.25604	1.24695
Soil dummy 4	2.55172	2.16922
Soil dummy 5	5.15957	2.06011
Soil dummy 6	-2.54280	-5.24153
Soil dummy 7	-5.12473	-1.34694
Year dummy 1997	64.01679	4.70546
Year dummy 1998	43.01561	1.11222
Year dummy 1999	-62.12425	-2.29520
Year dummy 2000	-32.43402	-1.49254
Year dummy 2001	-22.05206	-7.59341
Year dummy 2002	28.91310	5.44040
Year dummy 2003	48.04247	6.15846
Year dummy 2004	-54.21492	-3.56691
Year dummy 2005	33.25481	-1.75057
Year dummy 2006	10.08801	0.40121
Year dummy 2007	61.00224	1.13331
Year dummy 2008	53.12342	1.07971
R-squared	0.83162	

Source: Authors' own calculations.

Now, for the sensitivity analysis following the IPCC (1996) measures, we turn to the simulation of climate change impact on net revenue for the 2°C increase in mean temperature and 7 per cent rise in mean rainfall based on the basic regression results in Table 8.1. The consequential impacts by the representative month by seasons are depicted in Table 8.3. As seen from the regression results, there are considerable variations for both temperature and rainfall effects on the net revenue change. A 2°C increase in temperature for any representative month with no other change results in a decline in net revenue by ₹ 1,490 for January, ₹ 603 for April and ₹ 198 for July. Conversely, the net revenue increases in the month of October by ₹ 814. Similarly, in conformity with the regression results, a 7 per cent rise in precipitation is seen as beneficial during the growing period of *rabi* crops and harvesting period of *kharif* crops. These are associated with increases in the revenue by ₹ 111 for January and ₹ 91 for October. However, simulation of monsoon precipitation in July has almost no effect on farm revenue. A moderately adverse effect on revenue by about ₹ 93 is observed for rising precipitation in April (during pre-monsoon season associated with the summer crops). Note that, these simulation results for India are obtained from the average value over 12 years by aggregating statewide values (see Appendix Table A-8.3 for region-wise meteorological data for India). These are representative of the seasonal months (see Table 8.3). Despite the fact that this is an indirect way of measuring the impact of climate change on the incidence of poverty, yet it provides some clear direction as to the reaction of consumption expenditure to such outcomes of climate change that the global forums have continually suggested thus far.

Table 8.3

Simulation of Climate Change Effects on Consumption

(in ₹)

	January	*April*	*July*	*October*
Temperature effects (+ 2°C increase)	– 29.35	– 15.83	– 11.20	+ 17.12
Precipitation effects (+ 7% increase)	+ 5.76	– 8.96	– 0.16	+ 4.03

Note: Estimated average consumption (monthly per person in real term) is ₹ 347.82

The sensitivity analysis shows that a simulation of climate change for 2°C increase in temperature and 7 per cent rise in rainfall are quite significant (Table 8.2). There is considerable variation in consumption for climate-induced changes in net revenue. The 2°C increase in temperature, *ceteris paribus*, during a particular season leads to a decline in per capita monthly consumption expenditure by ₹ 29 for January, ₹ 16 for April and Rs.11 for July and subsequently for other months. For example, a moderately adverse effect on consumption by about ₹ 4 is observed for higher precipitation in April. Clearly, these simulations are amenable to change in both directions. The reduction in consumption, however, is still a predominant outcome of such changes, which in view of the empirical and simulation results would make a case for those month-wise specifications when lower precipitation reduces crop production.

Concluding Remarks

We find considerable impact of the climate variables on net land revenue and hence, consumption of the rural population across India. Looking at the marginal climate effects by seasons, it appears that January, April and July temperatures have negative influence, while the October temperature effect is positive. Our empirical result shows that the rainfall coefficients move in the expected direction although not as intensively as one expects with temperature, substantiating the agronomic explanations. However, simulation of monsoon precipitation in July has almost no effect on farm revenue. Finally we find a moderate variation in consumption resulting for climate-induced change in net revenue. To address the challenges on sustainable economic development and poverty, adaptation and mitigation strategies are required which may include financial incentives for improving land management, focus on carbon content, efficient use of fertilisers and irrigation, and similar measures. These incentives are expected to create positive association with sustainable development and with efforts required to reduce climate-related vulnerability.

To reiterate, we have estimated the economic implications of climate change for the Indian agriculture. Since India is home to a large indigenous tribal population and rural poor, who in turn are heavily dependent on local natural resources like forest and coastland with extensive biodiversity and sensitivity to climate change, the results may have deeper region-specific implications than the generalised ones. In future, we intend to use a similar structure for estimating the likely impacts of projected climate change on consumption of natural resources. This may help to develop and implement adaptation strategies for both biodiversity conservation and livelihood security of the resource-dependent people. In view of the dearth of studies focusing on effects of climate change on consumption-related outcomes, the study provides some direction in this chapter. While, earlier evidence for India covered the northern states and the Western Ghats (Deshingkar, 1997; Ravindranath *et al.*, 1997), the present study generates results for 17 major states for a period spreading over a decade. Our results show that climate change could impart moderate to large-scale impact on forest biodiversity and crop production over a wide range of varieties. The impact of climate change on the consumption is an offshoot of how the crop production is affected over several months of the year through two principal sources, namely: the rise in surface temperature and the unusual incidence of precipitation. The simulation of these changes ranging from 2°C and 7 per cent rise in temperature and precipitation respectively shows that the consumption level falls significantly. The consequence of such changes on the number of people in the BPL category should be immediate. The policy propositions should therefore, not only aim at mitigating these effects on a much bigger scale, clearly beyond considerations of one such country, but also look into internal readjustments for better environment-economic outcomes. In order to cope with the stress from projected climate change patterns, the immediate priority should also be to educate and train the indigenous and vulnerable people and promote community based asset generation such that the moral hazard of monitoring resource maintenance and replenishments is minimised. This will also strengthen public-private partnerships through scientific interventions in crop production in the longer run.

References

Beek, C.L.V., G.B. Meerburg and R.L.M. Schils (2010). "Feeding the World's Increasing Population while Limiting Climate Change Impacts: Linking N_2O and CH_4 Emissions from Agriculture to Population Growth", *Environmental Science and Policy* 13: 89-96.

Brine, K., R. Liechenko, U. Kelkar, H. Venema, G. Aandahl and H. Tompkins (2004). "Mapping Vulnerability to Multiple Stressors: Climate Change and Globalization in India", *Global Environmental Change* 14: 303-13.

Chaudhuri, S. and U. Mukhopadhyay (2009). *Revisiting the Informal Sector: A General Equilibrium Approach*. New York: Springer-Verlag.

Deshingkar, P. (1997). *Adapting to Climate Change in a Forest based Land Use System: A Case Study of Himachal Pradesh, India*. Stockholm: Atmospheric Environmental Issues in Developing Countries, Stockholm Environment Institute.

Fankhauser, S. and R.S.J. Tol (2005). "On Climate Change and Economic Growth", *Resource and Energy Economics* 27: 1-17.

FAO (2005). *Fertilizer Use by Crop in India*. Rome: Food and Agriculture Organization of the United Nations (Land and Water Development Division).

Forsyth, T. (2000). "Vulnerability to Climate Change: Theoretical Concerns and a Case Study from Thailand", *Discussion Paper*. Environment and Natural Resource Programme, Kennedy School of Government, Harvard University.

GoI (2003). *Tenth Five-Year Plan: 2002-07*. New Delhi: Planning Commission, Government of India.

Hanjra, M., A. Qureshi and M. Ejaz, (2010). "Global Water Crisis and Future Food Security in an Era of Climate Change", *Food Policy* 35(5): 365-77.

Harris, J.R. and M.P. Todaro (1970). "Migration, Unemployment and Development: A Two-Sector Analysis", *American Economic Review* 60(1): 126-42.

Hertel, T.W., M.B. Burke and D.B. Lobell (2010). "The Poverty Implications of Climate-induced Crop Yield Changes by 2030", *Global Environmental Change* 20: 577-85.

Intergovernmental Panel on Climate Change (IPCC) (1996). *Climate Change 1995*. Contribution of Working Group II. Cambridge: Cambridge University Press.

———. (2001). "Climate Change 2001: Impacts, Adaptation and Vulnerability: Summary for Policymakers", *Report of Working Group II of the Intergovernmental Panel on Climate Change*. Geneva: Intergovernmental Panel on Climate Change.

———. (2007). *Climate Change 2007*. *http://www.ipcc.ch/*

Jacoby, H., M. Rabassa and E. Skoufias (2011). "On the Distributional Implications of Climate Change: The Case of India", *Policy Research Working Paper*. Washington, DC: World Bank.

Kramer, A.M. (2007). "Adaptation to Climate Change in Poverty Reduction Strategies", Occasional Paper of Human Development Report Office, *Human Development Report* 2007/08. United Nations Development Programme.

Kumar, K.S.K. and J. Parikh (2001). "Indian Agriculture and Climate Sensitivity", *Global Environmental Change* 11: 147-54.

Marjit, S. and S. Kar (2011). *The Outsiders: Economic Reform and Informal Labour in a Developing Economy*. Oxford University Press.

Sanghi, A. and R. Mendelsohn (2008). "The Impacts of Global Warming on Farmers in Brazil and India", *Global Environmental Change* 18: 655-65.

Oldeman, L.R. (1992). "Global Extent of Soil Degradation", *Bi-annual Report* 1991-92. Wageningen, The Netherlands: International Soil Reference and Information Centre,.

Rathmann, R., A. Szklo and R. Schaffer (2010). "Land Use Competition for Production of Food and Liquid Bio-fuels: An Analysis of the Arguments in the Current Debate", *Renewable Energy* 35: 14-22.

Ravindranath, N.H., R. Sukumar and P. Deshingkar (1997). *Climate Change and Forests: Impacts and Adaptation (Regional Assessment for the Western Ghats, India)*. Stockholm: Atmospheric Environmental Issues in Developing Countries, Stockholm Environment Institute.

Ravindranath, N.H., N.V Joshi, R. Sukumar and A. Saxena (2006). "Impact of Climate Change on Forests in India", *Current Science* 90(3): 354-61.

Ringler, C. (2010). "Summary", *EuroChoices* (The Agricultural Economics Society and the European Association of Agricultural Economists) 9(3): 16-21.

Rosenzweig, C., M.L. Parry, G. Fischer and K. Frohberg (1993). "Climate Change and World Food Supply", Research Report No. 3 (Environmental Change Unit). University of Oxford. *http://www.ciesin.org/docs/004-046/004-046.html*

Scherr, S.J. (2000). "A Downward Spiral? Research Evidence on the Relationship between Poverty and Natural Resource Degradation", *Food Policy* 25: 479-98.

Schlenker, W. and M.J. Roberts (2009). "Nonlinear Temperature Effects Indicate Severe Damages to U.S. Crop Yields under Climate Change", *PNAS (Proceedings of the National Academy of Sciences of the United States of America)* 106(37): 15594-8. *http://www.pnas.org/content/106/37/15594.*

Skoufias, E., M. Rabassa and S. Olivieri (2011). "The Poverty Impacts of Climate Change: A Review of the Evidence", *World Bank Policy Research Working Paper* 5622. Washington, DC: World Bank.

Tirado, M.C., M.J. Cohen, N. Aberman, J. Meerman and B. Thompson (2010). "Addressing the Challenges of Climate Change and Biofuel Production for Food and Nutrition Security", *Food Research International* 43: 1729-44.

Tol, Richard S.J. (2009). "The Economic Effects of Climate Change", *Journal of Economic Perspectives* 23(2): 29-51.

UN (1996). *World Population Prospects: The 1996 Revisions*. New York: United Nations, Department for Economics and Social Information and Policy Analysis.

United Nations (2006). *Population Ageing 2006*. Geneva: Department of Economic and Social Affairs, Population Division.

UNDP (2009). *Climate Change: Perspectives from India*. S. Narain, P. Ghosh, N.C. Saxena, J. Parikh and P. Soni (eds.). India.

UNEP (2010). *UNEP Year Book 2010: New Science and Developments in Our Changing Environment*. Nairobi: Division of Early Warning and Assessment (DEWA).

Winter, M., P. Gaskell and C. Short (1998). "Upland Landscapes in Britain and the 1992 CAP Reforms", *Landscape Research* 23: 273-88.

Appendix A-8.1

Table A-8.1

Consumption of Organic and Inorganic Fertiliser in India

	Bio-fertiliser (tonnes)	*Inorganic Fertiliser (million tonnes)*
1969-70	NA	1.98
1992-93	1600	12.15
2003-04	10000	16.80

Note: Data source is Fertiliser Association of India (2003-04), except for inorganic fertiliser 1992-93 which is from the Planning Commission of India database.

Table A-8.2

Estimates of Greenhouse Gas Emissions in India, 2007

('000 tonnes)

		CO_2	CH_4	N_2O	CO_2 *Equivalent*
India		1497029.20	20564.20	239.31	1727706.10
Energy sector		992836.30	4266.05	56.88	1100056.89
Industrial sector		405862.90	14.77	20.56	412546.53
Agri-cultural sector	Total	0	13767.80	146.07	334405.50
	Enteric fermentation	0	10099.80	0	212095.80
	Rice cultivation	0	3327.00	0	69867.00
	Soils	0	0	140.00	43400.00

Note: Data source is India: Greenhouse Gas Emissions 2007, a report by the Indian Network of Climate Change Assessment, Ministry of Environment & Forests, Government of India (2010).

Table A-8.3

Basic Data for the Meteorological Stations in India

State	*City*	*Latitude (°N)*	*Longitude (°E)*	*Altitude (m)*	*Sea Distance (Mile)*
Andaman	Port Blair	11.66	92.74	79	5
Andhra Pradesh	Anantpur	14.65	77.61	350	170
	Hyderabad	17.40	78.51	545	174
	Masulipatnam	16.19	81.14	3	2
	Tirupathy	13.64	79.43	162	42
	Vijayawada	16.51	80.67	21	42
	Vishakhapatnam	17.68	83.21	3	4
Arunachal Pradesh	Pasighat	28.05	95.33	155	426
Assam	Dibrugarh	27.46	94.93	111	392
	Guwahati	26.14	91.74	54	225
	Silchar	24.81	92.79	97	163
Bihar	Bhagalpur	25.15	87.01	37	239
	Gaya	24.45	84.57	116	184
	Patna	25.36	85.06	60	163
Chhattisgarh	Ambikapur	23.10	83.15	602	265
	Jagdalpur	19.05	82.02	553	126
	Raipur	21.14	81.39	298	248
Delhi	New Delhi (Faridabad)	28.35	77.12	216	512
	New Delhi (Palam)	28.34	77.60	217	533
Goa	Panjim	15.29	73.49	60	6
Gujarat	Ahmedabad	23.04	72.38	55	59
	Baroda	22.18	73.15	34	25
	Bhuj	23.15	69.4	80	29
	Rajkot	22.18	70.47	138	49
	Surat	21.19	72.83	12	1
Haryana	Hissar	29.1	75.44	221	533
	Karnal	29.42	77.02	236	621
Himachal Pradesh	Dharmsala	32.16	76.23	1211	710
	Manali	32.23	77.08	1900	776
	Shimla	31.06	77.10	2202	660

contd...

...contd...

Jammu & Kashmir	Jammu	32.40	74.50	367	715
	Srinagar	34.05	74.50	1587	801
Jharkhand	Jamshedpur	22.50	86.10	142	91
	Ranchi	23.19	85.19	652	171
Karnataka	Bangalore	12.58	77.35	921	171
	Belgaum Samra	15.51	74.37	747	61
	Gadag	15.25	75.38	650	117
	Gulbarga	17.21	76.51	458	212
	Hassan	13.00	76.09	960	82
	Mangalore	12.55	74.53	102	1
	Mysore	12.18	76.42	767	85
Kerala	Cannanore	11.86	75.35	12	1
	Kozhikode	11.15	75.47	5	7
	Palakkad	10.77	76.65	93	43
	Thiruvanan-thapuram	8.29	76.57	64	7
Lakshadweep	Amini Divi	11.07	72.44	4	1
	Androth	10.83	73.68	5	1
	Minicoy	8.18	73.00	2	1
Maharashtra	Akola	20.42	77.04	309	279
	Aurangabad	19.51	75.24	579	177
	Mahabaleshwar	17.56	73.40	1382	51
	Mumbai	19.07	72.51	15	9
	Nagpur	21.06	79.03	309	360
	Nasik	20.02	73.50	18	50
	Parbhani	19.08	76.8	414	260
	Pune	18.32	73.51	559	71
	Solapur	17.40	75.54	479	186
Manipur	Imphal	24.46	93.54	781	200
Meghalaya	Cherrapunji	25.15	91.44	1313	173
	Shillong	25.34	91.53	1598	199
	Tura	25.3	90.16	349	198
Mijoram	Aizwal	23.36	93.00	1132	102

contd...

...contd...

Madhya Pradesh	Bhopal	23.17	77.21	523	302
	Gwalior	26.14	78.15	207	438
	Indore	22.43	75.48	567	194
	Jabalpur	23.12	79.57	393	464
	Khajuraho	24.85	79.93	283	502
Nagaland	Kohima	25.67	94.12	1261	263
Orissa	Balasore	21.31	86.56	20	10
	Bhubaneshwar	20.15	85.5	46	30
	Gopalpur	19.16	84.53	17	3
	Jharsuguda	21.55	84.05	230	190
	Sambalpur	21.28	83.58	148	160
Pondicherry	Pondicherry	11.93	79.83	1	1
Punjab	Amritsar	31.38	74.52	234	646
	Bhatinda	30.11	75.00	207	569
	Chandigarh	30.39	76.48	308	626
	Jullundur	31.19	75.34	228	650
	Ludhiana	30.56	75.52	247	631
Rajasthan	Abu	24.48	72.80	1219	159
	Ajmer	26.45	74.66	486	321
	Bikaner	28.01	73.34	224	396
	Jaipur	26.92	75.82	390	371
	Jaisalmer	26.54	70.55	242	281
	Jodhpur	26.25	73.03	217	276
	Kota	25.14	75.86	274	276
	Udaipur	24.57	73.53	514	180
Sikim	Gangtok	27.34	88.61	1676	362
Tamil Nadu	Chennai	13.00	80.11	16	3
	Coimbatore	11.02	77.03	400	74
	Kanyakumari	8.05	77.30	37	4
	Kodaikanal	10.14	77.28	2343	84
	Madurai	9.55	78.07	133	37
	Uthagaman-dalam	11.24	76.44	2623	42
Tripura	Agartala	23.53	91.15	16	50

contd...

...contd...

Uttar Pradesh	Agra	27.10	78.02	169	462
	Allahabad	25.27	81.44	98	434
	Bareilly	28.22	79.24	173	681
	Gorakhpur	26.45	83.22	77	292
	Kanpur	26.26	80.22	126	543
	Lucknow	26.45	80.53	128	538
	Varanasi	25.18	83.01	76	385
Uttaranchal	Dehra Dun	30.19	78.02	682	637
	Joshimath	30.34	79.34	1890	704
	Mukteswar	29.28	79.39	2311	654
	Nainital	29.23	79.30	1938	654
West Bengal	Cooch Behar	26.31	89.47	46	285
	Darjeeling	27.02	88.27	2128	346
	Kolkata	22.57	88.37	6	21
	Malda	25.03	88.14	31	203
	Sri Niketan	23.39	87.42	59	120

Note: The latitude, longitude and altitude presented here are based on the measurement available in online software at url: *http://www.altitude.nu/* and the distance from the state geographical centre to nearest shoreline is derived using the online software at url: *http://www.freemaptools.com/radius-around-point.htm*

9

ARINDAM BANIK, PRADIP K. BHAUMIK,
SHEIKH MD. MONZURUL HUQ AND
BHUBAN B. BAJRACHARYA

Trade in Health Services in South Asia

An Examination of the Need for Regional Cooperation

Introduction

South Asian countries have large intra-regional trade in health services. However, a large part of the health services trade in the region is informal, whereas the formal health services trade, which is rather small in size, faces a large number of barriers—implicit or otherwise. The measurement of barriers to trade in services, and the gains associated with removing such barriers has been of keen interest in recent years, particularly in the context of inclusion of services and investment in South Asian Free Trade Agreement (SAFTA). In general, barriers to trade in health services are unlike tariffs. They are typically regulatory barriers, rather than explicit taxes. The underlying economic rationale for policy reforms is that the removal of barriers to trade in services is likely to result in lower prices, improved quality, and higher competitiveness. As with trade in goods, restrictions on trade in services reduce welfare because they create a wedge between domestic and foreign prices, leading to a loss of consumer surplus. Health services liberalisation exerts an economy-wide influence as the services constitute strong inputs to all other economic activities, including trade.

Some studies identified several challenges related to the implementation of General Agreement on Trade in Services (GATS) commitments.[1] It seems useful to mention here that through the GATS, the member states of the World Trade Organization (WTO) have the option to commit themselves to liberalise health services. Article I of the GATS, following Bhagwati (1984) and Sampson and Snape (1985), discusses a four part typology of trade in health services. In terms of the GATS, health services include: medical and dental services, services provided by midwives, nurses, physiotherapists and para-medical personnel, hospital services, and other human services.

The four modes of GATS delivery of health services are: (i) cross-border supply: where the service is provided remotely from one country to another, such as telemedicine via Internet or satellite, or international health insurance policies;[2] (ii) consumption abroad: where individuals use a service in another country, such as patients travelling to take advantage of foreign health care facilities;[3] (iii)

1. Interestingly, multilateral liberalisation of trade in goods has taken place for the last half century, however, liberalisation of trade in services began only in 1994 with end of Uruguay Round . The GATS is the first and the only set of multilateral rules covering international trade in services. The agreement was concluded at the Uruguay Round (1986-1993). It came into force in January 1995. The GATS sought to gradually liberalise and expand trade in the service sector. It had a "built in agenda" mandating members to kick off progressive liberalisation negotiation on services from January 2000. The Guidelines and Procedures of Negotiations were adopted by the Council for Trade in Services on March 2001 as provided in the GATS Article XIX: 3, see Kelegama (2009).

2. The rising competition for foreign patients, due not only to economic but also cultural policy reasons has been accompanied by initiatives in the marketing of medical institutions. Such initiatives, sponsored by governments, universities, or private firms, consist of dissemination of information on the institutions and patients. For example, the so-called "health tourism fairs" are one of the most common mechanisms used by governments and institutions, either directly or through marketing agencies. Likewise, a telemedicine link has been established between Apollo Hospitals at Hyderabad, Delhi, and Chennai in India and Lahore Medical Imaging Center, Lahore in Pakistan. This is the first telemedicine link between India and Pakistan. A link of this kind is an excellent effort and it will go a long way in bringing together the medical community and people of the two countries. This will enable people of Pakistan to have easy access to specialists and super specialists without travelling to India. The telemedicine link has been launched as a move to facilitate exchange of medicare and health facilities at reduced cost in South Asian countries. The Apollo Telemedicine Networking Foundation has also established telemedicine centres in Nepal and Sri Lanka.

3. A good number of patients come to India from Bangladesh, Nepal, Bhutan, Sri Lanka, Pakistan, and Afghanistan for medical treatment every year. Likewise, many patients come to Pakistan from Afghanistan for medical treatment. Lack in domestic health infrastructure forces the Bangladeshi patients to move to India for treatment. In general, Mode 2 (consumption abroad) is the most popular mode through which trade in health services has been taking place between the two countries.

commercial presence: where a foreign company sets up operations within another country in order to deliver the service, such as hospitals, health clinics or insurance offices;[4] and (iv) presence of natural persons[5]: where individuals such as doctors, nurses or midwives travel to another country to supply a service there on a temporary basis.

There is a dearth of analytical research in estimating barriers to trade in health services, particularly in the context of South Asia. This chapter observes that an in-depth study focusing exclusively on health services trade will not only strengthen overall services trade capacity of the South Asian region but will also promote global and regional trade.

The chapter is aimed at assessing the potential in health services and economic costs of barriers to trade in health services in select South Asian economies such as Bangladesh, India and Nepal. In addition, the chapter examines the structure and nature of health services in both India and Nepal. As an extension, this chapter will also analyse the impact of liberalisation and regulatory reforms on economic welfare. For example, in order to promote telemedicine in selected South Asian economies, this chapter will attempt to highlight the barriers and also provide the way forward to eliminate such barriers.

The remainder of the chapter is laid out as follows. Section 2 discusses a review of literature of the study. Section 3 elaborates a brief overview of the dynamic properties of service trade liberalisation in South Asia. We discuss methodology in Section 4. The country

4. For instance, in an effort to enhance domestic capabilities in medical services as well as reduce foreign exchange costs derived from outflows of patients, several Asia Pacific countries are allowing foreign medical institutions to establish 'local branch campuses' or 'subsidiaries'. For example, India's Apollo Group has opened branches in Bangladesh and Sri Lanka; Escorts Heart Centre in Bangladesh, Nepal and Sri Lanka.

5. International trade in health services focuses on the mobility of patients; no comprehensive information on the movement of medical professionals is adequately available. A similar lack of information exists in relation to cross-border supply of medical education services. As mentioned, ample demand for health services triggered by the needs of the labour market, and the emergence of new technologies are rapidly expanding the market share of telemedicine. Such an expansion is likely to have a growing international component, but its potential for changing the current patterns of trade in the sector is difficult to assess at this stage.

cases are discussed in Sections 5 and 6 with an emphasis on issues of identification. In Section 7, we analyse data based on field work. Section 8 contains conclusions and policy recommendations.

Review of Literature

The literature on trade in services remains vast in general but is found to be small in health services, specifically in the context of South Asia. However, a few of them may be considered as notable contributions. The aforementioned studies by Rahman (2002), De (2006), De and Bhattacharya (2007) focus on health-related infrastructure issues and then discuss dominance of informal trade in this context. For example, Rahman (2002) found that about 57 per cent of total Bangladeshi patients seeking treatment abroad actually went to India in 1999. This is because medical services facilities in Bangladesh are inadequate, and the quality of the services in India is relatively better than that of Bangladesh. More interestingly, about 20 per cent of estimated 50,000 Bangladeshi patients went to India officially for treatment without valid visas. In most of the cases, they did not seek visa on medical grounds in order to avoid hassles, and took tourist visa to enter India for medical treatment. The findings are consistent with numerous examples of patients and case studies (De and Bhattacharya, 2007). In another interesting study, Kelegama and Mukherjee (2007) find that Indian doctors face problems in obtaining work permit in Sri Lanka for their stay in that country.

Banik, De and Bhaumik (2009) have recently studied Service Trade Restrictive Index (STRI)[6] in the context of five South Asian

6. The STRI methodology which translates qualitative information on services barriers into an aggregated quantitative score by sector is based on four modes defined by the GATS. This categorisation also allows one to capture the issue of complementarity and substitution between modes. The authors have gathered qualitative information through questionnaires completed by government agencies and various country reports that are available in the region as well as supplementary research. The qualitative information has been used to determine the values of the different components of the sectoral aggregate and modal indexes. The weight of each component has been determined through pair-wise comparison. The transition from qualitative to quantitative analysis involves many benefits, but is not without risks. The two main benefits of synthesising qualitative information in a quantitative index are first, to enable the comparison of restrictions across countries at the sectoral level, and second, to determine the impact of barriers on trade in services and on different variables of economic

contd...

economies such as India, Pakistan, Nepal, Sri Lanka and Bangladesh. The authors focused their analysis based on sectors such as education, health, travel and tourism, telecom (fixed and mobile), and transport sectors (air and maritime). They found that trade restriction in health sector varies across South Asian countries. For example, aggregate scores for select South Asian countries range from 0.23 (Nepal, the least restrictive) to 0.41 (Pakistan, the most restrictive). Pakistan's score is primarily attributed to consumption abroad (Mode 2) and movement of natural person restrictions (Mode 4). On close investigation, it appears that Central Bank's lengthy formalities to allow foreign exchange for nationals' treatment in other countries beyond limit is the major impediment. Bangladesh follows with an aggregate STRI score of 0.35, comprised of restrictions across Modes 2 and 4, but almost full openness in Mode 2. India's aggregate score of 0.33 reflects the sector's relative openness, carrying restriction in Mode 4.

Trade in Health Services: An Overview

A better health services enables countries to face the challenges of environment and global commercial integration. Evidence confirms that expanding economic opportunities for people living in developing and LDCs (least developed countries) raises their incomes. The key to expanding their economic opportunities is to help them build their assets. Human capabilities such as health are of intrinsic value and also have powerful effects on material wellbeing. Broad access to such facilities is also important to the material prospects of people. And the trade in health services can reduce their vulnerabilities. Therefore, the challenges for South Asian countries are to achieve gender equality in health—national commitment, and to recognise each others' standards—international commitment.

...contd...

performance. This provides a more objective basis for domestic policy debates, as well as for bilateral, regional and international negotiations through more transparent evaluations of reciprocity in concession-making. The main risk, however, of such an exercise that a traditional researcher faces when moving from a qualitative information on policy to a synthetic quantitative index: some dose of subjectiveness. The methodological improvements proposed by researchers on these subjects such as the use of pair wise-comparison techniques try to minimise the subjectivity.

In case of national commitment, the prospects for achieving gender equality in health vary considerably between countries. There has been more progress in gender equality in health (World Bank, 2005). Still, more than a third of developing countries will not achieve gender parity in health, and most of them risk not meeting the Millennium Development Goal (MDG) in 2015 if they do not take immediate action to extend health services to cover poor people. The risk is greatest for Sub-Saharan Africa and South Asia, the regions reporting the slowest progress in universal health.

In case of global commitment, progress toward mutual recognition of health services differs across countries. While developed countries were successful in recognising each other's medical services, the problem gets more acute in the case of developing and LDCs where progress has been very limited. Specifically, a strong asymmetry persists in terms of standards and contents of the medical services across the countries and regions. In addition, changes in the domestic and international market structures have promoted the appearance of activities closely related to health services. These new activities are designed to support health processes or systems without being 'instructional activities' per se. Some of the examples are, exchange programmes in health services and health and education services. In some countries, these activities are considered to constitute health services. Given the pace of change in the sector, definitional issues have also appeared as an important issue in many countries.

Health services also exist as a 'private consumption' item with a price determined freely by the providing institutions. Private sector expenditure on medical institutions reveals significant variations among Organisation for Economic Co-operation and Development (OECD) countries, ranging from 2 per cent or below of total expenditure on health in Portugal, Sweden and Turkey, to over 22 per cent in Germany, Japan, the United States (US), and Korea (WTO, 2001). Private sector expenditure is particularly significant at the tertiary level of health amounting, for instance, to over half of total private expenditure on health in Japan, Korea and the US.

Health services has become the single largest sector in many economies worldwide. It not only provides the bulk of employment and income in many countries, but it also serves as a vital input for producing other goods and services. So, an efficient health services sector is crucial for the overall economy. And because of this, agreement on opening up health services markets is crucial to the success of the current global trade talks.

Such market opening will bring gains to all economies, including the developing world, as long as it is done in a carefully considered way. But opening up health services markets is a particularly complex challenge. For one thing, any discussion of trade in health services has to include the thorny question of in- and out-migration issues (e.g., whether a qualified medical professional can freely move from one country to another to provide services to the patients).

In South Asia, Afghanistan, Bangladesh, and Sri Lanka are showing an interest in health services. A cooperative framework may facilitate South Asian Association for Regional Cooperation (SAARC) countries to tap advanced expertise available in some countries such as India through telemedicine and tele-diagnostic, tele-radiology, and tele-pathology services to hospitals in other SAARC countries (SAARC Secretariat, 2008). Trade in health services can be enhanced through Mode 2 (patients seeking treatments in other countries), Mode 3 (investment in labs and hospitals) and Mode 4 (temporary movement of health professionals like doctors and specialists). As mentioned earlier, cross-border informal trade in health sector plays a very important role in the case of services.

Another problem is that there is analytical literature which purports to show that when intermediation services are explicitly represented in their true economic form, rather than being represented in ad-valorem equivalent form, the two fundamental theorems of welfare economies need not hold. Because of this property, welfare impacts from liberalisation in services trade (even in small open economies) can be negative rather than positive as generally presumed in the goods like models used in the literature. Ryan (1990) study may be considered as an early piece to point this out. Chia and Whalley (1997) provided an example of welfare worsening liberalisation in the case of trade liberalisation in banking services. Bhatterai and Whalley (1998) have shown how explicitly modeling telecoms liberalisation in a network structure can change perceptions as to the division of the gains from liberalisation between small and large countries. The implication seems to be that only limited confidence can be attached to results obtained from the ad-valorem equivalent modeling used in numerical literature because the analytical structures used rule out alterative results. This problem would arise even where the results of individual studies are not contradictory to one another. Nevertheless, due to lack of information on cross-country trade in health services, we have not come across any concrete study with a clear focus on how to measure barriers to trade in health services in case of South Asian countries.

Methodology and Data

Methodological discourse towards assessing barriers to trade in health services follows a wide spectrum of studies on the services trade sector. A balanced and appropriate measure(s) has been considered in this chapter. In order to judge the relative strengths of the health service providers, a primary survey on selected health service providers has been carried out in the study region.

The study is based on a primary survey in India whose information was gathered from patients, doctors, and hospitals involved in trade in health services. We conducted a detailed survey of foreign (South Asian) patients who came to India to receive health services due to India's growing importance in supplying health services in the region. We surveyed a sample of 190 such patients based on convenience sampling procedure. Detailed information regarding their diseases, treatments, costs and payments was collected based on a questionnaire designed to capture all relevant data on patients including their perception on some aspects of trade in health services. Similarly, we surveyed 20 hospitals and 12 doctors. Three different questionnaires were used. On the demand side, we developed two country case studies such as Bangladesh and Nepal highlighting the key issues in trade in health services in order to identify some policy suggestions.

The country case studies such as Nepal and Bangladesh will use both secondary and primary information. In the context of health export status in Nepal, the study will use South Asia Watch on Trade, Economics and Environment (SAWTEE) database of 50 foreign patients having been treated in Nepal during the period of 2007.

Trade in Health Services in Bangladesh

Trade in health services of Bangladesh, more specifically Bangladesh's import of health services, constitutes an important segment in total bilateral trade between Bangladesh and neighbouring countries (Rahman, 2002). The available health services data on payments and receipts collected by the Bangladesh Bank in different years show that receipts were low in most of the years and net medical services show negative figures for 2003-2007. Strikingly, FY (fiscal year) 2009 depicts a positive balance (net medical services) and this provides a positive indication of the growth in health trade for the year (Table 9.1).

A large number of Bangladeshi patients are going to foreign hospitals, despite the financial costs and the cumbersome process of getting visas, obtaining foreign exchange, arranging transportation, accommodation, food and locating right health service providers (Rahman, 2002). From neighbouring countries perspective (e.g., India) Bangladesh is a country with high service seeking potential. Bangladesh mainly imports health services from foreign countries. A large number of Bangladeshi patients seek medical services in foreign countries such as India, Thailand and Singapore.

There is a dearth of reliable data or information on imports of health services in Bangladesh. There is no reliable data on important indicators such as number of individuals seeking services in India, reasons for the import of such services, modes of payments, structure of expenditures and quantum of foreign exchange spent etc. The lack of data actually hinders adequate understanding of the state, scope, and dynamics of this type of trade among countries under the SAARC region and other foreign countries.

Table 9.1

Medical Services Trade in Bangladesh (Value Unit in US$)

	FY2003	*FY 04*	*FY 05*	*FY 06*	*FY 07*	*FY 08*
Invisible receipts	0	9823	39924	10309	11219	1734875
Invisible payments	522745	588712	603834	429881	251044	480859
Net medical services	-522745	-578889	-563910	-419572	-239825	1254016

Source: Database, Statistics Department, Bangladesh Bank, 2009.

Table 9.1 also depicts that although a substantial number of service trade related requests have been made by several countries, to date no country has made any request to Bangladesh to liberalise its health and social service sector under the GATS mode. It reveals that a relatively large number of requests were made for telecommunication services, financial services, business services and transport services.

Health Service Trade in Bangladesh under Four Modes Potentials and Barriers Facing Cross-border Supply of Trade (Telemedicine, Mode 1)

There are several telemedicine service providers in Bangladesh and a few of them are working at the cross-border level. These are mainly private level initiatives and they mainly import telemedicine services from foreign countries. Some of these health care providers give services both at the domestic and international levels. A study, after analysing some telemedicine projects and their activities, opines that Bangladesh has much potential in telemedicine services (Nessa *et al.*, 2008). This study, after reviewing existing functions of the service providers, proposed a prototype telemedicine network for Bangladesh.

One of the largest telemedicine service providers in the country is Medinova Telemedicine. This is a project of the Medinova Health Care based in the capital city of Dhaka. Through this service, a private hospital like Medinova is connected with super-speciality hospitals in India such as AIIMS in New Delhi, Apollo Hospital in Chennai, Shankar Netralaya, Max Cardiac hospital, Kranti Kidney Hospital in Kerala, and CARE in Hyderabad. The facility of the services allows tele-consultation and video conferencing between Bangladeshi doctors and specialists in India.

It has been gathered through field study that Bangladesh has potential for health service imports and exports through Mode 1. Telemedicine has the potential to deliver health services to countries in the SAARC region using state-of-the-art technology. It may also be considered as an opportunity for economic development of the country. Bangladeshi hospitals can provide best possible treatment to their patients through telemedicine. Telemedicine discourages movement of Bangladeshi patients to foreign lands as they can receive the medical services from foreign doctors without moving to a foreign land, and check illegal (unreported) money transactions to India and other foreign countries which are mostly carried through informal channels (Rahman, 2002). The implementation and use of this technology may be a tool to stop a huge amount of illegal foreign exchange outflow from the country each year.

Some service providers opined that several factors hinder the implementation process of telemedicine services in Bangladesh. Resistance from doctors who feel threatened by alternative approaches, high initial expense of setting up some telemedicine systems, difficulty in justifying high costs, reimbursing insurance, legal liability issue etc., obstruct the process of the development and implementation of telemedicine services in the country. Another barrier is the lack of privacy and security regulations. Telemedicine is capital intensive, and a possible diversion of resources from basic preventive and curative services could occur. This service may also impair equity if it caters to a small section of the population, for example only the urban affluent of the country. Besides, most patients still prefer to see their physicians so the trust on the accuracy of findings generated through telemedicine needs to be built up (Dacanay and Rodolfo, 2005). Partnering between a local healthcare provider and a reputable institution in the target market may help overcome this barrier.

Telemedicine may also have some detrimental effect if its basic aspects are not considered while implementing this service mode. Incompatible information infrastructure, poor diagnostic and imaging studies, weak hospital infrastructure may hinder the development of telemedicine services in Bangladesh. Telemedicine may create an obstacle in resolving the cases about malpractice liability and coverage (Rafiq *et al.*, 2005).

Although health service trade through Mode 1 has much potential for Bangladesh, it is observed from field study that poor computer literacy among physicians, low technical expertise, lack of motivation and interest, technology phobia, and lack of initiatives from the government impedes the development and expansion of telemedicine services in Bangladesh.

Consumption Abroad (Mode 2)

To identify reasons for the import of health services by Bangladeshi patients, costs in treatment among domestic private and public hospitals and foreign hospitals are compared. The cost of treatment of five diseases (coronary bypass graft surgery, breast lump removal, knee joint replacement, cataract surgery, IVF (in vitro fertilisation) cycle and hernia correction are compared among United States, United Kingdom, Singapore, India and Bangladesh (Figure 9.1). The data for cost of treatment from both private and public hospitals in Bangladesh have been collected through field survey and compared with published data of the four other countries.

This situation is compounded by lack of drugs, long travel and waiting time (HEU, 2003 quoted in Andaleeb *et al.*, 2007). A study done by World Bank (2005) observed that Bangladeshi patients perceived a private hospital to have the best quality at all levels. On the other hand, a public hospital was considered to be of low quality, and NGO hospital at the *Upazilla*[7] level was considered to have the best quality.

It is observed that an increasing number of foreign patients from developing countries go to India and also some developed countries for treatment. Bangladeshi patients perceive foreign healthcare services to be more reasonably priced (ICDDRB, 2007). Relatively better and low-cost treatment in India, and proximity are principal reasons for patients going to India from neighbouring countries such as Sri Lanka, Bangladesh, and Nepal. A large part of transactions for

7. Administrative unit like Police Station.

trade in health services for Bangladesh, for example, goes unreported (especially in case of India) since such transactions are carried mostly through informal channels and therefore, not reflected in the balance of payments accounts.

Figure 9.1

Global Cost Differences for Cardiac Surgery

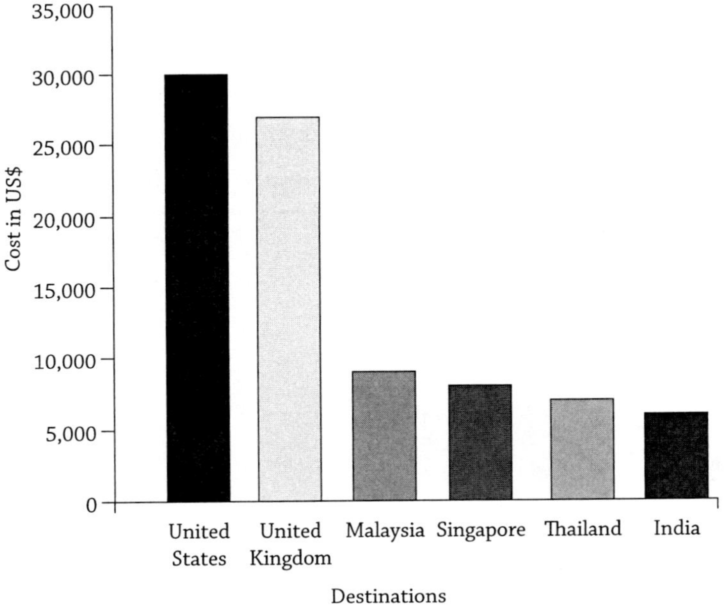

Health Care Seeking Behaviour of the Bangladeshi Patients: An Application of Mean Score of Relative Importance (MSRI) Method

To analyse the relative importance of the factors which motivated Bangladeshi patients to seek services from various types of hospitals mentioned before, MSRI analysis was carried out. MSRI technique, which is a descriptive statistical technique, was administered to analyse data. The formula of MSRI is given below (Huque, 2001).

$$MSRI = \frac{\Sigma W_i + (n-f)N}{n}$$

where,

ΣW_i = Total sum of cardinal weights assigned to different degrees of importance for the factor in question pointed out by the respondents.

n = Total size of sample.

f = Total number of respondents pointed out the factor in question (i.e. the frequency of the factor).

N = Total number of factors contributing to satisfaction (or dissatisfaction).

Table 9.2

Ordinal Degrees and Cardinal Weights

Ordinal Degree	*Cardinal Weight*
I (1st)	1
II (2nd)	2
III (3rd)	3
IV (4th)	4
V (5th)	5
VI (6th)	6
VII (7th)	7
.	.
.	.
XVII (17th)	17

Firstly, ordinal weights were assigned to different degrees of importance indicated by the respondents. Afterwards, the cardinal weights were assigned to different degrees of importance to calculate mean score of relative importance (Table 9.2).[8]

The study sees the health related service factors from service quality (Service Quality or SERVQUAL) point of view. Parasuraman *et al.* (1988), Zeithaml and Bitner (2006) note that there are five dimensions of consumer's service quality judgement when marketing perspectives are taken into consideration. These dimensions are: (i)

8. The formula used in the present study is more robust than a simple weighted average method (Alam, 1986; Haque, 2001).

reliability; (ii) responsiveness; (iii) assurance; (iv) empathy; and (v) tangibles. These dimensions are discussed below.

Reliability

Reliability is defined as the ability to perform the promised service dependably and accurately. In the broadest sense, reliability emphasises on promises about delivery of services, problem resolution ability, pricing, and other core service attributes of the company.

Responsiveness

Responsiveness is the willingness to help customers and to provide prompt service. This dimension emphasises attentiveness and promptness in dealing with customer requests, questions, complaints, and problems.

Assurance

Assurance is defined as employees' knowledge and courtesy, and the ability of the firm and its employees to inspire trust and confidence.

Empathy

Empathy is defined as the caring, individualised attention the firm provides its customers. The essence of empathy is conveying through personalised or customised service that customers are unique and special.

Tangibles

Tangibles are defined as the appearance of physical facilities, equipment, personnel, and communication materials. All of these provide physical representations or images of the service that customers, particularly new customers, will use to evaluate quality.

Total 3 health service factors were classified according to SERVQUAL dimensions. The classification of these factors is given in Table 9.2. Table 9.4 depicts the consolidated MSRI results of the three types of hospitals. These are government hospitals, private hospitals in Bangladesh, and hospitals located in India (coded as BD_Govt_MSRI, BD_Private_MSRI, and INDIA_MSRI respectively).

Table 9.3

Hospital Related Service Factors and Dimension of SERVQUAL

Hospital Related Service Factors	*SERVQUAL Dimension*
F1. Competency of the doctors	Reliability
F2. Competency of the nurses	Reliability
F3. Pathological laboratory equipped with all kinds of testing facilities	Tangible
F4. Waiting time to get appointment is short	Responsiveness
F5. Low treatment cost of the hospital	Reliability/cost
F6. Hospital is visually appealing	Tangibles
F7. Ambulance facility	Tangibles
F8. Hospitals has modern medical equipments	Tangibles
F9. Good quality food	Tangibles
F10. Accommodation cost low	Reliability/cost
F11. Specialist doctors are available	Reliability
F12. Hospital staffs respond promptly when needed	Responsiveness
F13. Follow-up treatment good	Empathy
F14. Doctor listens to one's problem attentively	Assurance
F15. Nurses are very caring and willing to respond when needed	Assurance
F16. Easy to get bed/cabin in the hospital	Assurance
F17. Non-repetitive pathological test	Assurance

Analysis of the MSRI Result: Patients from Government Hospitals in Bangladesh

It can be seen from the Tables that patients ranked competency of the doctor and availability of specialist doctors as their prime reasons (Rank 1) for visiting government hospitals. Patients who visited government hospitals ranked low cost treatment with 2 and short waiting time with 3. Government hospitals are always the last resort for poor patients who want low-cost treatment. These attitudes of the patients can be examined from service quality perspectives. It seems that reliability, responsiveness, and cost of treatment were the prime motivating factors behind selecting government hospitals.

Table 9.4

Comparative Analysis of MSRI

Name	*F1*	*F2*	*F3*	*F4*	*F5*	*F6*	*F7*	*F8*	*F9*	*F10*	*F11*	*F12*	*F13*	*F14*	*F15*	*F16*	*F17*
BD_Govt_MSRI	2.67	7.75	7.50	4.67	4.50	8.83	9.67	4.92	12.75	4.83	2.00	5.42	6.58	5.92	7.33	6.58	13.50
BD_Private_MSRI	1.43	4.79	4.71	3.14	7.43	10.14	14.29	4.29	14.79	10.71	2.57	5.93	4.79	4.79	2.71	5.36	11.07
INDIA_MSRI	1.75	4.44	5.00	15.44	13.63	10.25	16.63	5.38	16.31	16.31	1.81	3.44	1.81	2.63	3.19	16.56	5.31

Patients of government hospitals did not judge quality of food (F9) as an important factor in choosing these hospitals. They, in fact, did not consider repetitive pathological test (F17) as an important factor for selecting the hospitals.

Analysis of MSRI Result: Patients from Private Hospitals in Bangladesh

Competency of specialist doctors (F1) was the most important criterion for the patients to choose private hospitals in Bangladesh. The patient identified those specialist doctors (F11) who listen to the problems of the patients (F14) with care. It was the second most important decisive factor in selecting private hospitals. Reliability and assurance dimensions were also important service quality aspects that motivated patients to receive services from private hospitals. Short waiting time to receive an appointment was the third most important criterion to decide on private hospitals.

It can be observed from Table 9.4 that 'relative waiting time to see the doctor' is high in case of private hospitals when compared with government hospitals. It seems that there were some tangible elements (modern equipment or F8, and good pathological facilities or F3) which actually attracted patients to choose private hospitals. Like government hospitals, quality of food (F9) did have any important bearing on selecting private hospitals.

Analysis MSRI Result: Patients from Hospitals in India

The cost factor (F5) had low level of significance for the patients, who visited India to receive treatment (Table 9.4). Bangladeshi patients had to wait for long to get doctors' appointment (F4), but finally received reliable treatment with high levels of assurance and empathy. Most of the patients selected Indian hospitals for the specialist doctors that were available there (F11) and their high level of competency (F1). In addition to this, these hospitals provided good follow-up treatment (F13). Indian doctors listened to the patients' problems with care.

Prompt and good nursing services were also important determinants which allured the patients to choose Indian hospitals. Patients who selected India as their destination for treatment did not bother much about the accommodation cost (F10) and quality of food (F9) (see Table 9.5)

Table 9.5

Service Quality Factors, MSRI Ranking and SERVQUAL Dimensions

Type of Hospitals	*Factors*		*Weight*	*SERVQUAL*	*Rank*
Government Hospitals, Bangladesh	Specialist doctors available	F11	2.00	Reliability	Rank 1
	Competency of doctors	F1	2.67	Reliability	
	Low treatment cost of the hospital	F5	4.50	Reliability/ Cost	Rank 2
	Waiting time to get appointment is short	F4	4.67	Responsive-ness	
	Accommodation cost is low	F10	4.83	Reliability/ Cost	Rank 3
	Hospital has modern medical equipments	F8	4.92	Tangibles	
	Hospital staff respond promptly when needed	F12	5.42	Responsive-ness	Rank 4
Private Hospitals, Bangladesh	Competency of the doctors	F1	1.43	Reliability	Rank 1
	Specialist doctors are available	F11	2.57	Reliability	Rank 2
	Doctors listen to one's problem attentively	F14	2.71	Assurance	
	Waiting time to get appointment is short	F4	3.14	Responsive-ness	Rank 3
	Hospital has modern medical equipments	F8	4.29	Tangibles	Rank 4
	Pathological facilities equipped with all types of testing facilities	F3	4.71	Tangibles	Rank 5
	Competency of nurses	F2	4.79	Reliability	
	Follow up treatment is good	F13	4.79	Empathy	

contd...

...contd...

Hospitals in India	Competency of the doctors	F1	1.75	Reliability	Rank 1
	Specialist doctors are available	F11	1.81	Reliability	
	Follow up treatment good	F13	1.81	Empathy	
	Doctors listens to one's problem attentively	F14	2.63	Assurance	Rank 2
	Nurses are very caring and willing to respond when needed	F15	3.19	Assurance	Rank 3
	Hospital staffs respond promptly when needed	F12	3.44	Responsive-ness	
	Competency of nurses	F2	4.44	Reliability	Rank 4

Consumption Abroad: Opportunities and Risks

The specific nature of health consumption generates barriers to patients' mobility. The psychological cost of going abroad can be high for the patient. It is not the consumer's choice that always defines the nature, scope etc. of the health service consumption but also the physician's instructions. The problem of follow-up and after care when the patient is back home considerably increases the cost (and the risk) of this type of international transaction.

Commercial Presence: Opportunities and Barriers

It is anticipated that FDI (foreign direct investment) in health sector, will bring additional resources and expertise to improve the range, quality, and efficiency of services offered. It is understandable that this depends on regulation that exists. The presence of increased health technology through FDI may encourage the Bangladesh Government to invest in such technology and to improve the condition of health services in the public sector.

The commercial presence in health care services in Bangladesh can generate additional resources for investment, and upgrading of health care infrastructure and technologies. Nevertheless, concerns remain about the possible negative effects of FDI, including the question of market power, technological dependence, capital flight, and profit outflow. It is also observed that in respect of mode 3 the

Table 9.6

Identified Strength and Weaknesses of the Public, Private and NGO Health Service Providers in Bangladesh

Type of Services	*Cost*	*Perceived Quality*	*Technical Quality*	*Subjective Performance*	*Accessibility*	*Price*
Public	Lowest costs found at the national level. Highest costs found at the district level	Lowest perceived quality scores	Slightly lower technical quality than private facilities, increasing with level			Lowest prices at all levels
Private	Lowest costs found at the district level. Highest costs found at the national level	Best perceived quality scores at all levels	Technical quality Increasing with level		High levels have higher accessibility scores from the facility's standpoint, but lower scores from the patient's standpoint	Highest prices at all levels, increasing with the level of attention
NGO	Shows a similar cost than private and public facilities at the *Upazila* level	Best perceived quality scores at the *Upazila* level	Best technical quality scores	Best subjective performance scores	Have the highest accessibility score from the patient's standpoint	Low prices

Source: The World Bank, 2005.

services are usually non-tradable and an influx of foreign enterprises such as companies from India and East Asian countries (e.g. Thailand and Malaysia) can cause significant outflow of investment income from Bangladesh. This may lead to negative effects on the Bangladesh's balance of payments (Khor, 2006).

Liberalisation of Trade in Health Services in Bangladesh: Challenges and Opportunities

It is generally observed that services trade is considerably heavily restricted compared to trade in merchandise trade. As international health service transactions include FDI and the movement of labour, as well as long-established cross-border transactions, any policy that impedes service producers and consumers act together through any of these channels (or modes of supply) is considered an hindrance to trade (Findlay and Warren, 2000).

While addressing the issue related to GATS and its influence on the health policy of Bangladesh, it is observed that GATS may have some adverse affect on the health service policy of the country. The GATS actually works in the following manner: GATS commit WTO members to successive rounds of negotiations with a view to achieving a progressively higher level of liberalisation in their service sectors. To achieve this, WTO members make liberalisation requests of other member countries in secret, bilateral meetings in Geneva so as to open up to competition those sectors which are of most interest to their own service providers (Khor, 2006).

When a country fully commits a given sector e.g. health service sector under the GATS, it accepts two types of legal obligations. It actually grants 'market access' to foreign competitors, and refrains itself from establishing barriers to trade, such as quotas that limit the number of providers of a given service (physicians, hospitals etc). It also abstains from establishing barriers to the volume of service supplied by each provider (e.g., number of beds). If Bangladesh commits fully, it agrees to treat foreign competitors no less favorably than the suppliers from its own country (Belsky *et al.*, 2004).

Although, developing countries officially have the right to decide whether to commit a sector to GATS, in practice they come under intense pressure in these negotiations to meet the demands of more powerful WTO members—pressure which the smaller and poorer countries are often powerless to resist.

From a health policy perspective, measures that restrict market access may be more important than measures that restrict national treatment (Blouin, 2006). Restricting market access may serve legitimate health policy objectives, such as limitations on the number of service suppliers in a geographical area based on an economic needs test (Blouin, 2006). If Bangladesh would like to open its health sector to foreign providers it should consider 'experimenting with liberalisation outside of GATS before making GATS commitments as policy reversal remains easier if the experiment produces unsatisfactory results (Khor, 2006).

Liberalisation of trade in health services can create opportunities for Bangladesh, but may also aggravate pre-existing problems. Moreover, once liberalisation is locked in under international trade agreements, reversing policies becomes difficult. This may be true for a poor country like Bangladesh. It is understood that making inappropriate commitments to liberalise health services under GATS may result in the loss of policy space for Bangladesh.

Trade in Health Services in Nepal

This part of the study analyses the trade in health service in South Asian through Nepal's perspective. Nepal is a landlocked LDC in South Asia. The Government of Nepal is cognizant about the benefit of global economic integration. In this regard, the country in 2004 acceded to the WTO through the normal process of accession. In the same year, it also joined the regional trading agreements such as the SAFTA and the Bay of Bengal Initiative for Multi-Sectoral Technical and Economic Cooperation (BIMSTEC). Further, the country has bilateral preferential trade agreement with three countries (India, Tibet and Pakistan).

Against this background, the study will focus on the status of health services trade of Nepal with other South Asian countries and analyse the barriers of smooth flow in the health service trade. The study will primarily focus Mode 2 and Mode 3 since Mode 2 is

Table 9.7

Brief Outline of Trade in Health Services in Bangladesh

Macroeconomic and Trade Environment	*State of the Domestic Health Care System*
• Bangladesh is a LDC with GDP per capita US$ 1,500 (2008). • Liberal market access and national treatment policies allowing up to 100% foreign equity participation in most sectors and does not require a Economic Needs Test.	• Health status indicators: population growth rate 1.292%; Birth Rate: 28.86 births/1000 people; Death Rate: 8 deaths/1000 people; Infant Mortality Rate: 59.02/100 live births; Total Fertility Rate: 2.74%.
Mode 1: Cross-border Supply of Health Services	*Mode 2: Consumption of Health Services Abroad*
• Telemedicine services across borders are currently practiced by some hospitals and private organisations. • No restrictions exist on services and products available on the Internet for personal use. • There does not exist any government policy on telemedicine services. As a result, no controls/obstacles to use this service. • IT infrastructure is good; the rate of internet subscribers is around 7.3 persons/1000 people. • Bangladesh has no existing GATS commitments in Mode 1 in health services	• Bangladesh is a net importer of health service. Countries receiving Bangladeshi patients are mainly India, Thailand, Singapore, and Malaysia. • No restrictions on private citizens going abroad for consumption of health services • No existing or proposed GATS commitments in any health related sub-sectors under Mode 2

contd...

...contd...

Mode 3: Foreign Commercial Presence	*Mode 4: Movement of Health Professionals*
• Commercial presence requires that foreign service providers incorporate or establish the business locally in accordance with the relevant provisions of Bangladesh laws, rules and regulations. There is no fixed ratio of equity between local and foreign investors. Foreign equity to the extent of 100% is allowed. • Difficult to identify FDI in health sector as all private hospitals. • Ministry of Commerce and Industry is responsible for regulating FDI in health. Licensing of premises and its compliance with standards is the responsibility of MoH. • Bangladesh has no existing or proposed GATS commitments on Mode 3 in health services.	• In Bangladesh, the entry and residence of foreign natural persons (service providers) are subject to Bangladesh's immigration and labour laws, regulations, guidelines and procedures. There is no restriction is issuing work permits to foreign nationals in Bangladesh. The employment of foreign natural persons for the implementation of the foreign investment shall be agreed upon by the contracting parties and approved by the Government and such personnel shall be employed in higher management and specialised jobs only. • There is no restriction on professionals to move abroad for temporary job. • Bangladesh has no existing or proposed GATS commitments on Mode 4 in health services

most used one in health trade in the global context (Chanda, 2002) and FDI inflow through Mode 3 is important in the health sector of developing countries due to the investment and technology transfer in the country (Maskay *et al.*, 2006). Nevertheless, the study will also touch on the health trade potential through other two modes.

Nepal is net importer of health service by itself but there are several health service sectors in which country has comparative advantage. However, these health services are properly exploited for economic benefits of the country. Furthermore, there is a need to identify the constraints to supply the health service via each mode. So, the study will analyse: (i) policy framework of Nepal in health service; (ii) the status of Nepal in term of health export and import; and (iii) address the constraints on supply of health service via each mode.

There is no authentic recording of health service trade in Nepal so data in all four modes are not available. Nepal Rastra Bank (NRB) (Central Bank of Nepal) maintains the record of foreign exchange transaction by purpose which again is underestimated due to substantial informal health trade of Nepal. So, this country study has tried to present a glance of health trade in reference to information collected via own information[9] and some secondary source.

Policy Framework of Health Services

The public health system focuses on providing health services emphatically to the rural as well as urban areas. It is organised as a system of public and private health institute which is interlinked through a network of: (i) public hospitals at district, zone, regional and central level; (ii) health posts at village development committee (VDC) and ward level; (iii) private health institution; (iv) national disease specific health institution; and (v) Ayurvedic and other health institution (Figure 9.1). National Health Policy (NHP) (1991) has organised the public health system of Nepal from the lower tier to the upper tier (Figure 9.2). Furthermore, it is important to note

9. Own information indicates interviews, focus group discussion, and opinion survey by the study team.

how the existing organisational structure of Government of Nepal's Department of Health Services (DoHS) relates to the different administrative levels as a public health care network.

Figure 9.2

Flow Chart of Health Service Providers in Nepal

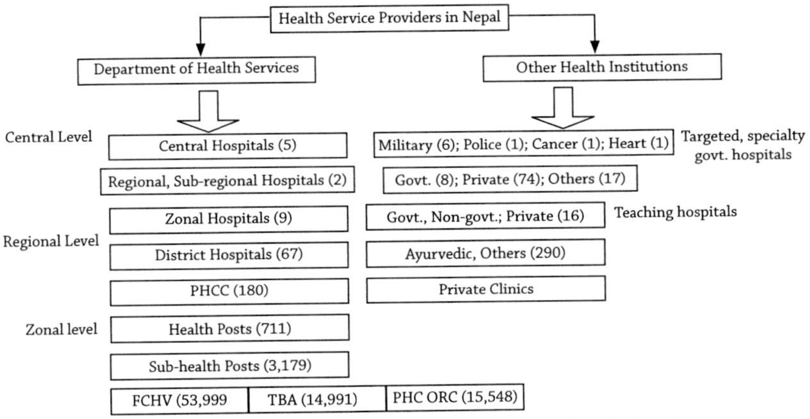

Note: FCHV: Female Community Health Volunteer; PHCC: Primary Health Care Centres; TBA: Traditional Birth Attendant; PHCORC: Primary Health Care Outreach Clinic.

The basic health services are largely provided by the public sector and the specialised services are open to both the public and private sector. The non-government sector incorporating 'for profit' institutions, NGOs (non-governmental organisations) and mission hospitals provided 41 per cent of the total beds in 2003 (MoH, 2003) which are however, mostly concentrated in the urban areas. Together with the liberal policy shift, the Government of Nepal is taking a very proactive approach for the development of the private sector with a view of promoting public private partnership with particular emphasis for the private sector on tertiary care.[10] Nepal Health Service Act, 2053 BS and Nepal Health Service Rule, 2055 BS are the legal documents to govern the health service in Nepal. Presently, six councils related to Health sector are instituted in Nepal under

10. Three Year Interim Plan also includes the strategy of managing and coordinating human, financial and physical resources for the quality improvement of the services provided under the partnership of private, government and non-government sector.

special law and regulation of respective council in order to govern and supervise the health service.

Establishment of Health Institutions

Nepal Health Service Act, 1997 and Nepal Health Service Regulation, 1997 govern the establishment of health institution in Nepal (Dixit, 2004). The concerned act and regulation has provision of establishment of health service institution, recruitment of health staff and supervision of health institutions. The act and regulation also incorporate allopathy, *ayurveda* and homeopathy along with health staff of all level (doctors, health workers, assistant health workers, and others). Specifically, along with these legal provisions, Industrial Enterprises Act (IEA) 1992 governs the setting up of private profit making heath institutions and the Trust Act or Social Welfare Act governs in term of setting up other non profit and non-governmental health institution. In terms of registration, the government hospitals are registered in Department of Health (DoH) under the Government of Nepal's Ministry of Health and Population, private profit making hospitals are register in Department of Industry (DoI) under the Government of Nepal's Ministry of Industry, Commerce and Trade (MoICT) after the consent of DoH the non profit and non governmental hospital are registered with Social Welfare Council (SWC) under Ministry of Women, Children and Social Welfare (MoWCSW) after the consent of DoH. Some Diseases specific hospitals owned by government are also established under its own act. For instance, B.P. Koirala Memorial Cancer Hospital has been established under B.P. Koirala Memorial Cancer Hospital Act, 1997 and Saheed Ganga Lal National Heart Center has been Saheed Ganga Lal National Heart Centre Act, 1997. After registration in concerned Department, the health institution needs to be registered at Inland Revenue Office to obtain a Permanent Account Number and obtain permission for trademarks, patents, and designs if necessary.

FDI Provision in Health

Foreign Investment and Technology Transfer Act (FITTA), 1992 govern the FDI in health sector under which FDI inflow needs to be registered and approved from Department of Investment after the consent of DoI, DoH and Company Registrar's Office (CRO). Foreign investors are required to undertake following steps: (i) incorporating at CRO; (ii) registering and approval from DoI and DoH and (iii) registering and approval from the Department of Investment. In the FITTA and any other FI related government document there is no clear documentation on the approval procedure so FI approval is granted case by case. To facilitate the forementioned procedures, the One Window Committee (OWC) was constituted at the MoICT of Government of Nepal but it is less functional because government has not clearly mentioned the authority and responsibility of the committee. Foreign investors can own up to 100 per cent equity in private health firms and are entitled to repatriate the investment amount and other earnings. Furthermore, to facilitate business transactions, foreign exchange restrictions have been relaxed. Foreigners and companies are now allowed to open and operate foreign exchange accounts in any of the domestic commercial banks. Likewise, there is the provision for business visas for foreign investors for up to 5 years. Provisions also exist for providing non-tourist visas to carry out studies for investment along with residential visas for foreign investors.

Qualification and Licencing Criteria of Medical Practitioner

Nepal Medical Council (NMC) established under Nepal Medical Council Act (NMCA), is the responsible body to regulate and maintain the standard of the medical and dental doctors in Nepal. Likewise, Nepal Nursing Council established under Nepal Nursing Council Act (NNCA) is the responsible body to regulate and maintain the standard of the nurses and assistant health worker of Nepal. These councils are responsible to recognise the medical certificate of concerned health personal and supervise the concerned medical teaching institutions. In terms of South Asia, NMC has recognised the medical degree (MBBS and Post Graduate) from 6 Bangladesh's Universities, over 100 Indian Universities, 9 Pakistani Universities and 1 Sri Lankan University. NMCA also allows foreign medical professional to practice in Nepal for one year after securing permission from NMC.

Provision of Visa for People's Movement

Visa provision is one of the most important factors to influence services trade via Mode 2. Nepal has visa free provision for India, with its border being porous and open. The residents of countries other than India can apply for three months tourist visa in the Nepali embassy of the country of residence and extent such visa for further three months. If there is no Nepali embassy in the country of residence then the applicant can apply for free visa for three days at the border point entry and receive the tourist visa from Department of Immigration within these three days.

Table 9.8

Nepal's Health Sector Commitment in GATS

Sector or Sub-sector	*Limitation in Market Access for Each of the Modes*	*Limitations on National Treatment for Each of the Modes*
Health related and social services A. Hospital services (CPC 9311) and direct ownership and management by contract of such facilities on a 'for fee' basis.	1) None 2) None 3) None, except only through incorporation in Nepal and with maximum foreign equity capital of 51 percent. 4) Unbound, except as indicated in the horizontal section. Medical experts can work with the permission of NMC for a maximum of one year.	1) None 2) None 3) None 4) Unbound, except as indicated in the horizontal section.

Source: http://www.wto.org/english/tratop_e/serv_e/serv_commitments_e.htm

Nepal's Commitment in GATS

Nepal is silent in term of Mode 1 under the market access limitation. The limitation on National Treatment includes: (i) none, except with respect to foreign exchange provided to foreigners (excluding those categories of persons covered by commitments in this agreement) to pay for any cross-border services for Mode 1; (ii) none for Mode 2; (iii) none except approval from concern department for Mode 3; and (iv) unbound except for measures concerning the categories of natural persons referred to in the market access column for mode four. Nepal has also made an additional general commitment in term of environmental impact and repatriate. Nepal has made specific commitment only in hospital services. The specific commitments in hospital services are revealed in Table 9.7.

The GATS commitment for 51 per cent cap on FDI on hospital is of no practical relevance as the FDI policy allows for 100 per cent cap on FDI for hospital.

International Trade in Health Service

NRB study (2005)reveals that the health service accounts marginal share in the service trade of Nepal. The share of health in service trade in 2004 is relatively low[11] (only 0.8%) which however is expanding in terms of FDI flow, attracting 28.2 percent of total FDI flow in service sector in 2004. NRB data suggests that Nepal is a net importer of the health treatment services in terms of Mode 1 and 2 on aggregate, and there is also an increasing trend in FDI approval.

The major health export and import diseases of Nepal are also provided in Table 9.9. The Nepalese patient of cancer, neuro, kidney, liver and heart diseases generally travels to a foreign country, particularly India, for treatment. On the other side, the Indian residing near border come to hospitals located in Terai region of Nepal for treatment. Basically they come to Nepal for pathology, general medicine and gastroenterology. Moreover, Nepal also exports health services in eye related diseases and *ayurveda*.

Mode 1: The recent rapid development in telecommunication technologies and health informatics has been changing the picture dramatically. Telemedicine, the practice of medical care using interactive audio, visual and data communications, includes medical

11. Tourism is the dominant sectors contributing one third of the total trade in services and one half of the total FDI flow to the service sector in Nepal.

care delivery, consultations, diagnosis and treatment, as well as the transfer of medical data. In the key informant interview with an official from the Nick Simon Institution, it was revealed that there are together around 25 hospitals in Nepal that provide telemedicine facilities and all of them are either government funded or charity hospitals. Om Hospital, was the only private hospital that had once initiated this service but later terminated this service. No health service institutions in Nepal provides telemedicine facilities to foreign countries.

Table 9.9

Major Disease with Health Import and Export of Nepal

Major Disease and Related Health Services that Nepalese Treat in Foreign Land	*Major Diseases and Related Health Services that Foreign Peoples Treat in Nepal*
• Cancer	• Pathology (In Terai Belt)
• Neuro Related Diseases	• General Medicine (In Terai Belt)
• Kidney Related Diseases	• Gastroenterology (In Terai Belt)
• Liver Related Disease	• Eye
• Heart Related Disease	• Ayurvedic

Source: Key Informant Interview.

Mode 2: Nepal has substantial outflow of patient to foreign country, especially India, as Nepal has limited capacity in providing services in many diseases. In the key informant interview with senior doctors and medical professionals, it was found that the major diseases prevalent in Nepal which lag overall resources are: cancer, neuro related diseases, kidney diseases and liver diseases. So, the patient of these diseases travel to foreign countries, especially India, for treatment. The information collected from the field survey and other related secondary sources postulates a glace of patient outflow from Nepal for treatment (Table 9.9).

SAWTEE (2008) has well discussed about the foreign patients coming to Nepal for various health services from five health service providers/institutions. The patients are generally economically less well off as the SAWTEE database suggests that their mean income is around ₹ 7000. Consumers of health services mainly from India

Table 9.10

Patient Flow from Nepal to Foreign Country

Source of Information	*Flow of Patient*	*Remarks*
Bajracharya and Bajracharya, 2008	Average of 2 to 3 patient per day to Indian cities	Migrant Movement Survey conducted in Nepalgunj and Danghadi (two bordering cities with India in mid and far Western region of Nepal) using purposive sampling of 25 respondent collected in 2 days
Handicap International, 2008	Average of 9 to 11 patient per day to Indian Cities	Migrant Movement Survey conducted in Bairahawa (bordering cities of with India in central region of Nepal) using purposive sampling of 100 respondents collected in 4 days
Hospital Agents (Apollo Hospital, Delhi; Bangkok Hospital, Bangkok)*	Average of 4 to 5 patients go to Bangkok and Apollo Hospital for treatment	Collected by study team during key informant interview
Cancer Patient Association of Nepal*	In last three years, average of 8 to 10 patients per year consult the Association regarding procedure to treat in different Indian cities	Collected by study team during key informant interview
Nepal Kidney Association*	In last year, average of 4 patients went to India for treatment	

Note: * Collected during Key Informant Interview.

belonged mostly to low and middle income groups which limit the expansion of services and choices for the consumers. Wealthy patients in particular might wish to take advantage of advanced, specialised treatments unavailable in the home country or perceived as better quality, or to avoid long waiting lists in the home country (Maskay *et al.*, 2006).

Eye care providers have some strategies to export the services through different levels of income of the consumers. An eye hospital at Biratnagar has choices for the consumer ranging from NRs. 900, 1700, 2500, 3500, 5000 and to 8000 for cataract services at the same provider. However Koshi, and BPKIHS are able to provide very limited choices. Not only limited service choices within the same provider but also limited choices for selection of providers in Nepal are major obstacles to expand the services for high income groups. Due to this they turn to Patna and Darbhanga for consumption of health services while Nepalese institutions provide services for the low and middle income groups.

Mode 3: There have been flows of health related FDI into Nepal, the first (a nursing home with Chinese FDI) was granted permission for operation in 1991. In this regard and even after about one and a half decade, the operating FDI of the seven firms total about Rs. 1.6 billion (approximately US$ 231 million) and the four firms have been approved by the government of Nepal and are in course of operation. The situation of health related FDI for 2005 is provided in Table 9.11.

Table 9.11

General Characteristics of Foreign Health Service Consumers

Statistics	*Age*	*Years of Schooling*	*Monthly Income (₹)*	*Persons Accompanied with the Consumer*
Mean	41	5	7390.74	3
Median	45	4	5550.00	3
Mode	60	1	3000.00	2
Std. deviation	20	4	8938.43	1
Minimum	1	1	1500	0
Maximum	80	16	30000	8

Source: SAWTEE, 2008.

Mode 4: There is a regular flow of Indian specialists visiting Nepal to provide services to Nepalese patients through private hospitals and nursing homes in Nepal. Furthermore there are a substantial number of foreign medical professionals coming to Nepal as visiting professors. SAWTEE (2008) presents a case study of private medical college where 4 to 5 foreign visiting professors are present in each academic year. Table 9.12 also represents substantial number of foreign medical professional working in Nepal.

Table 9.12

Foreign Direct Investment in Health Services

Category	*Number of Firms*	*Foreign Investment*	*Local Employment*	*Foreign Employment*
Operating	7	1617	877	138
Approved	4	1445	1524	1531
Total	11	3062	2401	1669

Source: Maskay *et al.*, 2006.

Barriers to Health Services Exports

During the field survey, some service consumers mentioned the absence of ward facility at some service providers, lack of adequate information about the service providers, and limited choices of service providers as existing disincentives related to the health services and providers. Similarly, a few respondents mentioned security problems/unpredictable situation in the country and paying an exorbitant amount for transportation (particularly in Kathmandu taxis) as the major disincentives which they suffered. Moreover, though the study could not capture non-Indian foreigners, service providers informed that they are facing an additional disincentive of limited choices in food items. Besides these, no other specific disincentives have been gauged from the field survey while examining it from the consumers' perspective.

In fact, with regards to movement of the patients, one of the most important barriers is emotional insecurity of patients who do not wish to be far from their families, and are particularly sensitive of possible cultural and linguistic differences. However, the patients from India did not face any such problems including language, discrimination in providing consultation services, and cultural both within and beyond the service providers while receiving health services in Nepal.

Trade in Health Services in India: A South Asian Perspective

A survey of 190 patients who had come to India from other South Asian countries to avail of medical services was conducted to understand the trade related barriers and their effect on actual patients. This section captures the essential aspects of the survey.

Tables 9.13 and 9.14 present a socio-demographic and socioeconomic profile of the patients. We can see that an overwhelming majority (about 79.5%) of the patients is male and more than half are in the age group 40-59. Not so surprisingly, about 95.8 per cent of the patients are from Bangladesh and about 61.0 per cent of these foreign patients have studied up to SSC/HSC or above.

The majority of patients come from single earning member households and for such households the average number of dependents is 4.97. It must be very difficult for such households to travel to another country for the treatment of one of its members—particularly when we also observe that the average income per household for such households is only 2,35,623.40 in local currency (which effectively means Bangladesh Taka). For double income households, the average number of dependents per earning member is 3.18 but the average income per household is about 5,00,000 units of local currency.

Figure 9.3

Income Source Disribution

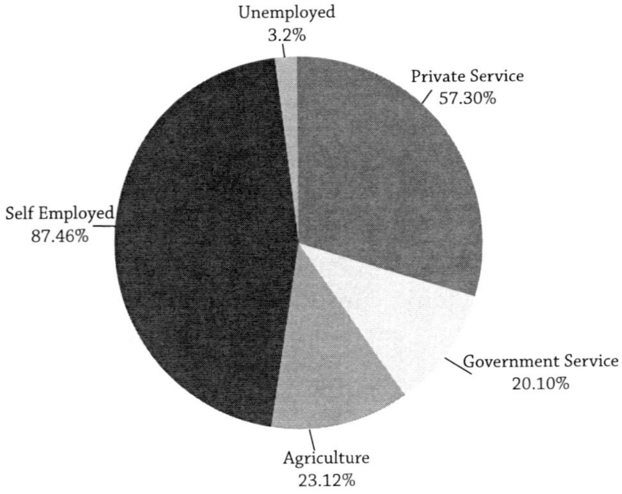

Table 9.13

Socio-demographic Profile of Sample Patients (No.)

	Gender			Marital Status				Education							Countries						
Age Categories (years)	Male	Female	Total	Un married	Married	Widowed	Sptd/ Divorced	Cannot read/ write	Can read/ write	Some schooling (Up to 4 yrs)	5-9 yrs of school	SSC/ HSC	Tech Trg (fml/ infml)	Others	1	2	3	4	5	6	7
Juvenile Upto 19	9	6	15	15	0	0	0	7	1	3	4	0	0	0	0	15	0	0	0	0	0
Youth 20-39	42	17	59	14	45	0	0	1	2	2	9	27	3	15	0	55	1	0	1	1	1
Middle-aged 40-59	84	15	99	5	94	0	0	0	8	11	20	46	3	11	2	96	0	0	1	0	0
Old 60 yrs and above	16	1	17	0	17	0	0	1	2	1	2	5	4	2	0	16	0	0	0	0	1
Total	151	39	190	34	156	0	0	9	13	17	35	78	10	28	2	182	1	0	2	1	2

Countries: 1=Afghanistan, 2=Bangladesh, 3=Bhutan, 4=Maldives, 5=Nepal, 6=Pakistan, 7=Sri Lanka.

Table 9.14

Socioeconomic Profile of Sample Patients

Number of Earning Household Members (Including Respondent)	*No of Patients*	*Adults*	*Children*	*Total Members*	*No of Dependents*	*Average Income per Household Per annum in Taka (For Bangladeshi Patients only)*
0	2	2	2	4	NA	375000
1	94	335	132	467	4.97	235419.56
2	61	281	107	388	3.18	502965.58
3	17	118	38	156	3.06	691875
4	8	77	26	103	3.22	495714.28
5	6	55	14	69	2.30	1060000
6	2	29	11	40	3.33	890000

Figure 9.3 shows the source of household income for the sample patients. The majority (87 out of 190 or 46%) is self-employed, followed by another 30 per cent in private service. About 12 per cent have agriculture as their source of income. Surprisingly, about 10 per cent of the patients are in government service in their respective country which implies a perceived lack of medical facilities even for government servants.

Profile of Diseases

Table 9.15 reveals that the largest number of patients come to India for cardiac (49) and cancer (45) treatment. Orthopaedic (21) and kidney-related (22) treatment also form a significant percentage of the sample of foreign patients.

Table 9.15

Disease Types

Type of Disease	*No of Patients*
Cardiology	49
Orthopaedics	21
Ophthalmology	6
Cancer	45
Kidney related	22
Neurology	11
Others	36

Table 9.16 shows the age-wise distribution of diseases among the sample patients. We notice a little bimodality among cardiology patients—both juvenile (under 19) and middle-aged patients outnumber youth in the sample. The dominance of males across all age groups and across all disease categories is also clearly visible—the only exception being patients who are between 20 and 39 years old and do not have any of the stated diseases. This could be due to gynaecological problems faced by the female youth patients.

Table 9.16

Age-wise Distribution of Patients

Age (Years Completed)	*Type of Disease*	*No of Patients*	*Male*	*Female*
Juvenile (Up to 19)	Cardiology	12	7	5
	Ophthalmology	1	0	1
	Kidney related	1	1	0
	Others	1	1	0
Youth (20-39)	Cardiology	7	5	2
	Orthopaedics	12	12	0
	Ophthalmology	2	1	1
	Cancer	7	4	3
	Kidney related	9	9	0
	Neurology	3	2	1
	Others	19	9	10
Middle-aged (40-59)	Cardiology	23	18	5
	Orthopaedics	8	7	1
	Ophthalmology	2	1	1
	Cancer	34	31	3
	Kidney related	11	10	1
	Neurology	6	5	1
	Others	15	12	3
Old (60 yrs and above)	Cardiology	7	7	0
	Orthopaedics	1	0	1
	Ophthalmology	1	1	0
	Cancer	4	4	0
	Kidney related	1	1	0
	Neurology	2	2	0
	Others	1	1	0

Figures 9.3(a) to 9.3(d) show the disease distribution of patients under different age groups. We find that 80 percent of the juvenile patients are cardiology patients whereas there is no such clear dominance among the youth patients—the highest percentage of patients in this age group is from the disease category ‘others’. Cancer is the most common disease among middle-aged patients and cardiology is the cause for treatment in India for 44 per cent of old patients.

The disease distribution shown in Figures 9.3(c) and 9.3(d) suggests that cardiology and cancer seem to be the diseases for which most of the patients are coming to India. However, a gender-wise reclassification shows that while cardiology is a common disease among both male and female patients, cancer is not that common a disease among female patients. In fact Figure 9.4(a) and 9.4(b) show different disease profiles for male and female patients.

Figure 9.3(a)

Patients Distribution under the Age Group "Upto 19 Years"

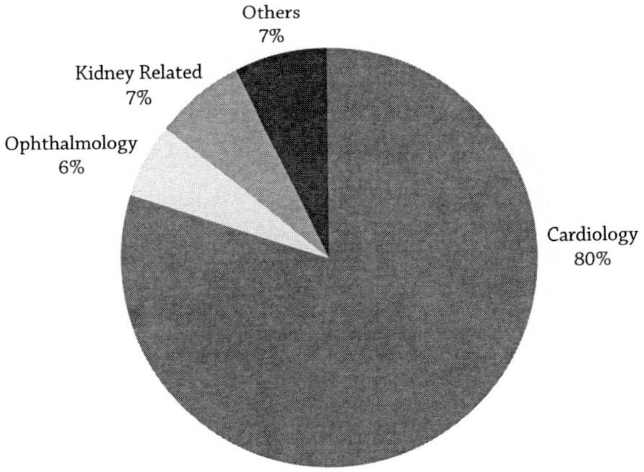

Figure 9.3(b)

Patients Disribution under the Age Group "20-39 Years"

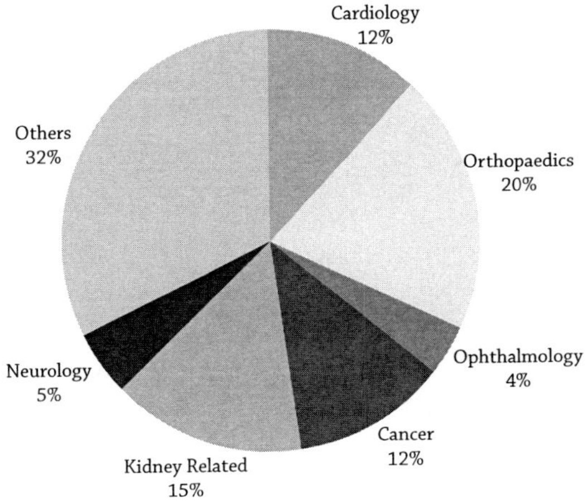

Figure 9.3(c)

Patient Distribution under the Age Group "40-59 Years"

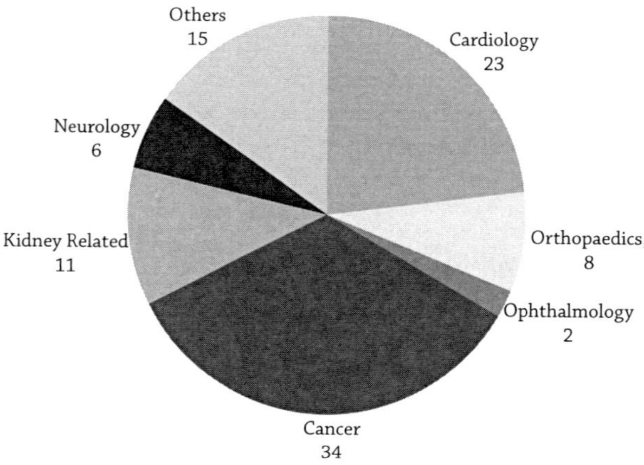

Figure 9.3(d)

Patients Distribution under the Age Group "60 Years and Above"

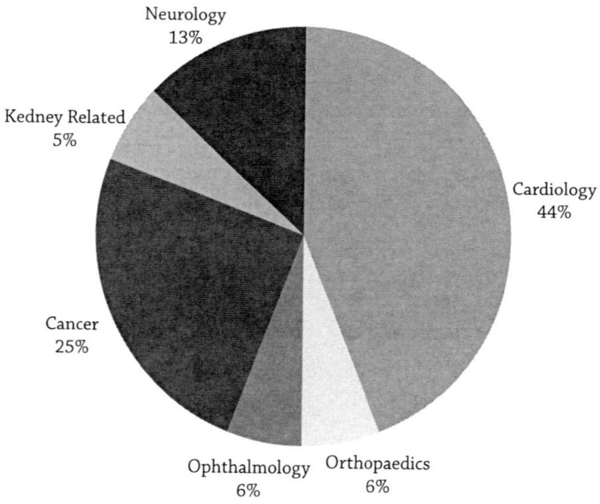

Figure 9.4(a)

Reporting Disease among Males

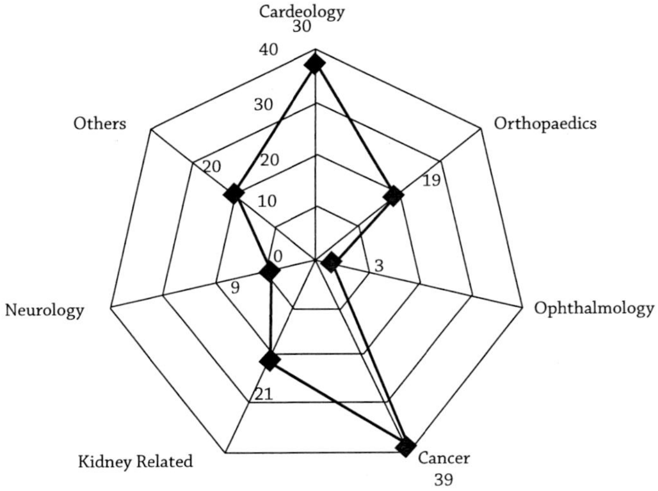

Figure 9.4(b)

Reporting Diseases among Females

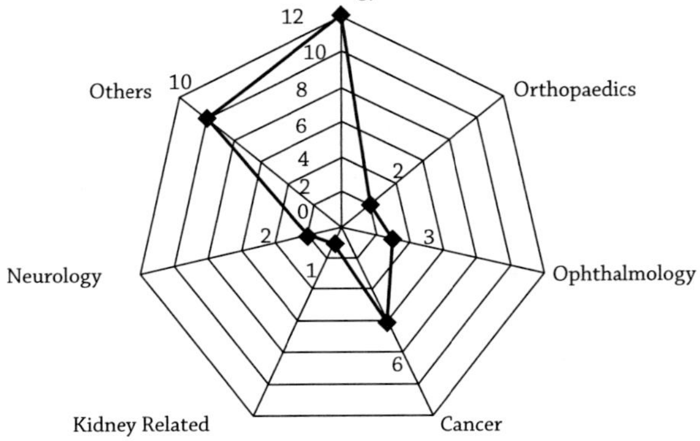

In Table 9.17 we analyse the average household income of Bangladeshi patients under different age groups and are undergoing treatment for different types of diseases. We do not find any common pattern for household income either based on the age of the patient or on the disease category.

Table 9.17

Disease and Economic Characteristics of Bangladeshi Patients

Age (Years Completed)	*Type of Disease*	*No of Patients*	*Avg Income (in Bangladesh Taka)*
Juvenile (Up to 19)	Cardiology	12	276833
	Ophthalmology	1	100000
	Kidney related	1	120000
	Others	1	40000
Youth (20-39)	Cardiology	6	477333
	Orthopaedics	12	661250
	Ophthalmology	1	150000
	Cancer	7	180000
	Kidney related	9	456667
	Neurology	3	241333
	Others	17	785530
Middle-aged (40-59)	Cardiology	22	355818
	Orthopaedics	8	351250
	Ophthalmology	1	480000
	Cancer	33	312697
	Kidney related	11	452182
	Neurology	6	263500
	Others	15	310400
Old (60 yrs and above)	Cardiology	7	320514
	Orthopaedics	1	120000
	Ophthalmology	1	300000
	Cancer	3	223333
	Kidney related	1	180000
	Neurology	2	690000
	Others	1	1680000

For example, the average household income is very high (16,80,000 and 7,85,530 respectively) for 'youth' and 'old' patients who reported to be undergoing treatment for other diseases ('others'), whereas for the same category of disease, the average household income is only 40,000 among juvenile and 3,10,400 among middle-aged patients.

Disease Diagnosis and Treatment

Figure 9.5 reveals that the vast majority of patients got their diagnosis done in their home country. Apparently, the local doctors advised them to go abroad for better treatment in view of insufficient facilities and expertise in the home country.

Figure 9.5

Patients Reporting Diagnosis of Disease

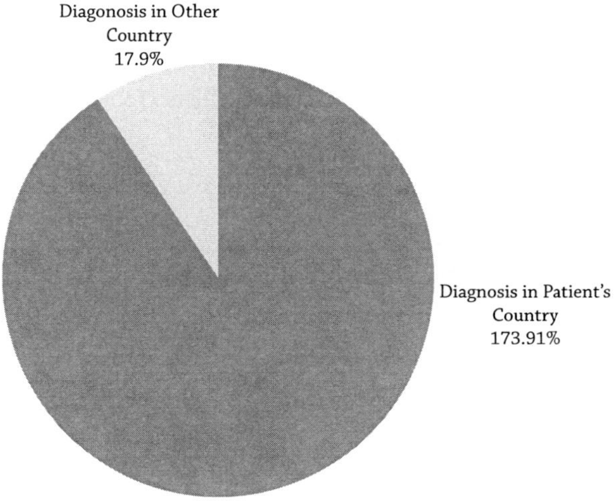

Figure 9.6

Patients' Disease Diagnosis Distribution

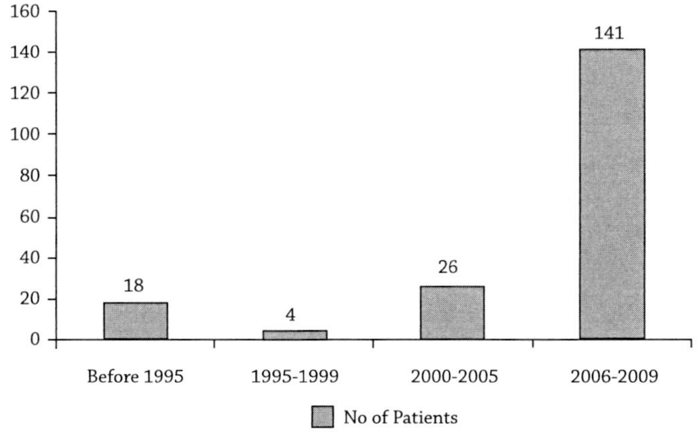

Not only was the diagnosis done in home country, in many cases we find that the patient knew about the disease diagnosis, but could not come earlier due to lack of resources as revealed in Figure 9.6. These could be both financial and non-financial. Many non-financial resources may be employed to overcome the different barriers to trade in health services.

Figure 9.7 shows that there is positive correlation between the annual household income and the amount spent on medical treatment in India, although the slope of the line of best fit is quite low. This figure is only for Bangladeshi patients as the amount spent is in local currency (Bangladeshi Taka). The richer patients tend to spend a higher amount on an average.

Figure 9.7

Scatter Diagram of Annual Household Income and Amount Spent for Medical Treatment

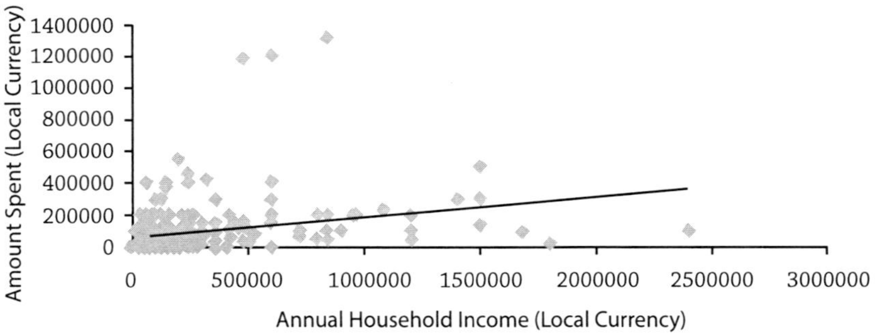

Barriers and Obstacles

We now analyse the barriers to Mode 2 trade in health services in South Asia. Figure 9.8 shows that while a clear category of medical visa is available, not all patients come under this category. In fact, as many as 15 per cent of the patients have entered India on tourist visas perhaps because getting a medical visa is more difficult and time-consuming in their perception, i.e. the transaction cost of getting a medical visa is much higher than that of a tourist visa whereas there is no added value for the same.

Figure 9.8

Information Barrier (Visa Barrier)

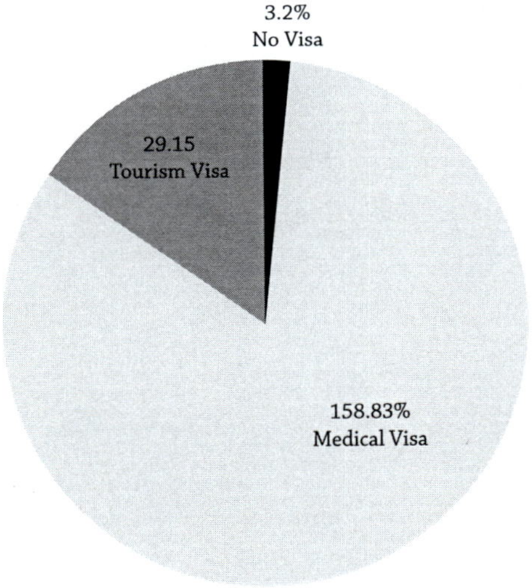

Figure 9.9 highlights another major barrier in terms of the duration and number of entries permitted by the patient's visa. Over 85 per cent of the patients have entered India on one month single-entry visa. It is reasonable to assume that the related uncertainty and anxiety would be adding to the cost associated with the patient's treatment in India.

Figure 9.9

No. of Medical Patients Who Came to India under Different Categories

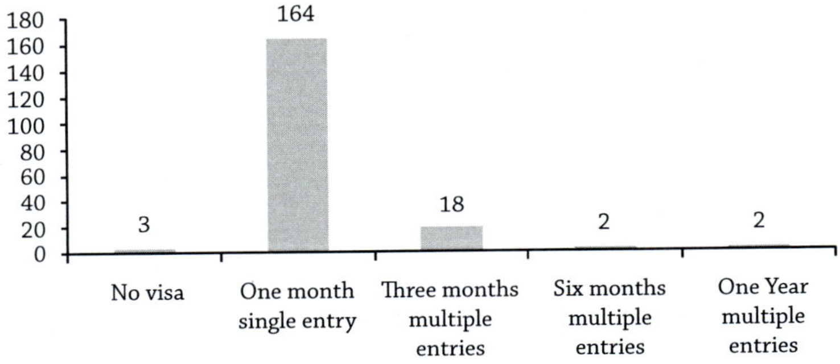

The time and cost incurred to get the Indian visa is reported in Figure 9.10. Although some (35) patients got their visa in one day, a large number of the patients (63) reported that it took them more than three days to get the same while another 55 reported to have got their visa in three days.

Figure 9.10

Patients Reporting Time Taken to Get Visa

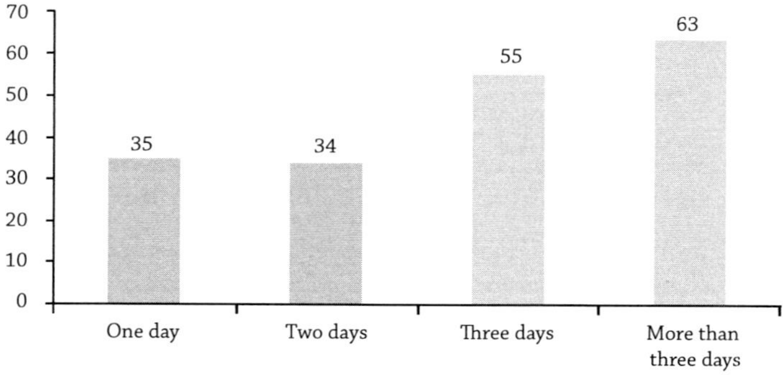

Figure 9.11 reinforces the reasons for these patients to come to India for their treatment. A vast majority (104 out of 190) of patients reported that they came to India because of its inexpensive and high quality doctors—a pull factor—while 49 and 30 reported the absence of good quality doctors and medical infrastructure, respectively, in their home country—a distinctive push factor. The pull factor can also be interpreted to cause welfare gain among the population of patients in the neighbouring South Asian country.

Figure 9.11

Decision-making Factors for Coming to India for Treatment

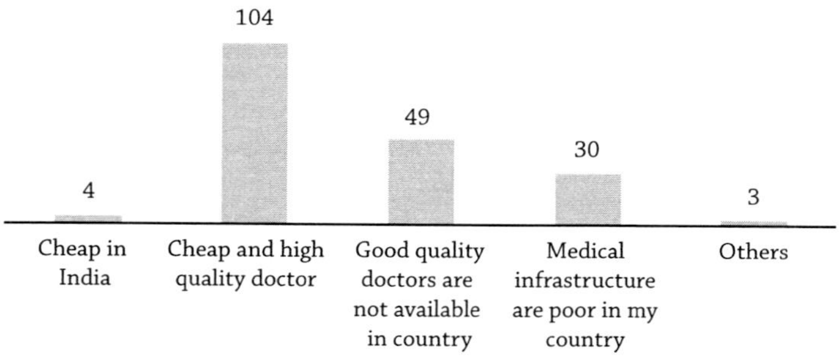

An overwhelming majority (97%) of the patients were not able to carry unlimited amount of foreign exchange from their respective country for medical treatment as reported by the respondents themselves (Figure 9.12).

Figure 9.12

Carrying of Unlimited Foreign Currency

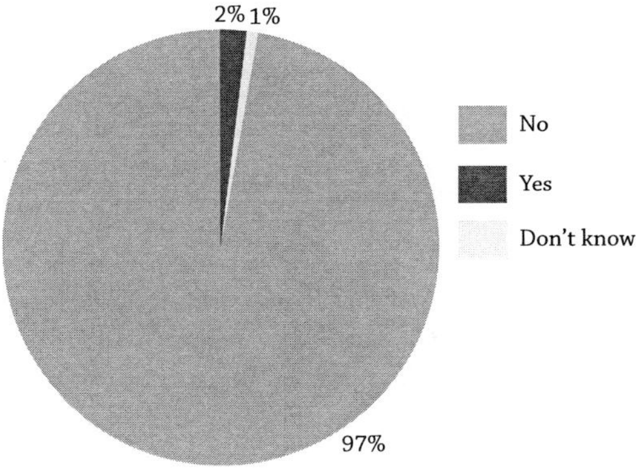

However, only nine per cent of the patients reported to have used the informal route to bring foreign currency to India for their treatment as shown in Figure 9.13. Apparently, most patients are able to bring all the foreign exchange they need for the treatment through the formal route itself.

Figure 9.13

Patients Reporting Remittance through Informal Route

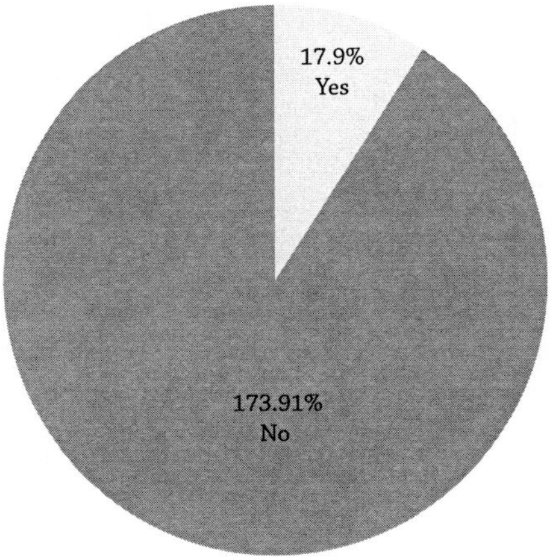

Table 9.18 shows the mode of travel used by the patients to reach their home country border. Most Bangladeshi patients have travelled by road to reach their nearest border implying that they crossed the land border; while for patients from most other countries, it has been the air border. The rail route is not preferred much by Bangladeshi patients.

Table 9.18

Patients Reporting "Amount Spent to Get Visa"

Categories	*No of Patients Reporting*	*Total Amount Spent*	*Average Amount per Patient*
Direct	165	33300	201.81
Indirect	22	9470	430.45

The next few charts assess the major obstacles to a foreign patient receiving medical services in India on a scale of 1 to 5 (1–minor obstacle and 5–major obstacle) as reported by the patients. A vast majority of patients feel that visa is a major obstacle to trade in medical services—the average score is 3.84 on a 5 point scale of 1 to 5 as seen in Figure 9.14. The bimodality of the distribution is interesting and suggests that there are two subpopulations within the patient population. For example, for patients who know someone in the embassy it is easy and for patients who don't it is very difficult to get their Indian visa and so becomes a major obstacle.

Figure 9.14

Visa as on Obstacle

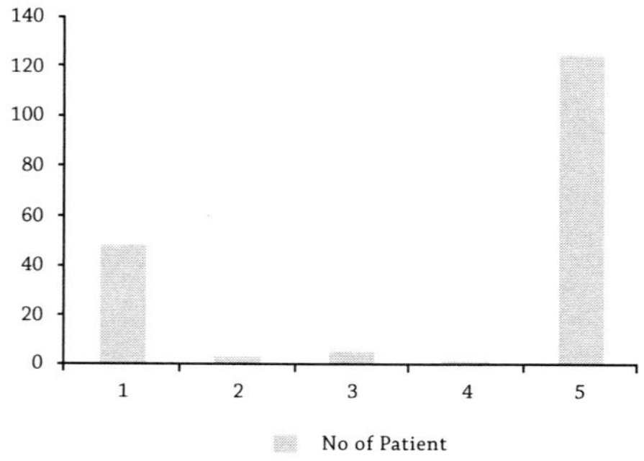

According to Figure 9.15, the absence of right information regarding medical facilities in India and the details regarding the processes and the treatments is seen as a serious obstacle by many patients. The average score on this count works out to 1.99.

Figure 9.15

Right Information to Come to India about Medical Facilities as an Obstacle

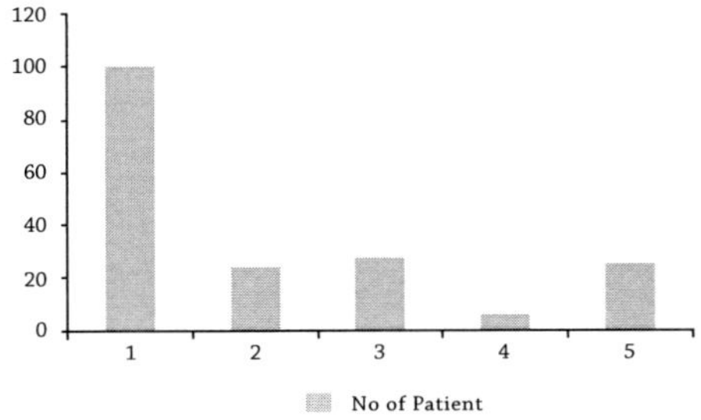

Non-availability of Indian rail ticket in the patient's home country is given a score of 5 on a five-point scale by 172 patients as shown in Figure 9.16. This raises the average score to 4.77.

Figure 9.16

Non-availability of Indian Rail Ticket as an Obstacle

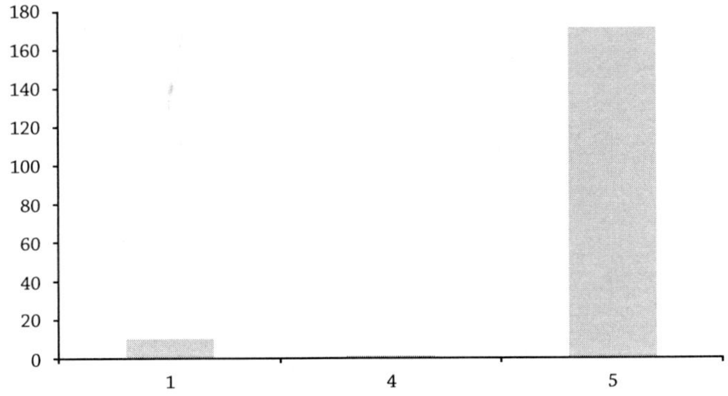

An integrated agency to streamline trade in health services and handle all aspects of a foreign patient's availing of health services in India is felt lacking by many patients. In fact, many of them have felt the lack of such an integrated agency as an obstacle and the average score is 3.10 computed from the distribution shown in Figure 9.17.

Figure 9.17

Non-availibility of Intergrated Agency as an Obstacle

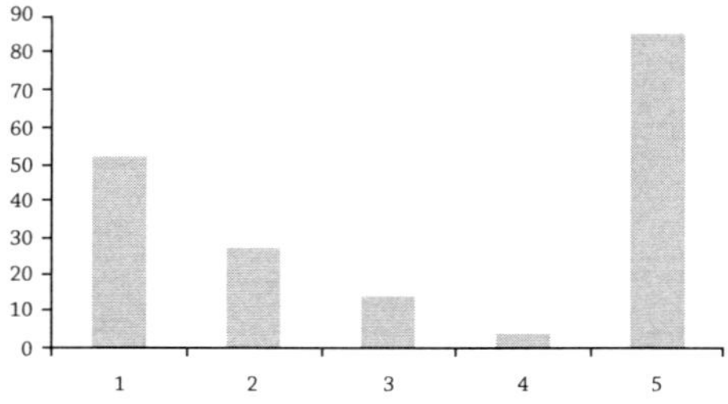

Suggestions and Perceptions

Almost all the patients have responded very favourably to some of the suggestions made to them as shown in Figures 9.18 to 9.21. As many as 99 per cent agree that common medical insurance should be available for treatment in any SAARC country, while 100 per cent of them feel that hospitals should offer comprehensive packages.

Figure 9.18

Medical Insurance for All SAARC Countries

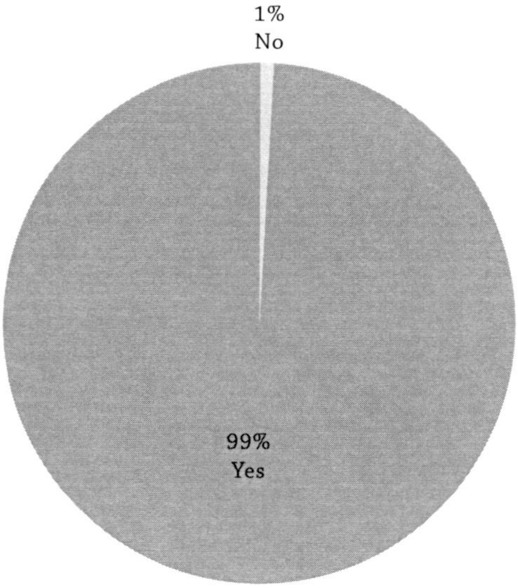

Figure 9.19

Follow up Services in Your Country's Hospitals/Institutions

Figure 9.20

Liaison Outlets at Home Country

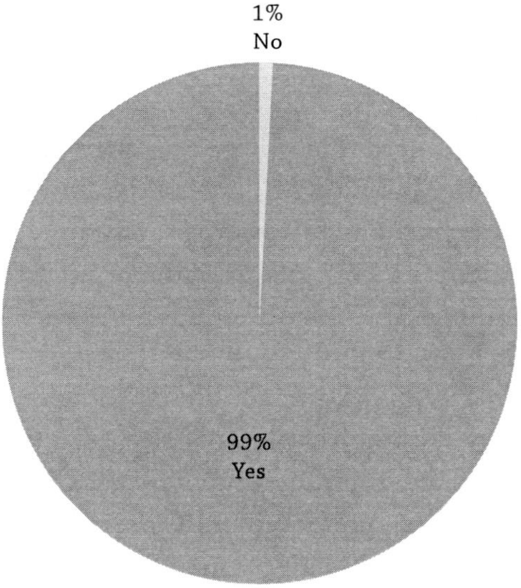

Figure 9.21

Comprehensive Package by the Hospitals

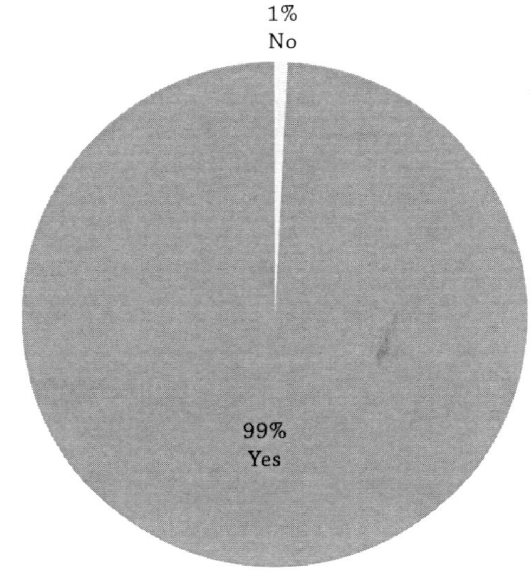

Similarly, 99 per cent of the patients feel that Indian hospitals should establish liaison outlets in their home country as well arrange to provide follow-up services in hospitals and/or institutions of the patient's home country.

Figure 9.22 presents the opinion of the respondent patients on different aspects of trade in health services including various barriers to such trade. An overwhelming majority of (96.8%) patients are happy with the medical treatment but feel the barriers are unnecessary. Surprisingly as many as 73.2 per cent have no particular view on current account convertibility and only 24.2 per cent feel that their country should have it. 77.9 per cent feel that doctors should be able to move freely to another country to offer their services while another 73.7 per cent feel that there should be standardisation of skill among medical personnel to help their movement across countries. 70 per cent patients feel that there should be dual taxation treaty to help medical professionals and another 76.8 per cent have expressed the view that if their country removed the barriers to trade in health services, there will be more welfare gains.

Figure 9.22

Perception-1

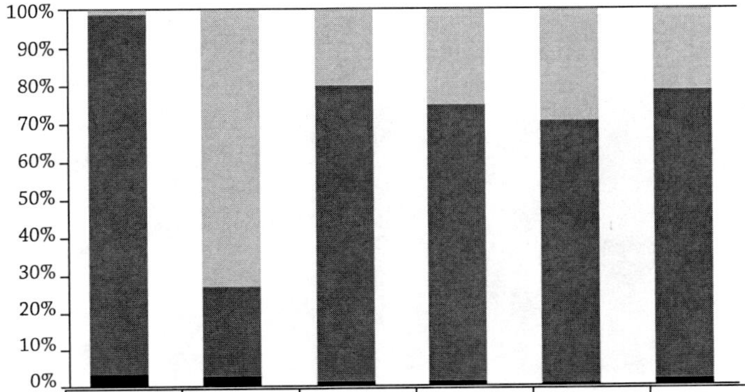

	Happy with the Medical Treatment but the Barriers are Unnecessary	Current Account Convertibility	Doctors (Skilled should Move Freely	Standardisation of Skill	Dual Taxation Treaty for Medical Professionals	Welfare
Cant Say	2	139	40	48	56	41
Yes	182	46	148	140	133	146
No	6	5	2	2	1	3

Figure 9.23 presents some more perceptions of the patient respondents. According to 77.9 per cent of the respondents, visa issues are complicated. About 40 per cent patients reported that they have been cheated by the informal foreign exchange traders while only 19.5 per cent reported not being cheated by them. A clear 80 per cent of the patients have opined that their medical insurance policy should be valid across all SAARC countries. 64.7 per cent patients feel that the airfare is too high and 93.7 per cent stated that access to medical services is needed for all citizens of South Asian nations.

Table 9.19 summarises the charges of different medical services and also the average actual payments made by them, including any discount received by the patients. All the patients made the payments by cash. The unit prices vary across a wide range and by and large the actual payments are close to the unit prices.

Figure 9.23

Perception-2

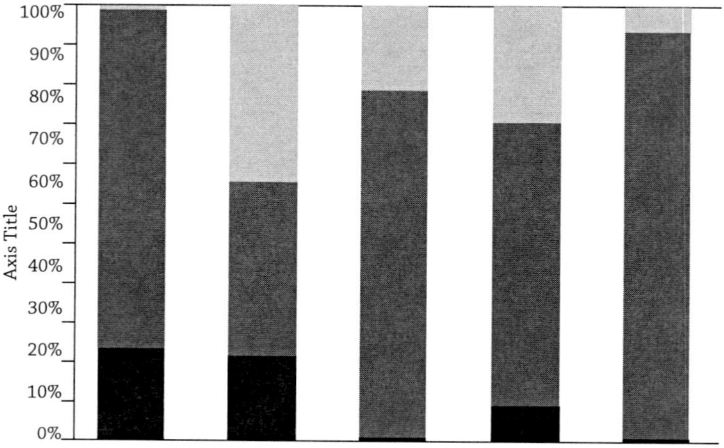

	Visa Issues are Complicated	*Informal Foreign Exchange Traders Cheated*	*Medical Insurance Policy should be Applied to SAARC*	*Airfare is too High*	*Access to Medical Services to all Citizens of South Asia*
Cant Say	2	77	37	51	11
Yes	148	76	152	123	178
No	40	37	1	16	1

Table 9.19

Mode of Travel to Reach Home Country Border

Country	*Travel to Nearest Border*	*No. of Patients*	*Total Cost (in Local Currency)*	*Avg. Cost in Local Currency*
Afghanistan	By air	2	NA	NA
Bangladesh	By air	22	55250	2630.95
	By rail	4	1710	427.50
	By road	156	133565	856.19
Bhutan	By road	1	2000	2000.00
Nepal	By air	1	3500	3500.00
	By road	1	300	300.00
Pakistan	By Air	1	NA	NA
Sri Lanka	By Air	2	NA	NA

Table 9.20

Charges for Getting Medical Services

Sr. No	*Service*	*Average Unit Price*	*Average Actual Payment Including Test (Rs.)*	*Average Discount if Any*	*Payment Mode*
1	High-risk open heart surgery	255200	255200		Cash
2	Balloon heart surgery	79800	79800		Cash
3	Bypass surgery (avg.)	149478	149478	27321	Cash
4	Angiography	10000	10000		Cash
5	Double valve change	255000	255000	25000	Cash
6	TGA operation	180000	180000		Cash
7	Open heart surgery and angiogram	180000	180000		Cash
8	Cataract operation	15600	15600		Cash
9	Kidney stone operation	45000	45000		Cash
10	Kidney transplant	215000	235000		Cash
11	Operation of spinal cord	35000	59250		Cash
12	Plate setting operation	80000	80750		Cash
13	Package operation for bone marrow	200000	200000		Cash
14	Ultrasound operation	54000	54000		Cash
15	Elbow operation	35000	35000		Cash
16	Appendix operation	30000	30000		Cash
17	Operation fees (neuro)	75000	115000		Cash
18	Plate setting operation	80000	80750		Cash
19	Other orthopaedic operation	69000	69000		Cash
20	Chemotherapy	25000	40167		Cash
21	Cancer related tests (CT scan,MRI, X-ray, Blood test, Biopsy etc. avg)	14977	14977		Cash
22	Asthma test	10000	10000		Cash
23	Bone marrow transplant	2000000	2000000		Cash
24	Skin allergy test	2000	2300		Cash
25	CT Scan	9000	9000		Cash
26	MRI	6500	6500		Cash
27	Doctor's fee (avg)	400	400		Cash

Table 9.21

Mode 1, Mode 2 and Mode 4 Services from Hospitals

		Mode 1		*Mode 2*		*Mode 4*	
City	*Name*	*Countries Offered Telemedicine Services**	*No of Cases (Telemedicine) during Last Two Years*	*South Asian Patient Coming from*	*No of Patients during Last Two Years*	*Countries Visited by Your Hospital Doctors to Offer Professional Services*	*No of Doctors from SAARC Countries that Visited Your Hospital in Last Two Years*
Bangalore	Manipal Health System	none	0	Bd, Bh, Np, SL	300	none	0
	Narayana Hrudayalaya	Bd, Bh, Np, SL	3000	Bd, Bh, Np, SL	3000	Bd, Bh, Pk	30
	Sri.Jayadeva Institute of Cardiology	none	0	Bd, Np, SL	200	none	0
Chennai	Apollo Hospitals	Bd, Ml, Np, SL	10000-12000	Bd, Bh, Ml, Np, Pk, SL, Af	2500	Bd, Ml, SL	25
	Chetinad Health City	none	0	Bd, SL	100	none	0
	Christian Medical College	none	0	Bd, Bh, Ml, Np, Pk, SL, Af	10000	none	0
	Global Hospitals & Health City	Bd	300	Bd, Ml, SL	100	none	0

contd...

...contd...

	Lifeline Multispeciality Hospital	none	0	Bd, Ml, Np, SL	86	Ml, SL	10
	MIOT	none	0	Bd, Ml, Np, SL, Af	300	none	0
	Sri Ramchandra Medical Centre	Bd, Bh, Ml, Np, Pk, SL, Af	700	Bd, Bh, Ml, Np, Pk, SL, Af	200	SL	15
Delhi	All India Institute For Medical Sciences	none	0	Bd, Bh, Np, Pk, Af	2000	Bd, Bh, Ml, Np	50
	Apollo Hospitals Delhi	Bd, Np, Pk, Af	0	Bd, Bh, Np, Pk, Af	1000	none	0
	Escorts Heart Institute & Research Centre	none	0	Bd, Pk, Af	500	none	0
	Jaipur Golden Hospital	none	0	Bd, Pk, Af	100	none	0
	Rajiv Gandhi Cancer Institute and Research Centre	none	0	Bd, Bh, Np, Pk, Af	800	none	0
Kolkata	Kothari Medical	none	0	Bd		Bd	50
	Peerless Hospital & B.K.Roy Research Centre	none	0	Bd, Bh, Np	600	none	0

contd...

...contd...

	Rabindranath Tagore International Institute of Cardiac Sciences	Bd	12000	Bd, Bh, Np	3000	none	0
	Ruby General Hospital Ltd.	none	0	Bd, Bh, Np	1500	none	0
Mumbai	Tata Memorial Hospital	none	0	Bd, Ml, Np, Pk, SL, Af	1200	none	0

Note: * Bd – Bangladesh; Bh – Bhutan; Ml – Maldives; Np – Nepal; Pk – Pakistan; SL – Sri Lanka; Af - Afghanistan

Table 9.22

No of Patients Treated in Last Five Months (before 1 June 2009)

Month	*Total No of Patients*	*Country of Origin*										
		Bangla-desh	*Pakis-tan*	*Nepal*	*Afghan-istan*	*Mal-dives*	*Sri Lanka*	*Bhutan*	*US*	*EU*	*Gulf*	*Others*
January	524	274	11	26	19	8	42	12	7	8	59	58
February	441	188	16	26	16	13	45	10	6	6	41	74
March	538	279	11	19	18	7	37	9	9	7	48	94
April	477	264	14	27	12	7	23	7	8	6	54	55
May	490	290	6	12	11	7	32	3	3	9	38	79
Total	2470	1295	58	110	76	42	179	41	33	36	240	360

Hospitals

Table 9.20 captures different aspects of medical services offered by our sample of Indian hospitals to foreign patients. We have tabulated the information using the WTO classification of trade in services.

All the 20 hospitals surveyed reported receiving patients from some SAARC country or the other. South Indian hospitals from Bangalore and Chennai are more active in offering telemedicine services. Only 6 of the 20 hospitals reported that their doctors go to some neighbouring country to render professional services and 1 each has stated that their doctors have gone to only Bangladesh or only Sri Lanka. Similarly, only 6 hospitals reported that any doctor from another SAARC country visited them over the last two years. Mode 3 services are relatively fewer and could not be captured through the questionnaires administered to the Indian hospitals.

Doctors

The questionnaire for doctors was administered to 65 doctors and some of the information is presented in Table 9.21. The information given by doctors corroborates the information gathered from the patients that a very large number of the patients come from Bangladesh. In our sample we found that Sri Lanka sent the second highest number of patients, followed by Nepal from within the SAARC. But overall, a large number of patients also come from the gulf countries.

Figure 9.24 reveals that only 20 per cent of the doctors surveyed travel to SAARC countries to treat patients. This percentage is still fairly high considering that Mode 4 services trade is perhaps the most restrictive among all the four modes. The break-up in terms of which neighbouring countries do these 13 (out of the 65 surveyed) travel to is shown in Table 9.22.

Figure 9.24

Doctors Travel to SAARC

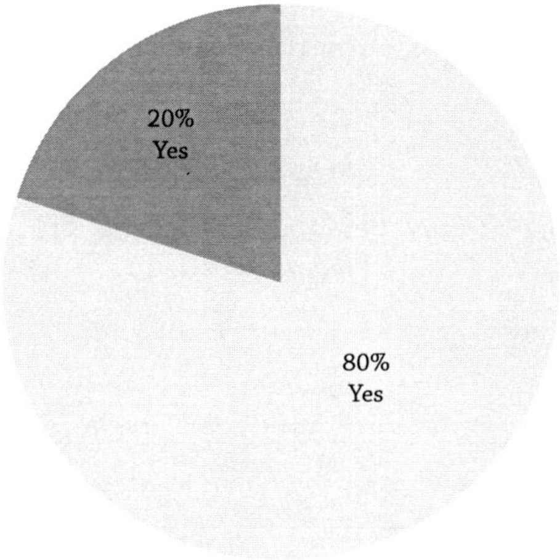

Out of 13 doctors that reported to have travelled to a neighbouring country to offer medical services, 10 of them reported to have travelled to Bangladesh. None of the doctors reported to have travelled to Pakistan or Afghanistan.

The doctors were asked to rate on a 10-point scale how important each of the five given possible reasons was in their decision not to move to SAARC countries. Figures 9.25 through 9.32 capture the responses of the 65 doctors.

Figure 9.25

Security Environment Perception

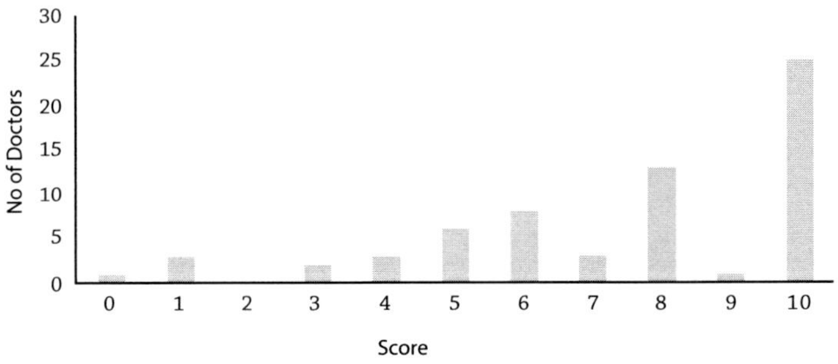

Security environment comes out as a strong demotivating reason in Figure 9.28. The mean score is 7.43 out of a possible 10. Figure 9.29 conveys that the attractiveness of the Indian market is reason enough for some doctors not to move to SAARC countries. The average score is 9.

Figure 9.26

Indian Market Perception

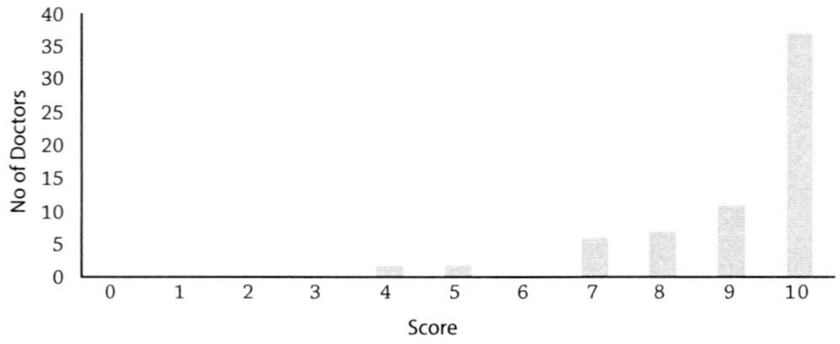

The hassles of getting an employment permit does not appear to be a strong enough reason as the average score is 6.98 as shown in the distribution captured in Figure 9.30. Similarly, complicated visa process also does not appear to be a strong reason to dissuade travel to other SAARC countries because the average score on this count is only 4.29 computed from the distribution shown in Figure 9.28. Finally income tax policies and complications thereon are not perceived to be a strong reason by the doctors. They have awarded an average score of only 3.86 to this reason.

Figures 9.27

Employment Permit Perception

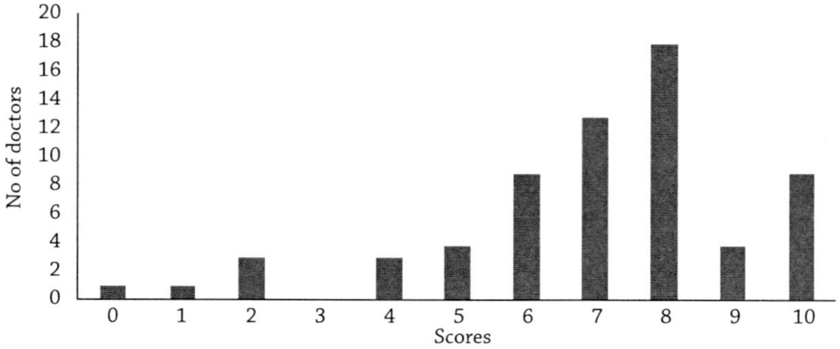

Figure 9.28

Complicated Visa Perception

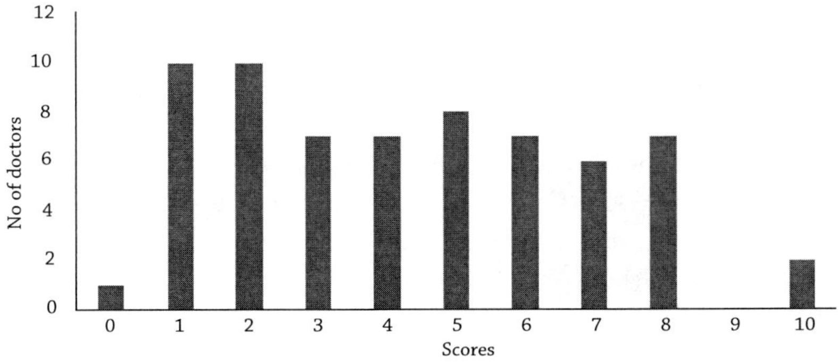

Figure 9.29

Income Tax Policy Perception

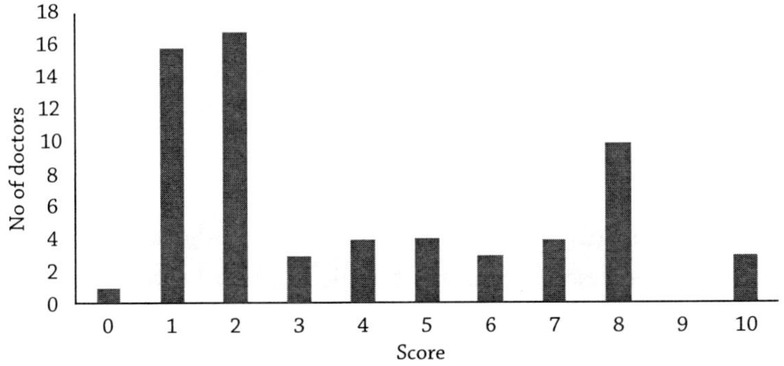

Summary and Conclusions

This study was conducted in three South Asian countries—India, Bangladesh and Nepal. In order to gain insights into the trade in health services in India, the study examines the opinions of patients, hospitals owners and doctors involved in this service trade. A total of 190 foreign patients from SAARC countries that came to India to receive medical services, 20 hospitals across five metros, and 65 doctors active in offering professional services were surveyed using three structured questionnaires. Two case studies were carried out in two countries (Bangladesh and Nepal) to examine the demand aspects of health service trade. This study also aims to profile the health service sector of these two countries which might affect trade in health services. It focuses on the liberalisation of health services and assesses the challenges and opportunities posed by the liberalisation of trade on the provisions of health services and options for national policy makers. It further makes an effort to examine the barriers in health service trade in the two relatively small countries of South Asia. An effort is made to explore possible regional cooperation in health service trade among the above three countries of the SAARC region. The evidence is actually useful in order to understand commitments and challenges regarding trade in health services in the SAARC region.

The study opines that there exists a gender bias among the foreign patients coming to India for medical treatment. An overwhelming majority (about 79.5%) of the patients is male and more than half are in the age group of 40-59. Not so surprisingly, about 95.8 per cent of the patients are from Bangladesh. The largest number of patients (46%) is self-employed followed by another 30 per cent in private service. About 12 per cent of the patient's sources of income are agriculture. Surprisingly, about 10 per cent of the patients are in government service in their respective country which implies a perceived lack of medical facilities even for government servants.

The largest number of patients coming to India is for cardiac (49) and cancer (45) treatment. Orthopaedic (21) and kidney-related (22) treatment also forms a significant percentage. A little bi-modality among cardiology patients—both juvenile (under 19) and middle-aged patients outnumber youth in the sample is noticed by the study. The dominance of males across all age groups and across all disease categories is also clearly visible—the only exception being patients who are between 20 and 39 years old and do not have any of the stated diseases. This may be due to gynaecological problems that are faced by the female youth patients.

Majority of the patients get their diagnosis done in their home country. Apparently, the local doctors advise them to go abroad for better treatment in view of insufficient facilities and expertise in the home country. In many cases, the issue of travelling to India for treatment comes after several months of diagnosis.

As many as 15 per cent of the patients were found to have entered India on a tourist visa, implying that the higher transaction cost of getting a medical visa is much more than the higher perceived value for the same. Over 85 per cent of the patients have entered India on a one month single-entry visa. The related uncertainty and anxiety would be adding to the cost associated with the patient's treatment in India. About 11 per cent of the patients admitted to using the services of a broker or a middleman for their visa.

A vast majority (104 out of 190) of patients reported that they came to India because of its inexpensive and high quality doctors—a pull factor—while 49 and 30 reported the absence of good quality doctors and medical infrastructure, respectively, in their home country—a distinctive push factor. Regarding remittance of foreign exchange, the higher income households do bring in slightly higher amounts through the informal route. There is no particular relationship between the rates at which Indian rupee is bought by the Bangladesh patients and their respective household income.

This study also studied the major obstacles to a foreign patient receiving medical services in India on a scale of 1 to 5. It turns out that visa is a major obstacle to trade in medical services (average score 3.84). Neither language nor a central bank permission for remittance nor information regarding medical facilities in India is perceived to be a major obstacle. However, non-availability of Indian rail ticket in the patient's home country is given a score of 5 on a five-point scale by 172 patients.. This raises the average score to 4.77. An integrated agency to streamline trade in health services and handle all aspects of a foreign patient's availing of health services in India is felt lacking by many patients. In fact, many of them have felt the lack of such an integrated agency as an obstacle.

An overwhelming majority of patients (96.8%) are happy with the medical treatment but feel that the barriers in this respect are unnecessary. Surprisingly, as many as 73.2 per cent have no particular view on current account convertibility and only 24.2 per cent feel that their country should have it. Between 70 and 80 per cent patients feel that doctors should be able to move freely to another country, that there should be standardisation of skill among medical personnel, that there should be dual taxation treaty to help medical professionals and that if their country removed the barriers to trade in health services, there will be more welfare gains. According to 77.9 per cent of the respondents, visa issues are complicated. About 40 per cent patients reported that they have been cheated by the informal foreign exchange traders while only 19.5 per cent reported not being cheated by them. A clear 80 per cent of the patients have opined that their medical insurance policy should be valid across all SAARC countries and another 64.7 per cent patients feel that the airfare is too high.

All 20 hospitals surveyed reported receiving patients from some SAARC country or the other. South Indian hospitals from Bangalore and Chennai are more active in offering telemedicine services. Only 6 hospitals reported that any doctor from another SAARC country visited them over the last two years. As expected, none of the hospitals are having any Mode 3 medical service.

Doctors corroborate the information gathered from the patients that a very large number of the patients come from Bangladesh. In our sample we found that Sri Lanka sent the second highest number of patients, followed by Nepal from within the SAARC. But overall, a large number of patients also come from the gulf countries. Only 20 per cent of the doctors surveyed travel to SAARC countries to treat patients. This percentage is still fairly high considering that Mode 4 services trade is perhaps the most restrictive among all the four modes.

Security environment comes out as a strong demotivating reason, discouraging movement of doctors. The attractiveness of the Indian market is reason enough for some doctors not to move to SAARC countries. The hassles of getting an employment permit, complicated visa process or income tax policies, and complications thereon also do not appear to be strong enough reasons. In summary, Mode 4 service seems to have the highest potential to offer the maximum welfare gain in South Asia.

The case study on Bangladesh reveals the fact that telemedicine services may help Bangladesh to provide better services to its people, side by side checking illegal money transfer to neighbouring countries. Telemedicine may assist more consumers in getting access to faster, better and possibly cheaper diagnostic medical services, including some therapeutic services. It should be borne in mind that there may be weak consumer protection and for this reason additional inter-country agreements are needed.

It is understood that telemedicine and teleconferencing services between the SAARC countries can help to import and export services and accordingly benefit and improve the services of both private and public hospitals of the SAARC region. Currently, Bhutan and India have already entered into the network and are reaping the benefit of this technology. Unfortunately the Bangladesh government has not taken any effective initiative in this respect and the country still remains outside the SAARC telemedicine network. Countries like Bangladesh, Nepal, and Afghanistan, for example, can join in the regional group like SAARC telemedicine network, and provide its citizens faster, superior and cheaper diagnostic medical services, including some therapeutic services through regional telemedicine services.

It is observed that Mode 2 provides quality treatment to Bangladeshi patients and there is little doubt that a huge amount of foreign exchange of Bangladesh outflows to foreign countries, often through illegal channels as Bangladeshi patients spend huge amount of foreign exchange in India and East Asian countries like Thailand and Singapore for receiving treatments.

The study opines that commercial presence in health services (Mode 3) can create supplementary resources for investment in and upgrading of health care infrastructure and technologies of the country. The availability of private capital in the country may reduce the total burden on government resources and may help to generate employment. Inflow of foreign capital in certain parts of the health system (e.g., establishment of hospitals with modern facilities) may reduce the burden on government resources and allow the public sector to relocate its resources toward the patients with less ability to pay. The presence of foreign commercial firms (with higher levels of pay and/or better equipment and premises) may entice Bangladesh health personnel away from public facilities: an 'internal' brain drain.

For this reason there is a need to formulate effective public policy to check it and to impose limitations on FDI in health services.

There are also other possible negative effects of FDI in health services in Bangladesh e.g., excessive technological dependence, capital flight and profit outflow. All these may lead to negative effects on Bangladesh's balance of payments. It may also make foreign medical services affordable to wealthy persons and to those with expensive medical insurance. It is generally observed that foreign private health service providers try to offer services which are not offered by the public sector. These services are usually given to attract affluent customers.

The study further observes that FDI actually enhances commercialisation of the health care sector of Bangladesh. Bangladesh, therefore, should take a step back and deeply study the above issues of the risk and benefits of commercialisation of its health sector and then decide whether this sector should be opened up to foreign investment.

It is noted that temporary movement of personnel (Mode 4) may assist Bangladesh and other SARRC countries in receiving essential healthcare services. It is felt that Bangladesh would be benefitted substantially through increased export of service providers (e.g. doctor and nurses) through TMNP (Temporary Movement of Natural Persons). It has been noticed that there exist severe disparities in the number of health personnel among SAARC countries. TMNP may make health services more accessible and affordable, thus increasing the welfare of the SAARC countries. In this respect some constructive knowledge spillover effects are also possible. TMNP can assist in reducing these disparities and the shortages of health professionals. Bhutan has already shown interest in employing Bangladeshi doctors in the hospitals of their country. This is a significant signal for Bangladesh indeed. Bangladesh can adopt an effective domestic health policy in this respect. For opening up markets in the SAARC region and also in the developed countries, Bangladesh government should identify the current capacity of supply of health professionals within the country.

A special type of visa may be introduced for the SAARC countries in this respect. Indian proposal on GATS Visa is gradually becoming popular with both developed and developing members who successfully distinguished between temporary provision of service supply and migration (Bhattacharya *et al.*, 2003). Some developing countries e.g., Tunisia, earn huge amount of foreign exchange through health service trading. Tunisia has probably the highest potential for health services exports in the Middle East and North Africa (MENA) region (Lautier, 2008) and a country like Bangladesh can follow the model of Tunisia in this respect.

Bangladesh government should also devise a long term plan for health service trade. Identification of market and negotiations for market access should be linked with health professional's skill development plan. The number one priority in upcoming negotiations for Bangladesh in health service trade should be TMNP under mode 4. The liberalisation of health sector with limited opening of mode 4 in the SAARC region will bring positive result in reducing deficit in trade in health services, improving quality of health services, and enhancing technology transfer. The policy of exporting health service providers through TMNP requires plans for attraction of returned migrants, an essential element of which is to help them to be effectively absorbed into the domestic labor market (Raihan and Mahmood, 2004). It is also understood that in designing health service trade in future under SAFTA, it is vital to protect the interests of the smaller and weaker economies of the SAARC region for example, Bangladesh and Afghanistan, so that these countries can constructively engage themselves in benefiting from access to a free trade area.

This study makes some observations and recommendations basing on Nepal case study. Health services at most of the public institutions in Nepal are subsidised by the government and services are generally provided from public good perspective. This implies that such public institutions are less important from the trade viewpoint. Therefore, greater involvement of the private sector particularly in operating teaching hospitals and tertiary care, and liberalisation of the policies for exporting health services are necessary for exporting the services.

Most of the patients arrived in Nepal from India belong to low-income households. Interestingly, a few of them are ready to pay fees higher than the local citizens under the condition of additional benefits such as accommodation, food etc. Therefore, provision of at least two or three levels of fee structure with differing facilities particularly at specialty and high cost treatment providers should be arranged to attract high income foreign people for service consumption. Rather than the general services, Indian patients are found to be interested in the specialty and chronic problem related services. Therefore, department with relevant services targeting Indian patients should be established particularly in the hospitals which are nearer to India. In doing so, priority should be given to the illness requiring high-cost treatment so that volume of the trade would be large.

Effective information channel needs to be developed to attract larger flow of the patients from the foreign land. Many patients are facing problems in identifying an appropriate service provider because of the non-availability of the information regarding available services and the cost structure in different institutions.

It is noted by the study that a different stratum of patients can be attracted in Nepalese hospitals if some unique features can be incorporated in the domestic service system. For this purpose, more focus should be given on research activities for exploring the locally available natural resources that are useful in the treatment and at the same time for developing unique country-specific methods of treatment and promoting traditional methods of treatment. Quality of the services is one of the most important elements to attract patients in a particular health institution. Therefore, the Nepal Government should make necessary provisions for assuring quality of the health services.

Some of the advanced countries such as the US and Canada have high demand for low cost health service providers, particularly from developing countries. To fulfill this gap in those countries and for the promotion of service export through the bilateral agreements, efforts should be made to attract FDI to raise the production of human resources in the domestic country. By these means, export of health service can be facilitated mainly via Mode 4.

Despite the increasing inflow of non-Indian tourists, health tourism is found virtually limited to Indian service consumers in Nepal. Therefore, there is a need to integrate health services with the tourism for exporting services to non-Indian foreigners via second mode. For this purpose, gradually tourists can be attracted for the treatment purpose in the country by making them familiar with the domestic service system through the arrangement of health services in the tour package, etc.

Management tie-up and the expansion of the network of the domestic service providers with the reputed foreign health service providers and insurance companies is important for exporting services via both second and third modes. The Nepalese Government can encourage this primarily through policy adjustments. In the present context of increasing role played by the private sector, the purpose of regulating the health services in the country and registering medical practitioners according to their qualifications by establishing a medical council as provisioned in NMCA seems relevant. Initiatives should be taken in this line to ensure quality services and to bring homogeneity in the services which are important elements in attracting foreign patients for service consumption.

This study has put forward some policy implications. The findings of the study suggest that there exists a huge arbitrage opportunity for the local professionals and other local service providers in a particular economy due to demand and supply gap. To achieve greater economic welfare, the barriers have to be removed, defined by Modes 3 and 4. The organisation of a regional skills council for standardisation of skills would be very important to take advantage of the arbitrage opportunity. Once these are identified, then investments may be encouraged and in the process movement of natural persons without barriers such as simplified visa, favourable work permit, dual taxation, among others, may be resolved. This is a kind of win-win situation in the light of economic welfare gains in the region.

The study has four strong policy implications for services trade sector in South Asia. Firstly, due to abundance of trained and skilled professionals in health services India has advantage in cross-border supply (i.e. in Modes 1 and 2). Therefore, opening up of cross-border supply of services in these sectors would strengthen services trade flows through Modes 1 and 2 in the region. The member countries and their highly skilled population can also be benefited with the help of an integrated region. Secondly, with regard to trade in services under Mode 3 (commercial presence), South Asian countries should further liberalise FDI and adopt transparent domestic regulations in the areas of health services. Besides, domestic reforms and liberalisation would lead to generate higher FDI under Mode 3 in the region. Thirdly, SAARC region is one of the most important exporters of services through the movement of natural persons (Mode 4). Bangladesh, India, Pakistan and Sri Lanka have large endowments of labour at all skill levels and have a comparative advantage in exporting services through this mode of supply. South Asian countries should therefore expect liberalisation of movement of natural persons for professional services from developed and other developing countries. Fourthly, many have argued that the level of education is below the performance required to integrate entrants to the labour force. The modes are important implications for understanding technology spill over in health sector across South Asian economies.

What emerges is that South Asian countries have to take cautious but forward looking steps in order to remove the trade restrictions in services trade in general and health sector in particular. These are the sectors which drive services trade in many of the South Asian countries and also provide employment. Therefore, adequate reforms may not only remove the barriers to services trade but also generate higher services trade in the region, through which the region may achieve higher income and employment. This will ultimately strengthen the overall services trade capacity of the region, which is remarkably skewed at present.

Trade liberalisation, under multilateral broad based negotiations is important because it provides an opportunity for the countries to gain visible benefits for their exporters from opening up of markets.

The WTO has proven a powerful means for countries to promote economic growth and development resulting in creation of new jobs and narrowing the development gaps. This study envisages that SAARC as a regional trading bloc can also promote growth, generate employment and strengthen overall development of the region.

As the next step, an assessment of the impact of the different reforms engaged by the sample countries would be useful. However, such an evaluation is not an easy task given the multiplicity of direct and indirect effects. Ex-ante and ex-post qualitative and quantitative assessments must be conducted at the sectoral level but also at the economy-wide level to capture the interaction between the various sectoral reforms and the impact on other sectors.

The world as we know today will undergo major changes by the middle of this century. The countries that are unable or slow to respond will have to make room for others that can move quicker, and innovation will be the key differentiating factor. In the long term, it may even be possible for some economies to survive only on the basis of their capital or technology, but labour alone may be unable to provide this sustenance. By bringing a large part of their population to the economic marketplace, the South Asian nations may set free their innovation potential which has so far not found any route to reach the market. When this happens, the region will surely be a different place with many possibilities.

References

Alam, S.M.I. (1986). "Job Satisfaction: A Case Study of Working Women in Different Garment Factories in Dhaka City", *Journal of Management Business & Economics* 12(1): 72-88.

Andaleeb, S.S., N. Siddiqui and S. Khandakar (2007). "Patient Satisfaction with Health Services in Bangladesh", *Health Policy and Planning* 22: 263-73.

Bajracharya, Bhuban B. and Rojan Bajracharya (2008). Endline Evaluation of the Community Based *Trafficking Prevention Initiatives Project*. Kathmandu: Technical Review Group Pvt. Ltd.

Bangladesh Bank (various issues). *Bangladesh Bank Enterprise Survey*.

Banik, Arindam, Prabir De and Pradip K. Bhaumik (2009). "Measuring the Barriers to Trade in Services in South Asia: An Empirical Exercise". *Mimeo*. International Management Institute. November.

Belsky, L., R. Lie, L. Mattoo, E.J. Emanuel and G. Sreenivasan (2004). "The General Agreement in Trade in Services: Implications for Health Policymakers", *Health Affairs* 23(3): 137-45.

Bhagwati, J.N. (1984). "Why are Services Cheaper in the Poor Countries", *The Economic Journal* 94(374): 279-86, June.

Bhattacharya, D. (2005). "Least Developed Countries in Trade Negotiations: Planning Process and Information Needs", Paper 52. Dhaka, Bangladesh: Centre for Policy Dialogue.

———. (2002) "Foreign Direct Investment in South Asia: Promises and Pitfalls", Paper presented for the *Roundtable on Government-Industry Partnership: Sourcing Foreign Direct Investment for Poverty Alleviation in SAARC Countries*. Paradise Island, Maldives. 29 September to 1 October 2002.

Bhattacharya, D., M. Rahman, A. Raihan, M.A. Tipu and F.A. Khatun (2003). "Ongoing WTO Negotiations and Bangladesh's Interests: Insights from CPD's October 2002 Tracking Mission to Geneva", *CPD Occasional Paper* 34. Dhaka: Centre for Policy Dialogue.

Bhattarai, Keshab and John Whalley (1998). "'The Division and Size of Gains from Liberalization of Service Networks", *National Bureau of Economic Research Working Paper* 6712.

Blouin, C. (2006). *International Trade in Health Services and the GATS*. Presentation at the CEEC, La Havana. July 13-14.

Chanda, R. (2001). *Movement of Natural Persons and the GATS*. Report written for the Indian Council for Research on International Economic Relations. Excerpt published by Oxford, UK: Blackwell Publishers.

———. (2002). *Trade in Health Services*. New Delhi: Indian Council for Research on International Economic Relations.

———. (2003). "Social Services and the GATS: Key Issues and Concerns", *World Development* 31(12): 1997-2011.

Chia, Ngee Choon and John Whalley (1997). "A Numerical Example Showing Globally Welfare-Worsening Liberalization of International Trade in Banking Services", *Journal of Policy Modelling* 19(2): 119-27.

Dacanay, J.C. and M.C.L. Rodolfo (2005). "Challenges in Health Services Trade: Philippines Case", *Discussion Paper Series* No. 2005-30. Philippines: Philippines Institute for Development Studies.

De, P. (2006). "The Growth of International Trade in Services: Some Implications", *Journal of International Logistics and Trade* 4(2).

De, P. and B. Bhattacharyay (2007). "Deepening India: Bangladesh Economic Cooperation: Challenges and Opportunities", *Discussion Paper* # 130. New Delhi: Research and Information System for Developing Countries (RIS).

Dixit, Hemang (2004). *Health in Quest: Nepal*. Kathmandu.

Drager, N.D (n.d.). *Trade in Health Services and GATS*. Department of Ethics, Trade Human Rights and Health Law, World Health Organization (WHO).

Findlay, C. and T. Warren (eds.) (2000). *Impediments to Trade in Services: Measurement and Policy Implications*. New York: Routledge.

———. (2000). "Introduction", in C. Findlay and T. Warren (eds.), *Impediments to Trade in Services: Measurement and Policy Implications*. London: Routledge. pp.1-20.

Handicap International (2008). *Situation of Physically Disable in Central Terai of Nepal*. Kathmandu.

Haque, M. Shamsul (2001). "The Diminishing Publicness of Public Service Under the Current Mode of Governance", *Public Administration Review* 61(1): 45-66.

Haque, S.M.R. (2000). "Consumers' Perception on Health Service Marketing of Private Hospitals in Dhaka Metropolitan Area". Unpublished Masters' Thesis. Savar, Dhaka, Bangladesh: Department of Business Administration, Jahangirnagar University.

ICDDRB (2007). "Use of Household Income and Consumption Data as a Measure of Poverty in Rural Bangladesh", *ICDDRB Scientific Report No.* 99. Dhaka. (mimeo).

Kelegama, S. (2009). *Trade in Services in South Asia*. Sage India.

Kelegama, Saman and Indra Nath Mukherji (2007). "India-Sri Lanka Bilateral Free Trade Agreement: Six Years Performance and Beyond", *RIS Discussion Paper*. New Delhi. *http://www.ris.org.in/dp119_pap.pdf*

Khor, M. (2006). *UNCTAD Panel Debates State of WTO Services Negotiations*. Geneva. 10 February.

Lautier, M. (2008). "Export of Health Services from Developing Countries: The Case of Tunisia", *Social Science & Medicine* 67: 101-10.

Maskay, Nephil Matangi, Rajan Krishna Panta and Bishnu Prasad Sharma (2006). "Foreign Investment Liberalization and Incentives in Selected Asia-Pacific Developing Countries: Implications for the Health Service Sector in Nepal", *Working Paper Series* No. 22. Asia-Pacific Research and Training Network on Trade. *http://www.unescap.org/tid/artnet*

Ministry of Health (1991). *National Health Policy*. Kathmandu, Nepal.

Nessa, A., M. A. Ameen, S. Ullah and K.S. Kwak (2008). "Applicability of Telemedicine in Bangladesh: Current Status and Future Prospects", Conference Proceedings of *Third International Conference on Convergence and Hybrid Information Technology*. pp. 948-53.

Parasuraman, A., V.A. Zeithamal and L.L. Berry (1988). "SERVQUAL: A Multiple Item Scale for Measuring Consumer Perception of Service Quality", *Journal of Retailing* 64: 12-40.

Rafiq, A. and C.R. Merrell (2007). "Telemedicine for Access to Quality Care on Medical Practice and Continuing Medical Education in a Global Arena", *The Journal of Continuing Education in the Health Professions* 25: 34-42.

Rafiq, M., M. Rafique, A. Hussain, M. Altaf (2005). "Studies on Heritability, Correlation and Path Analysis in Maize (*Zea mays L.*)", *J. Agric. Res.* 48(1): 35-38.

Rahman, Mustafizur (2000). *Bangladesh-India Bilateral Trade: An Investigation into Trade in Services*. Paper prepared for SANEI. Dhaka: Centre for Policy Dialogue.

———. (2002). "Bangladesh-India Bilateral Trade: An Investigation into Trade in Services", in T.N. Srinivasan (ed.), *Trade, Finance and Investment in South Asia*. New Delhi: SANEI and Social Science Press.

Rahman, M.M., M. Shahidullah, M. Shahiduzzaman and H.A. Rashid (2002). "Quality of Health Care from Patient Perspectives", *Bangladesh, Medical Research Council Bulletin* 28: 87-96.

Raihan, A. and M. Mahmood (2004). "Trade Negotiations on Temporary Movement of Natural Persons: A Strategy Paper for Bangladesh", *CPD Occasional Paper Series:* 36. Dhaka: CPD.

Raihan, A. (2005). *Liberalizing Trade in Services: Negotiating Strategy for Bangladesh*. Dhaka, Bangladesh: Centre for Policy Dialogue (CPD).

Raychaudhuri, A., R. Acharyya, S. Marjit, M. Rahman, M.A. Tipu and D. Bhattacharya (2002). *Trade Potentials of South Asian Economies under the New Global Trade Regime: The Role of Some Non-price Factors—A Case Study of India, Bangladesh and Sri Lanka*. Project Report for South Asia Network for Economic Research Institutes (SANEI), India.

Raychaudhuri, A. and P. De (2007). "Barriers to Trade in Higher Education Services: Empirical Evidence from Asia-Pacific Countries", *Asia-Pacific Trade and Investment Review* 3(2): 67-98.

———. (2008). "Barriers to Trade in Higher Education Services in India in the Era of Globalisation: An Empirical Exercise", *Economic and Political Weekly* 43: 1368-90.

Ryan, C. (1990). "Analysing Service Quality in the Hospitality Industry using the SERVQUAL Model", *Services Industries Journal* 11(3): 324-43.

SAARC Secretariat (2008). *Report of the Regional Consultation Meeting on the Draft Study on Potential for Trade in Services under SAFTA Agreement*. 6-7 February. New Delhi.

Sampson, G.P. and R.H. Snape (1985). "Identifying the Issues in Trade in Services", *The World Economy* 8(2): 171-81.

SAWTEE (2008). *Nepal's Export Potential in Services: Health, Education and High- end Retail Services*. Kathmandu.

World Trade Organisation (WTO) (2001). *Guide to the GATS: An Overview of Issues for Further Liberalisation of Trade in Services*. The Hagu:e Kluwer Law International.

World Bank (2003). *Private Sector Assessment for Health, Nutrition and Population (HNP) in Bangladesh*. Report No: 27005-BD. Washington, DC: World Bank. pp.6-7.

———. (2007). *South Asia Growth and Regional Integration*. Washington, DC: The World Bank.

———. (2005). "Comparative Advantages of Public and Private Health Care Providers in Bangladesh", *Bangladesh Development Series Paper* No. 4. www.worldbank.org.bd/bds

———. (2006). "India-Bangladesh Bilateral Trade and Potential Free Trade Agreement", *Bangladesh Development Series Paper* No. 13. *www.worldbank.org.bd/bds*

WTO (2007). *Challenges and Opportunities in Global Services Trade*. International Trade Statistics.

Zeithamal, V.A. and M.J. Bitner (2006). *Marketing*. 4th ed. Singapore: McGraw-Hill/Irwin.

10

SAFDAR SOHAIL, NOORULAIN HANIF
AND MALIHA QUDDUS

Quantification of Barriers to Services Trade in Pakistan

Introduction

The service sector has emerged as an important sector in the world economy and contributes significantly to the global GDP (gross domestic product), constituting around 60 per cent of global output and 30 per cent of global employment. In many developing countries, services account for 50 per cent or more of GDP, with agriculture and industry accounting for less than half of total production.[1]

Like other South Asian nations, Pakistan too has witnessed a major transformation in its economic structure with the share of the service sector rising to nearly 54 per cent in the economy in the fiscal year 2008-09. Pakistan, however, is not a very important player in the global trade in the services sector. According to World Trade Organization (WTO) Statistics 2012,[2] Pakistan ranked 85 and 63 in terms of export and import of commercial services respectively. Pakistan's share in global services exports is 0.07 per cent and imports are 0.18 per cent.

In Pakistan, the services sector registered a growth rate of 3.7 per cent in 2012-13 against a growth of 5.3 per cent in 2011-12. This performance is mainly contributed by finance and insurance at 6.6 per cent, general government services at 5.6 per cent, housing services at 4.0 per cent, other private services at 4.0 per cent,

1. See World Bank's *World Development Indicators* and presentation by Pranav Kumar on "Services Negotiations in the Doha Round: Concerns of South Asia", in Colombo 9-10 March 2005.

2. *http://stat.wto.org/CountryProfile/WSDBCountryPFView.aspx?Language=F&Country=PK*

transport, storage and communication at 3.4 per cent and wholesale and retail trade at 2.5 per cent.[3]

Pakistan's exports of services were US$ 5,455 million in 2010-11 as compared with US$ 5,229 million in 2009-10. Import figure of services for 2010-11 was US$ 7,590 million whereas in 2009-10 it was US$ 6,911 million. Services trade in communication, computer & information services, insurance services, personnel, cultural and recreational services, government services (i.e. remittances received by foreign missions in Pakistan, military units and agencies, and international organisations) stood in surplus. But trade in transport services, tourism, financial, construction, royalties and licence fees were in deficit.[4]

Pakistan's objectives for its services sector are reflected in the comprehensive liberalisation regime being negotiated at the WTO, and in Pakistan's opening commitments offer. Pakistan has made significant progress in implementing its liberalisation commitments in many services. But implementation is not yet complete and has not been without problems.

In Mode 4, the liberalisation has not progressed in a way that allows developing countries like Pakistan to use their comparative advantage in low and medium skill labour-intensive services, since strict and discretionary visa and licensing requirements, lack of recognition of qualifications, burdensome procedures, and economic need tests act as barriers.

The South Asian Association for Regional Cooperation (SAARC) member countries, being cognizant of the growing importance of the services sector, welcomed the signing of the Agreement on Trade in Services and hoped that this would open up new vistas of trade cooperation and further deepen the integration of the regional economies. They called for the early ratification of the Agreement. The leaders also called for the early conclusion of negotiations on the specific schedule of commitments under the Agreement.[5]

---

3. *Economic Survey of Pakistan 2012-13.*
4. *www.commerce.gov.pk*
5. 16th SAARC Summit Declaration, Thimphu 2010.

However, despite the rising significance of the service sector in South Asia, trade in services has not significantly grown within the region. At the global level, however, the SAARC countries have significantly liberalised their services sector and concomitant FDI (foreign direct investment) policies in several sectors permit 100 per cent FDI. Intriguingly, the commitments at the South Asian Free Trade Area (SAFTA) level do not cover some of those services which have been opened up to foreign international participation. Thus, the commitments for the region clearly portray the failure on the part of SAFTA members to lock into the existing liberalisation. There is no wonder, therefore, that despite recent talks and initiatives, the share of intra-regional trade and investments is still quite modest.

Scope of the Study

At present there is very little intra-industry trade in the major service sectors in different SAARC countries as the South Asian countries trade more with international firms and involve in intense intra-industry competition at the regional level. Over the last two decades, in fact, there has been no significant profit shifting from global to regional firms as it could only take place with more intra-industry trade and cooperation at the regional level, resulting in some sort of regional import substitution.

It is seen that the SAARC countries have been rather slow in appreciating the importance of liberalisation in services. One major obstacle in this regard is the absence of credible studies and data in the service sector, especially in the case of Pakistan. This has been a major constraint for Pakistan in developing effective promotional strategies to enjoy full potential of services liberalisation. This also hampers Pakistan's effective participation in trade negotiations at different forums. The presence of relatively higher levels of trade barriers in South Asia in the services sector has resulted in increased trade through informal channels, especially in health and education sectors.

The main purpose of the chapter is to assess the barriers to Pakistan's trade in services in key sectors such as telecommunications, health, education and transport. The study has been designed to take the policy discussion on regional economic integration forward, and improve the policy and regulatory environment at home. A special focus has been paid to explore the trade potential that exists between India and Pakistan. However, the non-availability of sector specific data was a big challenge in conducting the study. For meeting the challenge, the study generated the required data relating to barriers in services trade through sector specific surveys and interviews from all the major stakeholders throughout the country. The details are given in the next section.

The rest of the chapter is structured as follows: Section 2 discusses in brief the data and the methodology. Section 3 provides an analysis of the telecom sector while section 4 covers the higher education sector. Section 5 provides the analysis of the health sector and section 6 gives the details of the transport sector. Sector specific recommendations are given at the end of each section. Finally, the chapter concludes with an analysis of existing barriers to trade in services, and the potential of increasing trade within the SAARC region, particularly trade between India and Pakistan.

Data and Methodology

The methodology adopted for the collection of data was a combination of stakeholder analysis and expert opinion. The process included the designing of questionnaires, identification of respondents, field visits, interviews, collection of data, scoring and weighting of measures. In translating qualitative information into numerical values, the first step was to select a scoring strategy for the information collected through the survey, of which nearly 90 per cent contained descriptive information regarding the presence or absence of regulations/restrictions. In order to overcome the challenge of transforming all measures into numerics, we had to incur some loss of variation as a rich variety of possible outcomes was reduced to a 0-1 score in order to gain simplicity and tractability.

The required data for studying the domestic regulations, barriers to trade, and the impact of recent liberalisation were not easily available. Therefore, a fresh survey was conducted for each sector. The respondents included major service providers in the country, regulatory authorities, and other stakeholders to get updated and accurate information comments, and opinions about each sector. The process included the designing of questionnaires, identification of key respondents, field visits, interviews, meetings with various government officials and ministries, collection of data, and scoring and weighting of measures.

The surveys helped to understand various types of barriers faced by the service providers which were considered as proxies for South Asian potential investors, study the impact of recent reforms on the performance of the sectors and the economy as a whole, and obtain relevant information on bi-lateral barriers to service trade.

Telecom Sector of Pakistan

Overview of Telecom Sector

The telecommunication sector is considered as the backbone of the economy as it interlinks the other services sectors such as IT and financial services. According to the *Economic Survey of Pakistan 2008-09*, telecom sector contributes upto three per cent to the national GDP. The sector also contributes a handsome amount to the national exchequer through taxes and duties. According to the report by the Pakistan Telecom Authority (PTA),[6] the total telecom revenue was Rs 411 billion in 2011-12. The sector has expanded phenomenally and the prices of telecommunication services have come down significantly. As a result, the telecom sector of Pakistan has come to be seen as a successful model of liberalisation in Pakistan.

The telecom sector in Pakistan is expected to grow fast in the coming years. According to a forecast by United Nations (UN), Pakistan's population is expected to rise to 190 million by 2018. Assuming that future cellular coverage reaches 95 per cent of all urban population and 30 per cent of rural population (and taking into account the relative geography and population density of each province), there is expected to be a demand

6. *http://www.pta.gov.pk*

of approximately 25 million cellular subscriptions by 2018,[7] indicating a tremendous potential for growth in the sector in future. Sensing these opportunities, the sector has been a beneficiary of unusually high investment. Total telecom investment during the year 2012-13 was US$ 4.51 million and the share of the telecommunication sector in GDP was 2.0 per cent.[8] Telecom companies in Pakistan have invested over US$ 8 billion during the last four years, out of which the mobile sector investment share accounts for 66 per cent of the total investment. These investments were followed by high level of imports of telecom equipment. According to the Pakistan *Economic Survey* (2008-09), telecom imports comprised 3 per cent of total imports.

Liberalisation of Telecom Sector

According to WTO (2008), the telecom sector of Pakistan has been totally transformed. In order to examine the scope and depth of the liberalisation process in the telecom sector in Pakistan, it is useful to understand the nature and importance of the key milestones. The process of development and liberalisation started in earnest in the early 1990s. There is a common perception that before the liberalisation of the telecom sector, telecommunication services were available at higher costs and the quality was poor mainly due to lack of competition. The process of development and liberalisation was accompanied by the development of regulatory policies and institutions to ensure the liberalisation of the sector in such a way as to guarantee freedom of competition, prevent monopoly, and provide the best telecommunications services at the lowest prices possible.

The telecom deregulation and cellular mobile policies resulted in large investments and new players entering the telecom market. Since July 2003, the regulators have handed out more than 900 fixed, mobile, and long-distance licenses to some 50 companies, enhancing the teledensity in Pakistan to 52.8 per cent and the number of mobile subscribers increasing from 8 million in 2003 to over 76.6 million

7. Government of Pakistan (2004).

8. *http://www.pta.gov.pk*

by the end of 2007. The expansion of telecom services has made the sector a major provider of skilled jobs as its exponential growth has resulted in the creation of 80,000 jobs directly and 500,000 jobs indirectly.

Framework for Measuring Services Trade Barriers

The general impression regarding the efficiency of telecommunication regulatory infrastructure in opening up the telecom sector to genuine competition is quite positive in Pakistan, except in the area of exports. It was expected that after the liberalisation, the telecommunication sector would become an important exporter of services, which did not materialise. The importation in the telecommunication sector, on the other hand, has grown significantly. But the FDI and/or importation of telecommunication services or equipment from South Asia is negligible.[9] The intra-regional prices of communication services at the moment are higher than inter-regional prices in most SAARC countries. The cheapest prices from Pakistan are $0.03 (fixed and mobile), offered to many non-SAARC destinations, including the US and Hong Kong China. The lowest SAARC prices are to Bangladesh, $0.12 (m) and India, $0.12 (f). The cheapest intra-SAARC price is four times that of the cheapest extra-SAARC price.

The cheapest prices from Sri Lanka are $0.10 (m) and $0.21 (f); they are not offered to SAARC destinations. The lowest SAARC prices are $0.14 (m to India) and $0.32 (f) to most SAARC countries. The neighboring SAARC countries cost 40-50 per cent more than the distant US.

Surprisingly, the tariffs apart from other factors which impact upon the decisions to invest abroad or export, the importation of services/FDI from South Asia into Pakistan might be facing restrictions/trade barriers. It is usually difficult to measure the impact of barriers/restriction on trade in services, especially when the required information regarding these restrictions is not readily available in general and particularly due to a very low/almost non-existent flow of trade or FDI. The present chapter tries to fill the gap

9. This understanding is based on the basis of interviews with the industry representatives; the disaggregated data is not available at the moment.

to an extent by gathering and analysing information on restrictions by using the survey.

Index of Restrictiveness for Telecom Sector

Scores are assigned for each restriction on the basis of nature of restriction and how stringent it is (the more stringent the restriction, the higher the score). The index score ranges from 0 to 1. The key respondents of this survey were representatives from all major service providers (both domestic and foreign) and the regulatory authority, PTA.[10] The index of restrictions is given in Table 10.1.

Analysis of Survey Results

General

According to our survey from PTA, there is no discrimination between foreign and local telecom operators citing the fact that out of the five mobile operators four are foreign owned. The only potential barrier for foreign entrance especially for services like satellite, radio Wi-Fi devices, and security clearance has to be obtained from various security agencies. In case of India, the level of restrictiveness is 1; though it is understood that few Indian companies ever took interest in entering the Pakistan market.

Other barriers are horizontal and apply to all foreign firms regardless of the sector they operate such as they have to face language barriers, work permit for entry, environment, contacts and security problems. One of the biggest problems highlighted by the service providers is their lack of information about the rules and regulations as the documents containing the rules and regulations are not easily available. For example, in February 2009, PTA enacted Sim Registration Regulation which was viewed unfavorably by the industry as they believed this was against the clauses of their Licence Agreements. The new clause clashes with their contracts with the PTA, which had allowed them to keep their clients' information secret. The response of mobile companies to this measure was

10. In order to better understand the barriers and discrimination (if any), both the domestic and foreign telecom operators were interviewed for the purpose of the analysis.

Table 10.1

Index of Restrictions

Score	*Extent of Restrictiveness*
0.00	Does not restrict at all
0.25	Somewhat restricts
0.50	Fairly restrictive
0.75	Moderately restrictive
1	Completely restrictive

Barriers	*Ranks*				
	0.00	*0.25*	*0.50*	*0.75*	*1.00*
Licensing procedure			✔		
Licensing cost			✔		
Transparency in licensing procedure	✔				
Inter-connection agreements		✔			
Tariff regulations					✔
Anti-competitive rules	✔				
Equipment standards requirements			✔		
Pricing policy	✔				
Government policies instability					✔
Security situation of country				✔	
Corruption at govt. level					
Other regulatory constraints by government				✔	
Difficulty in finding reliable and competent business partner	✔				
High bureaucratic red tape			✔		
Culture & language	✔				
Lack of competent work force	✔				

Source: Assessment by Pakistan Institute of Trade and Development (PITAD) Research and Survey Team.

strongly worded as saying, "This was not part of the agreement when we paid hundreds of millions in licence fees; Licence terms cannot be changed just like that."

However, PTA contends that all regulations are enacted after a thorough consultation process, involving all major stakeholders. They believe that there is a lack of coordination within the industry regarding these regulations. As the foreign impact is different compared to the local impact, so the foreign service providers usually face more of the bureaucratic hurdles.

The Pakistan National Accreditation Council (PNAC) deals with unfair practices by domestic and foreign service providers through consultation and awareness. To accommodate the local service providers, the council has taken initiative to train, raise awareness, and provide consultation to enhance competitiveness.

All mobile operators are expanding their networks at a much faster pace owing to the fact that most of the densely populated metropolitan cities are now covered—with almost 100 per cent penetration. These companies are now increasing their coverage to those uncovered areas where mobile networks have not reached.

Licensing Procedure

According to the survey results, majority (85 per cent) of our respondents agreed that the system of licensing is quite simplified now and they are satisfied with the procedure. Initially the number of fixed line licenses Local loop (LL) and Long-Distance and International (LDI), was open and unlimited, subject to meeting the PTAs licensing requirements, but currently there is a seven year 'watch' period on issuing new licenses, including for cellular services. The results of the survey are given in Table 10.2.

Table 10.2

Licensing Procedure

Restrictive unsatisfactory	*Unrestricted satisfactory*
15%	85%

While the PTA does not normally consider licensee applications before it releases a public invitation, expressions of interest can be lodged at any time. Criteria for issuing a licence include economic viability, Pakistani ownership, and contribution to universal service goals, and other social or economic development objectives.

According to our survey report, 12 LDI licenses were awarded to the new operators. All of these 12 LDI companies are now operational, carrying international traffic to and from Pakistan. Issuance of these licenses has allowed the mobile and WLL (wireless local loop) carriers to construct their own long distance backbone networks as well as operate an international gateway. All carriers believe that they have sufficient of their own traffic to justify this network and even go beyond the 14 telecom region points of presence. Competition in the LDI sector has already brought down the tariffs for the international incoming and outgoing calls.

WLL operators were offered 20 years licenses with a view to increase the penetration rates in the underserved areas. As far as restrictions of new entrance are concerned, the Government of Pakistan lifted restrictions on basic telephony services.

New licenses are awarded by the Ministry of Information Technology. On the basis of market readiness, an open policy is followed for the issuance of class licenses. Class licenses are granted to applicants who meet the objective criteria (as published by PTA). Companies must register with the Security and Exchange Commission of Pakistan (SECP). Carriers can hold both LL and LDI licenses.

The other set of barriers, i.e. high fixed capital costs and economies of scale (accrued to incumbent operators) are minimised by PTA's invitation to international telecom operators in local market. This has ensured that financial constraints do not become a problem. As the incumbent could use interconnection network as a catalyst to ignite anti-competitive practices, PTA has devised interconnection guidelines for each service to avoid such practices.

Impacts of Liberalisation

An analysis of the impact of liberalisation is given below.

Mobile Cellular Operators

The mobile cellular services started in the 1990s when the government awarded licenses to two cellular mobile companies i.e. M/s Paktel and M/s Pak Com (Instaphone) for the provision of cellular mobile telephone in Pakistan. Third cellular licence was issued in 1992 by the Ministry of Communication to M/s Pakistan

Mobile Communications Limited (PMCL) 'Mobilink'. The Mobilink established GSM (Global System for Mobile Communication) network. In order to meet the increased demand for cellular phone, PTA issued licence to M/s Pakistan Telecommunication Mobile Limited (Ufone) for provision of GSM service in 2001.

The progress in cellular subscriber base was remarkable in the year 2001. Today mobile network coverage is reaching to almost 90 per cent of the total population. Especially with the introduction of the CPP (calling party pays) regime, the growth rate is calculated to be 142 per cent. In order to further boost the mobile phone sector, the government drastically reduced the royalty for mobile operators from 4 per cent of the gross revenue to only 1.5 per cent in 2001. These measures helped in increasing the cellular penetration to 3.3 per cent in June 2004 (crossing the fixed line density of 2.9 per cent in the same year).

In 2004, mobile licenses to two new companies (Warid and Telenor) were awarded through open bidding against auction bidding price of US$ 291 million each. As per the new mobile policy, these licenses were kept technology neutral so that the operators could decide the best possible option. The introduction of these two mobile operators gave a tremendous boost to the mobile phone subscriber base in Pakistan which increased by a phenomenal 182 per cent. On average, 2.3 million subscribers were added every month during 2006-07. In 2008, China Telecom acquired Paktel and Instaphone, and is providing services under the name of Zong.

After experiencing phenomenal growth for the last couple of years, the telecom sector of Pakistan is now experiencing positive but slow growth in terms of revenue, subscribers and teledensity, reaching 60.6 per cent at the end of the third quarter in March, 2009.

Foreign Direct Investment

FDI plays an important role in development of countries like Bangladesh especially through bringing about technological improvements, poverty reduction and raising living standards. It is also considered as one of the largest source of private capital flow in developing countries.

Pakistan has introduced wide-ranging reforms to attract inflow of foreign investment. In the 1990s, the flow of FDI started to decline but later on in 2000 the government aggressively pursued trade and investment reforms to remove various irritants affecting business and investment climate. The trend of FDI in the telecom sector is given in Table 10.3

Table 10.3

Trends of FDI in Pakistan

(US$ million)

	FDI in Telecom	*Total FDI*	*Share of Telecom (%)*
2008-09	815.0	3,720.0	21.9
2009-10	373.6	2,199.4	17.0
2010-11	79.2	1,574.0	5.0
2011-12	361.4	820.6	-44.0
2012-13	-408.0	1,576.0	-25.89

Source: Pakistan Telecom Authority 2014.

In Pakistan, FDI in the telecom sector is often quoted as a success story of liberalisation. However, there are two sides to the coin. The downside is that the volume of FDI masks the disproportionate repatriation of profits from the telecom sector. Profits repatriated from the sector, on average, account for 8.74 per cent of total profits repatriated from Pakistan. These repatriations reached their peak in 2007 when the sector repatriated profits worth $151.1 million which was 18.7 per cent of total profits repatriated by companies from Pakistan.

Access to Telecom Services

Today telecom access, which was a mere 4 per hundred inhabitants in 2002, stands at 23.1 per hundred inhabitants. The mobile subscriber base has reached 30 million whereas on average 2 million new connections are added per month in the total subscriber base. Mobile services have become more affordable to common people due to increased competition and reduced prices. Similarly, services like WLL and broadband are becoming popular in the country. Fixed line subscribers are also increasing and tariffs of all telecom services have been drastically reduced. The minimum tariffs for mobile-mobile, mobile-fixed and NWD (nation wide dialing) calls have dropped more than 50 per cent as compared with tariffs in 2004-05. Some calling cards are providing international calls at as low as Rs 1.99 per minute and NWD calls at Rs 0.63 per minute.

Impact on Labour Demand and Supply

The effects of trade liberalisation on demand and supply of labour can be seen by assessing the level of employment, changes in wages and conditions of employment. A detailed analysis of the sector reveals that the fundamental structural reforms in the telecommunication sector have contributed positively towards creating employment opportunities in the country. In 2004, the government declared the telecommunication sector as a priority area for employment generation and poverty reduction. At present, this is the fastest growing sector of the economy and the pace is likely to accelerate even further in the next few years, creating more jobs and raising the incomes of the people. Moreover, indirect employment is being generated through franchises, venders and distributors of the telecom companies.

In most educational institutions, telecom engineering is a separate department with substantial enrollment. The students have bright prospects for employment in the sector. Better education standards and training methods will have obvious benefits to this growing industry. It is observed that the impact of the expansion of the telecom sector and the reduction in rates has significantly contributed to the welfare especially of the middle class.

Conclusions and Recommendations

For the telecom sector, it can rightly be said that the deregulation has proved fruitful. The fruits of these deregulation and liberalisation policies in the telecom sector of Pakistan are now being enjoyed by the people in the form of increased consumer choices, greater access, better quality in general, value added services, and affordable prices. The technology is changing rapidly and its transfer to the local market is even faster. The private sector is taking advantage of the situation. The segment of society which has benefited the most by this process is the consumer. Before the liberalisation of the sector, getting a telephone connection was a momentous task for an ordinary customer. Now, the customer has a wide variety of telecommunication services to choose from. Telecom rates have reduced drastically and communication has become easier for people using the latest technology at affordable price. The policy makers are hoping for positive outcomes from trade liberalisation including rapid economic growth and poverty reduction. Liberalisation of the telecom sector in Pakistan has attracted increased FDI inflows, brought about technological changes, and generated employment opportunities. However, since the liberalisation process started only a few years back, it will take some time for the market to mature, and the benefits leverage economic growth and competitiveness further.

In order to promote intra-regional trade, it is important that all SAARC countries reduce their tariffs for the member countries. Presently, the intra-regional prices of communication services are higher than inter-regional prices in most SAARC countries. This will be an important milestone towards the promotion of regional trade and making SAFTA beneficial for its people as they will start communicating, interacting and doing business with each other.

The role of regulatory authorities is also very important in the removal of distorting barriers. The regulatory authorities of SAARC countries should also cooperate and coordinate with each other in order to promote intra-regional communication services, trade, dispute resolution, and maintain a level playing field. It is one of the high potential sectors and business-to-business contact can also be helpful in producing the necessary will to move forward.

Higher Education Sector

Trade in Education Services

Education has emerged as one of the largest service sector in terms of shares in GDP and employment in many economies across the world. It not only provides the bulk of employment and income, but also serves as a vital input for producing other goods and services making it a crucial sector for the overall economy. Thus, the question of opening up the market for education services has become an important issue for countries like Pakistan (Raychaudhuri and De, 2007).

During negotiations for education service commitments, a number of delegations highlighted the political sensitivity of the sector due to its 'public good' element and high degree of government involvement. In this regard, there was a common understanding that the negotiations and the resulting commitments made would not replace public sector education. It was agreed that the existence of private providers should not amount to displacement of public education services, but complement.[11] Some believe that the sensitivities vary from one sub-sector to another, with adult and other education services being less sensitive. Keeping this in mind, the negotiating proposals presented were limited to higher education, adult education and training.[12]

Profile of Pakistan's Higher Education Sector

In Pakistan, higher education refers to education above grade 12, which generally corresponds to the age bracket of 17-23 years. The higher education system in Pakistan is made up of two main sectors: universities/DAI (degree awarding institutes) sector and the affiliated colleges sector.

---

11. Council for Trade in Services, *Education Services*, Special Session, Section I/8(a). JOB(05)/203.
12. See WTO Council for Trade in Services (2000). Commitments are sought by this proposal only from countries that permit private education, rather than from countries that maintain exclusively public systems. Members are invited to accord full market access and national treatment in the areas concerned.

The higher education sector is predominantly public in nature with public HEIs (higher education institutions) dominating both the university/DAI and college sectors The period from 1990 to 2000 saw a steady increase of 11 universities in the public sector and a similar number in the private sector bringing the total number of universities to 44 from 22 in the last decade. The DAIs increased from 3 to 4 in the public sector and from 0 to 6 in the private sector. The total number of institutions rose from 25 in 1990 to 54 in the year 2000. Towards the end of the last decade, two universities only for women were also established: one in the public and the other in the private sector.

There are also two public sector distance learning institutes: Allama Iqbal Open University (AIOU) and Virtual University (VU) which in 2006-07 enrolled a total of 199,660 students (AIOU enrolled 190,447 students, and VU enrolled 9,213 students).[13]

Regulatory Regime

The higher education (HE) sector in Pakistan falls under the purview of:

- Ministry of Education, which formulates the National Education Policy.
- Higher Education Commission (HEC), which is the primary regulatory body for the HE sector. The aim of the commission is to reform higher education and transform Pakistan from an agriculture-based economy to a 'knowledge-economy'.

A major component of the HEC's reform agenda was to establish research centers at universities. However, these heavily funded research centers or facilities did not have a core group of active researchers, neither was there a serious discussion on the utility and meaningfulness of such centers.

Survey Results

Mode 1: The sample for this mode consisted of the government owned AIOU. The university was asked a series of questions designed

13. *www.hec.gov.pk*

to assess the barriers to trade under Mode 1. The purpose of the survey was to determine the reasons why AIOU failed to attract more enrollments from foreign based students. According to the survey, regulations on the preparation of course materials and regulations on the management of students' academic work were non-existent and the few regulations that existed were not at all restrictive. Regulations on the establishment of education resources (e.g., library) were 'somewhat restrictive' in terms of the associated costs. Requirement for legal compliance of all the electronic media used for the presentation of course materials was not restrictive. Regulations on premise requirements were also not restrictive. The university was of the view that the requirement of establishing regional centers was somewhat restrictive primarily due to the fact that AIOU does not have an extensive online presence. This increases its reliance on the establishment of a regional centre where tutorial courses were conducted by its (physically present) tutors. The university was of the view that this problem could largely be mitigated through an increased online presence.

Mode 2: The sample for this survey consisted of foreign students enrolled in various academic programmes in Pakistani universities. The respondents were asked a series of questions to determine the barriers they faced at the time of enrollment in Pakistani universities. Nearly 30 per cent of the students were required to make some sort of financial deposits with their respective universities while 70 per cent of the students believed that the initiatives by the government to promote higher education in Pakistan (in terms of course quality, faculty, and infrastructure) were effective. On the other hand, about 60 per cent of the students were of the opinion that the government was not providing any incentive for foreign students to enroll in Pakistani academic institutions. An overwhelming majority (70%) of the students believed that the inadequate international recognition of Pakistani degrees was a major barrier in attracting foreign students. Pakistan does not impose any restriction on student employment which is reflected in the responses with 70 per cent of the students ranking this barrier as not restrictive.

The HEC has made it mandatory for all foreign students, desirous of seeking admission to Pakistani universities, to obtain an equivalence certificate of their degrees from the Inter Board Committee of Chairmen (IBCC). Around 80 per cent of the students were of the view that this requirement was not restrictive while 10 per cent of the respondents thought it otherwise. The students from African and Central Asian countries are required to get clearance from the Interior Division of the Government of Pakistan.

Nearly half of the respondents opined that the grant of a student visa by Pakistani authorities was not a barrier for foreign students whereas 40 per cent of the students thought that the process was very restrictive (Figure 10.1). Further analysis revealed that all respondents who identified this factor as 'completely restrictive' were Chinese Muslim students studying in the International Islamic University (IIU). When asked to explain the reasons for rating this factor as completely restrictive, a majority of the students indicated that they were only granted a single entry visa for three months which had to be renewed and/or extended for the duration of the degree after clearance from the Ministry of Interior.

Assessment by PITAD Research and Survey Team

The students were asked to rank all the above mentioned factors in terms of their importance, with 1 being the least important and 7 being the most important. The grant of visa received a ranking between 4 to 7 by 80 per cent of the students with 40 per cent of them ranking it as the most important whereas 50 per cent of the respondents rated this factor as completely restrictive or fairly restrictive. Therefore, not only is the requirement for visa restrictive, it is also very important in assigning weights and scores for the construction of TRI (Trade Restrictiveness Index).

Degree equivalence was ranked as important by 40 per cent of the respondents although 80 per cent of the respondents believed that this requirement was not at all restrictive. Another factor, the international recognition of Pakistani degrees was ranked between 4 and 7 by 60 per cent of the respondents and 70 per cent of the students believed that this was an impediment in attracting foreign students to Pakistan.

Figure 10.1

Enormity of Barriers to Higher Education

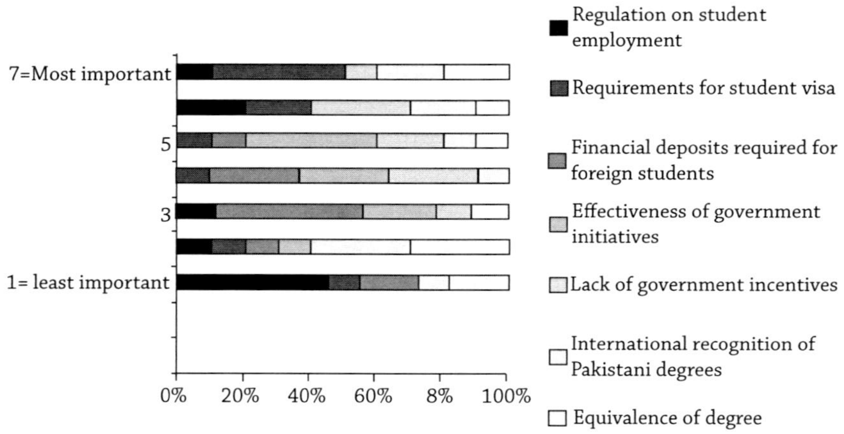

Note: Assessment by PITAD Research and Survey team.

In order to obtain a more objective picture of the barriers faced by the foreign students, the HEC, university administrations and foreign embassies were also consulted. The HEC mentioned that it had clearly laid down and published on its website the steps for the admission of foreign students and the steps for renewal of visa. According to the laid out procedures, after obtaining admission in a Pakistani university, the student has to approach the Pakistani Mission in his/her respective country for a visa. The Mission then forwards all the concerned documents to the Ministry of Foreign Affairs in Islamabad for further processing. The Ministry of Foreign Affairs forwards these documents to the Ministry of Interior for security clearance. The Ministry of Interior as per the relevant policy has to complete all the processes within four weeks and send the visa to the Mission concerned.[14] The University administrations contacted were of the view that they followed the guidelines provided by HEC in "letter and in spirit" and did not add any further conditions for the admission of

14. "Steps for the Admission of Foreign Students" document obtained from Higher Education Commission.

foreign students. The foreign missions, however, corroborated more or less the feedback from the foreign students.

When the university administrations were asked about the enrollment of students from the SAARC region their response was that the number of students from the region in Pakistani universities was negligible with an average of only 2 to 3 students from Nepal every year. There were a sizable number of Afghan students but most were naturalised citizens of Pakistan.

Mode 3: The sample for this survey consisted of Universities with foreign collaboration or twinning arrangements and the HEC. The HEC representatives were interviewed regarding the process of and the requirements for establishing foreign universities and twinning arrangements (with foreign universities). The HEC officials maintained that they had published all procedures and guidelines for establishment of a new university/institution as well as procedures for inspection. The application and licence processing fees are also mentioned in a comprehensive document also available on its website (HEC, 2007). According to HEC and after a review of the pertinent legislation, it seemed that there was no discrimination between foreign universities willing to establish branch in Pakistan and Pakistani owned universities.

As far as the foreign collaboration and twinning arrangements are concerned, HEC specifies all such forms of collaborations and has laid out an approved policy governing these arrangements.[15] The HEC claims that such collaboration is available provided that the affiliate foreign university is recognised and has a good academic standing. It welcomes collaboration with renowned foreign universities and fast tracks the process. However, it is wary of what it refers to as "bogus colleges" existing only on paper.[16] The regulation in this regard is relatively reasonable with the HEC requiring that the universities undertaking such arrangements have provision in their respective charters.

15. *Source:* "Approved Policy of HEC for Foreign Collaboration".

16. Interview with Director General A&A, Higher Education Commission Pakistan.

Universities with foreign collaboration and twinning arrangements were asked questions regarding the procedural barriers they faced. Further detailed interviews were conducted in order to explore other non regulatory barriers that restricted foreign investment under Mode 3. Most of the universities surveyed believed that the requirement for programme approval and renewal of approval was not a barrier to foreign investment under Mode 3. Accreditation by HEC was cited as a major barrier by most of the universities surveyed, with 20 per cent believing that it was completely restrictive in attracting foreign investment in their institutes. When asked to rank the reasons why accreditation was restrictive, almost 90 per cent of the respondents ranked bureaucracy and politics at HEC as the most important factor; whereas the procedure for accreditation and requirement to deal with different government agencies were ranked the lowest. Accreditation fees was also not considered a barrier by most respondents as the fees required were rather low, i.e. approximately US$ 1,500. The requirement for local incorporation was not considered a barrier by most respondents.

As per the services liberalisation commitments in the WTO regime, Pakistan allows for 60 per cent foreign equity participation in Mode 3. India and Sri Lanka allow foreign equity up to 100 per cent and Nepal allows foreign equity of 80 per cent. Compared with SAARC members, this seems unattractive. As far as restrictions on foreign equity were concerned, 50 per cent of respondents thought that these restrictions were a barrier while the other half thought it otherwise. The reasons for this could be that higher education in Pakistan is less dependent on foreign investment with a trend towards foreign-linked programmes that have no links with foreign equity investment.

Pakistan's offers in General Agreement on Trade in Services (GATS) state that there will be no national treatment with regards to subsidies, i.e. Pakistani owned private universities and foreign universities are ineligible for government subsidies. Nearly 80 per cent of the respondents believed that the government did not provide any incentives or support for attracting foreign investment. When the respondents were asked to rank the barriers in terms of importance, accreditation by HEC was ranked as the most important factor followed by lack of government support and incentives for the sector. The respondents were then asked a series of questions regarding non-regulatory barriers. The major issues identified by most respondents rated in terms of importance were:

- Lack of paying customers: According to respondents the most important non regulatory barrier to foreign investment in Pakistan's HE sector was the absence of a large market. Any foreign university operating in Pakistan (with all the requisite infrastructure and foreign faculty) would have to charge fees of approximately US$ 10,000 to US$ 12,000—for which a market does not exist. This is due to the fact that at this fee level, foreign university branch campuses in Pakistan directly compete with foreign universities. Most respondents opined that at such high fee levels, the students would rather opt to travel abroad than obtain a degree from a second tier university branch campus.
- Land: The minimum land and endowment requirements imposed to private educational institutions to establish a campus are 10 acres (3 acres in city, and 7 acres in city fringes) depending upon the location, having potential for further development. Under national treatment commitment, all real estate acquisition by non-Pakistani entities is subject to authorisation depending upon the location and purpose of such acquisitions. Respondents believed that these requirements further increased the costs of setting up foreign owned branch campuses.
- Security situation: The security situation has been cited as a major barrier to foreign investment. For example, the Middlesex University which was in talks with a local partner to establish a branch campus in Islamabad had to withdraw from the plan due to major security concerns.
- Grant of charter from the Federal Government or the Provincial Government: After the completion of all the formalities, the HEC recommends the case for grant of charter to the Federal Government or the Provincial Government, as the case may be. A major barrier at this stage

(and one that was acknowledged even by the HEC officials) is that cabinet approval takes a very long time and the process may not be transparent.

Mode 4: The sample for this survey comprised of foreign faculty members teaching in Pakistani universities, university administrations, and the HEC. The questions for the foreign faculty members and university administrations were designed to ascertain the barriers faced under Mode 4. All the respondents were of the view that the requirement for a permit to teach and a permit to work in Pakistan was not a barrier to movement of natural persons since the authorities had placed no such regulations. There were also no quotas imposed by the HEC or university administrations on the employment of foreign nationals with respondents from the National University of Modern Languages (NUML) which boasts of a very large foreign faculty, stating that they could have a 100 per cent foreign faculty members if they so required. About 90 per cent of the respondents stated that the equivalence of degrees was not a barrier since there were no such requirements imposed either by the HEC or the University administrations. Visa requirements also did not pose any restrictions on the entry of foreign faculty. In most cases, the foreign faculty members interviewed mentioned that visa requirements did not pose any restrictions. Apart from regulatory barriers, the respondents were asked about other barriers they faced in Pakistan. A major barrier according to both university officials and foreign faculty members was the security situation and travel advisories which were preventing many faculty members from traveling to Pakistan.

When the universities were asked about foreign faculty from the SAARC region they informed that there were currently no faculty member from the region. NUML, which employs a large number of foreign faculty, mentioned that it did not have a single faculty member from the region. Even though the University had a Hindi programme, it did not employ a single faculty member from India.

Increasing Higher Education Trade between Pakistan and SAARC Countries

Across the region, the higher education sector manifests interesting similarities. All South Asian countries lack adequate resources to provide their population with quality higher education. Due to their other more pressing priorities like poverty reduction programmes, health care and basic education, in the short or medium term, they are not able to allocate adequate resources to quality higher education for those who are willing to join higher education as usually happens in advanced countries. In light of the above circumstances, pooling of regional resources could provide a big boost to the higher education sector in South Asia.

Conclusion and Recommendations

There were no major barriers identified for Mode 1 and the AIOU could create its own distance learning programme provided the infrastructure constraints are overcome. The recognition of Pakistani degrees abroad however, is a major barrier for the foreign students in Pakistan. For some foreign nationals, the issuance of visa is also restrictive due to the government policy of issuance of visas for only three months rather than for the entire duration of the degree. Foreign investment in Pakistan is restricted due to the absence of a large market and security situation. The minimum land requirement imposed on universities and the grant of charter to universities are also inhibitive factors. Surveys and interviews suggest that these barriers are non-discriminatory between local and foreign ownership. It is found that the only discrimination foreign and private universities face is the absence of government support and subsidies. No major regulatory barriers exist for Mode 4 as there are no visa restrictions, no requirements for work/teaching permits and recognition of degrees. The only factor that prevents the foreign faculty from travelling to Pakistan is the adverse security climate and travel advisories by respective governments.

The large number of students from Pakistan studying in universities abroad is indicative of the huge potential demand for higher education services in the country. Excess demand and common linguistic ties in the region provide a unique opportunity for trade in higher education in the region for all modes of supply. Moreover, Pakistan, India and Sri Lanka have made commitments in the higher education sector. In order to encourage trade in higher education, there is a need to take major initiatives at the SAARC level. For example, for promoting trade under Mode 1, the SAARC Consortium of Open Distance Learning (SACODil) was established and India's Indira Gandhi National Open University (IGNOU) also offered concessional fees to students from South Asia. However, SACODil seems to have failed to articulate and implement any visionary plans for transforming trade under Mode 1. It is important therefore to give fresh impetus to new initiatives in this regard.

Health Sector

Overview of Trade in Health Services

International trade in health services has been opening possibilities for increasing economic contribution of the health sector to the national economies of many developing countries. Governments from both developed and developing countries are exploring different options including the implementation of export strategies for health services and the liberalisation of business ownership to maximise resource endowments and competitive advantages. This endeavour requires facing the challenge of reconciling trade objectives like foreign currency generation with those of granting their populations universal access to quality health care at an affordable cost.[17]

Balancing trade objectives with public health interests is a recurrent theme in the literature on trade in health services. According to Woodward *et al.* (2002), liberalisation of health services "may facilitate access to high-level services by the better off; but it may also divert human resources from public services to more profitable, private services for the elite or foreign markets, thus reducing staffing levels, lowering staff quality, and/or raising salary costs for the public sector."

A report by the Save the Children is highly critical of liberalising trade in health services and concludes that the market disciplines

17. "Trade policies and export of health services: a development perspective" by David Díaz Benavides

included within GATS undermine national efforts to develop public health systems, and calls for the Agreement to be revised (Hillary, 2002). Due to the sensitivities involved in trade in health services, the trade in health services is minimal, particularly when compared with other traded services (Woodward *et al.*, 2002). However, a study by Rupa Chanda (n.d.) asserts that the health care sector is among the most rapidly growing sectors in the world economy.

In general, health services are traded in the following ways:

Mode 1: Cross-border delivery of health services through telemedicine can enable healthcare providers in one SAARC country to provide services to a consumer in another SAARC country. Trade under this mode is likely to grow in future with the advent of new medical and communications technologies.

Mode 2: Trade in health services via consumption abroad is typefied by medical tourism.

Mode 3: Commercial presence in health services through foreign direct investments in hospitals and healthcare centres.

Mode 4: Trade via movement of health service providers between countries.

Of the four sub-sectors, medical and dental services are the most heavily committed (54 members), followed by hospital services (44 members) and services provided by nurses, midwives and others (29 members). Overall, this pattern suggests that it is politically easier or economically attractive for administrations to liberalise capital intensive and skills-intensive sectors than labour-intensive activities (Adlung and Carzaniga, 2002).

One study by the Asian Development Bank (ADB), "Trade in Health Services", states that SAARC members would be willing to undertake more liberal commitments at the regional level, on the premise that all seven countries make liberal commitments under the GATS. The study asserts that the SAARC members should be undertaking deeper commitments at the regional level rather than the multi-lateral level due to two prime reasons. First, the small size of the SAARC group would enable it to benefit from liberalisation fairly quickly. Second, the risk of opening up the health sector at the regional level would be drastically reduced as compared with the multi-lateral level (ADB-UNCTAD, 2008).

It is therefore imperative that the governments develop a comprehensive strategy for trade in health services in order to balance commercial interests with the provision of low cost and efficient health care to all its citizens.

Profile of Health Services in SAFTA

The World Economic Forum's *Global Competitiveness Report* ranks Pakistan at number 116 (out of 134 countries) in terms of the health and primary education sector. India ranks at number 100, Bangladesh at 105, Nepal 107 and Sri Lanka at 53.[18] Apart from Sri Lanka, the ranking achieved by the remaining SAFTA members is fairly low.

Sectoral Profile of Pakistan's Health Services

According to the *Economic Survey of Pakistan* (2008-09), the Government of Pakistan spent a paltry 0.5 per cent of GNP (gross national product) on health care. The government recognised the need to enhance allocations in this area and mainstreaming "alternative approaches to health financing."[19] The public sector dominates Pakistan's health sector and the country has one of the largest public sector owned service delivery infrastructure in the world. However, dual job-holding is common due to the differences in incentives in the public *vis-á-vis* the private sector. As a result, the role of the private sector has been increasing in the provision of health services. A survey undertaken by the WHO estimates that around two-thirds of Pakistan's population buys health care through out of pocket expenditures from the private sector.[20] As opposed to this, there is no regulatory framework in place for the private sector. Efforts are underway to address the currently prevailing service

---

18. World Economic Forum (2008). "Table 10.6 Basic Requirements: Health and Primary Education", *Global Competitiveness Report 2008-09.*
19. "Health and Nutrition", *Economic Survey of Pakistan 2008-09.*
20. *Trade in Health Services in Pakistan: A Country Case Study*, WHO/SEARO.

delivery challenges by developing alternative service delivery and financing options at the basic health care and hospital levels.

Constitutionally, health is a provincial subject in Pakistan with clearly demarcated roles, responsibilities and prerogatives at each level of the government. The Federal Government is mandated with policy-making, coordination, technical support, research, training and seeking foreign assistance. The provincial and district departments of health are responsible for the delivery and management of health services.

Some key challenges facing Pakistan's health sector are:

- Neglect of linkages with the private sector.
- Neglect of quality and equity dimensions in health service delivery.
- Lack of inter-sectoral coordination and limitation of prevalent sectoral approach.
- Lack of institutional capacity including measurement and monitoring skills.
- Insufficient levels of resource allocation for the health sector.

Regulatory Regime

The health sector falls under the purview of the Ministry of Health and is regulated by the Pakistan Medical and Dental Council (PMDC). The PMDC, established under the Pakistan Medical and Dental Council Ordinance 1962, is the authority responsible for the regulation of the medical and dental profession in Pakistan. The Pakistan Nursing Council established under the Pakistan Nursing Council Act 1952 is the authority responsible for registration and licensing of nurses and midwives. Only persons possessing degrees recognised by the relevant Councils and registered with such Councils can practice the profession of medicine, dentistry and nursing in Pakistan.

Survey Results

Mode 1: The sample for this survey consisted of hospitals that had established telemedicine links with international institutions. The experts interviewed were of the opinion that there were no regulatory or legal issues that they faced. No permission was required from the government to set up a telemedicine link and the only problem that they infrequently encountered was technical problem.

Mode 2: The sample for this survey consisted of leading private hospitals in Pakistan (both foreign and Pakistani owned). The survey was designed to assess the barriers that prevented foreign patients from coming to Pakistan for treatment. All the respondents ranked visa restrictions low on the restrictiveness scale indicating this was not an issue in Pakistan. The lack of portability of health insurance, according to some respondents, was not relevant for Pakistan and the South Asian region with 80 per cent of the respondents rating it the lowest on the restrictiveness scale. When asked whether the movement of patients in the region was restricted due to a lack of capacity to pay by the consumer, most respondents believed that this was not a restrictive factor and a market did exist in the region. The absence of specialised healthcare facilities in Pakistan as a barrier to attracting foreign patients was rated as quite restrictive or fairly restrictive by 70 per cent of total respondents. When asked to identify any other factors that restricted foreign patients, some respondents identified high cost of treatment in Pakistan compared with India as a major inhibitor. The average cost of a kidney transplant in a leading private hospital in Pakistan was nearly three times as high as in India.[21] Other respondents also believed that lack of awareness about the Pakistan's health sector was restricting patients from travelling to the country. Health practice in Pakistan was not presented in international forums at all or if done so it was on a very limited scale. The respondents were also asked to rank the barriers in terms of their importance. Visa restriction was ranked as the least important followed by lack of capacity to pay (by consumers), lack of portability of health insurance, cost of treatment and awareness of Pakistan's health care sector. The absence of specialised healthcare facilities was ranked the highest by most respondents.

---

21. According to officials at Shifa International Hospitals Ltd.

Table 10.4

Barriers to Trade in Health Services

Mode 2		
Barrier	*Is the Barrier Highly Restrictive? (Rating between 3 and 5)*	*Comments*
Visa restrictions	No	10 per cent ranked it as somewhat restrictive; 80 per cent ranked it as not restrictive at all
Lack of portability of health insurance	No	Respondents believed that the issue was not relevant for Pakistan
Lack of capacity to pay	No	70 per cent rated it as somewhat restrictive
Absence of specialised healthcare facilities	Yes	40 per cent fairly restrictive; 30 per cent as quite restrictive
High cost of treatment in Pakistan	Yes	Some respondents believed that the cost of medical treatment was higher than in India.
Awareness about Pakistan's health sector	Yes	Identified as a major barrier; Pakistan should be represented at international forums.

Source: PITAD Research and Survey Team.

Mode 3: The respondents for the survey were the leading foreign owned for profit private hospitals operating in Pakistan. The survey was designed to assess the reasons why Pakistan was not attracting foreign investment. The procedure for registering a hospital was rated as either somewhat restrictive or not at all by the respondents. The same ratings were assigned to the requirement for local incorporation by foreign hospitals. All the respondents were of the opinion that restrictions on foreign equity were not a barrier to trade and investment in Pakistan; the reason being that for setting up hospitals Pakistan allowed foreign investors to hold 100 per cent equity on a repatriation basis. When asked whether the government had provided any incentives/loans/support for attracting foreign investment in health services, the respondents replied in the negative. The respondents were asked to identify other factors that, in their perception, were inhibiting foreign investment under Mode 3. Some believed that there was generally a lack of interest among investors regarding investment in this sector. Secondly, some thought that the cost of treatment was generally high in Pakistan. Ranking the barriers in terms of their importance, the respondents believed that procedure for registering an institution was the least important factor followed by requirement for local incorporation. Lack of interest by foreign investors was rated the highest by the respondents. It should be noted here that the survey could not collect the views of the PMDC and the Ministry of Health despite repeated attempts.

Table 10.5

Procedural Restriction in Health Services

	Mode 3	
Barrier	*Is the Barrier Highly Restrictive? (Rating between 3 and 5)*	*Comments*
Procedure for registering a hospital	No	80 per cent of respondents rated it as somewhat restrictive; 10 per cent rated it as not at all restrictive
Requirement for local incorporation of hospital	No	Same as above
Lack of interest by investors	Yes	50 per cent of respondents identified this as a barrier
High cost of treatment	Yes	A few leading hospitals identified this as a barrier

Source: PITAD Research and Survey Team.

Mode 4: The sample for this survey comprised of leading foreign owned for profit hospitals operating in Pakistan. The survey was designed to assess why Pakistani hospitals failed to attract foreign doctors. Visa restrictions were rated by 60 per cent of the respondents as quite restrictive whereas 20 per cent of the respondents thought that visa restriction was fairly restrictive. A mixed response was received for the recognition/equivalence of degrees as a barrier. While 40 per cent of the respondents believed that it somewhat restricted foreign doctors, the remainder ranked it as quite restrictive. In the Pakistan Medical and Dental Council Ordinance 1962, Section 13 relates to the power of the Council to enter into negotiations with appropriate authority within or outside Pakistan for settling a scheme of reciprocity for the recognition of medical and dental qualifications. Section 14 provides that the Federal Government after consulting the Council may accord recognition to a medical qualification granted by a medical institution outside Pakistan.[22] For the purpose, PMDC has a Recognition Committee headed by the Vice President of the Council which is responsible for equating and recognising various degrees, which have not been mentioned in various schedules of the Ordinance and obtained by doctors from countries outside Pakistan. The Committee determines equivalence of foreign degrees with the Pakistani degrees. It also evaluates the teaching experience gained by Pakistanis in teaching institutions located in foreign countries. Foreign experience counts as an added value for appointments in medical and dental colleges in Pakistan.

Table 10.6

Enormity of Barriers in Health Sector

	Mode 4	
Barrier	*Is the Barrier Highly Restrictive? (Rating between 3 and 5)*	*Comments*
Visa restrictions	Yes	60 per cent of the respondents cited as quite restrictive while 20 per cent respondents thought that visa restrictions were fairly restrictive.
Recognition of degrees	Yes/No	40 per cent of respondents rated it as somewhat restrictive; 60 per cent rated it as quite restrictive
Requirement of work permit	No	Rated as low by all respondents

Source: PITAD Research and Survey Team.

22. *http://www.supremecourt.gov.pk//sub_links/judgements/CP2206of20*

The requirement for a work permit was rated low by all respondents. When asked whether highly qualified foreign doctors had to sit for an examination before being eligible to practice in Pakistan almost all respondents replied in the negative. When asked to identify other barriers, some respondents cited security concerns while others believed that there was no plan by the government to attract expert medical knowledge into the country. When asked to rank the barriers in terms of their importance, visa restrictions were cited as the most important followed by the absence of a government plan to attract foreign qualified doctors.

Conclusions and Recommendations

The foregoing analysis reveals that within the SAARC region in general and Pakistan in particular, trade in health services is fairly liberalised with no regulatory constraints on the movement of patients across borders (falling under Mode 2); while few restrictions on investments in the health sector (under Mode 3) and arrangements are in place at the institutional level for the recognition of medical degrees (affecting Mode 4).

The major barriers in Mode 2 are not regulatory but stem from the lack of specialised healthcare facilities, the lack of promotion of Pakistan's health sector and the high cost of treatment in Pakistan as compared with India. Out of these factors, the lack of awareness about Pakistan's health sector is considered as the most important factor. Therefore, the following policies are recommended:

- the government should formulate a regional medical tourism policy.
- the government should arrange health shows in regional markets.
- the government should provide incentives to institutions promoting and marketing Pakistan's healthcare portfolio in international markets.

Even though Pakistan is a large market there is still little foreign investment in its health care sector. Survey results show that the regulatory barriers are not impeding investors who are generally ambivalent towards investing in this sector. For Mode 4, some of the major barriers identified relate to visa restrictions and the absence of a sound government policy for attracting foreign doctors. In the health care industry, professional human capital remains the core service element. The government should work on a master plan to attract professionals and expatriates by providing, for instance, 'Special Citizen' status to doctors/medical researchers.

For the SAARC region, there is a significant potential for trade in health services under different modes. For Mode 1, the Lahore Imaging Centre has a telemedicine link with India and there are numerous prospects for trade under this mode since it is least impacted by adverse security situation. As evidence suggests, there is a movement of patients across borders in the region, but through informal channels. All members should frame a comprehensive policy that would deal with timely issuance of medical visas to patients aiming at promoting health tourism.

The policies of India and Pakistan generally prohibit FDI in other countries which should be revised at least for the health sector. Since all SAARC countries are net exporters of midwives, nurses, physiotherapists, and other skilled medical personnel which limit the potential in this category, there is a vast potential for travel of specialist doctors for which the member countries could frame a 'specialist exchange programme'.

Transport Services

Economic and industrial development processes demand rapid as well as mass transportation of goods and raw materials. The more easily the passengers and goods get to the destination, the more rapid is the pace of development of a country. The transport and communication systems need continuous expansion and maintenance of the network of railways and highways as well as the rolling stock.[23]

The determinants of export performance largely rely on external and internal factors. External factors include market access conditions while internal factors refer to supply side conditions. The supply side,

23. *www.energy.com.pk*

for the most part, is affected by transport costs and service quality (including speed and reliability of delivery), entrepreneurship, capital and labour costs, and product quality as well as the role/performance of export promoting institutions. These supply capacity elements have a significant and positive impact on export performance and thus, in turn, on the competitiveness of export products.

High trade cost such as transportation charges, documentation requirements, and clearance delays at the borders has a negative effect on trade. However, improved transport and trade facilitation measures bring obvious win-win outcomes for the trading partners,

Geographically, Pakistan is surrounded by landlocked countries like Afghanistan and the Central Asian States. Transit trade takes on immense importance, demanding smooth and quick flows across borders in which Pakistan has a key role to play. The transit proposals attain a higher level of importance keeping in view the nature of political relations and security situations in the area.

Trade facilitation is not a difficult area for Pakistan on account of major customs reforms undertaken under 'CARE'—a programme implemented with the help of the World Bank. Pakistan needs to roll over CARE countrywide.

South Asia has a strong comparative advantage in its service sector, which accounts for a significant and growing share of the region's total output, mainly due to a combination of strong demand and effective reforms undertaken by the South Asian countries. However, due to lack of adequate research on services trade policy and limited availability of data on international trade in services, policy makers have limited guidance as to how liberalisation of trade and investment in services should proceed at the regional level.

The present study looks into the issues related with transport services in Pakistan from the trade facilitation perspective, i.e. trade specific impediments to efficient trade and transport logistics for Pakistan in South Asia.

Regional cooperation in transport services can play a crucial role in addressing critical problems of hindering trade in goods. A better cooperation in services like transport and trade facilitation can transform landlocked countries such as Bhutan and Nepal into land-linked countries and regions. While Pakistan could be the gateway for all South Asian countries to access one another's market through the land route, Pakistan and India can play an important role as transit states for the rest of South Asia to access Central Asia's market.

Overview of Transport Services in South Asia

Exports of transport services, along with travel services, account for over 50 per cent of the global trade in services.[24] Transportation services constitute the major component of services trade in South Asia. South Asian exports of transportation services grew much faster than those from Asia and the world during 1995 to 2008. As an outcome, South Asia contributed around 7.7 per cent and 1.5 per cent of transportation services exports of Asia and the world respectively in 2008, compared with 6.9 per cent and 1.1 per cent in 1995. In the case of Sri Lanka and India, transportation services exports have grown much faster than imports during 1995 to 2008. Except for Nepal, South Asian countries show rising trend in exports of transportation services during 2000 to 2008. The largest exporter of transport services in South Asia is India, which experienced a rapid growth in exports of transport services over the period 1995 to 2008. In 2008, India's total exports of transportation services were over US$ 6 billion, contributing about 76 per cent of the total regional transportation services exports. Pakistan, Bangladesh and Sri Lanka are other important South Asian players in trade of these services. All the South Asian countries, including India, have a deficit in trade in transportation services.

Travel services relate to tourism which has emerged as an important and fast-growing source of foreign exchange earnings in many developing countries including those in South Asia. In fact, South Asia has witnessed much faster growth in trade in travel services, both in exports and imports, compared to Asia and the world as a whole. The largest exporter of travel services among South Asian countries is India. In 2008, India earned about US$ 7.85 billion from travel services compared with US$ 2.58 billion in 1995. Maldives and Sri Lanka also have a surplus in travel services trade.

24. WTO (2006). *WTO Annual Report*.

The growth rate of exports in the case of Sri Lanka is also higher compared with growth rate of imports as in the case of Bangladesh.

Under Mode 3, though there is some investment by India in other SAARC members, there is no FDI between India and Pakistan. This is attributable to the stated policies of both countries to prohibit any foreign investment from their respective countries. Though the political circumstances are not very conducive, the relevant firms of these countries should seriously explore the possibilities of joint ventures, as they could make huge gains once the level of trust improves.

Table 10.7

Index of Revealed Comparative Advantage in Transportation Services

	2000	*2001*	*2002*	*2003*	*2004*	*2005*	*2006*	*Average (2000-2006)*
Afghanistan								
Bangladesh	0.47	0.41	0.47	0.32	0.31	0.42	0.34	0.39
Bhutan								
India	0.50	0.50	0.55	0.57	0.49	0.47	0.52	0.51
Maldives	0.25	0.24	0.21	0.21	0.20	0.31	0.28	0.24
Nepal	0.51	0.49	0.51	0.43	0.31	0.39	0.46	0.44
Pakistan	2.58	2.39	1.41	1.26	1.48	1.35	1.62	1.73
Sri Lanka	1.80	1.21	1.75	1.79	1.77	2.01	2.36	1.81

It is believed that increased trade relationship can play a vital role in normalising the political relationship between the two countries. This will, therefore, benefit millions of people living in both countries as the resources would be diverted from less desirable areas, such as defense spending, to poverty alleviation initiatives. Given the likely impact of trade liberalisation between the two countries, the unavailability of any established estimate of potential trade and the items likely to be traded is unfortunate.

Barriers in Transportation Sector

Poor infrastructure, along with protective policies, corruption and red tape is a major obstacle that impedes economic growth of

South Asia. Investment climate surveys have pinpointed transport as a particular problem for regional and international trade in South Asia. Bottlenecks are encountered in all modes of transport infrastructure and services: poor condition of roads, lack of intra-regional connectivity between the national road networks, unreliable and overall costly road transport services, underinvestment in railways (which has led to the excessive use of road transport), unrealised high potential for rail and inland water freight transport, inadequate road and rail connectivity of ports with the hinterland, and others. Trade between India and Pakistan accounts for about US$ 2 billion a year, but with improved transport infrastructure and removed trade barriers it could grow substantially.

Increasing transport facilitation is seen as one of the main avenues of increasing the trade potential within the region. To quote ADB-UNCTAD (2008) report, "High trade costs such as transportation charges, documentation requirements and clearance delays at the borders have a discouraging impact on trade and production similar to trade restrictions such as tariffs and quotas."

Poor access to transport infrastructure and services also leaves hundreds of millions of people in South Asian countries without access to basic social and economic services. This poor access, especially in the rural areas, contributes to a sense of isolation from the economic mainstream, leading to a greater incidence of poverty among the region's large rural populations. Only 57 per cent of South Asia's rural population has access to all-season roads. It is therefore critical to maintain existing transport infrastructure and services while simultaneously investing in new and improved services.

South Asia is also prone to natural disasters and conflict, requiring substantial investment in the reconstruction and rehabilitation of transport infrastructure. Reconstruction in war-torn Afghanistan, the aftermath of the December 2004 tsunami in Sri Lanka, India and the Maldives, earthquakes in Pakistan in October 2005, as well as 2004 floods in Bangladesh, are typical examples of the region's needs in disaster reconstruction, management and collaboration.

Transport Services in Pakistan

Transport is an important sector in Pakistan's economy, accounting for 10 per cent of gross domestic product and 20–25 per cent of investment in the annual public sector development programme. The provision of infrastructure facilities for transportation is largely the responsibility of the public sector agencies. There were advantages in the past in having such facilities delivered by the public sector.

According to an estimate, the bulk of Pakistan's international trade, about 40 million tonnes per annum of dry and liquid cargo, is transported by road along the main corridor, Peshawar-Lahore-Karachi, called the National Trade Corridor (NTC). Almost all of this trade (95%) is handled by the two seaports of Karachi and Port Qasim, located about 50 km from each other. Pakistan's trade is characterised by a concentration of movements within the country (mainly along the NTC), small numbers of export destinations and import origins (mainly three regions) and a simple supply chain structure.[25] This should provide ideal conditions for improving trade procedures and logistics services.

The sustained economic growth and trade competitiveness of Pakistan heavily depends on improvements in its trade environment through harmonisation, simplification and standardisation of trade procedures, and improvements of logistics services. Strategic investment in infrastructure is necessary for Pakistan to take advantage of the geopolitical situation in the region and benefit from regional cooperation in trade and commerce.

However, the transport sector is constrained by key issues that include multimodal share distribution, preservation of existing assets, project prioritisation, portfolio management, effective public or private sector initiatives, and adequate and stable funding. The government has made efforts in the past to articulate a comprehensive transport policy that encompasses all sub-sectors.

Survey Results

The details of survey results are discussed below.

25. The supply chain most often involves direct movement between the factory and port or via an inland container depot.

Maritime Transport

Extensive interviews were conducted with trade facilitation experts to identify various issues at Pakistan's ports. According to experts' opinion, there are three main parties that directly affect port efficiency, i.e. port authorities, customs and carrier agents. A survey was conducted which consisted of custom officials, port authorities, shipping companies, exporters and importers. The respondents were asked a series of questions that were designed to assess the barriers that existed at Pakistan's ports.

One survey was conducted with importers importing through ports and Karachi International Container Terminal (KICTL), one of the biggest container terminal operators in Pakistan. About 75 per cent of the respondents rated lack of port capacity as fairly restrictive as the ports were currently operating at or near maximum capacity. Also, Pakistani ports did not have the capacity to handle large vessels (sea was not dredged). KICTL, however, assigned a higher value to this factor in terms of restrictiveness and rated it as quite restrictive.[26] Absence of risk management by Customs was rated high in the restrictiveness index by 90 per cent of the respondents including KICTL. The modus operandi of custom authorities is to check every container arriving at the port which invariably leads to long delays and clogging of ports. Adopting risk management techniques in Customs' procedures would expedite the clearance of goods. The time taken to clear goods in Customs using old-fashioned procedures can amount to as much as one or two weeks. New risk management techniques will release 80-90 per cent of the goods within a few hours (UNCTAD, 2008). Lack of coordination between different government agencies at port (narcotics, health department etc.) was also rated as fairly restrictive by 70 per cent of the respondents including KICTL. According to the respondents, some government agencies like railways have no presence at port. Some importers also expressed their concern over the fact that once a container was cleared by Customs it had to be reopened by

---

26. *1 = does not restrict at all; 2= somewhat restricts; 3= fairly restrictive; 4= quite restrictive; 5= completely restrictive*

the narcotics department leading to long delays. Inefficiency of carrier agents at ports was rated as restrictive by 90 per cent of the respondents. After clearance by Customs, goods cannot be released until the carrier agent has confirmed the receipt of payment by the importer. In most countries, this clearance takes less than 15 minutes but in Pakistan this procedure takes about 48 hours.[27]

Responses regarding the absence of EDI-IT (Electronic Data Interchange-Information Technology) at ports had a mixed response with 30 per cent of the importers rating it low with 20 per cent rating it high as completely restrictive. KICTL on the other hand, rated it as fairly restrictive according to them with the advent of the Pakistan Customs Computerised System (PACCS) some of the system was already online. Inadequate road and rail connectivity and the absence of multimodal transport among South Asian countries were rated as fairly restrictive by most importers. The Pakistani authorities currently do not allow multimodal transport which has compounded the problems of many importers. For port infrastructure, most importers rated it as less restrictive but this factor was rated as completely restrictive by KICTL. Port location was rated low by most (70%) importers as restrictive. According to KICTL, port location was an issue because due to the absence of a deep sea port most large vessels had to dock at ports in the United Arab Emirates (UAE) and from there, cargo was loaded onto smaller vessels for their onward journey to Pakistan.

Another survey was carried out with the Customs' officials the results of which were similar to the ones obtained from the importers and KICTL. The following issues were flagged by the Customs authorities:

- Multiple customs systems: At present, two parallel processes, one is largely automated called PACCS and other is paper-based, though computerised, called One-Customs System are operational;
- Lack of coordination among various agencies at the port: For example, Customs and ports are integrated but shipping lines and warehouses are not integrated with them. For ports charges, trader has to pay separately whereas it could be aligned with customs duty payments rather easily.

27. Based on responses we received during our survey results.

- Lack of single-window type system whereby trader (importer or exporter) can interact with all regulatory authorities through one portal.
- Improper risk management processes: The system is still heavily dependent on human discretion (say in Customs) leading to delays and corruption opportunities. Officials were of the view that risk management practices based on principles defined in the Revised Kyoto Convention (RKC) of the WCO (to which Pakistan Customs is a signatory) will immensely help in trade facilitation. The RKC is based on two important pillars: (i) formal forums for dialogue between customs and trade; and (ii) adoption of risk management principles. Incidentally, Pakistan Customs has the tools and systems available but has not yet defined risk management processes to make use of these tools.
- Unorganised and unprofessional shipping agents and freight forwarders, mostly in the form of one desk operator's agents.

After rating barriers in terms of their restrictiveness, respondents were asked to rank the barriers in terms of their importance from most important to least important. The results are summarised in Table 10.8.

Table 10.8

Severity of Barriers in Maritime Transport

Barrier	*Ranking (9 = Most Important, 1 = Least Important)*
Absence of risk management by Customs	9
Lack of coordination between different government agencies at port	8
Absence of computerisation/EDI-IT at ports	7
Inefficiency of carrier agents	6
Absence of multimodal transport	5
Inadequate road and rail connectivity to ports	4
Limited port capacity	3
Location of port	2
Lack of port infrastructure	1

Source: PITAD Research and Survey Team.

Road Transport

The respondents for this questionnaire were customs officials, exporters and importers trading through the Wagah border with India, and the Ministry of Commerce officials of the government. The questions were designed to assess the problems that were encountered when trading with India via Wagah. When asked as to what extent the poor road condition restricted trade, 50 per cent of the respondents rated it as fairly restrictive and 50 per cent rated it low on the restrictiveness scale. Lack of bi-lateral transport and multi-lateral transit agreements was rated by 70 per cent of the respondents as quite restrictive. Security and political uncertainty in the South Asian region was rated high on the restrictiveness scale, all respondents were of the view that the cumbersome procedures at border posts and lack of investment in road infrastructure in the region were a direct consequence of the security situation. Transhipment of cargo at the border was rated high in the restrictiveness index by 80 per cent of the respondents with 50 per cent rating it as completely restrictive. Inefficient immigration and Customs' offices at border posts were rated as fairly restrictive by 70 per cent of the respondents. A mixed response was received for the existence of a single gate for goods and customers at Wagah, with 40 per cent saying that it was fairly restrictive while 20 per cent rating it as completely restrictive. Limitation on the number of trucks that could go across each day at Wagah was rated as fairly restrictive by 80 per cent of the respondents. Absence of computerisation/EDI-IT at border posts was also rated as fairly restrictive by almost 80 per cent of respondents. Lack of baggage scanning facilities at border posts and poor conditions of vehicles were rated low on the restrictiveness scale.

After rating barriers in terms of their restrictiveness, respondents were asked to rank the barriers in terms of their importance from most important to least important. As can be seen, on average, respondents thought that the most restrictive barrier was the security and political situation followed by transhipment of cargo (Tables 10.9 and 10.10). The least important barrier was the poor condition of vehicles and baggage scanning facilities at the border posts.

Table 10.9

Barriers in Road Transport Services

Barrier	*Is the Barrier Highly Restrictive? (Rating between 3 and 5)*	*Comments*
poor road conditions in the region	Yes/No	50 per cent rated it low on the restrictiveness scale while 50 per cent rated it as fairly restrictive
Lack of bi-lateral transport and multi-lateral transit agreements	Yes	70 per cent of respondents rated as quite restrictive; 20 per cent rated it as fairly restrictive
Security and political uncertainty in the South Asian region	Yes	100 per cent of respondents rated it between 3 and 5
Transhipment of cargo at the border	Yes	50 per cent rating it as completely restrictive; 30 per cent rating it as either quite restrictive or fairly restrictive
Inefficient immigration and custom offices at border posts	Yes	70 per cent of respondents rated it as fairly restrictive
Existence of single gate for goods and passengers at Wagah border	Yes/No	40 per cent of respondents saying that it was fairly restrictive; 20 per cent rating it as completely restrictive.
Limitation of number of trucks that could go across each day (at Wagah border)	Yes	Rated as fairly restrictive by 80 per cent of respondents.
Absence of computerisation/EDI-IT at border posts	Yes	Rated as fairly restrictive by almost 80 per cent of respondents.
Lack of baggage scanning facilities at border posts	No	70 per cent of respondents rated it as either somewhat restrictive or does not restrict at all.
Poor condition of vehicles	No	Same as above

Source: PITAD Research and Survey Team.

Table 10.10

Severity of Barriers in Road Transport

Barriers	*Ranking (9 = Most Important, 1 = Least Important)*
Poor road conditions	3
Lack of bi-lateral transport and multi-lateral transit agreements	8
Security and political uncertainty	9
Transhipment of cargo	7
Absence of computerisation/EDI-IT at border posts	6
Immigration and custom offices at border posts	5
Existence of single gate for goods and passengers at Wagah border	4
Limitation of number of trucks that could go across each day (at Wagah border)	2
Poor condition of vehicles	1

Source: PITAD Research and Survey Team.

In many respects, Pakistan's external transport and trade facilitation systems provide an adequate level of connection with the global economy:

- Sea freight rates for both container and bulk cargoes are in line with regional and international levels, taking into account the size of the container flow.
- Sea transit times are slightly better to some major markets than for its competitors and worse for others, but this is largely a feature of geography and distance.
- There is an adequate supply of road transport which, for break bulk and bulk cargo, offers some of the lowest road freight rates in the world, but with low service levels.
- Where service quality is important, Pakistan's exporters have improvised relatively effective (if rather ad-hoc) arrangements with the road transport industry to monitor the flow of exports and ensure delivery times at port, though at significantly higher freight rates than are normal.
- While Customs was traditionally a major constraint with very cumbersome and time consuming manual systems, it is

beginning to achieve significant improvements in clearance times and is in the process of further major streamlining of procedures. It is however still perceived as a problem by port users.

Conclusions and Recommendations

For increasing exports competitiveness, Pakistan needs to adopt a systematic approach that takes into consideration both common and trade specific impediments to efficient trade and transport logistics.

The Government of Pakistan has made considerable progress in the facilitation of international trade. These improvements include measures taken to simplify and modernise Customs procedures, and to increase the quality of logistics services. It has also focused on the infrastructure side of the supply chain by upgrading roads and ports facilities, in particular along the Peshawar-Lahore-Karachi corridor.

The transport development programme of Pakistan is based on a broad strategy that includes establishment of a multimodal transport system with emphasis on asset management with consolidation, upgrading, rehabilitation and maintenance of the existing system, and enhanced private sector participation in sector development and institutional capacity building, with the use of modern technology, procedures and processes to increase sector efficiency. The strategy also takes into account the regional and domestic dimensions, particularly in relation to rail, road and ports and shipping sub-sectors, enhancing regional connectivity to improve links to the Central Asian states, Iran, Afghanistan and India.

Sustained efforts must continue (including Trade and Transport Facilitation Project, TTFP) to reform customs and trade procedures. All these measures for trade facilitation need to be taken by Pakistan with a view to promoting and enhancing legitimate trade in a secure and safe environment. Regardless of progress in the WTO in trade facilitation area, Pakistan is already compliant of majority of measures expected to be included in the future trade facilitation agreement.

A sound domestic regulatory regime can be important in providing a conducive policy environment for businesses to trade in different services. Domestic regulations are also important, for instance in Mode 3 in terms of better governance that safeguard investments of a long term nature. This distinction between the positive aspects of domestic regulations with those that may act as barriers to trade in services is important to keep in view while making any assessment of domestic regulatory regime *vis-à-vis* services sector and FDI in the SAARC region. It follows that such an understanding would also have important implications for policy negotiations among SAARC countries for expanding trade in services.

Regional cooperation in transport services can play a crucial role in addressing major problems hindering trade in goods as well. A better cooperation on services like transport and trade facilitation can transform landlocked countries such as Bhutan and Nepal into land linked countries and regions. While Pakistan could be the gateway for all South Asian countries to access one another's market through the land route, Pakistan and India can play an important role as transit states for the rest of South Asia to access the Central Asia's market.

At present the South Asian countries are at early stages of creating synergies in the transport sector. Transportation is one of the major barriers in enhancing trade among SAARC countries. Even with more doses of liberalisation of goods, the traded volumes could be restricted by the ways and means of transportation.

Appendix A-10.1

Services Trade Restrictiveness Index

The appendix discusses the results of the Service Trade Restrictiveness Index (STRI) estimated by Banik *et al.* (2009) for the SAARC region. The methodology adopted by this study for the construction of STRI is to identify the barriers through expert opinion and assigning weights based on a pair-wise comparison. A widely accepted criticism of this methodology is the element of subjectiveness that it brings into the analysis. Being cognizant of this methodological flaw, our study instead sought to conduct a detailed stakeholder analysis coupled with expert opinion. The primary purpose of the entire exercise being the provision of reliable input for the construction of an STRI similar to the one constructed by Banik *et al.* (2009) Extensive surveys enabled us to ensure the robustness of the information collected for the selected sectors in Pakistan.

Results for the mobile services sector in Pakistan reveal relatively low scores especially for Mode 3 (FDI). The results are fairly similar for most SAARC countries as all have liberalised this sector. However, low STRI scores for Mode 3 in telecom belie the level of restrictiveness between India and Pakistan both of whom have policies that forbid FDI in their respective countries. If this factor was accounted for, it would have produced higher scores in the STRI. In the trade in services, as with tariffs in the case of merchandise trade, it is seen that the level of protection differs across partners with a different level of protection applied to different countries. Therefore the STRI fails to take into account bi-lateral protection levels which according to our results are very inhibitive between India and Pakistan. We believe that a possible area of research (based on information collected from the methodology used in this research) could be the construction of bi-lateral STRIs which would be a more realistic measurement of service trade barriers.

Table A-10.1

Mode Wise Service Trade Restrictiveness Index Scores and Rank for Pakistan, 2009: Selected Services Sectors

	Score	*Rank*	*Score*	*Rank*	*Score*	*Rank*	*Score*	*Rank*	*Score*	*Rank*
Telecom (Mobile)	0.00	N.A	1.00	1	0.43	4	0.53	1	0.50	1
Higher Education	0.62	1	0.67	1	0.67	2	0.52	2	0.55	2
Health	0.20	2	0.58	1	0.04	2	0.51	1	0.41	1
Maritime Transport	0.50	2	0.00	2	0.54	2	0.63	2	0.57	2

Source: ADB, 2009.

Figure A-10.1

Mode Wise Services Trade Restrictiveness Index Scores for Pakistan, 2009

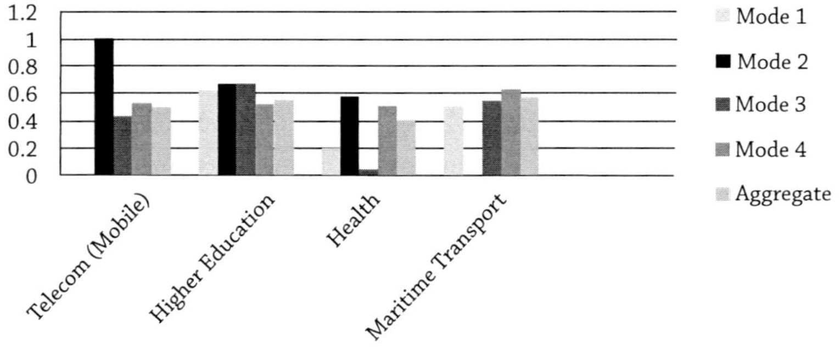

Source: ADB, 2009

For higher education, Pakistan has fairly low scores on the restrictiveness index across all four modes. For other countries, however, the STRIs reveal varying levels of openness across modes. India, for example, has relatively restricted sector in mode 4 (0.62) but lower restriction levels in mode 2 (0.22) partly explained by full current account convertibility in its BOP account. For the higher education sector, the findings show that for Mode 2 there is substantial discrimination against foreign students depending upon their country of origin. For example, it is found that most foreign students who rate the visa regime as highly restrictive are mostly from China.[28] In the

28. According to Interior Ministry sources, mainly Chinese Muslim students require a stricter security clearance due to security concerns of the Chinese Government.

health sector, Pakistan's score is primarily attributed to consumption abroad (mode 2) and movement of natural persons' restrictions (mode 4). On close investigation, it appears that State Bank's (central bank) lengthy formalities to allow foreign exchange for nationals' treatment in other countries beyond limit is the major impediment. We find a major divergence in the STRI scores for Mode 1 which after a thorough analysis reveals that there are absolutely no barriers for health trade under this mode even with India. In the maritime transport sector, the results are fairly in line with our findings, Pakistan's aggregate score is 0.57, this compares favourably as compared with India which has an aggregate score of 0.65. In all SAARC members, the highest number of restrictions is placed on Mode 4.

We believe that the compilation of the STRI could be further enriched by enhancing the quality of the data. It may be argued that the data collection methodology used in our study which also seeks to identify bi-lateral trade barriers would result in the construction of an STRI which is more meaningful to policy makers and negotiators alike.

Recommendations

Pakistan is well aware of the benefits of liberalisation of the services sector, in terms of new entrants, local as well as foreign, and the important gains likely to stem from increased competition and efficiency of production, as Pakistan has experienced in its 'telecommunications sector'. The Government of Pakistan is following a conscious policy, as have other developing countries, of liberalising its trade and investment regimes to promote growth especially through increasing value added exports. Pakistan's experience with autonomous liberalisation in the services sectors has been viewed rather positively.

The SAARC process is moving towards deeper integration with the inclusion of services in the negotiation process. However, there is a near consensus among the SAFTA observers that concrete measures to facilitate trade and economic cooperation in South Asia are yet to show results and that there is much more to be done to translate the ambitions into reality (Panagariya and Pitigala, 2006).

For Mode 1, our survey results indicate the absence of any regulatory barriers and the presence of few technical barriers; moreover, trade under this mode is not affected by the security situation in the region. This begets the question: why trade under this mode is not taking off particularly for education and health? We believe that there needs to be a sound policy at the intra-government level to promote Mode 1 with the development of a coherent strategy for the promotion of trade under this mode and expediting the existing initiatives.

A first step towards achieving higher trade in Modes 2 and 4 is to remove visa restrictions and enhance the free movement of natural persons across borders. According to survey results in the education and health sector services, trade is restricted due to problems in obtaining visas.

Under Mode 3, whereas there is some investment by India in other SAARC members there is no FDI between India and Pakistan. This can be attributable to the stated policies of both countries to prohibit any foreign investment from their respective countries. Though the political circumstances these days are not very conducive, the relevant firms of these countries should seriously explore the possibilities of joint ventures, as they could make huge gains once the level of trust improves.

During the course of this research it was observed that a major stumbling block is a dearth of services trade statistics in the SAARC region which could potentially be used by the countries to delay their commitments in the sector. With respect to Pakistan, the absence of credible service sector data at the firm level and mode-wise data on trade in services in Pakistan has been a major constraint in developing effective promotion strategies for the service sector. This is also hampering effective participation of Pakistan in trade negotiations at different forums.

Therefore, we strongly recommend an improvement in the statistical coverage of service sector with disaggregated data to make clear to the policymakers the value and scope of services trade. Moreover, we believe that there should be uniformity of data organisation across the SAARC region. For the purpose, there should be a mobilisation of stakeholders at the SAARC level to build an effective strategy for data development and help in devising national statistics of trade in services on a format suggested by United Nations Interagency Task Force on Statistics of international trade in services.

In the domain of services, the involvement of private sector has been very limited; both at the level of private sector-government as well as at the business-to-business levels, especially in Pakistan. Our surveys have produced significant awareness on the South Asian prospects and challenges in the services sector. This has also enabled us to identify the key stakeholders. Our extensive surveys have created a genuine interest and keenness in reducing the restrictiveness of trade in services between India and Pakistan in particular and among South Asian countries in general for enhancing mutually beneficial intra-industry trade.

Our study has shown that, in terms of services, Pakistan is the least integrated in South Asia and can benefit from higher levels of trade. Therefore, it needs to prepare itself much more to enhance its trade in services.

References

ADB-UNTAD(2008). "Trade in Services and South Asia: An Overview", *Quantification of Benefits from Economic Cooperation in South Asia.*

———.(in press). "Quantification of Benefits from Trade Integration in South Asia", India Study.

Adlung, R. and A. Carzaniga (2002). *Health Services under the General Agreement on Trade Services.* World Health Organization.

Banik, Arindam, Prabir De and Pradip K Bhaumik (2009). *Measuring the Barriers to Trade in Services in South Asia: An Empirical Exercise.* ADB.

Benavides, D.D. (2002). *Trade Policies and Export of Health Services: A Development Perspective.* World Health Organization. p.54.

Bohm, A., Marcelo Follari, Andrew Hewett, Sarah Jones, Neil Kemp, Denis Meares, David Pearce and Kevin Van Cauter (2004). *Forecasting International Student Mobility: A UK Perspective.* London: British Council.

Chanda, Rupa (2001) "Trade in Health Services", *Working Paper* No. 70, ICRIER, November. Available at *www.icrier.org/pdf/WP-RUPA.pdf*

———. (n.d.) *Trade in Health Services.* World Health Organization. Originally published in the *Bulletin of the World Health Organization* 80(2): 158-163 (2002).

Czinkota, M.R. (2005). *Loosening the Shackles: The Future of Global Higher Education.* Prepared Statement for the WTO Symposium on Cross-border Supply of Services. Geneva

Dayal, D., A. Das, R. Banga, K. Iyengar and S. Ahmed (2008a). *Quantification of Benefits from Economic Cooperation in South Asia.* pp.xvii-xviii. Macmillan India Ltd.

———. (2008b). "Health and Related Services", Chapter 14 in *Quantification of Benefits from Economic Cooperation in South Asia.* New Delhi: Macmillan. p.150.

Government of Pakistan (2004). *Mobile Cellular Policy.* IT & Telecommunication Division, Ministry of Information Technology.

———. (2009a). "Health and Nutrition", Chapter 11 in *Pakistan Economic Survey 2008-09.* Islamabad, Pakistan: Ministry of Finance. p.169.

———. (2009b). "Growth and Investment", Chapter 1 (Table 1.5: Sectoral Share in GDP) in *Pakistan Economic Survey 2008-09.* Islamabad, Pakistan: Ministry of Finance.

———. (2009c)."Trade and Payments", Chapter 8 in *Pakistan Economic Survey 2008-09.*Islamabad, Pakistan: Ministry of Finance.

Hasnain, K. and A.H. Toor (2008). *Higher Education Commission (HEC): A General Appraisal of Major Schemes and Related Recommendations*. Islamabad: Quaid e Azam University.

Higher Education Commission (2007). *Guidelines for the Establishment of a New University or an Institution of Higher Education*. 5th ed. Islamabad.

———. (n.d.) *Approved Policy of HEC for Foreign Collaboration*. Islamabad.

———. (n.d.) "Number of Graduates Produced by Distance Learning Universities during 2004-05 to 2006-07". Retrieved April 4, 2009 from *http://hec.gov.pk/stats.html*

Hillary, J. (2001). *Is Trade in Services under GATS the Way forward for Health Care in Developing Countries?* Save the Children Fund.

International Trade Centre (ITC) (2005). "Medical and Health Services", in *Services Capacity Report*. EC Trade Related Technical Assistance Programme for Pakistan.

Isani, U. and M.L. Virk (2005). *Higher Education in Pakistan: A Historical and Futuristic Perspective*. 2nd ed. Islamabad: National Book Foundation.

Jahangir, K. (2008). *Management of Higher Education Reforms in Pakistan: An Implementation Perspective*. National University of Modern Languages. pp.80-82.

Larsen, K., J. Martin and R. Morris (2002). "Trade in Educational Services: Trends and Emerging Issues", *Working Paper*, OECD.

Lodhi, Adnan (2007). *2007 Sees Improvement in Education Sector*. Retrieved April 14, 2009 from *http://www.dailytimes.com.pk/default.asp?page=2008%5C01%5C02%5Cstory_2-1-2008_pg7_39*

Mattoo, Aaditya and Randeep Rathindran (2005). "Does Health Insurance Impede Trade in Health Care Services?" *World Bank Policy Research Working Paper* No. 3667.

Ministry of Commerce (n.d.) *Study on Trade in Services*. Government of Pakistan. p.87.

Mirza, Zafar (n.d.). *Trade in Health Services in Pakistan: A Country Case Study*.

NIEPA (2006). "Privatization and Commercialization of Higher Education", Conference Proceedings of National Seminar. May 2. New Delhi: National Institute of Educational Planning and Administration.

Nielson, Julia and Daria Taglioni (2004). "Services Trade Liberalisation: Identifying Opportunities and Gains", *Trade Policy Working Paper* No. 1. Paris: OCED.

Nishtar, S. (2008). *National Trade Policy 2008-09: The Trade Health Interface*. Retrieved April 19, 2009 from *http://www.heartfile.org/pdf/34_Trade_Policy.pdf*

Panagariya, Arvind and Nihal Pitigala (2006). "Preferential Trading in South Asia", *World Bank Working Paper Series* 3813.

Qamar, Abid (2005). "Trade between India and Pakistan: Potential Items and the MFN Status", *SBP-Research Bulletin* 1(1).

Rahman, M. (2000). *Bangladesh-India Bilateral Trade: An Investigation into Trade in Services*. Draft Report. South Asia Network of Economic Research Institute (SANEI).

Raychaudhuri, A. and P. De (2007). "Assessing Barriers to Trade in Education Services in Developing Asia-Pacific Countries: An Empirical Exercise", *Working Paper Series* No. 34.

Rehan, Selim (ed.) (2008). "Chapter 1: Table 5 Revealed Comparative Advantage of Services Subsectors in South-Asia", in *Domestic Preparedness for Services Trade Liberalisation: Are South Asian Countries Prepared for Further Liberalisation?* Jaipur: CUTS International.

UNCTAD (2008). "Risk Management in Customs Procedures", *UNCTAD Trust Fund on Trade Facilitation Negotiations Technical Note* No. 12. November.

UNESCO (2004). "Higher Education in a Globalized Market", *Education Position Paper* (ED-2004/WS/33).

WHO/SEARO (2004). *Interregional Workshop on Trade and Health*. New Delhi, 12-13 October.

World Economic Forum (2008). "The Global Competitiveness Index: Prioritizing the Economic Policy Agenda", "2.2: Country/Economic Profiles: Pakistan", "Table 6 Basic Requirements: Health and Primary Education", "Section V: Higher Education and Training—5.03 Quality of Education System; 5.04 Quality of Math and Science Education; 5.05 Quality of Management Schools; 5.06 Internet Access in Schools; 5.07 Local Availability of Specialized Research and Training Services; 5.08 Extent of Staff Training" and "Table 10.6 Basic Requirements—Helth and Primary Education" in *The Global Competitiveness Report 2008-09*. Geneva.

Woodward, D., N. Drager, R. Beaglehole and D. Lipson (2002). *Globalization, Global Public Goods, and Health*. World Health Organization.

World Bank (n.d.). "Healthcare Services?" *Mimeo*.

WTO (2008). *3rd Trade Policy Review of Pakistan.*

WTO Council for Trade in Services (2000). "Communication from the United States: Higher (Tertiary) Education, Adult Education and Training", (S/CSS/W/23), Special Session.

———. (2001). "Communication from Australia: Negotiating Proposal for Education Services", (S/CSS/W110), Special Session.

———. (n.d.). *Education Service.* Special Session JOB(05)/203, Section I/8(a).

WTO Working Party on Domestic Regulation Communication from China and Pakistan (n.d.). *Proposed Disciplines on Domestic Regulation under Article VI.4 of the GATS.* JOB (06)/158.

Websites

SAARC Consortium on Open and Distance Learning (2009). Retrieved April 14, 2009 from *http://www.saarc-sec.org/?t=2.9.2*

Prasad, S. *Telemedicine Takes World-class Healthcare to Rural India.* Retrieved June 28, 2009 from *http://www.zdnetasia.com/insight/specialreports/healthcare/0,3800005625,62043102,00.htm*

Apollo Hospitals Launches Telemedicine Link-up between New Delhi and Lahore (2004, October). Retrieved June 28, 2009 from *www.accessmylibrary.com/.../summary_0286-13522564_ITM*

Pakistan Medical and Dental Council v. Ziauddin Medical University & Other, December 15, 2006. Retrieved from *http://www.supremecourt.gov.pk//sub_links/judgements/CP2206of20*

Apollo Group Company Profile. Retrieved from *http://www.apollohospdelhi.com/apollo-group/group-companies.html*

http://stat.wto.org/CountryProfile/WSDBCountryPFView.aspx?Language=E&Country=IN

Text of 13th SAARC Summit. Retrieved form *www.saarc-sec.org*

Number of Universities/DAIs in Pakistan (1947 to 2007-08). Retrieved April 10, 2009 from *http://hec.gov.pk/stats.html*

WTO Trade Profile: Pakistan (April 2009). Retrieved from *http://stat.wto.org/CountryProfile/WSDBCountryPFView.aspx?Language=F&Country=PK*

WTO Trade Profile: India (April 2009). Retrieved from *http://stat.wto.org/CountryProfile/WSDBCountryPFView.aspx?Language=E&Country=IN*

Fee Structure (2009). Retrieved April 3, 2009 from *http://ignou.ac.in*

Ph.D Produced (November 2008) Retrieved April 10, 2009 from *http://hec.gov.pk/stats.html*

www.sbp.org.pk/Ecodata. Retrieved August 20, 2009.

11

KRISHNA PRASAD PANT

Health Costs of Dung Cake Fuel Use by the Poor in Rural Nepal

I

INTRODUCTION

Background

Dung cake (bricked and dried animal dung) is being used as a cooking fuel by poor people in many South Asian countries including Nepal, India, Bangladesh and Pakistan. For the rural farmers who rear large ruminant animals, dung cake fuel involves no explicit cost. The dung is available at an animal farm, and the opportunity cost of labour is very low for women and children in rural areas. Even households with no animals are found to collect dung from trails of animals and pasture land; and prepare dung cake with no out-of-pocket expenses. However, there are several other costs of dung cake fuel to the households, like health costs, decrease in farm productivity, and increased drudgery for women making and using dung cakes. Burning animal dung also releases carbon dioxide that contributes to the greenhouse gases (GHG) in the atmosphere. The health costs of the pollutants emitted from this fuel are feared to be very high. These costs include out-of-pocket expenses towards the treatment of illness caused due to the use of dung cake in addition to the wage loss due to the illness (Pant, 2012). The second problem is that dung is an important source of organic manure, which is very vital to agricultural productivity and by using dung as cooking fuel it decreases the plant nutrient availability for the farms, forcing farmers to either use costly and environmentally unsafe chemical fertilisers, or produce less food, leading to malnutrition in their families. It also brings about IAP (indoor air pollution) and deficiency of manure, which has an impact on the agricultural productivity as well as the soil quality (Pant, 2013). Thirdly, a study carried out by Rural Energy Development Programme (REDP) (2000) showed that the dung cake has increased the social burden on more than 78 per cent of the women and children in rural areas because of the extra work involved in making it in those areas of Nepal.

Dung cake fuel use is affected by several factors. The rural energy consumption pattern depends on geographical, cultural, social, and economic factors. The consumption pattern for energy and fuel-mix also varies considerably across different agro-climatic zones. For example, firewood, crop residue and dung cake consumption in the Western Himalayas is reported to be 1.95 kg, 0.14 kg and 0.22 kg per capita per day, respectively; whereas in the East Coast Plains and Hills, the consumption rate of these fuels is 0.60 kg, 0.08 kg and 0.13 kg per capita per day, respectively (Planning Commission, 1992). The share of animal dung fuel in Nepal accounts for 7.0 per cent of household energy consumption (MoPE, 2000). The National Living Standards Survey (2003-04) of Nepal shows that 10.33 per cent of the total households in the country are using dung cake as the primary cooking fuel. Considering there are 4.25 million households in the country (CBS, 2002), 0.44 million households use dung cake as the main cooking fuel. The proportion of households burning dung cake as the main fuel for cooking is higher in Terai districts as compared to those in the hills. Among the Terai districts, the problem is concentrated in over a dozen districts, namely Morang, Sunsari, Saptari, Siraha, Dhanusha, Mahottari, Sarlahi, Bara, Parsa, Nawalparasi, Rupandehi, Kapilvastu and Dang (CBS, 2004). The problem is found to be more severe in Kapilvastu district adjoining the Indian border.

Only 2.38 per cent (0.10 million) of the households use biogas (less polluting than any other solid fuel) that is generated out of the animal dung. Biomass is primarily used as fuel for cooking, space heating, and animal feed preparation. The plant is technically feasible, financially viable and environment friendly. In spite of such distinct benefits, many farmers still use dung cake and have not adopted biogas technology. One can argue that this is due to a lack of capital among the poor but institutional sources provide credits for establishing biogas. The government provides a subsidy of Rs 5,000 per plant in Terai districts under CDM (clean development mechanism) of the carbon trade. This subsidy comes to be about 20 per cent of the total cost of installation.

The reluctancy of farmers in Terai districts to adopt the biogas technology can be attributed to their ignorance of the health benefits. Planners and policy makers too, are not fully aware of the health benefits of switching cooking fuel from dung cake to biogas. Studies in the past have mostly focused on the health and environmental costs arising due to fuelwood consumption and the health costs of dung cake fuel use have been mostly ignored by many studies. Policy makers are lacking an important piece of information needed for energy and health planning. The study quantifies the health costs of dung cake fuel use among the rural poor.

The broad aim of this study is to develop linkages between poverty (taking dung cake fuel use as the main indicator of the poverty) and the health outcome. More specifically, the study includes the objectives of assessing the health effects of using dung cake as the cooking fuel; estimating the household health costs of dung cake fuel use and comparing it to the price of alternative cooking fuel (biogas); and exploring factors affecting the households' decision to use dung cake instead of biogas as the cooking fuel.

Health Costs of Dung Cake Fuel and Possible Interventions

When we visit a poor settlement during cooking hours, we can see a brown cloud of toxic dung-smoke hovering over the hut. These people rely on dung cake for cooking. They continue to burn cow dung which leads to the release of both toxic fumes and GHGs far worse than a modern coal-burning plant could ever produce (Borders, 2008). Studies show that the burning of biomass for heating and cooking results in high indoor particle concentrations. Smoke from cooking stoves burning biomass fuels contains carbon monoxide, fine particulates, nitrogen dioxide and hydrocarbons—all at concentrations far in excess of what is considered unsafe in outdoor air (USEPA, 2008). Burning of the dung cake also releases active metals. The high metal content of the dung cake may reflect both the presence of biological metals (especially iron and copper) in dung (Anthony, 1971) as well as metals associated with the local soil with which the animal dung is mixed to make briquettes.

The fine particles derived from the burning of the dung cake are highly oxidising and long-term exposure to airborne particulate matter has been associated with increased rates of ARI (acute respiratory infections), chronic obstructive lung disease, and cancer (Mudway *et al.*, 2005). Use of biomass fuels indoor leads to levels of IAP many times higher than international ambient air quality standards, exposing poor women and children on a daily basis to a major public health hazard (von Schirnding *et al.*, 2000). World Health Organization (WHO) estimates suggest that up to 6.5 per cent of the annual disease burden in developing nations is attributable to the burning of solid fuels in the indoor environment (WHO, 2001; Smith and Mehta, 2003). Exposure to IAP, especially to particulate matter from the combustion of biomass like wood, charcoal, agricultural residues and dung has been implicated as a causal agent of respiratory diseases in developing countries (Chen *et al.*, 1990; de Francisco *et al.*, 1993; Ellegård, 1996; Pandey, 1984a, 1984b; Pandey *et al.*, 1989a; 1989b; Smith *et al.*, 2000). The Worldwide recognition and size of IAP's estimated impact has prompted the World Bank (2001) and other international development institutions to identify reduction of IAP as a critical objective for the coming decade. Yet, the health effects of dung cake fuel are not well researched. Though the research on exposure to indoor smoke and its impacts on respiratory diseases in developing countries began in the 1960s and 1970s in India, Nigeria, and Papua New Guinea (Ezzati and Kammen, 2002), the evidence of causal links between cow dung cake burning and diseases is still not clear.

The poorest people continue to rely on dung cake for their household energy needs. IAP is a poverty related issue, and is believed to have a strong bearing on household income. The interventions for reducing IAP should not only be cost effective but also affordable for the poor. The poor decide to use dung cake fuels for cooking because they are cheaper than modern fuels and are generally easily prepared. But the health costs can be high—a point that is usually not understood or grossly ignored by most users of dung cake fuel. The indirect cost of solid fuel is borne by the users in several ways, like physical discomfort, risk of fire, and effects on health. While the physical discomforts are simply endured and the risk of fire is considered to be negligible by the users of dung cake fuel, they also lack the information to discern the linkage between dung cake fuel usage and its effects on their health. They cannot easily attribute their diseased conditions to the type of fuels they burn.

An intervention to reduce IAP can save lives. Smith (2000) makes a conservative estimate that nearly half a million premature deaths can be attributed annually to the use of biomass fuels. Literature presents conflicting ideas and postulations for prevention and mitigation of the problem of IAP in rural poor households in developing countries. Recent reports from Bangladesh by Dasgupta *et al.* (2006) link the level of IAP with wall and roof permeability, the location of the kitchen, and the kitchen's openness to other rooms in the house. They find that the construction of walls and roofs have significant effects on IAP concentration. However, it has also been pointed out that different sources of biomass fuel contribute very little to explaining differences in measured average IAP, thereby concluding that fuel choice is less important than the ventilation factors in poor households in explaining variation in IAP. The study argues that because ventilation changes are inexpensive, lack of awareness among the rural dwellers is the primary limiting factor for preventing the problem of IAP.

Treading a different path from these findings, Pitt *et al.* (2005) conclude that improving ventilation by increasing the permeability of roofs or walls has no significant effect on the health outcomes. They conclude that nearness to the stove is the major factor that can be used to explain health effects, and argue that the decisions of division of labour among the males and the females in a household are indicative of exposure at the individual level. These findings indicate that avoiding exposure to cook stove prevents health damage to some extent. This finding, however, can help only one individual of the family i.e., the cook. It can not help the entire household because generally in most households only one person in the family cooks food.

II

METHODOLOGY

The study has been conducted using primary data collected from a sample of 331 households and nationally representative data from 3912 households taken from Nepal Living Standard Survey 2003-04.[1] The primary data was collected from six Village Development Committees (VDCs) in Kapilvastu district. The VDCs were selected with the intention to find households using biogas and households using dung cake in the same villages and under similar setting to facilitate the comparison. Medical officers were consulted in District Hospital to find the nature of respiratory problems and their symptoms reported by the people. Physicians in the hospital reported that young, married, non-smoker ladies and old women in the district have chest damage and cough which resembles that found in chronic smokers. The problem is recursive and cumulative, eventually leading to COPD (chronic obstructive pulmonary disease).

Sampling

Household is the ultimate sampling unit. A sampling frame of households using dung cake as the main cooking fuel and another sampling frame of households using biogas as the main cooking fuel was constructed. The information on biogas households was obtained from four biogas companies working in the district. The largest intervention has been made by Rastriya Biogas Company with 705 units of biogas plants established by 2008. The second one is Bhrikuti Biogas Company which established 266 plants in the district. The third one is Public Biogas and the last is Tribeni Biogas that works in southern part of the district.

1. The NLSS household data was purchased from Central Bureau of Statistics (CBS).

Table 11.1

Sampling of Households

	Village Development Committee	Households using Biogas and Dung Cake			No of Sample Households		
		Biogas	Dung cake	Total	Biogas	Dung cake	Total
1	Gajehada	48	92	140	24	46	70
2	Motipur	160	10	170	80	5	85
3	Niglihawa	10	104	114	5	52	57
4	Badganga	20	10	30	10	5	15
5	Hathausa	36	76	112	18	38	56
6	Kopuwa	38	58	96	19	29	48
	Total	312	350	662	156	175	

The information on the dung cake users was obtained from key informants in the sample VDCs. From each sampling frame, 50 per cent of the households were selected using systematic sampling with random start. Thus, we had 175 dung cake user households and 156 biogas user households for survey and analysis. Each member of the sample households was surveyed for the symtoms of asthma and eye diseases.

Data

The household survey was conducted using a well structured, pre-tested questionnaire. The questionnaire included modules on fuel use, demographic structures, socioeconomic conditions, prevalence of respiratory and eye diseases, and costs of these illnesses. The survey was conducted for six weeks by a team of trained enumerators. Among the poorest in the rural Nepal, many of the diseases go untreated or at least not properly diagnosed. We focused on rural dwellers whose symptoms were apparent and visible, and surveyed the appearance of the symptoms of these diseases for one year.

Analytical Framework

The analysis has been done in the household consumption framework. Within given exogenous income and time, the households attempt to maximise their utility with consumption, leisure, and fuel attributes. Every fuel carries a cost to the household. Some fuels have direct costs, some have indirect costs, and some of them have both in different proportions. The biogas has direct costs of establishment and some labour costs for feeding dung and water to the digester every day. Dung cake fuel is prepared by the household itself and carries only the opportunity cost of using labour and applying manure to the crops. The time and budget constraints implicitly capture the opportunity costs. When the households operate in fuel markets, their decision price is determined by the market price. For non-market participants, the decision price of dung cake is the opportunity cost of preparation and drying, labour, and indirect health costs.

The study begins with the notion of household welfare represented by an indirect utility function, where utility is derived from leisure and the consumption of various goods and services. As health of the family members is affected negatively by dung cake, it is necessary to consider an expanded form of a household utility function that includes specific health-related variables. In the attempt to maximise fuel and health efficiency, when given full information, the households choose a combination of fuels keeping in view their budget and other resource constraints. The study attempts to generate evidences that help housholds to compare benefit and costs so that they adopt pollution reducing-interventions like biogas (consequently increasing household utility). The health effects of dung cake were analysed at the individual level whereas the household shadow value of the health and fuel choice decisions were analysed at the household level.

Health Effects of Dung cake and Biogas

For estimating the individual health effects of dung cake, a probit (probability unit) regression was run with dichotomous dependent variable of appearing ($y = 1$) and not appearing ($y = 0$) of respiratory disease symptoms. Individual health outcomes were regressed with dung cake fuel use, personal characteristics, and village characteristics. This model emerges from normal CDF (cumulative distribution function) (Gujarati, 2003: 608). The appearance of disease symptoms in i^{th} individual depends on an unobservable utility index I_i. This latent variable is also known as the normal equivalent deviate (n.e.d.) or normit and determined by one or more explanatory variables. The larger the value of the index, the greater is the probability of a disease appearing.

A probit model with a dichotomous dependent variable y_i and the continuous independent variable x_i are estimated in:

$$\Pr(yi = 1) = F(xib) \quad (1)$$

Here b is a parameter to be estimated, and F is the normal cumulative distribution function. The term 'xb' is called the probit score or utility index. Since 'xb' has a normal distribution, the probit coefficients are tested with Z test (Gujarati, 2003). The interpretation of a probit coefficient is that, a one-unit increase in the predictor leads to an increase of b standard deviations in the probit score.

Following probit, equation is estimated as the health function on pollution exposure, conditional upon personal and household characteristics, to estimate marginal effects and odd ratios:

$$\Pr(Hij = 1) = \alpha + \beta 1Fj + \beta 2Pij + \beta 3Kj + \beta 4Ej + \beta 5Vj + eij \quad (2)$$

Where, Hij is the incidence of respiratory disease symptom for person i in household j. The explanatory variables are a vector of fuels used by household j (Fj); a vector of person-specific attributes of person i in household j (age, gender, education, earning, smoking and working as cook) (Pij); vector of kitchen characteristics in household j (outside kitchen, ventilation, and cooking time) (Kj); vector of household characteristics in household j (ethnicity, family size, income, and asset) (Ej); vector of village characteristics where household j is located (distance to highway and distance to forest) (Vj); and the error term (eij).

Household Health Costs of Dung cake Fuel

The household shadow values of the respiratory health were estimated using cost of illness method. The costs of diagnostic tests (including X-ray and laboratory examinations), fees (charged by doctors and hospitals), costs of medicine, and travel costs (to and from the hospitals or health posts) for the treatments were estimated by a survey of the actual expenditures incurred by the households. The costs of additional dietary expenses resulting from illness were also included. The duration abstained from work and the time spent travelling, in the hospital, and caretaking were estimated and valuated using the opportunity cost of time lost. The total cost of illness thus estimated is the household shadow value of the health The product of the household shadow value of health and the marginal effect of dung cake on health gave us the lower bound for the health costs of burning dung cake. Finally, the health cost of dung cake fuel was compared with the cost of installation of biogas plant to improve the health of the rural poor.

Factors Affecting the Household Decision to Use Dung Cake

The household survey data and NLSS data were used for fitting a probit model separately to identify the factors affecting the household decision to use dung cake as the cooking fuel. The following probit model is estimated.

$$\Pr(dungfuel = 1) = b0+b1C+b2B+b3F+b4L+b5D+b6E+b7I+ b8Em+b9Ef+e \qquad (3)$$

Where, Pr(dungfuel = 1) is probability score of using dung cake as the main cooking fuel. The explanatory variables are number of cattle (C); number of buffaloes (B); family size (F); land holding (L); distance to forest (D); ethnicity (E); household income (I); male education (average years of schooling of males) (Em); female education (average years of schooling of females) (Ef) and error term (e). In nationally representative NLSS data some regional variables like Terai *versus* mountains and rural *versus* urban were also included to catch the fixed effects confounding to the decision variables.

III

EMPIRICAL FINDINGS

The results are presented in three sub-sections, namely health effects of dung cake fuel, its health costs, and the factors affecting the household decisions to use dung cake fuel. The factors affecting the dung cake use are divided into two categories—the results at

Table 11.2

Descriptive Statistics of Health Related Variables at Individual Level

Sr. No.	Variable	Unit	n	Mean	Standard Deviation	Minimum	Maximum
1	Dung fuel	Dummy	2142	0.57	0.50	0.00	1.00
2	Kitchen outside	Dummy	2142	0.37	0.48	0.00	1.00
3	Ventilation	Dummy	2142	0.73	0.44	0.00	1.00
4	Cooking time	Minutes	2142	60.72	21.79	20.00	
5	Male	Dummy	2142	0.49	0.50	0.00	1.00
6	Tribal	Dummy	2142	0.51	0.50	0.00	1.00
7	Age	Year	2142	26.55	18.71	0.50	89.00
8	Education	Years of schooling	2142	4.41	4.53	0.00	16.00
9	Earning member	Dummy	2142	0.34	0.47	0.00	1.00
10	Smoking	Dummy	2142	0.09	0.29	0.00	1.00
11	Working as cook	Dummy	2142	0.25	0.43	0.00	1.00
12	Ownership of television set	Dummy	2142	0.56	0.50	0.00	1.00
13	Household income	Rs '000	2142	44.88	87.07	0.00	
14	Family size	No	2142	7.67	3.07	1.00	18.00
15	Distance to highway	Km	2142	6.58	4.78	0.00	14.00
16	Distance to forest	Km	2142	6.01	5.26	1.00	19.00
17	Symptoms of asthma	Dummy	2142	0.03	0.17	0.00	1.00
18	Symptoms of eye diseases	Dummy	2142	0.08	0.27	0.00	1.00

Note: The mean at individual level for some variables may differ from the mean at the household level for the same variable due to unequal number of members in the households and their weighting effects.

Source: Field Survey 2009.

the district level and results at the national level and are discussed alongside.

Health Effects of Dung Cake Fuel

Health effects of dung cake fuel use were analysed for 2,142 individuals (49% males) from 331 sample households (the average age of family members being 27 years). The descriptive statistics show that 57 per cent of the sample individuals live in households that use dung cake fuel (Table 11.2). It is hypothesised that use of dung cake fuel increases respiratory health problems. Similarly, 37 per cent of the individuals live in households that have a kitchen outside the house. A separate kitchen is expected to decrease health problems. Literature claims that ventilation reduces the effects of indoor smoke (Dasgupta *et al.*, 2006) and as high as 73 per cent of the population lives in houses with ventilated kitchen. It is hypothesised that longer the hours of cooking, higher the air pollution and more the number of respiratory health problems. The average cooking period per meal is about one hour. As the females mostly stay indoor as compared to males, it is believed that effect of indoor smoke on males is less. Tribal communities are more traditional as compared to other communities. Thus, it is believed that tribal communities suffer from respiratory diseases more than other communities. More than half of the sample individuals were from tribal communities.

Education is expected to reduce health problems. Average years of schooling of the individuals under study was 4.41 years. 34 per cent of the individuals were earning members of the family. Earning members are supposed to be more sensitive to their health conditions as compared to non-earning members. The respiratory health problems are hypothesised to be low among the working members. Smoking is another confounding factor that is believed to affect the respiratory health of the people, but only 9 per cent of the individuals were reported to be smokers. 25 per cent of the individuals worked as cooks in their family. There was more than one person cooking food in each household. Those who cook are feared to suffer more from respiratory illnesses.

Larger the family size, more the quantity of food that needs to be cooked. Thus, a larger amount of fuel is burnt and there are more respiratory health problems.

Ownership of television set is taken as an indicator of household assets. Nearly 56 per cent of the individuals lived in houses that had television sets. The average household income was Rs 44,880 per year. Higher income is expected to reduce respiratory health problems.

Average distance to the highway from the house was 6.58 km. The distance to the highway is taken as a proxy for outdoor air pollution and it is hypothesised that farther the dwelling house from the highway, fewer are the respiratory health problems. As the forest regenerates fresh air, distance to the forest is taken as another variable that affects respiratory health. People living near the forests are expected to be healthier than those living far from the forests. The average distance from the forest is about 6 kilometers.

After a discussion with the medical practitioners working at the district hospital of Kapilvastu, it was found that asthma and eye diseases are the major diseases the users of dung cake fuel are suffering from. Therefore, the symptoms of asthma and eye diseases were taken as the dependent variables. The two symptoms of asthma include: 'need to stop for breathing when walking at own pace' and 'wakening at night by attack of shortness of breath'. The asthma symptoms were reported by three per cent of the sample individuals. Similarly, redness in eyes, watery eyes, and difficulty to see in light are taken as symptoms of the eye disease. More than eight per cent of the individuals reported these symptoms. These health variables were regressed with individual, household, and village-related variables as discussed above.

Asthma Disease and Dung cake Fuel

Estimation of a probit regression develops mathematical relationship of asthma symptoms to dung cake fuel use and other related variables. The use of dung cake fuel significantly increases the probability of developing asthma symptoms (Table 11.3).

Use of dung cake fuel increases the probability of developing asthma by 1.5 per cent. Other confounding factors affecting asthma were also estimated. The risk of asthma significantly increases with an increase in age and an increase in the distance

Table 11.3

Effects of Dung Cake Burning and Other Variables on Asthma Disease: Dependent Variable: Symptoms of Asthma

	Variable	*Coeffi-cient*	*dF/dx*	*Standard Error*	*z*	*P>|z|*	*95% Confidence Interval*	
1	Dung fuel	0.367**	0.015**	0.183	2.000	0.045	0.008	0.726
2	Kitchen outside	-0.083	-0.003	0.132	-0.630	0.532	-0.342	0.176
3	Ventilation	-0.068	-0.003	0.145	-0.470	0.639	-0.353	0.216
4	Cooking time	0.001	0.000	0.003	0.290	0.768	-0.005	0.006
5	Male	0.117	0.005	0.147	0.790	0.427	-0.171	0.405
6	Tribal	-0.227*	-0.010*	0.137	-1.660	0.098	-0.495	0.042
7	Age	0.023***	0.001***	0.003	6.750	0.000	0.016	0.029
8	Education	-0.014	-0.001	0.017	-0.850	0.396	-0.048	0.019
9	Earning member	-0.201	-0.008	0.137	-1.470	0.143	-0.469	0.068
10	Smoking	-0.126	-0.005	0.183	-0.690	0.489	-0.485	0.232
11	Working as cook	0.067	0.003	0.154	0.440	0.663	-0.235	0.369
12	Television	-0.057	-0.002	0.144	-0.400	0.693	-0.339	0.225
13	Household income	0.000	0.000	0.001	-0.420	0.673	-0.002	0.001
14	Family size	-0.020	-0.001	0.023	-0.910	0.365	-0.065	0.024
15	Distance to highway	-0.026	-0.001	0.019	-1.370	0.171	-0.063	0.011
16	Distance to forest	0.027**	0.001**	0.013	2.030	0.043	0.001	0.054
17	Constant	-2.503***		0.348	-7.190	0.000	-3.186	-1.821
	LR chi2(16) = 79.96 (p=0.000)		n = 2142				Pseudo R2 = 0.141	
	Log likelihood = -244.24							

Source: Field Survey 2009.

from the forest. As age increases, the effect of pollution cumulated over the years reaches the threshold level in later

Table 11.4

Effects of Dung Cake Burning and Other Variables on Eye Diseases
Dependent Variable: Symptoms of Eye Diseases

	Variable	*Coefficient*	*dF/dx*	*Standard Error*	*z*	*P>|z|*	*95% Confidence Interval*	
1	Dung fuel	0.449***	0.047***	0.129	3.480	0.000	0.196	0.701
2	Kitchen outside	0.131	0.015	0.093	1.410	0.160	-0.051	0.313
3	Ventilation	0.019	0.002	0.108	0.170	0.862	-0.193	0.231
4	Cooking time	-0.005**	0.0005**	0.002	-2.050	0.040	-0.009	0.000
5	Male	-0.056	-0.006	0.109	-0.510	0.612	-0.270	0.159
6	Tribal	0.033	0.004	0.102	0.330	0.744	-0.166	0.233
7	Age	0.024***	0.003***	0.003	8.910	0.000	0.018	0.029
8	Education	0.008	0.001	0.012	0.700	0.484	-0.015	0.031
9	Earning member	-0.099	-0.010	0.101	-0.980	0.325	-0.296	0.098
10	Smoking	-0.031	-0.003	0.137	-0.230	0.820	-0.300	0.237
11	Working as cook	0.213*	0.025*	0.110	1.940	0.052	-0.002	0.428
12	Television	-0.074	-0.008	0.102	-0.720	0.471	-0.274	0.127
13	Household income	-0.001*	0.0001*	0.001	-1.610	0.107	-0.002	0.000
14	Family size	-0.016	-0.002	0.016	-1.030	0.301	-0.047	0.014
15	Distance to highway	-0.028**	-0.003**	0.013	-2.160	0.031	-0.053	-0.003
16	Distance to forest	0.017*	0.002*	0.010	1.780	0.075	-0.002	0.037
17	Constant	-2.025***		0.255	-7.950	0.000	-2.525	-1.526
	LR chi2(16) = 146.23 (p=0.000)		n =2142				Pseudo R2 = 0.127	
	Log likelihood = -503.37							

Source: Field Survey 2009.

years. Forests provide fresh air that reduces risk of developing an asthmatic condition. The households away from forests have no such amenities, hence see a significant increase in the problem of asthma. Asthma is, however, lesser of an issue among tribal communities. In addition to living near forests, they may have traditional and indigenous medicines or food practices that reduce the incidence of asthma. This equation estimated is statistically significant and explains over 14 per cent of the variations in development of asthma disease among the rural poor.

Against the general perception, household assets, income, and smoking habit do not significantly affect the symptoms of asthma. It can be concluded from the analysis that stopping the use of dung cake fuel can decrease the problem of asthma among rural dwellers.

Eye Disease and Dung Cake Fuel

Eye disease is another problem the users of dung cake fuel were suffering from. The results of the probit analysis show that dung fuel increases the symptoms of eye diseases significantly by 4.7 per cent (Table 11.4).

The other variables aggravating the problem are the age of the individual and working as a cook. Per year increase in age increases the probability of having eye diseases by 0.3 per cent. Similarly, working as a cook increases the probability of eye disease by 2.5 per cent. Distance to the forest also increases the problem of eye diseases. Every kilometre increase in the distance to the forest increases the risk of eye diseases by 0.2 per cent. It can be presumed that the households in the vicinity of forests may be supplementing the dung cake with firewood that generates lesser smoke.

Household income and distance from the highways significantly decrease the incidence of eye diseases. The household income affects the wellbeing in complex ways, often leading to better living that decreases the risks of diseases. The distance to the highway is taken as an indicator of outdoor pollution in villages. Near the highway, the outdoor air pollution is high, and as we go further into villages the level of outdoor air pollution decreases, thus decreasing the problem of eye diseases.

Cooking time per meal, however, gives an unexpected result: longer the cooking time, lesser is the problem of eye disease. This is because leaving the fire unattended leads to cooking for a longer duration but at the same time reduces the exposure to smoke.

It can be safely inferred that the use of dung fuel increases the incidence of eye diseases among the rural people in general, and the family cook in specific. As the comparisons are made between households using dung cake fuel and biogas fuel, there is little possibility that other dirty fuels confound the results.

Health Costs of Dung Cake Fuel Use

Cost of illnesses is estimated using a household survey of the costs incurred due to diseases. The cost headings include hospital and doctor fees, laboratory costs including X-ray, blood examination and others as appropriate, purchase of medicines, dietary expenses resulting from the illness, and wage lost due to illness. The wage lost includes the work days lost due to illness and time spent by family member(s) to take care of the patients.

Household Shadow Value of Health

Among the sample individuals, 2.9 per cent were suffering from visible symptoms of asthma disease. The cost of illness study shows that, on an average, one case of asthma costs Rs 5,312 per annum (Table 11.5). The largest portion of this cost (76.6%) goes into buying medicine.

Since the hospital and doctors fees are not high in Nepal, particularly in government hospitals (they are highly subsidised), this cost comes out to be only about 10 per cent. As the cost benefit analysis is done at the household level, the public sector expenditures are not included in the estimates. Additional dietary expense is the third largest factor that contributed to the costs of the asthma illness. As the wage rate is very low (about Rs 12 per hour), the wage lost due to illness of the patient and the care taker is very low (less than 1% of the total costs). It can be concluded that out-of-pocket expenses are much higher (due to asthma) than the imputed value of labour.

Table 11.5

Shadow Value of Asthma Disease

	Cost Heading	*N*	*Mean (Rs)*	*Per cent*	*Standard Deviation (Rs)*	*Minimum (Rs)*	*Maximum (Rs)*
1	Hospital/Doctor Fees	62	544.68	10.3	1570.25	0	10,000
2	Laboratory Costs	62	174.68	3.3	365.95	0	2,000
3	Medicine purchase	62	4069.52	76.6	13853.26	0	100,000
4	Dietary expenses resulting from illness	62	501.61	9.4	2553.51	0	20,000
5	Wage lost due to work days lost due to illness	62	15.23	0.3	54.65	0	360
6	Wage lost due to time spent by family member(s) on care taking	62	6.31	0.1	20.48	0	100
	Total		5312.03	100.0			

Source: Field Survey 2009.

The results showed that 8.2 per cent of the people were suffering from eyerelated diseases. Each case of the eye disease, on an average, costs Rs 2,249 per annum (Table 11.6). In this case, the treatment of eye disease as well the major portion of the cost goes into buying medicines (78.1%). Fees of hospitals and doctors account for 8.5 per cent. Similar amount goes to the dietary expenses due to the illness. The imputed value of the wage lost is very small. This is because in many cases people work in spite of eye diseases.

Every case of asthma costs individuals Rs 5,312 per annum (Table 11.5). Use of dung cake fuel increases the risk of asthma in the sample individuals by 1.5 per cent (Table 11.3). The use of dung cake fuel thus increases the risk of asthma by Rs 79.68 per annum. Since the size of household was 6.58 (Table 11.2), the increase in the risks of asthma disease due to burning dung cake fuel amounts to Rs 524 for each household per annum.

Table 11.6

Shadow Value of Eye Diseases

	Cost heading	*N*	*Mean (Rs)*	*Per cent*	*Standard Deviation (Rs)*	*Minimum (Rs)*	*Maximum (Rs)*
1	Hospital/Doctor Fees	176	191.78	8.5	550.65	0	5,000
2	Laboratory Costs	176	104.66	4.7	922.14	0	12,000
3	Medicine purchase	176	1755.48	78.1	8575.07	0	100,000
4	Dietary expenses resulting from illness	176	188.86	8.4	1530.02	0	20,000
5	Wage lost due to work days lost due to illness	176	5.33	0.2	21.53	0	200
6	Wage lost due to time spent by family member(s) on care taking	176	2.84	0.1	13.31	0	100
	Total		2248.95	100.0			

Source: Field Survey 2009.

Similarly, every case of eye disease costs the individual Rs 2,249 per annum (Table 11.6). Use of dung cake fuel increases the risk of eye disease by 4.7 per cent (Table 11.4). Thus, the use of dung cake fuel increases the risk of eye disease by Rs 106 per annum. The increase in the risks of eye diseases by burning dung cake fuel amounts to Rs 695 per household per annum.

Taking the two diseases of asthma and eye diseases, the annual value of loss of health for each household is Rs 1220 per annum. This does not include the pain and suffering of the patients and their kin.

Household Costs for Fuel Switching

For households in rural areas, the best alternative to dung cake fuel is the biogas plant. The same dung can be fed to the biogas plant to generate cooking gas through anaerobic gasification. In the study area, a biogas plant was introduced 15 years ago. Over 47 per cent of the sample households use biogas plants successfully. The average cost of construction of biogas plant is Rs 22,425 per plant (of average dome size 6.87 cubic metre) and the subsidy obtained is Rs 3,287 per plant (Table 11.7). As the average life of a biogas plant is 30 years (Pant, 2007) the annual depreciation of biogas plant is Rs 748 per plant.

The annual cost of a biogas plant (Rs 748) is much lower (61.3%) than the health costs of using dung cake fuel (Rs 1220). It means the alternative fuel biogas plant is available at half the cost of the health problems it can help to avoid. Additional benefits of the biogas are safety, comfort, and prestige. Yet, the rural households are reluctant to adopt biogas plant as an alternative to the dung cake fuel.

Table 11.7

Cost of Construction of Biogas Plant

	Variable	*Unit*	*N*	*Mean*	*Standard Deviation*	*Minimum*	*Maximum*
1	Size of biogas plant	m^3	156	6.87	1.58	4.00	15.00
2	Year of use	year	156	5.92	3.40	0.50	15.00
3	Cost of construction	Rs	156	22,425.81	6,698.05	9,000.00	50,000.00
4	Subsidy actually obtained	Rs	156	3,287.74	2,878.72	0.00	9,000.00

Source: Field Survey 2009.

When the dung cake users were asked whether they want to establish a biogas plant, 58.3 per cent declined. Among those who wanted to establish a biogas plant, 85.1 per cent felt the need to take a loan for the purpose. A loan for a biogas plant is readily available through priority sector lending of the Agriculture Development Bank and commercial banks.

Switching from dung cake fuel to biogas cooking fuel is also a gender-sensitive issue. In rural Nepal, cooking is generally done by females and biogas makes the cooking service much easier than the dung cake burning. Cooking with dung cake fuel takes longer time (zero order correlation between the dung cake fuel and cooking time is 0.16). Yet another aspect is the dung cake preparation and drying is done mostly (96%) by females and the involvement of males in this act in negligible (Table 11.8). However, the involvement of males in feeding dung to biogas plant is much higher (56.4%). In this way, the adoption of biogas plant instead of dung cake fuel can make the life of the females in villages much easier.

The dung slurry after the use in biogas can be used in farming whereas that which is burnt as dung cake is reduced to ash. The small amount of ash after burning the cake is rich in potassium (a plant nutrient) but other major nutrients like nitrogen and phosphorus are lost. As the dung in biogas plant is already digested crops can absorb it quickly. An another benefit of the biogas plant is that it helps in the reduction of the release of GHGs. Avoiding the use of dung cake fuel reduces the release of carbon dioxide (the main GHG), and feeding dung to biogas plant reduces the release of methane, another important GHG.

Table 11.8

Gender Involvement in Biogas and Dung Cake Making

	Gender	Feeding Dung Fuel to Biogas Plant		Preparing Dung Cake	
		Frequency	%	Frequency	%
1	Male	10	6.4	2	1.1
2	Female	68	43.6	168	96.0
3	Both	78	50.0	5	2.9
	Total	156	100.0	175	100.0

Source: Field Survey 2009.

It means switching from dung cake to biogas has several benefits for the households as well as the society. The households can reduce their health expenditure, make their family healthier, and increase crop productivity. This decision is women-friendly as well. The society will be benefitted from the reduction of the emission of GHGs. Other benefits are safety, comfort, and prestige of using biogas. Why are a large number of rural households still using dung cake fuel for cooking their food? Next section attempts to answer this question by using household level data.

Factors Affecting the Household Decisions to Use Dung Cake Fuel

The study analysed the primary household data from Kapilvastu district and also the household data from NLSS 2003-04 to make the results nationally representative.

Factors Affecting Dung cake Fuel Use in Kapilvastu District

The household survey was conducted for 331 households in the rural areas, out of which 53 per cent households were using dung cake for cooking and rest were users of biogas plant (Table 11.9). On an average, a household keeps 1.34 heads of adult cattle and 1.30 heads of buffaloes. The animals give dung that is equally needed for dung cake making and the biogas plant. As the animals in the rural areas are major assets, it can be hypothesised that larger the number of animals the wealtheir is the household and lesser is the probability of using dung cake as fuel. The average family size is 6.58 persons per household which is slightly higher than the national average of 5.2 persons (CBS, 2002). Similarly, the land holding size is 0.76 hectare that compares with the national average of 0.79 per household (CBS, 2006).

The average distance from the household to the forest is 5.78 km. More the distance from the forest, more costly it is to collect fuelwood and may lead to higher probability of using dung cake fuel by the poor households. About 47 per cent of the sample households belonged to tribal communities, particularly Tharu. The tribal communities are more tradition bound are thus assumed to continue with their habit of burning dung fuel.

The average household income of the sample households was Rs 42,161 per annum. With the increase in income, it is expected that the use of dung cake fuel will reduce. Males were found to be more educated than females. Average male education was 5.31 years of schooling whereas female education was 3.55 years of schooling. Education is hypothesised to reduce the use of dung cake fuel for cooking. These variables are fitted to probit model to explain the use of dung cake fuel by the rural households.

Table 11.9

Descriptive Statistics of Variables at Household Level

	Variable	*Unit*	*n*	*Mean*	*Standard Deviation*	*Minimum*	*Maximum*
1	No of cattle	No	331	1.34	1.36	0.00	6.00
2	No of buffalo	No	331	1.30	1.42	0.00	11.00
3	Family size	No	331	6.58	2.74	1.00	18.00
4	Land holding	Ha	331	0.76	0.99	0.00	10.20
5	Distance to forest	Km	331	5.78	5.18	1.00	19.00
6	Tribal ethnic groups	Dummy	331	0.46	0.50	0.00	1.00
7	Household income	Rs '000	331	42.16	81.19	0.00	820.00
8	Male education	Years of schooling	331	5.31	3.40	0.00	16.00
9	Female education	Years of schooling	331	3.55	2.72	0.00	11.00
10	Dung cake fuel use	Dummy	331	0.53	0.50	0.00	1.00

Source: Field Survey 2009.

Probit analysis using dichotomous dependent variable dung cake (1 for using dung cake fuel and 0 for using biogas) explains the factors affecting the use of dung cake fuel. The results show that increase in the number of cattle increases the use of dung cake fuel whereas the number of buffaloes decreases the use of dung cake fuel (Table 11.10). Every unit increase in the number of cattle increases the probability of using dung cake fuel by 8.5 per cent, whereas every unit increase in the number of buffaloes decreases the probability of using dung cake by 5.0 per cent. This is because buffalo dung is softer than cow dung and more suitable for feeding in biogas plant than the preparation of dung cake. Moreover, buffaloes are reared by well off farmers who are more likely to be able to afford biogas.

Every kilometre increase in the distance of the household from the forest increases the probability of using dung cake fuel by 2.1 per cent. This is because of the shortage of fuelwood in the villages that are far away from the forest. Similarly, tribal households have 30 per cent more probability of using dung cake fuel than non-tribal households. It means the practice of burning dung cake fuel is mostly tradition bound.

As expected an increase in household income significantly decreases the use of dung cake fuel. Education is another strong variable that decreases the use of dung fuel. An increase in male schooling decreases the probability of using dung cake fuel by 4.4

Table 11.10

Factors Affecting Household Decision for Use of Dung Cake as Cooking Fuel in Kapilvastu District

	Variable	*Coefficient*	*Marginal Effect (dF/dx)*	*Standard Error*	*z*	*P>|z|*	*95% Confidence Interval*	
1	No of cattle	0.214***	0.085***	0.071	3.020	0.002	0.075	0.352
2	No of buffalo	-0.125**	-0.050**	0.060	-2.080	0.037	-0.242	-0.007
3	Family size	0.017	0.007	0.037	0.460	0.642	-0.056	0.090
4	Land holding	-0.037	-0.015	0.098	-0.380	0.705	-0.229	0.155
5	Distance to forest	0.052***	0.021***	0.018	2.920	0.004	0.017	0.087
6	Tribal ethnic groups	0.758***	0.295***	0.186	4.080	0.000	0.394	1.122
7	Household income	-0.002*	-0.001*	0.001	-1.660	0.097	-0.005	0.000
8	Male education	-0.110***	-0.044***	0.030	-3.670	0.000	-0.168	-0.051
9	Female education	-0.242***	-0.096***	0.041	-5.950	0.000	-0.321	-0.162
10	Constant	0.688**		0.331	2.080	0.037	0.040	1.337
	LR chi2(16) = 201.24 (p=0.000)		n=331				Pseudo R2 = 0.440	
	Log likelihood = -128.27							

Source: Field Survey 2009.

per cent whereas an increase in female schooling decreases the probability of dung fuel use by 9.6 per cent. It can be inferred that education is a strong variable that encourages the switch from dung cake fuel to biogas, and female education is much stronger than male education. The probit function estimated is strong and explains 44 per cent of the variations in the fuel choice. The land holding and the family size of the household are not found to affect the use of dung cake fuel for cooking.

The analysis of the factors affecting the dung cake fuel use shows that the practice can be reduced by educating people, particularly women, and intervening through income-generating activities. Tribal communities need focused support for altering the practice of dung cake burning. As the distance to the forest increases dung cake burning, plantation of trees on barren lands in villages and low quality farmlands can also reduce the burning of dung cake. Support to keep buffaloes needs to complement the support for biogas promotion for increase the adoption of biogas.

Factors Affecting Dung cake Fuel Use in Nepal

Fitting the model with NLSS data makes the results nationally representative. Factors affecting the household decisions to use dung cake fuel are analysed at the national level, comparing households that use dung cake with those that do not. The number of households using biogas, however, is not sufficiently large to compare with the dung cake users as we did with district level data. Probit analysis was done using dichotomous dependent variable dung cake (1 for using dung cake fuel and 0 otherwise).

The descriptive statistics of the variable used in the national level analysis are presented in Table 11.11. On an average, a household in Nepal maintains 1.51 cattle and 0.75 buffaloes. The family size is 6.65—ranging from 1 person to 44 persons. This is slightly higher than the national figure of 5.20. The land holding per household is 0.56 hectare if we consider the non-farm household too in the sample. This is slightly smaller than the national average of 0.79 hectare per farm household. The average household income is Rs 93,884 per household. This is because the data is nationally representative and includes households from urban areas as well. The dispersion of income is very high. There is a difference the education of between males and females. On an average a male has got 4.71 years of education whereas a female received only 2.88 years of schooling. This pattern was also observed in the sample data. The structure of house represents the basic economic wellbeing of the households. Around 28 per cent of the households in Nepal still live in a house with a thatched roof. The sample is nationally representative and 41.7 per cent of the households are from Terai and rest from middle and high mountains. Over 70 per cent of the sample households are from rural areas and the rest are from urban areas. The results show that 10.3 per cent of the total households in Nepal are still using dung cake as their main cooking fuel.

It is a shameful fact that over 10 per cent of the Nepalese households still rely on animal dung cake for their cooking fuel. It is difficult to answer why this practice still continues. Using nationally representative sample data generated by NLSS 2003-04 we attempt to identify some socioeconomic factors that compel people to use dung cake fuel. It is clear from the results that the number of cows increases the use of dung cake fuel and the number of buffaloes does not (Table 11.12). The results of the variable 'cow' are consistent with those from the micro-level results presented in Table 11.10, whereas the effects of buffaloes are not significant at the national level. This is because buffalo dung is less suitable for making dung cake. Another important variable is the 'family size'. The larger the family size, the larger is the probability of using dung cake fuel. This relates population control to the environmental health. Control of the population can decrease the exposure to the IAP caused by burning dung cake. Land holding also significantly affects the use of dung cake fuel. The more large the land, the more easy farmers might feel in producing enough food to feed their family even with low use of organic matter like cow dung.

Table 11.11

Descriptive Statistics of the Variables taken from NLSS Survey (2003-04)

Sr. No.	*Variable*	*Unit*	*n*	*Mean (Rs)*	*Standard Deviation (Rs)*	*Minimum (Rs)*	*Maximum (Rs)*
1	No of cows	No	3912	1.517	2.185	0	25
2	No of buffalo	No	3912	0.750	1.181	0	14
3	Family size	No	3912	6.649	3.640	1	44
4	Land holding	Ha	3912	0.558	0.962	0	19.837
5	Household income	Rs '000	3912	93.884	298.590	0	5480
6	Male education	Years of schooling	3677	4.712	3.921	0	17
7	Female education	Years of schooling	3808	2.875	3.273	0	17
8	House with thatched roof	Dummy	3912	0.280	0.449	0	1
9	Terai area	Dummy	3912	0.417	0.493	0	1
10	Rural area	Dummy	3912	0.702	0.457	0	1
11	Dung cake fuel use	Dummy	3912	0.103	0.304	0	1

Source: NLSS household data.

At the national level the household income does not affect the use of dung cake. This finding refutes the belief that people use dung fuel due to their destitute poverty. This is not only due to poverty but due to other socioeconomic factors and the situational context of rural areas that the rural people are using dung cake fuel. Education is the key factor affecting the use of dung fuel. Though the male education is not significant at the national level analysis, the female education strongly affects the use of dung cake fuel. This result is consistent with the sample study as presented in table 11.10. A thatched roof in the house significantly increases the probability of using dung cake fuel. Dung cake fuel use is more prevalent in Terai areas than in the hills and mountains. It is obvious that the rural areas use dung cake fuel more than the urban areas. The explanatory variable fitted in the model explains over 35 per cent of the household decisions to use dung cake as the cooking fuel. It means the habit of using dung cake fuel is explained more by situational contexts like geographic areas, livestock farming, demographic structure, and education than the income.

Table 11.12

Factors Affecting Household Decision for Use of Dung Cake as Cooking Fuel in Nepal

Sr. No.	*Variable*	*Coefficient*	*Marginal Effect (dF/dx)*	*Standard Error*	*z*	*P>|z|*	*95% Confidence Interval*	
1	No of cattle	0.032*	0.0012*	0.018	1.810	0.070	-0.003	0.067
2	No of buffalo	0.038	0.0015	0.034	1.120	0.263	-0.029	0.105
3	Family size	0.026***	0.0010***	0.009	2.890	0.004	0.008	0.044
4	Land holding	0.057*	0.0022*	0.032	1.770	0.077	-0.006	0.120
5	Household income	0.0001	0.000005	0.000	0.940	0.345	0.000	0.000
6	Male education	-0.001	-0.00006	0.013	-0.110	0.912	-0.027	0.024
7	Female education	-0.110***	-0.0042***	0.019	-5.920	0.000	-0.146	-0.073
8	Thatched roof	0.404***	0.0193***	0.080	5.080	0.000	0.248	0.560
9	Terai area	2.265***	0.1940***	0.155	14.610	0.000	1.961	2.569
10	Rural area	0.536***	0.0169***	0.110	4.870	0.000	0.320	0.752
11	Constant	-3.605***		0.205	-17.600	0.000	-4.006	-3.203
	LR chi2(16) = 878.54 (p=0.000) Log likelihood = -798.77		n=3573				Pseudo R2 = 0.355	

Source: NLSS household data.

IV

CONCLUSIONS

This chapter explored the health effects and health costs of the dung cake fuel and identified the factors affecting the household decisions to use dung fuel. The dung cake fuel is used by 10 per cent of households in Nepal with a large concentration in Terai district. The analysis was done particularly in relation to the use of biogas as an alternative choice that is being used by less than 3.0 per cent households. The study is based on the primary data from a survey of 175 dung cake user households and 156 biogas user households, and NLSS data for 3912 households.

The study used the probit model to econometrically measure the adverse health outcomes resulting from dung cake fuel use, household health costs as the shadow value of respiratory health in the household utility function, and the effect of various factors that account for the households decision to use dung cake. The results of the study explain why dung cake is preferred over biogas despite the fact that the latter technology is subsidised and may be preferable from a social cost-benefit point of view. The study quantified the relationship between dung cake fuel use and health of the family members. Dung cake fuel use is found to increase asthma and eye diseases significantly among rural dwellers. It also estimated the household shadow value for major diseases such as asthma and eye diseases caused by dung cake fuel in the rural poor people.

Switching the cooking fuel from dung cake to biogas serves the households through health and productivity benefits, and the society through reduced emission of greenhouse gases. In this study, reduced health cost (Rs 1220) per annum due to the fuel switching is estimated to be much larger than the price (Rs 748) of alternative clean fuel the biogas. The study estimated that the burden of health costs to the poor is attributable to the use of dung cake, and provided a basis for adoption of cleaner fuels like biogas.

The chapter also assessed the factors affecting the use of dung cake by people and explored the options suitable for them. It analysed the factors affecting the use of dung cake fuel for cooking food, and found that tribal people in rural areas largely depend on dung fuel.

'Income' is a strong variable at local level. 'Education', particularly female education, is the strong variable that can reduce the use of dung cake fuel. The problem is more severe in rural areas in the Terai region where forests are not readily accessible. The results will be supportive in formulating household energy policy, agriculture policy, and health policy for the poor rural households. Creating awareness of the health costs of dung cake fuel among people in rural areas, particularly tribal communities can reduce the use of this dirty fuel, and thus improve the health of people, increase the productivity of farms, and reduce the emission of GHGs.

References

Anthony, W.B. (1971). "Animal Waste Value—Nutrient Recovery and Utilization", *Journal of Animal* Science 32: 799-802.

Borders, M. (2008). "Environment, Killing Me Softly", *10 Ways Mainstream Environmentalism Hurts the Developing World. www.aWorldConnected.org.*

CBS (2002). *Population Census 2001, National Report*. Kathmandu: Central Bureau of Statistics. pp.112-3.

———. (2004). *Nepal Living Standards Survey 2003/04, Statistical Report*. Volume 1. Kathmandu: Central Bureau of Statistics. p.31.

———. (2006). *Monograph: Agriculture Census Nepal 2001/02*. Kathmandu National Planning Commission, Central Bureau of Statistics.

Chen, B.H., C.J. Hong, M.R. Pandey and K.R. Smith (1990). "Indoor Air Pollution in Developing Countries", *World Health Statistics Q* 43: 127-38.

Dasgupta, S., M. Huq, M. Khaliquzzaman, K. Pandey and D. Wheeler (2006). "Indoor Air Quality for Poor Families: New Evidence from Bangladesh", *Indoor Air* 16: 426-44, www.blackwellpublishing.com/ina.

de Francisco A., J. Morris, A.J. Hall, J.R.M. Armstrong Schellenberg and B.M. Greenwood (1993). "Risk Factors for Mortality from Acute Lower Respiratory Tract Infections in Young Gambian Children", *International Journal of Epidemiology* 22: 1174-82.

Ellegård, A. (1996). "Cooking Fuel Smoke and Respiratory Symptoms among Women in Low-income Areas in Maputo", *Environmental Health Perspective* 104: 980-5.

Ezzati, M. and D.M. Kammen (2002). "Household Energy, Indoor Air Pollution, and Public Health in Developing Countries", *Resources for the Future*, Issue Brief, 02-26. Washington, DC.

Gujarati, D.N. (2003). *Basic Econometrics*. 4th edition. New Delhi: Tata McGraw-Hill.

MOPE (2000). *State of Environment* Nepal 2000. Kathmandu, Nepal.

Mudway, I.S., S.T. Duggan, C. Venkataraman, G. Habib, F.J. Kelly and J. Grigg (2005).

"Combustion of Dried Animal Dung as Biofuel Results in the Generation of Highly Redox Active Fine Particulates", *Particle and Fibre Toxicology 2(6).http://www.particleandfibretoxicology.com/content/2/1/6*

Pandey, M.R. (1984a). "Prevalence of Chronic Bronchitis in a Rural Community of the Hill Region of Nepal", *Thorax* 39: 331-6.

———. (1984b). "Domestic Smoke Pollution and Chronic Bronchitis in a Rural Community of the Hill Region of Nepal", *Thorax* 39: 337-9.

Pandey, M.R., J.S. Boleji, K.R. Smith and E.M. Watfula (1989a). "Indoor Air Pollution in Developing Countries and Acute Respiratory Infection in Children", *Lancet* 1: 427-9.

Pandey, M.R., R.P. Neupane, A. Gautam and I.B. Shrestha (1989b). "Domestic Smoke Pollution and Acute Respiratory Infections in a Rural Community of the Hill Region of Nepal", *Environment International* 15: 337-40.

Pant, K.P. (2007). "Valuing Interventions to Reduce Indoor Air Pollution—Fuelwood, Deforestation, and Health in Rural Nepal". The Pakistan *Development Review* 46(4) (Part II): 1169-87.

———. (2012). "Cheaper Fuel and Higher Health Costs among the Poor in Rural Nepal," AMBIO: *A Journal of the Human Environment 41(3): 271-83. http://www.ncbi.nlm.nih.gov/pmc/articles/PMC3357850/*

———. (2013). "Misuse of Domestic Resources Increases Import Dependency: Case of Dung Cake Fuel and Demand for Chemical Fertilizers in Nepal," *World Journal of Science, Technology and Sustainable Development* 10(1): 42-54.

Planning Commission (1992). *Eighth Five Year Plan (1992-97)*. New Delhi: Planning Commission, Government of India.

Pitt, Mark M., Mark R. Rosenzweig and Md. Nazmul Hassan (2005). "Sharing the Burden of Disease: Gender, the Household Division of Labor and the Health Effects of Indoor Air Pollution", *CID Working Paper* No. 119. Center for International Development Harvard University. March.

REDP (2000). *An Impact Study of REDP Program, 2000*. Kathmandu, Nepal: Rural Energy Development Programme.

Smith, K. (2000). "National Burden of Disease in India from Indoor Air Pollution", *Proceedings of the National Academy of Science* 97(24): 13286-93. www.pnas.org

Smith K.R., J.M. Samet, I. Romieu and N. Bruce (2000). "Indoor Air Pollution in developing Countries and Acute Lower Respiratory Infections in Children", *Thorax* 55: 518-32.

Smith, K.R. and S. Mehta (2003). "The Burden of Disease from Indoor Air Pollution in Developing Countries: Comparison of Estimates", *International Journal of Hygiene and Environmental Health* 206: 279-89.

USEPA (2008). *National Ambient Air Quality Standards*. US Environmental Protection Agency. www.epa.gov/air/criteria.html

von Schirnding, Y., N. Bruce, K. Smith, G. Ballard-Tremeer, M. Ezzati and K. Lvovsky (2000). "Addressing the Impact of Household Energy and Indoor Air Pollution on the Health of the Poor—Implications for Policy Action and Intervention Measures", *Draft Working Paper*. Prepared for Commission on Macroeconomics and Health.

WHO (2001). "World Health Organisation". *World Health Report*. Geneva: WHO.

World Bank (2001). *Making Sustainable Commitments: An Environment Strategy for the World Bank*. Washington, DC: World Bank.

12

NISHA ARUNATILAKE, SUWENDRANI JAYARATNE, PRIYANKA JAYAWARDENA, ROSHINI JAYAWEERA AND DUSHNI WEERAKOON[1]

Impact of Remittances on the Household of the Emigrant and on the Economy of the Migrant's Country

Sri Lanka

Introduction

Sri Lanka has experienced varying forms and intensity of migration in post-independence decades. The number of people leaving the country, both for political and economic reasons, increased significantly in the 1980s. At present, close to two million Sri Lankan citizens are estimated to have migrated for foreign employment. The estimated outflow of migrants exceed the number entering the labour force annually.[2] The bulk of such migrants are to be found in Middle Eastern countries. Lack of adequate livelihood and employment opportunities at home is the prime driver for most of such out-migration. Skilled migrants—estimated to make up about 22 per cent of all migrants—on the other hand mostly seek better employment/financial opportunities abroad.

Migrant remittance flows into Sri Lanka are significant and rising. Remittance inflows have come to account for nearly 8.0 per cent of Sri Lanka's GDP (gross domestic product) in 2007 (US$ 2.5 billion), second only to export earnings from goods (US$ 7.7 billion) and far above that of average FDI (foreign direct investment) inflows of 1.5 per cent

---

1. Authors' names are in alphabetical order. Authors are thankful to the South Asia Network of Economic Institutions (SANEI) for funding this study.
2. Based on Sri Lanka Bureau of Foreign Employment (SLBFE) and Department of Census and Statistics Labor Force Survey data.

of GDP. The macroeconomic implications are significant in terms of the contribution to GDP growth, easing Sri Lanka's foreign exchange constraints and pressure on the exchange rate by providing valuable BoP (balance of payment) support. In 2006-07, for instance, if not for remittance inflows, Sri Lanka would have had to grapple with an annual average current account deficit of 11.5 per cent of GDP as opposed to the actual of 4.5 per cent of GDP.

At the micro level, remittances have been an important flow of income for poorer households. Remittances have also shown to push households out of poverty. However, the effect of remittances on household welfare can be either positive or negative, depending on the characteristics of the migrant and their household. Remittances from abroad have increased demand for health and education services, especially at the high end. In communities where there is high concentration of migrants, investments in high-end private sector health facilities have increased and there is increased demand for health services. Studies have found that households of migrant workers tend to become dependent on regular remittances for their daily sustenance with some husbands/parents giving up income generating activities. This has resulted in a number of social problems such as abuse of remitted funds, neglect of children, and behavioral changes of family members.[3]

Over the years the government has facilitated labour migration to ease employment and foreign exchange shortfalls in the country, with the relaxation of regulations on travel and foreign exchange convertibility to facilitate overseas work and remittances. These efforts have resulted in an increase in the remittance flows and the number of emmigrants over time.

Sri Lanka along with other developing countries has been pushing for liberalisation of Mode 4 or movement of natural persons under the General Agreement on Trade in Services (GATS) given that developing countries including Sri Lanka possess a comparative advantage in their trade through Mode 4. However, progress on this issue has been poor at the multi-lateral level. In the meanwhile, Sri Lanka has managed to sign bi-lateral agreements to secure employments

3. See Hettige (1991).

for Sri Lankans on a limited basis in a number of countries such as Malaysia and South Korea to name a few. The government is hoping to raise remittance to US$ 4 billion by 2010 and to US$ 6.5 billion by 2016 by changing the skill mix of migrants and the composition of country destinations. Recognising the economic importance of worker remittances, the government has already appointed a high-level committee to study issues and recommend appropriate policies as well as measures to enhance worker remittances.[4]

Chapter Objectives

The main research ideas focused upon in the chapter are as follows:

(i) Impact of remittances on the macro economy.

(ii) Impact of remittances on the household of an emigrant.

(iii) Remittance flows and enhancing the quality and reach of infrastructure.

Unlike an extensive body of research that examines the relationship between growth and sources of foreign capital—primarily aid and FDI—the literature on the relationship between economic growth and remittances remains very sketchy. To some extent this is partly due to underlying assumptions that remittances are by and large used mostly for consumption purposes by individual households and, therefore, have a limited impact on long-term growth. Nonetheless, given the significant increase in remittance flows over recent decades, such inflows can have a major economic impact on recipient economies, including on the efforts to reduce overall poverty.

With remittance inflows accounting for nearly 8.0 per cent of GDP in Sri Lanka, the developmental impact can be significant. Notwithstanding deficiencies in the quality and coverage of remittance flows, the study uses secondary data to examine trends in the volume of remittances over time, and assess whether stable growth of such inflows has had any significant impact as a source of external development finance for the country. In doing so, the analysis details the degree to which Sri Lanka has come to rely on such inflows to bolster currency reserves, finance imports, enhance the ability of banks to finance loans and thus overall investment in

4. Central Bank of Sri Lanka (2006).

the country. In brief, the analysis attempts to understand the role of remittances in ensuring macroeconomic stability and growth prospects for the Sri Lankan economy.

The chapter then attempts a quantitative examination of the impact of remittance flows at a more micro level. To examine the impact of remittances on the household of the emigrant, the study uses household data for this purpose. First, the chapter provides an overview of the contribution of migrant remittances to household incomes. Using descriptive and distributional analysis, it examines the types of households receiving migrant remittances, and examines the equalising effects of remittance incomes. Next, choosing a variety of household level education, health, and other behavioural indicators, such as school attendance of children, health status of household members, and alcohol consumption of household members, the study examines the impact of remittances of households.

Under the third research question, two important questions that arise—albeit with some degree of overlap—are:

(i) what can countries do to increase remittance inflows through formal channels?

(ii) what strategies can countries adopt to maximise their developmental impact?

First, the chapter examines the state of formal and informal infrastructure for remittances in the country. Then, it explores the effectiveness of each of these institutions as well as assesses the range of services offered by them to migrant workers to channel funds from abroad to home. Thereafter, the chapter explores possible means by which the government as well as the private sector could enhance the use of the formal remittance system, given that a substantial amount of remittances go though the informal channels at the moment. The study also examines how the services provided through formal channels can be directed towards maximising the benefits of remittances to improve family welfare. All in all, the chapter aims to highlight both the potentials as well as challenges in this regard, and add to the current literature on remittance systems.

Trends in Migration and Remittances

History of Migration Trends

Sri Lanka has experienced varying forms and intensity of migration in post-independence decades. Following independence in 1948, the question of "stateless" plantation labour brought to Sri Lanka by British colonial powers from Southern India was to be addressed through an agreement for repatriation. Under the Sirimavo-Shastri Agreement of 1964 between the governments of India and Sri Lanka, an estimated 337,000 people were repatriated from Sri Lanka during the period 1977-1982. From 1983, with the onset of a civil conflict in the country, there was also a significant exodus from the ethnic Tamil community. Much of the early wave of such out-migration were of those seeking asylum in neighbouring India as well as a large exodus to developed countries, primarily to Europe and Canada. Over time, the numbers of such people leaving the country for political reasons were joined by those seeking to out-migrate for economic reasons as well. For instance, a significant number of Sri Lankans have increasingly sought permanent migratory status in developed countries such as Australia following efforts by those countries to attract particular skilled migrants.

Temporary migration for purposes of employment abroad began to be a significant source of labour out-migration in Sri Lanka only in the late 1970s. Changes in both the external environment and domestic policy shifts coincided to encourage such migration. A substantive programme of economic reforms instituted in Sri Lanka during 1977-78 saw the relaxation of a stringent exchange control regime that acted to curtail ease of foreign travel. While inflows of foreign currency were permitted, Sri Lankans travelling abroad were allowed only a few foreign currency transactions. On the external front, the second oil price hike of 1979 opened up significant employment opportunities in labour-starved Middle Eastern economies that had begun to reap the benefits of petroleum. The initial trickle of migrant workers from Sri Lanka began to grow steadily from the early 1980s to reach an estimated 1.6 million by 2008 (SLBFE).[5] The estimated outflow of migrants per annum of about 250,000 exceeded the number entering the labour force annually.

The early out-migrants were primarily unskilled labour. Indeed, the majority of temporary migrant workers from Sri Lanka have been female labour, providing their services as 'housemaids' in the Middle East. Mostly, lack of adequate livelihood and employment opportunities at home has been the prime driver for such out-migration. While there have been some marginal changes to the profile of out-migrants in more recent years—with more opportunities for skilled migrants emerging in labour-constrained economies of the European Union (EU) and the United States (US)—unskilled migrants still account for more than 75 per cent of the total, and female migrants continue to make up about 62 per cent of the total stock of migrants from Sri Lanka.

With the build up of migrant workers, migrant remittance flows into Sri Lanka have been rising steadily over time. At US$ 2.5 billion in 2007, they have come to be a major source of external development finance for the country. With remittance inflows accounting for nearly 8 per cent of GDP, their potential developmental impact on the economy also remains quite significant.

Recent Trends in Migration for Employment

Data on migration related statistics in Sri Lanka are not thorough. The primary data collating agency is the SLBFE. The SLBFE data captures those migrants that opt to register with the SLBFE prior to departure, as well as estimates of migrants seeking employment overseas through direct sources (captured via pre-departure immigration formalities.[6] Both estimates are thus, subject to some uncertainty—most likely to be an underestimate of the actual number of migrants. For instance, while migrants are encouraged to register via Licenced Agencies, it if often the case that many opt to

5. Sri Lanka Bureau of Foreign Employment, Sri Lanka Bureau of Foreign Employment. *http://www.slbfe.lk/* (accessed 1 August 2014).

6. Available data suggests that approximately 70 per cent of migrants have chosen to engage with registered sources while the remainder have gone through direct sources.

Table 12.1

Migrant Profile (2007)

	Stock of Migrants		*Flow of Migrants*	
	Male	*Female*	*Male*	*Female*
Total	622,300	1,020,155	102,629	114,677
By Age				
20-29			43.4	32.5
30-39			29.0	33.6
By skill				
Professional level	2.0	0.2	1.5	0.1
Middle level	5.9	1.0	3.2	0.5
Clerical & related	9.5	1.2	3.8	0.5
Skilled	41.8	10.5	42.5	5.2
Semi-skilled	0.5	0.0	3.1	0.2
Unskilled	40.3	7.6	45.9	4.4
Housemaid		79.4		89.1

Source: SLBFE.

engage with unlicenced operators. Similarly, information furnished in pre-departure immigration formalities may not necessarily yield systematic and accurate information. In a similar vein, published data does not capture undocumented migrants, although anecdotal evidence suggests that the numbers could be quite high and rising.

On the basis of available published data, it is estimated that Sri Lanka has a stock of nearly 1.6 million migrants currently (SLBFE). The annual gross outflow has increased steadily from about 20,000 in the mid 1980s to over 200,000 persons at present.[7] Available data suggests that nearly 62 per cent of the stock of migrants comprises female labour, although the share of female out-migrants annually has declined from an average of around 70 per cent of the total in the 1990s to less than 55 per cent by 2007. Of the female migrants, an overwhelming majority of the stock of female out-migrants (89%) remains housemaids to date, with hardly any change in the composition of skills of migrants over time.

7. Net figures are not available due to lack of information on returning migrants.

Unlike female migrants, a significant share of the stock of male migrants (around 42 per cent) is comprised primarily of skilled labour category. However, it is noteworthy that despite the higher numbers of male migrants in recent years, the skills composition has not seen any discernible shift.

The Middle East remains the major host destination. Of all migrants in 2007, over 90 per cent found their way to Middle Eastern countries, with housemaids making up 50 per cent of such out-migrants. The dominance of Middle Eastern countries as a destination for the bulk of Sri Lanka's migrants is also reflected in the origin of remittance inflows to the country (Table 12.2). North America and Europe were also important sources of remittance inflows in the 1980s. This is most likely related to the significant numbers of Sri Lankan nationals who migrated to countries in these regions—primarily as asylum seekers—following the outbreak of civil conflict in the country from the mid 1980s.

Whilst the share of total remittances from North America has continued to decline in the 1990s, Europe has emerged as a growing source in more recent years. This reflects in part the changes to the composition of out migrants from Sri Lanka in terms of both

Table 12.2

Source of Remittance Inflows to Sri Lanka

(in Per cent)

	1987	*1990*	*1993*	*1996*	*1999*	*2002*	*2005*	*2008*
Middle East	45.5	47.0	55.4	58.1	61.7	59.8	56.8	59.8
North America	20.5	19.5	12.1	8.4	7.3	6.7	6.5	3.9
European Union	16.1	16.5	14.9	14.7	13.6	17.1	18.5	18.0
Europe Other	5.0	4.8	4.8	5.6	5.6	5.6	7.0	4.4
South Asia	1.8	1.7	1.7	0.8	0.8	0.8	1.0	1.1
South East Asia	4.2	4.5	1.6	2.0	1.9	1.9	2.0	3.1
Far East Asia	4.1	3.2	7.7	7.3	6.1	4.9	4.5	6.0
Australia	1.5	1.8	1.0	1.0	1.0	1.1	1.5	1.9
Other	1.2	1.0	0.7	2.0	2.0	2.1	2.5	1.8
Total	100.0	100.0	100.0	100.0	100.0	100.0	100.0	100.0

Source: Central Bank of Sri Lanka, *Annual Report*, various issues.

gender and skills. Increasingly, more males with higher skills are out-migrating. To an extent, this reflects changes in the global labour market where many developed countries instituted 'visas for jobs' programmes to attract temporary job seekers to fill skill shortages in the home countries. More recently, the Sri Lankan Government too has been promoting the idea of encouraging more skilled immigrants, for instance, in areas such as health care.

Institutional Framework

Over the years, Sri Lanka has instituted a number of programmes and schemes that cover issues of governance in the process of labour migration, the protection and welfare of migrant workers and their families. The SLBFE Act, 1985 is the first major legislative recognition of labour migration.[8] Sri Lankan migrant workers overseas do not fall within the purview of national labour laws that govern and protect workers within Sri Lanka, and thus the SLBFE Act is the primary piece of legislation that applies to Sri Lankan workers migrating for overseas employment. Moreover, Sri Lanka ratified the international convention on the protection of the rights of all migrant workers and their families in 1996. The creation of a separate ministry, Ministry of Foreign Employment Promotion and Welfare (MFEPW), in February 2007 is another indication of the priority assigned to labour migration in Sri Lanka.[9]

The MFEPW is responsible for:[10]

- Formulation and implementation of foreign employment programmes.
- Promotion of foreign employment.
- Career guidance on foreign employment.
- Training for foreign employment.
- Welfare of migrant workers.
- Housing development programs for migrant workers.

8. Act No 21 of 1985 amended by Act No 4 of 1994 and The Sri Lanka Bureau of Foreign Employment Regulations (The Gazette of Sri Lanka, 1985-08-28, No. 364/9)

9. See Ministry of Foreign Employment Promotion and Welfare (2008).

10. *http://www.empro.gov.lk/main.php?pid=About*

- Wages, terms and conditions of foreign employment.
- Regulation of fee levying by employment agencies.
- Administration of SLBFE.

Improvement of the quality, skills and communication abilities of migrant workers are main goals of the ministry. A number of training programmes are conducted by the ministry to achieve these targets. This training abolishes the language barriers which most of the unskilled migrant workers face in the host countries. In addition, they are empowered through these programmes to ensure their rights and privileges in the destination. The main training body of the ministry is the SLFBE.

Sri Lankan Government has signed several MoUs to maximise the development impacts of migration and remittances. They are MoUs with Jordan, UAE, Bahrain, Qatar and Libia. Oman, Lebanon, and Kuwait are in the pipeline. In addition, Sri Lankan Government has a trade agreement with Government of South Korea to promote foreign employment. However, since MoUs are not binding, it is more meaningful for Sri Lanka to engage in bi-lateral agreements.

MFEPW has the overriding objective of activating government policy through identified agencies in a wider foreign employment promotion network.[11] There are two institutions coming under the purview of the MFEPW; namely, SLBFE and Sri Lankan Foreign Employment Agency (SLFEA).

Sri Lanka Bureau of Foreign Employment

SLBFE was established by Act of Parliament in 1985. The Act confers upon the SLBFE the legal mandate to be the governing authority for Sri Lanka's migrant labour force and to act as the lead agency for overseas employment administration. The law empowers the SLBFE to manage the emigration of workers through the licensing of employment agencies, data collection on migrant workers, setting of standards, negotiation of employment contracts, and ensuring

11. See Ministry of Foreign Employment Promotion & Welfare (2008).

provision of welfare measures for the protection of overseas Sri Lankan workers.[12]

With regards to the promotion of formal remittance channels, the SLBEF employs two methods. The first is through pre-departure training programmes and the second method is through government level recruiting conditions. There are five types of pre-departure or orientation progammes conducted by the SLBFE. They are:

(i) In-house training and orientation programmes for unskilled female migrant workers. This is for unskilled migrants for both Middle East countries (12 days) and non-Middle East countries (21 days).

(ii) 18 days training programme for migrant workers (male and female) who are going to South Korea. 12 days of training is for the Korean language, law, culture along with banking, health and SLBFE formalities. The other six days are for vocational training, depending on the selected job.

(iii) One day awareness programme for unskilled female workers who have previous experience in working abroad.

(iv) 18 days basic literacy course for those who are weak in writing in Sinhala and Tamil.

(v) 40 days industrial sewing training programme for both males and females.

These training programmes are conducted at the district level so that migrant workers have easy access to them. Most of the training programmes include creating awareness on banking. State owned banks are involved in these training programmes together with the SLBFE. Most of these orientation programmes have been conducted since 1995.

In government managed recruitment schemes such as those to South Korea, it is necessary for migrant workers to open an NRFC (Non-Resident Foreign Currency) account before leaving the country. In addition, they are provided bank loans, and migrant workers can repay their loan amount through NRFC accounts. This procedure supports efforts to enhance the use of formal money transfer system for remittances.

---

12. Ibid.

In addition to these two main strategies, the SLBFE promotes formal money transfer systems at the international airport, Sri Lankan embassies overseas, etc. To strengthen these activities, it employs agencies to carry our pre-departure orientation programmes.

Sri Lankan Foreign Employment Agency (Pvt) Ltd

The SLFEA was established in 1996 for the purpose of directing youth for foreign employment. This agency functions in association with local and foreign employment agencies to secure employment opportunities for the Sri Lankan youth with full state intervention. For example, the SLFEA is coordinating the recruitment of industrial trainees to send to South Korea, under the agreement between the Government of Sri Lanka and the Korean Federation of Small and Medium Businesses. It is also vested with the responsibility of devising and implementing methodologies related to accident, welfare and security of migrant workers. SLFEA also possesses a complete data bank and customer service facilities.[13]

Association of Licensed Foreign Employment Agencies

The Association of Licensed Foreign Employment Agencies (ALFEA) was established by an Act of Parliament in 1985 with the objective of ensuring and enforcing best ethical practices for foreign employment trade by strict disciplinary control of all stakeholders. It aims to work consistently towards development of more foreign employment opportunities for Sri Lankans.

This institution also provides pre-orientation programmes for migrant workers. These orientation programmes include the provision of knowledge on banking systems and the promotion of formal channels of remitting money. In addition, it warns migrant workers about the adverse effects of informal channels through their training programmes.

---

13. *http://www.empro.gov.lk/main.php?pid=About*

National Labour Migration Policy for Sri Lanka[14]

In addressing diverse developmental, economic, and social issues associated with labour migration, Sri Lanka has over the years, instituted a number of programmes and schemes that cover issues of governance in the process of labour migration, protection and welfare of migrant workers and their families. Despite a range of existing administrative and legal measures and regulations, maintaining the delicate balance between promotion of overseas employment and protection of national workers abroad has remained a challenge for the government. The Ministry of Labour Relations and Foreign Employment initially identified the need to articulate the Sri Lankan Government's policy on labour migration in a comprehensive policy document based on a long-term vision. In February 2009, the Sri Lanka National Policy on Labour Migration was launched by the MFEPW.

This policy aims to promote opportunities for all men and women to engage in migration for decent and productive employment in conditions of freedom, equity, security and human dignity. The National Policy on Labour Migration promotes and supports the migration of skilled men and women to secure work environments where the protection of fundamental human rights at work is upheld to the highest standards.

Data and Methods

Macro Impacts

As explained in an earlier section, the chapter poses two main research questions. The first of which is to assess the impact of remittances on the macro economy. For this part, the study uses secondary data to examine the trends in remittance flows and its overall support to sustain economic stability and growth in the economy. Existing literature will also be referred to where relevant. Macroeconomic data has been gathered from secondary sources, including data compiled by the Central Bank of Sri Lanka and data specific to migration from the SLBFE.

---

14. See Ministry of Foreign Employment Promotion & Welfare (2008).

Micro Level Impacts

Household survey data provides basic socioeconomic information on the migrants and their households. However, as these are nationally representative samples that do not focus on migrant families, the number of migrant families captured in these surveys are small. For this study we use Consumer Finance and Socio-Economic Survey (CFS) data carried out by Central Bank of Sri Lanka during 2003-04 period. CFS data consists of comprehensive data from households on income, expenditure, consumption, savings, investments and borrowings, as well as household data on demographic features, education, health, the labour force, housing conditions, household amenities and land ownership. A sample of around 12,000 households were surveyed covering most districts, except some district affected by conflict, of Sri Lanka. It includes migrant information on the purpose of travel, type of employment—if employed abroad, destination country and the duration of migration. Survey includes information on households with migrant members on 700 households in 2003-04.

This data has been used to order households according to income and to examine the distribution of remittances across households. The study also examines the impact of remittances on household income, expenditure and welfare as detailed below.

Impact of Remittances on Household Income, Expenditure and Welfare

Assessing the impact of remittances on households is made difficult by several factors. Only cross sectional household surveys are available for Sri Lanka. As a result, it is not possible for the analysis to compare a household's situation pre- and post-migration. Comparing households with at least one migrant worker to non-migrant households can result in biases, as certain household characteristics that influence the decision to migrate can also influence household living standards. To overcome these difficulties we use propensity score matching techniques to choose a control group of households that are similar to migrant-households (see Appendix A-12.1 for details).

The households with migrant workers (hereafter referred to s migrant households) may be characteristically different to those that do not have migrant workers (non-migrant households). This makes estimating the impact of remittances on households more complex. In order to overcome this problem we will use a propensity score matching technique to estimate the impact of remittances on chosen household impact indicators. The propensity scores for each observation in the sample will be estimated using standard probit models. Then the impact, I, of remittances on migrant households can be shown as:

$$I=\sum_{j=1}^{P}\left(Y_{ij}-\sum_{i=1}^{NP}W_{ij}Y_{ij0}\right)I_{P}$$

Where Y_{j1} is an outcome indicator, such as expenditure on education, for migrant household j, Y_{ij0} is the outcome indicator for the ith non-migrant household matched to the jth migrant household, P and NP are the total number of migrant and non-migrant household respectively and W_{ij} are the weights used to calculate the average value of the outcome indicators for non-migrants.

Remittance Inflows and their Development Effectiveness

Information regarding channels through which remittances are sent and the institutions involved in the process and the services/products offered by them to attract migrant remittances was gathered mainly by existing secondary information available on the subject. This information was corroborated with interviews with selected stakeholders, namely the formal institutions such as the commercial banks licenced to handle inward remittances, money transfer businesses, the post office as well as discussions with officials from government agencies such as the SLFEB, Central Bank of Sri Lanka, and NGOs (non-governmental organisations) working on migration issues. The interviews with stakeholders provide a deeper understanding of the potential and challenges in channeling funds through the formal system as well as suggest policy options available to the government which is keen on attracting greater flows of money into the formal system.

Results: Macro Level Developmental Impacts

Impact of Remittances on the Macro Economy

The benefits of migration to countries of origin are largely associated with remittance inflows. These are, for the most part, personal flows from the migrants to their families. As such, direct person-to-person flows tend to be well targeted to meet the needs of recipients. Where the bulk of migrants tend to be poor, such remittance flows can have a significant impact in generating welfare gains for migrants.

At the more macro level, remittance inflows are an important source of external financing for developing countries, often providing a steady source of capital in excess of funds generated through ODA (overseas development assistance), FDI and portfolio flows. More important of them all, remittance flows may also serve to stabilise recipient economies at times of economic downturns brought on by phenomena such as a natural disaster, financial crisis, political conflict, etc. In essence, where migrants send more money to families during crises, remittance inflows can be countercyclical to smooth macroeconomic shocks in the migrants' home countries. Thus, the overall developmental impact of remittances can be quite significant, although the benefits may be conditional on the broader economic context of the recipient country.

The rest of the section examines trends in the volume of remittances over time, and assesses whether stable growth of such inflows has held any significant impact as a source of external development finance for Sri Lanka. In so doing, the analysis details the degree to which Sri Lanka has come to rely on such inflows to bolster currency reserves, finance imports, enhance the ability of banks to finance loans and thus overall investment in the country, etc. In brief, the analysis attempts to understand the role of remittances in ensuring macroeconomic stability and growth prospects for the Sri Lankan economy.

Contribution of Remittances to Macroeconomic Stability

Sri Lanka has witnessed a steady increase in remittance inflows over the last two decades, rising from US$ 140 million in 1980 to US$ 2.5 billion by 2007—an increase from less than 4 per cent of GDP to 7.7 per cent of GDP over the same period (Figure 12.1). Sri Lanka saw its highest inflow of remittances in 2005—peaking at 8 per cent of GDP—in the aftermath of the December 2004 Asian tsunami natural disaster that claimed the lives of nearly 40,000 people and caused extensive displacement. Such remittance inflows to affected family members in recipient economies reflect the countercyclical nature of remittance flows referred to above.

Figure 12.1

Trends in Remittance Inflows

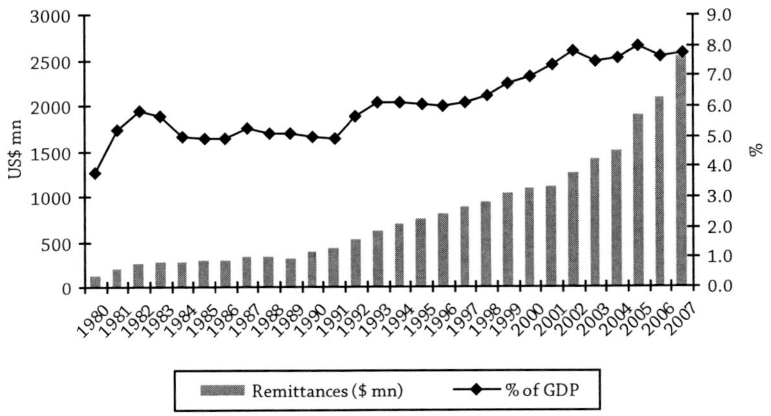

Source: Central Bank of Sri Lanka, *Annual Report*, various issues.

Remittance inflows have been one of the more stable sources of foreign capital inflows to Sri Lanka. Remittances were nearly twice the size of ODA received by Sri Lanka in 2007 and far exceeded the inflows of FDI that the country has received. In general, remittance inflows have also tended to be less volatile than that of private capital inflows and official flows. The inflow of ODA to Sri Lanka in particular has fluctuated considerably from year to year relative to that of remittances.

Remittance inflows have provided significant BoP support to the Sri Lankan economy. With import expenditure consistently outstripping export earnings growth, Sri Lanka has had to contend with persistent deficits on its trade balance (Figure 12.3). Remittances have proved to be an important and stable source of external finance to cushion the impact of a weak merchandise trade account. Indeed, as previously noted, remittances can have a stabilising effect at times of crises. For instance, as the Sri Lankan economy was subject to the external supply-side shock of a rapid rise in international oil prices during 2004-2008, a sharp deterioration in the trade account was offset by higher inflows of remittances.[15] While the increase in 2005 is explained by the post-

15. The sharp increase in remittance inflows in 2005 is largely associated with the December 2004 tsunami that claimed the lives of nearly 40,000 people in Sri Lanka.

Figure 12.2

Comparative Sources of Foreign Capital Inflows

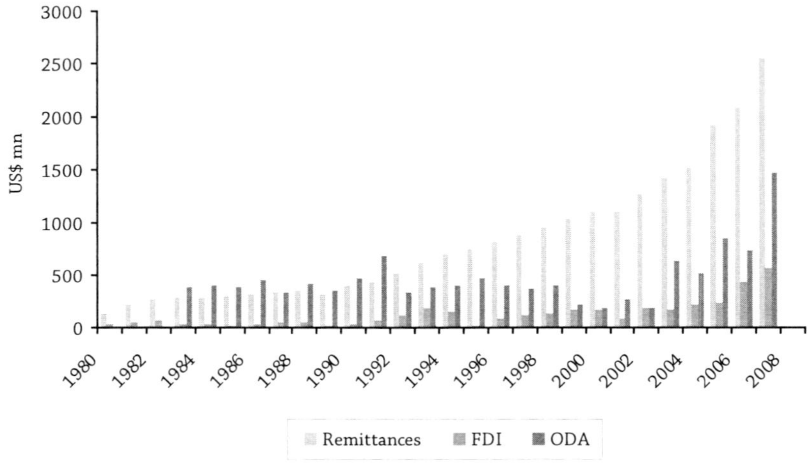

Source: Central Bank of Sri Lanka, *Annual Report*, various issues.

tsunami related inflows, remittance flows continued to remain robust in the wake of the boom in oil exporting countries of the Middle East. For instance, during 2005-2007, while export earnings growth averaged 12 per cent per annum, the growth in remittance inflows rose at an average of 19 per cent per annum.

While a sizeable surge in inflows that leads to a real exchange rate appreciation may hold adverse implications for the competitiveness of the export sector, there is little evidence to suggest that this has been a factor in Sri Lanka. Remittance inflows have been stable and persistent over a long period of time, negating any possible 'Dutch disease' effects.

Contribution of Remittances to National Savings

In addition to providing financial resources for households at the micro level, remittances are an important source of national savings that can lift the investment rate of a country. The savings take the form of direct investment, cash, or deposits into the financial system. A relatively low volume of domestic savings—averaging around 17 per cent of GDP—has been a constraining factor in attempts to lift

Figure 12.3

Remittances and BoP Support

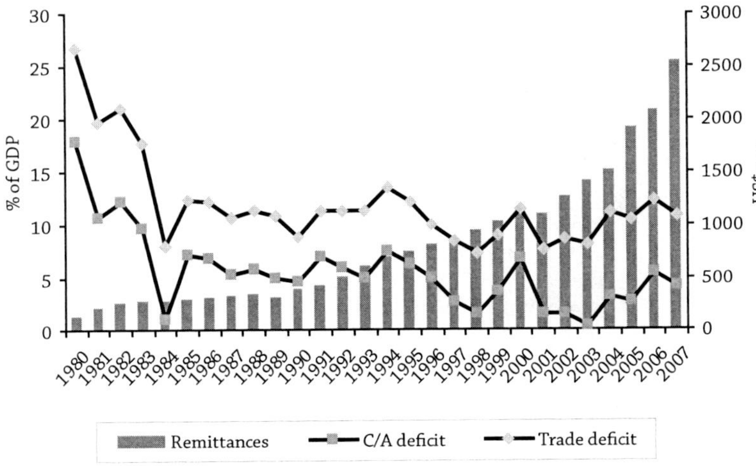

Source: Central Bank of Sri Lanka, *Annual Report*, various issues.

Sri Lanka's investment rate (Table 12.3). Due largely to remittance inflows,[16] Sri Lanka has managed to maintain a much higher rate of national savings and thus, a higher rate of total investment in the economy. While inflows that increase investment are likely to have a positive effect on economic growth, a good investment climate—including the presence of a well-developed financial system—will partly determine the extent to which remittances are invested in physical and human capital.

Table 12.3

Contribution of Remittances to Savings and Investment

(Per cent of GDP)

	1980-84	*1985-89*	*1990-94*	*1995-99*	*2000-04*	*2005-07*
Domestic savings	13.7	12.2	14.7	17.3	16.0	17.5
National savings	16.5	14.6	17.8	21.4	21.3	23.1
Investment	29.4	23.1	24.4	25.4	23.8	27.6

Source: Central Bank of Sri Lanka, *Annual Report*, various issues.

16. Captured by net private current transfers from abroad.

Table 12.4

Households Receiving Foreign Remittances

	No. of Migrant Hhs	*Sample Size*	*% Hhs Receiving Remit-tances*	*Remittances as a % of Hh income[1] in the Last Six Months*		*Level of Remittances (Rs) in the Last Six Months[1]*	
				Mean	*Std. Dev.*	*Mean*	*Std. Dev.*
Total	1,176	11,722	10.0	37.3	29.8	49,062	95,507
By Income Quintile							
1-poorest	129	2,346	5.5	36.1	26.1	9,597	7,691
2	180	2,345	7.7	32.2	27.9	14,709	12,977
3	210	2,343	9.0	38.2	30.2	25,436	20,128
4	270	2,344	11.5	36.1	27.8	36,669	29,006
5	387	2,344	16.5	37.3	29.8	99,661	151,044
By sector							
Urban	245	1,477	16.6	34.6	30.1	58,103	81,259
Rural	902	9,650	9.3	37.0	28.6	47,593	100,215
Estate	29	595	4.9	30.0	22.4	18,369	17,466
Total	1,176	11,722	10.0	36.3	28.8	49,062	95,507

Note: 1. Only migrant households were considered in the calculation. Calculations compare remittances in the last six months to household income in the last six months. Remittance incomes are included when calculating income quintiles.

Source: Own calculations using Central Bank, *Consumer Finance Survey Data 2003-04.*

Results: Micro Level Impacts

Impacts on Household Incomes and Expenditures

The World Bank (2006) finds that remittances can reduce poverty, improve a household's ability to withstand adverse shocks (for example, households receive higher levels of remittances during adverse health outcomes, crop failures, etc.), provide credit for household enterprises, and improve household investments on education and health.

Roughly, 11 per cent of households in Sri Lanka receive remittances from abroad. Compared to the national average, a higher per cent of urban households and richer households receive remittances from abroad (see Table 12.4).[17] Remittances account for roughly 36 to 37 per cent of the income of the household, on average. This amount remains more or less constant across different income quintiles. The remittances as a per cent of household income is lower for the estate sector (30%) compared to the other sectors. Roughly the remittance income received by households is Rs 8,177 a month (one-sixth of Rs 49,062) or 48 per cent of the mean household income (Rs 17,114)[18] per month for 2003-04.[19] These calculations are limited to money and goods received by households while their family members are abroad. Money and goods brought home by returnee migrants are not captured in these calculations. Given that most low skilled workers bring majority of their earnings in person when returning from abroad, the calculations for poorer households would be an underestimation of the actual benefits to the household.

Using household survey data in Sri Lanka, De and Ratha (2005)[20] find that remittances can help households to move to higher income deciles. However, households in the middle income deciles are more likely to move up along the income ladder than the poorest income deciles.

As indicated earlier, comparison of expenditures by migrant and non-migrant households needs to be done carefully as the characteristics of migrant households can be different from non-migrant households, and as these differences can influence the expenditure patterns. In order to control for such biases, we selected a group of households with characteristics similar to migrant households using propensity score matching techniques, referred to as the matched-non-migrant households. The comparisons for mean expenditure levels for non-migrant households in general as well as for matched-non-migrant households are given in Table 12.5. As

17. Remittance incomes are included when calculating income quintiles. It is possible that the income quintiles may change, if remittance incomes are not considered when calculating income quintiles.

18. *Central Bank Annual Report, 2005.*

19. These calculations include in-kind benefits received by households from relatives living abroad, but does not include money and goods brought home by returnee migrants.

20. As described in World Bank (2006).

Table 12.5

Comparison of Expenditure and Income by Migrant and Non-migrant Households (Hh), with Controls for Selection Bias Using Propensity Score Matching Techniques

Variable	*Method*[1]	*Migrant Hh*	*Non-migrant Hh*	*Differ-ence*	*S.E.*	*T-stat*
Expenditure (year prior to the survey)						
Total expenditure	Unmatched	248,432	198,157	50,275	4,216	12
	Matched	247,664	209,396	38,268	12,110	3
Food expenditure	Unmatched	95,110	82,805	12,305	791	16
	Matched	95,136	82,103	13,033	2,036	6
Non-food expenditure	Unmatched	117,411	89,231	28,180	2,780	10
	Matched	116,566	87,522	29,044	5,756	5
Expenditure on durable goods	Unmatched	19,850	13,935	5,916	1,763	3
	Matched	19,908	28,890	(8,982)	7,993	(1)
Health expenditure	Unmatched	8,915	7,138	1,777	559	3
	Matched	8,901	6,607	2,294	1,007	2
Education expenditure	Unmatched	7,145	5,048	2,098	447	5
	Matched	7,152	4,273	2,879	878	3
Income (six months prior to the survey)						
Income from properties[2]	unmatched	16,835	12,692	4,144	710	6
	matched	16,642	12,091	4,551	1,382	3
Income from Hh financial assets[3]	unmatched	7,345	4,001	3,344	1,354	2
	matched	7,361	3,652	3,708	2,226	2
Income from Hh physical assets[4]	unmatched	107,524	25,645	81,879	19,438	4
	matched	107,835	9,220	98,616	31,418	3
Number of income sources per Hh	unmatched	5.5	5.4	0.1	0.0	3.0
	matched	5.5	5.1	0.4	0.1	4.0
Education and health outcomes						
Morbidity rate age <=14	Unmatched	0.12	0.14	-0.02	0.01	-1.8
	Matched	0.12	0.11	0.01	0.02	0.3
School enrollment age>=5 & <=14	Unmatched	0.92	0.93	-0.02	0.01	-1.4
	Matched	0.92	0.94	-0.02	0.02	-1.1

Notes: 1. The control group in the unmatched method is all non-migrant households. The control group in the matched method is households that look similar to migrant households. In the matched method, the control group is selected using propensity score.

2. Rent/lease income from immovable property; movable property; imputed rent if resident in own house; income from property.

3. Savings accounts; term deposits; govt. securities; private sector investment.

4. Land and buildings; machinery, equipment etc.; livestock; physical stocks and receivables.

Source: Own calculations using *Consumer Finance 2003-04* data.

seen, in the matched sample, migrant households spent Rs 38,000 more annually than non-migrant households. This higher spending in total household expenditure is due to higher spending on food, non-food items, health, and education expenditure by migrant households. However, expenditure on durable goods was lower in

Table 12.6

Comparison of Expenditure and Income by Migrant and Non-migrant Households (Hh), with Controls for Selection Bias Using Propensity Score Matching Techniques

		Households				
Variable	*Method*[1]	*Migrant*	*Non-migrant*	*Difference*	*S.E.*	*T-stat*
Education and health outcomes						
Morbidity rate age <=14	Unmatched	0.12	0.14	-0.02	0.01	-1.8
	Matched	0.12	0.11	0.01	0.02	0.3
School enrollment age>=5 & <=14	Unmatched	0.92	0.93	-0.02	0.01	-1.4
	Matched	0.92	0.94	-0.02	0.02	-1.1
Health outcomes by sector						
Morbidity rate age <=14 (Urban)	Unmatched	0.12	0.12	0.00	0.03	-0.08
	Matched	0.12	0.08	0.04	0.07	0.6
Morbidity rate age <=14 (Rural)	Unmatched	0.12	0.15	-0.03	0.01	-2.02
	Matched	0.12	0.13	0.00	0.03	-0.18
Morbidity rate age <=14 (Estate)	Unmatched	0.11	0.09	0.02	0.05	0.34
	Matched	0.11	0.23	-0.11	0.13	-0.87
Education outcomes by sector						
School enrollment age>=5 & <=14 (Urban)	Unmatched	0.91	0.93	-0.01	0.03	-0.46
	Matched	0.91	0.97	-0.06	0.05	-1.09
School enrollment age>=5 & <=14 (Rural)	Unmatched	0.92	0.93	-0.01	0.01	-1.13
	Matched	0.92	0.93	-0.01	0.02	-0.49
School enrollment age>=5 & <=14 (Estate)	Unmatched	0.85	0.91	-0.06	0.06	-1.04
	Matched	0.85	0.88	-0.04	0.14	-0.28

Notes: 1. The control group in the unmatched method is all non-migrant households. The control group in the matched method is households that look similar to migrant households. In the matched method, the control group is selected using propensity score.

Source: Own calculations using *Consumer Finance 2003-04* data.

migrant households compared to matched-non-migrant households. All these differences are statistically significant at one per cent level except expenditure on durable goods which is significant at five per cent level.

Compared to matched-non-migrant households, migrant households received a higher level of income from properties, financial and physical assets. Furthermore, the migrant households receive income from a higher number of sources (i.e. migrant houses have a more diverse set of income sources). Having access to a diverse set of income sources is found to increase the coping strategies of households during shocks. The income from household physical assets was particularly high for migrant households. These estimates were also statistically significant at one per cent level. These estimates shows that at least, economically and on average, migrant households are better off compared to non-migrant households.

Impacts on Health and Education

Migration has mixed effects on health and education of the migrant households. On one hand, migration leads to greater investments in education and health due to increased wealth and better health knowledge. However, the health and education outcomes of households of migrants are mixed and are dependent on both the characteristics of the migrant and their household. Remittances, on one hand, provide better education and health opportunities to household members. However, migration of parents can leave families of young children with inadequate guidance and an additional burden of household responsibilities which can lead to higher school absenteeism, dropping out of school, poor nutrition and health care of children, especially in younger children, and substance abuse—especially in older children.[21] Given that Sri Lanka has a rapidly ageing population, the breakdown of traditional family support for elderly due to migration is a concern, both for households and policy makers.

21. IOM (2000).

Estimates for expenditure on health and education by migrant, non-migrant matched households show that on average, investments on health and education are indeed higher for migrant households (see Table 12.5) at statistically significant levels. However, school enrollment and morbidity level indicators did not show statistically significant differences between migrant and non-migrant households at the national or the sub-national sectoral levels (see Table 12.6). It is possible that although there is no statistically significant difference in these indicators at the national level there could be differences at the sub-national level among certain population groups.[22]

Results: Enhancing Quality and Reach of Remittance Flows to Sri Lanka

Enhancing Remittance Inflows to Sri Lanka

As discussed in the earlier sections of the chapter, the development impacts of migrant remittance inflows at both the macro and micro levels are significant. However, these impacts are to a great extent dependent on whether remittances are sent through formal or informal channels. Informal channels/informal money transfer systems[23] can be identified as money transferring mechanisms which are outside the conventional, regulated financial system.

In order to minimise the associated negative impacts of money channelled through informal channels, governments have undertaken measures to discourage and curtail informal money transactions. Development benefits of remittances at the country level can be maximised when it is channelled through formal channels as they open up paths for savings and investments.

---

22. Although the differences in education and health outcomes for more detailed indicators were examined (e.g., narrower age groups), these also did not result in any significant differences between the migrant and non-migrant households. For brevity, these results are not reported.

23. Informal transfers are also referred to as 'alternative remittance systems', 'poor man's private banking vehicle', 'underground banking', 'ethnic banking' and 'informal value transfer business'

The most significant drawback of informal remittances is the foregone foreign exchange for the recipient country. As illustrated in Figure 12.4, in an informal remittance transaction, the money sender in the host country contacts a middle man who is an agent of the informal system—this person might be a shopkeeper or a money lender in the town.[24] The money sender gives the middle man the money with the basic details of the recipient, like the name and the address.[25] The agent in the host country informs his agent to provide the due amount to the recipient or his bank account through a call or message. Within this system there is no physical movement of money. As a result, the foreign exchange may never reach the beneficiary's country or if it does, it is usually after a lag. As a result the country loses foreign currency which is crucial for BoP requirements, external reserves positions, etc.

The loss of government revenue is another disadvantage for the government when money is remitted informally. It is easy to evade taxes when using informal channels as the information (of transactions) never reaches the formal financial systems. And this leads to a loss of tax revenue to the government. Furthermore, informally channelled remittances are highly vulnerable to exploitation. Anonymity is possible through informal remittances and thus, there is a concern that financial flows are much more vulnerable to illegal activities (Institute of Policy Studies [IPS] of Sri Lanka, 2008).

At the household level, remittances that are informally channelled are more likely to be used for immediate consumption rather than for savings and investment. This is mainly due to the lack of motivation to save when money is received through informal channels. Contrary to this, if remittances are channelled through formal means, banking activities of remittance recipients and senders tend to gradually increase. These increased banking activities open up paths for savings and investments. Formal channels always motivate people to save their remittances rather

24. Many agents are known to run a legitimate business in addition to the financial services they provide.

25. However, if the money sender sent his money through this person several times and if he is familiar with the agent, this too is unnecessary.

Figure 12.4

Basic Informal Remittance Transaction

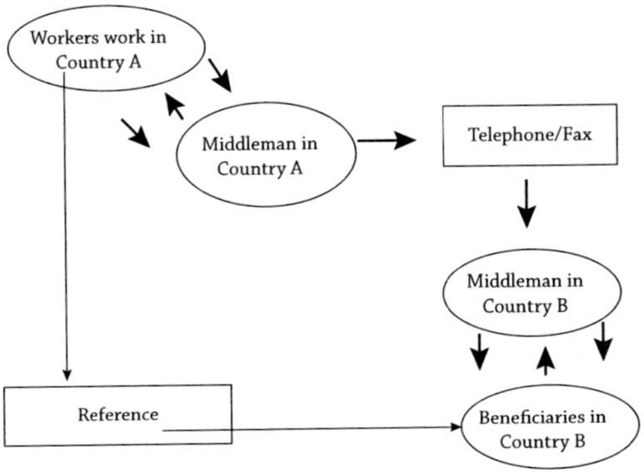

Source: Maimbo (2004).

than using them for immediate consumption. For example, 20 per cent of the remittances channelled through People's Bank in Sri Lanka cannot be withdrawn immediately. This restriction makes it necessary for customers to save some portion of the remittances they receive.

Remittance of money through formal channels could enhance a country's development process; however, in spite of these benefits and the varying government policies in place to encourage the use of formal channels, informal transfers are still prominent in many remittance-receiving countries (Siegel and Lucke, 2009).

Econometric analysis and available household surveys suggest that unrecorded flows through informal channels may conservatively add as much as to 50 per cent or more to recorded remittances (World Bank, 2006). These large numbers of informal transactions not only prevent remittances from being used productively but also increase the risk of such money being used for illegal activities such as money laundering and terrorism. In the case of Sri Lanka, Lasagabaster *et al.* (2005a) have estimated that unrecorded remittances could have been as much as 45 per cent of total private remittances in the mid-1990s.

The literature points to various reasons as to why migrants use informal channels to remit money. These include:

(i) Cost effectiveness—agents usually take a small commission, often lower than official bank rates. They often have low overheads and generate profit through small commissions and exchange rate speculations.

(ii) Efficiency and safety—transactions take very little time to be completed and is a safe, reliable way to move funds especially in countries plagued by political insecurity.

(iii) Flexibility and non-bureaucratic nature—informal channels are attractive to remitters who have tax, immigration and other legal concerns due to the informal nature of the transactions.

(iv) Anonymity—the transactions do not require documentation and does not usually have a paper trail, which makes it difficult to track these transactions.

Hernandez-Coss (2005; 2005a) study on the US-Mexico and Canada-Vietnam remittance corridors classifies transfer channel determinants under the broad headings of personal incentives, customer service incentives, and economic incentives. Personal incentives include anonymity/secrecy, cultural familiarity and personal contacts with economic incentives including speed, cost, secondary benefits and legal or regulatory environment.

Orozco (2003) based on a review of country experiences states that among other factors, access to information, cultural practices, and educational and income status of the recipient and sender influence the choice of transfer method. Amuedo-Dorantes and Pozo's study (2005) based on an econometric analysis identifies the migrant's legal status, sector of employment, family networks in the host country, and length of stay in the host country as important determinants.

Furthermore, many studies such as Buencamino and Gorbunov (2002), Higazi (2005) and Hear *et al.* (2005) find factors like cost, convenience, speed, security, trust and familiarity playing a major role in deciding the channels that migrants choose to transfer remittances.

In this background, this section of the chapter examines the current status of the formal and informal infrastructure for remittances in the country focusing on the services offered and their effectiveness. The section also examines how to encourage the use of formal channels. The services and their effectiveness can be examined using various indicators.

This study mainly uses the following indicators: (i) transaction cost; (ii) speed; (iii) outreach; and (iv) other incentives.

Transaction Costs

Transaction cost plays a large role in the choice of remittance method. It varies widely across different means of remitting money. The fee is determined by several factors such as competition and volume of the remittance. In general, transaction cost is relatively small for large remittances, but it is a concern for small remittance. Costs also vary across remitting institutions.

Speed

Speed is another important factor which determines the choice of money transfer system. Currently well developed technology has reduced the time taken for money transfers.

Outreach

Greater outreach of financial services is an important factor in attracting remittances to formal channels. It will reduce the time and travelling cost of the beneficiary as well as the time spent by the sender to reach the services. Outreach of different financial institutions varies depending on the cost of expansion.

Other Factors

There are several other factors which determine the choice of money transfer system of migrant workers. They include incentives provided (over the applicable general interest rates), investment opportunities, cultural familiarity and convenience.

The analyses in this chapter were based on information collected by both primary and secondary sources. The information gathered by existing literature was corroborated by interviews carried out with different stakeholders. Stakeholder interviews were carried out with selected main institutions—both government and private—involved in the areas of foreign employment and remittances. Seven commercial banks were interviewed—3 government and 4 private banks—in order to get an understanding of the different types of products and services they offer to the migrant workers. Two government agencies and the

ALFEA were interviewed to identify the government's role in attracting remittances to the country and also the role of the licenced agents in the process. Apart from the institutions, nine return migrants were interviewed (four from the Colombo district, two from Kandy district and three from the Kurunegala district). They were representative of both skilled and low skilled workers and belonged to the ethnic groups of Sinhala, Tamil and Muslims.

Formal Channels of Remitting Money in Sri Lanka and Extended Services

Formal (regulated) channels of remitting money are those that fall under a regulated financial system, with the three main channels of formal remittance services in Sri Lanka being the commercial banks, Money Transfer Businesses (MTBs) and Sri Lanka Post. Developments in institutions providing financial services and awareness of the services provided by them have played a major role in attracting foreign remittances through formal channels in Sri Lanka. Given that only formal transactions are recorded, increases in the inflow of remittances in to the country can be partly attributed to these developments. Under the Exchange Control Act of Sri Lanka, any licenced commercial bank is a full-fledged authorised dealer of foreign exchange. Apart from commercial banks, authorised dealers appointed by the Controller of Exchange, money changers and other persons appointed by the Central Bank can engage in limited foreign exchange transactions.[26]

Commercial Banks

Sri Lanka has a fairly large banking network with 22 licenced commercial banks operating in the country. These include 11 domestic banks who offer a wide range of products with especially the government banks distributed across the country including in the North and East. The 11 foreign banks on the other hand are more restricted to providing services to a relatively lower number of clientele in the main cities.

---

26. Money changes are authorised to purchase foreign currency notes and exchange them for any other currency but are not authorised to sell foreign exchange for Sri Lankan rupees.

Available Means of Remittances

It is possible to identify 3 main options that remitters can use to send money: (i) bank drafts; (ii) bank telegraphics (i.e. telex, Society for Worldwide Interbank Financial Telecommunication (SWIFT)); and (iii) exchange houses. Sending money through SWIFT is very fast but expensive. Nevertheless, it is the method used by most to transfer money from one bank to another. On the other hand, international drafts are one of the least expensive means of transferring money but take the longest time to process. Dollar drafts take about two weeks to be processed and other currencies take more than two weeks. Money sent through these means is either collected over the counter or is transferred to the relevant products offered by banks. One leading private bank quoted that 65 per cent of remittances they receive are over the counter transactions with no savings resulting from the transaction. According to the banks, apart from the rupee accounts the most popular foreign currency account is the NRFC account. NRFCs are popular since no bank charges are imposed and they are tax exempt.[27] Interviews with return migrants who have worked as housemaids show that their money have been sent mainly to rupee accounts whereas, the more educated and skilled workers have sent money to NRFC accounts.

Additionally, web based money transfer systems like 'e-Exchange', 'People's eRemittance', 'Bank of Ceylon (BOC) e-cash', 'Sampath e-remittance Service' have enabled Sri Lankan expatriates to make instant money transfers from many countries around the world. Furthermore, many banks are also linked with MTBs like Western Union and Money Gram, providing migrant workers and expatriates a range of products and services for remitting money. These MTBs have been able to attract customers not only through their quick services but also through special offers. For example, one commercial bank that has linked up with Western Union provides a free mobile phone for any transaction through the Western Union done via their bank. With the

27. However, if money is sent to a NRFC in a particular bank via another commercial bank a nominal fee of Rs 100 for a remittance amount of up to Rs 100,000 is charged. The exact amount charged may differ from bank to bank. However, the rates given here are those charged on average and have been extracted from interviews conducted with local banks only.

private banking sector providing services like 'Holiday Banking' and '365 Day Banking' facilities, the provision of services have improved.

Compared to bank drafts, all electronic based remittances services provide quick services. Remittance receivers can obtain money in one to two days and the sender can remit money from any part of the world.

According to banks most number of remittances is received from Middle Eastern countries like Saudi Arabia, UAE and Kuwait given that a majority of Sri Lankan migrant workers are in the Middle Eastern countries. However, in terms of value it is the European countries that lead. The difference lies in the fact that a majority of workers in the Middle East are low/semi-skilled with relatively low salary levels whereas to those in the Western/European countries.

Interest Rate or Other Incentives

Banks provide the facility for remitters to save money in foreign exchange accounts—both savings and fixed deposit accounts—with rates being negotiable in some banks for savings of large amounts. Some banks base their interest rates on the London Interbank Offered Rate (LIBOR) and offer rates that are 0.25 per cent to 0.5 per cent above the LIBOR rate in order to attract remittances. Furthermore, in a bid to attract the flow of foreign exchange to the country the government provides a 20 per cent bonus on interest earned in NRFC accounts.[28]

There have been no difficulties in withdrawing money at the receiving end with ATM (automated teller machine) facilities being provided for foreign currency accounts in many private banks. Accounts such as People's Banks 'Doodaru Ethera Isuru' also provide the facility for parents to open foreign currency accounts for their children with an interest rate higher than the prevailing NRFC/RFC (Resident Foreign Currency) interest rates.[29]

---

28. Nevertheless, the effectives of this bonus is questionable as it is paid on interest on all existent NRFC accounts in the country, not taking into consideration if they have been active or not in the recent years. As bankers point out, it might prove to be a loss to the country if the government has to pay more as bonus than the actual inflow of foreign exchange to the country.

29. NRFCs for children staying with parents abroad and RFCs for children whose parents are employed abroad but the children are in Sri Lanka.

Other incentives provided by banks in order to attract worker remittances include the provision of housing and self employment loans at low interest, credit card facilities, overdraft facilities, lottery schemes with higher chances of winning when the balance is higher, etc. The provision of insurance schemes is not common with only a few banks providing this incentive, for example the Millenium Shield Life Insurance cover of the Hatton National Bank. Many banks promote their services locally as well as in other countries where the concentration of Sri Lankan workers is high. Promotions are carried out through radio and television channels aired abroad, local magazines circulating in foreign countries, brochures and websites. For example, banking officers have programmes on radio channels and provide information on how to address banking issues. Some also sponsor and cover events such as the Independence Day and special programmes held during the festival periods.

Transaction Costs

When remitting money the sender has to bear a cost at the point of sending money as well as at the receiving point. This is with the exception of sending money to NRFCs and RFC. In order to encourage the flow of foreign exchange to the country no commission is charged for NRFC and RFC accounts and the money sent to these accounts is tax free. When sending money, the cost they have to bear at the remitters end is higher while the Sri Lankan bank charges are quite nominal. When money is sent to a bank to be transferred to an account in another bank, the bank charges a flat rate of Rs 500. However, if the money is sent to a rupee account maintained in that bank the charge is lower—between Rs 100-Rs 150. If money is taken over the counter, the fee is Rs 150.

The bank charges at the sending point can differ from country to country and according to the amount sent. For example at the time of writing, bank-to-bank charges from London were around UK£ 3 (Rs 555) for transactions up to UK£ 200 (Rs 36,944), UK£ 5 (Rs 924) for transactions between 200-1000 (Rs 36,944-Rs 184,720), UK£ 10 (Rs 1847) for transactions between 1000-5000 (Rs 184,720-Rs 923,600) and UK£ 20 (Rs 3694) for transactions over UK£ 5000 (Rs 923,600). If money is sent from UAE bank-to-bank charges are 15 dirham (Rs 469). However, if it is a draft the bank charges are 5 dirham (Rs 156).

Outreach

State and private banks offer their services through 2,068 branches and 2,665 other service outlets in the country (see Table 12.7 for details). Over the years the state banks, the BOC and the People's Bank (PB) have been able to attract a majority of remittances coming through the formal channel (see Table 12.8). This is mainly due to their ability to outreach; with the BOC having 303 branches and the PB 640 branches which facilitate remittances across the country including in the North and the East. In addition to this, PB has around 400 agents and correspondents in 105 countries. This wide network of the state banks has helped them gain a major share in the remittances market of the country.

Table 12.7

Distribution of Banks and Bank Branches

Total no. of LCB branches and outlets	4,733
Branches	2,068
Domestic bank branches	1,894
Main branches	1,355
Extension/Pay offices/Service counters	539
Overseas branches	12
Foreign bank branches and other outlets	174
Branches	41
Other outlets	133
Student savings units	2,665

Source: Central Bank of Sri Lanka, *Annual Report* (2008).

Several banks[30] have Sri Lankan Business Promotion Officers (BPOs) in foreign countries that are conversant in all three major languages used in Sri Lanka, Sinhala, Tamil and English. This is in order to facilitate transactions to their customers working in foreign countries. Given the number of Sri Lankans working, a majority of the BPOs are based in the

30. i.e. Sampath Bank, Commercial Bank, National Savings Bank.

Table 12.8

Remittances by Licenced Commercial Banks

(Million Rupees)

Institution	*2002*	*2003*	*2004*	*2004 (% of total)*
Bank of Ceylon	741.8	772.0	881.4	56.4
People's Bank	183.3	208.9	232.7	19
Seylan Bank	102.5	129.0	147.5	9.4
Hatton National Bank	42.7	57.5	81.6	5.2
Commercial Bank	63.7	79.6	93.4	6.0
Sampath Bank	58.8	75.4	76.1	9
Others	92	91.6	51.2	3.3
Total	1,287.0	1,410	1,563.9	100.0

Source: Lasagabaster *et al.*, (2005a).

Middle Eastern countries like UAE, Jordan, Qatar and Kuwait. As a large number of house maids work in these countries, the BPOs have been helpful in minimising language problems in communicating and filling up relevant forms. Apart from the Middle Eastern countries, some banks have BPOs operating in countries like Italy and London. Apart from the BPOs, Sri Lankan agents are also available in countries like Qatar, Hong Kong, Canada, Oman, Australia, Bahrain, and Kuwait, with a majority of them operating in Exchange Houses.

Money Transfer Businesses

The role of MTBs in providing remittance services to Sri Lankan migrants is becoming increasingly important. The leading MTB in the country, Western Union, has epanded its outreach and promotes its services extensively.

Outreach

Being in the industry for over 150 years Western Union currently has over 3,007 agent locations in Sri Lanka[31] including commercial

31. Sunday Observer (2009), *http://www.sundayobserver.lk/2009/02/15/bus14.asp*

banks. With its recent link with Sri Lanka Post they have been able to further strengthen their outreach: Western Union MTB facilities are available 641 post offices across the country. Further expansion of their services at the sub-post office level in the future will be beneficial for workers from rural areas. In addition, Western Union has invested in the infrastructural development of the Postal Department.

Money Gram is another MTB that operates in Sri Lanka with its services available through the branches of BOC, Hatton National Bank, Nations Trust Bank, Commercial Bank of Ceylon, Sampath Bank and Seylan Bank.

MTBs have been a quick and easy channel of sending and receiving money with a transaction taking a few minutes to process. A personal idenification is needed to remit money; however, the requirement of other documents vary from country to country. The receiver can receive the money by producing a reference/pin number together with identification (i.e. identity card, passport). Documentation needs are minimal and with services available in over 200 countries, MTBs have proved to be an increasingly popular means of sending money.

Sri Lanka Post

Sri Lanka Post is one of the oldest government departments, providing services for over 200 years (and international money transfer services since the 1960s). Despite their wide outreach which is also their biggest strength (see Table 12.7), their paper-based system has hindered their ability of providing quick and efficient money transfer facilities to the public. In the year 2004, the postal service dealt with remittances amounting to just US$ 8 million—less than one per cent of the total market.[32]

Outreach

There is a total of 4,737 post offices distributed across the country. The breakdown is given in Table 12.9.

---

32. Lasagabaster *et al.* (2005a).

Table 12.9

Post Office Network in Sri Lanka

Post Offices	641
Sub Post Offices	3412
Agency Post Offices	684

Source: Sri Lanka Post

Available Means of Money Transfer

There are 3 instruments that a migrant worker can use in order to send money via Sri Lanka Post (subject to limitations): (i) Money Orders (MOs); (ii) British Postal Orders (POs); and (iii) Western Union. These money transfer facilities are available in all 641 post offices around the country including the North and East.

(i) MO: Money order facilities can be used by Sri Lankan migrants in 6 countries: Japan, Maldives, South Africa, UAE, Malaysia and Singapore. Although the facility was also available in the US (till 2007) and West Germany it was subsequently discontinued by those countries as Sri Lanka Post is paper-based and does not have an electronic system. Currently, around 1000 international MOs are received per year. A majority of these MOs are sent by workers in Japan although these numbers have been decreasing. Japan too has expressed their preference of Sri Lanka moving to an electronic system with a proper data base of customers in order to improve efficiency and transparency of the transactions taking place. When money is remitted through a MO, a copy of it is sent to Sri Lanka Post which is then delivered to the beneficiary. After MOs are sent to Sri Lanka and received by the post office, it takes 2-3 days to send it to the local beneficiary. However, the time it takes to reach Sri Lanka Post from the above mentioned countries differs from country to country.[33] The beneficiary can get the money by producing it to the

33. For example, it takes just 4 days for a MO to reach Sri Lanka from Japan as they send them through express mail service whereas it takes as long as 1-3 weeks when one is sent from the UAE. Sri Lanka Post has no control over the time taken by post offices in other countries in sending the MOs.

particular post office to which it is sent, and should be able to confirm identity before receiving money.

(ii) British POs: Sri Lankans in UK can use British POs in order to remit their money. However, in this case the postal order which the remitter gets from the post office in the UK is posted directly by the remitter to the beneficiary in Sri Lanka after which the beneficiary can receive the money by producing the postal order at any of the 641 post offices. Although previously around 2000 British POs were received on average per month, this has come down drastically to about 200. This is mainly due to the faster electronic remitting services available now.

(iii) Western Union: Sri Lanka Post linked up with the money transfer system, Western Union from February 2009. The services are provided through the 641 post offices across the country. In order to provide their services Western Union has provided the computers that are needed although the human resources and other costs are borne by Sri Lanka Post. A transaction takes about five minutes on average after which money can be received by the beneficiary by producing the pin number to any post office. Although, this facility has been available only for about three months, Sri Lanka Post says it has already attracted a substantial amount of remittances.

It has to be noted that the exchange rate used by Sri Lanka Post for both MOs and POs is a weekly rate and not a daily rate. This rate is decided based on the Central Bank rates and, in addition 5 per cent is reduced from the exchange rate as service charge. The rate is weekly especially due to the administrative difficulties and costs Sri Lanka Post would have to bear if they were to have a daily rate (i.e. as there is no electronic system the rates would have to be faxed to all 641 post offices everyday). Based on the exchange rate fluctuations, the use of a weekly exchange rate may be advantageous or disadvantageous. Post offices provide services six days a week. The working hours differ from post office to post office with some post offices even working from 5 AM in the morning to 9 PM in the night.[34] This can be another incentive to use Sri Lanka Post given that a majority of banks (especially branches out of the cities) are closed on Saturdays. Other advantages of using Sri Lanka Post is to send MOs and POs include: (i) widest coverage and the ability to reach people in very rural areas; (ii) it is not profit based so services are provided at the lowest cost; (iii) money sent through MOs and POs are not taxed; (iv) no verification is sought from the sender like in the banks; and (v) it takes only 2-3 days to process after a MO reaches Sri Lanka.[35]

Sri Lanka Post is working on introducing the International Financial System (IFS), an electronic system which would enable them to be quicker and efficient in providing their services. This has been developed by the Universal Postal Union which has about 191 countries as its members.[36] This will not only enable Sri Lanka Post to provide a more efficient and quicker service to workers who remit money but it will also expand the outreach of services abroad. These services are currently available only in 7 countries.

Encouragingly, Sri Lanka Post is aware of the areas that they should develop in order to be a more attractive channel for remitting money. However, being a government department one of the major hindrances include the long and time consuming processes in getting funds and proposals accepted. Some existing rules and regulations[37] and also the lack of an IT skilled technical support in Sri Lanka Post poses a problem to the introduction of the IFS system.

34. Post offices are graded as supra-level, class 1, class 2, sub post offices and agency post offices. It is mainly the supra-level one's which provide long working hours.

35. This is subject to that a draft has all the necessary details filled correctly. There is about a month's delay in the process of verifying when incomplete addresses are given and in instances where the beneficiaries name is not given.

36. According to Sri Lanka Post, IFS is already available in 38 countries with 40 members in the testing process.

37. Sri Lanka Post cannot advertise its products in the media thereby, limiting dissemination of product information, etc.

Informal Remittance Systems in Sri Lanka, their Usage and Recent Trends

In different parts of the world, there are different types of informal transfer systems in operation, i.e. *fei ch'ien* in China, *hundi* in South Asia (Pakistan and Bangladesh), hawala in North Africa, Middle East and South Asia, *padala* in Philippines, *hui kuan* in Hong Kong and *phei kwan* in Thailand. Although names may differ, all these systems have a common operational method with *hawala* and *hundi* being the most common money transfer systems in South Asia. Global estimates suggests that informal channels continue to account for a significant share of remittance flows and this is likely to be the case for Sri Lanka as well (Institute of Policy Studies of Sri Lanka, 2008). There is no reliable information on informal money transfer systems in the country but estimates suggest that around 50 per cent of remittances are channelled through informal systems.[38]

Of the nine return migrants that were interviewed, only one had used an informal channel to send money to Sri Lanka and that too just once as the migrant did not send money regularly to Sri Lanka. It is interesting to note that although it was attempted to find migrants who had used informal channels to send money, during the course of the study, it was not successful. All those we spoke to had used formal channels to send money to their relatives back home. The interviews suggested that the usage of informal channels in Sri Lanka have lowered with improvements in the formal infrastructure over time and the better flow of information to the masses. The following analyses were based largely on literature as well as on interviews held with the banking sector and government agencies. Due to the unavailability of data and information on informal channels, the study was unable to determine the type of informal transfer system that is used more commonly in Sri Lanka. The authors feel that a large survey of return migrants that have used informal channels would have to be carried out to capture more details on informal money transfer channels.

38. Foundation for Development Cooperation (2007).

Reasons for Sri Lankan Migrants to Use Informal Transfer Systems

Absence or Non-performance of the Formal Financial Sector

Lasagabaster *et al.* (2005) have identified the absence or the non-performance of the formal financial sector to be a major reason for migrants to use informal money transfer systems. The study highlights that migrants from conflict affected areas in Sri Lanka prefer to use informal channels as the formal financial services available in these areas are limited. Remittance recipients in these areas also prefer to use the informal sector as they find it difficult to collect money from formal financial institutions.

However, in the recent past the formal financial sector has been developing fast with advanced remittance services being offered by a majority of institutions. Interviews illustrated that while skilled migrants are usually aware of formal remittance options all semi-skilled and unskilled migrant workers are informed about these services through pre departure trainings conducted by the SLBFE. Therefore, this study does not see conventional financial systems or migrants' unawareness about remittances services as reasons for the use of informal channels. With regards to the cost of transaction, most of the formal channels offer their services at a minimum cost as described previously in the study. However, the transaction cost at the destination countries can be high. As can be seen in Table 12.10, a migrant who is in UK has to bear a cost of US$ 16.28 to remit US$ 200 to Sri Lanka during the first quarter of this year. It is around eight per cent of the amount one remits.

Table 12.10

Average Total Cost of Remittance, 1st Quarter, 2009

	From	
Amount of Money (US$)	*Italy*	*United Kingdom*
200	15.38	16.28
500	27.28	23.98

Source: http://remittanceprices.worldbank.org/CountryCorridors/

In addition, the outreach of the conventional financial services is better in Sri Lanka. All government banks and most of the local private banks operate in the Northern and Eastern provinces in the country, with services to be expanded with the end of the conflict. Western Union, which is one of the leading money transfer Business in Sri Lanka has excellent outreach through its agreement with Sri Lanka Post. The quality of the local outreach of the formal financial services is not further questionable. In addition to the local outreach, the Sri Lankan financial sector has spread its wings to some extent in the global market. However, this branch network and correspondent banks together with business development agents are not sufficient to provide door-to-door services as the informal sector does. Therefore, seemingly the efforts to attract more remittances to the formal channels at the destination end are still in the initial stages. Most of the visited financial institutions identified stringent government rules in foreign countries and high costs in expanding services to other countries as major barriers for further improving their services.

Cultural Reasons

Cultural aspects, especially language barriers have been cited as a major reason for migrants to use informal channels. It is reported that in Italy about 45 per cent of migrant workers use informal channels to send their remittances as they are not familiar with the procedures and the language used in Italian banks (Giggi, 2006).[39] On the other hand, informal sector service providers are able to provide door-to-door service for their customers. Informal service providers in destination countries visit migrants' work place and collect money which they need to send to Sri Lanka. This system is mostly preferred by the women who work in the Middle Eastern countries where they are not permitted to go out often and remit their earnings due to cultural reasons in those countries. However, interviews revealed that the number of transactions via informal transfers is none/negligible from the Middle Eastern countries due to the strict regulations in those countries.

39. As quoted in Foundation for the Development Cooperation (2007).

However, in the interviews carried out for the current study it was suggested that language is not a main barrier in sending money through the formal channel for a majority of Sri Lankan workers. Remittances of salaries of many housemaids in Middle Eastern countries are done by the head of the households where they work, thereby eliminating the need for them to personally visit banks/exchange houses. However, in rare occasions where they visit these institutions they get the householder to write the required information in English which is then presented at the banks/exchange houses. The banking officers use these information to fill up the forms on behalf of the migrant workers. It was mentioned by some that Tamil speaking migrants have an advantage with many South Indian Tamil speaking people working in exchange centers/ banks in popular destination countries of Sri Lankans. Nevertheless, the SLBFE has taken measures to minimise the language barrier by making it compulsory for housemaids who are unable to read/write to come for training programmes where they are taught the basics, i.e. to write the basic information, to place a signature, etc.

Being Undocumented Migrants

Undocumented migrants are unable to work with formal financial institutions as they are unable to present the required documents. A study carried out by Foundation for Development Cooperation (2007) also confirms this phenomenon. It highlights that undocumented workers who migrate from Sri Lanka due to the civil war in the Northern and Eastern parts of Sri Lanka for more than 20 years have increased. Foundation for Development Cooperation (2007) states that the total number of workers who have left the country without official travel documents is estimated to be in the range of 700,000 to 1,000,000.

Workers with Expired Visa and First Time Migrants

Foundation for Development Cooperation (2007) identifies workers with expired visas and first time migrants as two groups who mostly use informal money transfer systems. There are some Sri Lankan migrants in destination countries who have expired visas and are waiting to renew it. This temporary condition may lead to them using the informal systems as they are unable to present the required documents. The other group on the other hand has all the documents needed to open an account in the host country. However, the banks in host countries ask for a minimum amount of money to be saved when opening an account which is not feasible for unskilled workers who work at lower wages. It takes several months for them to collect the required money. Simultaneously, they have to remit money to Sri Lanka to repay their loans borrowed to cover the migration cost and to feed others left behind at home. Therefore, migrant workers tend to use informal channels to remit money until they open bank accounts.

Tax Evasion and Avoidance of Exchange Control

Interviews with stakeholders revealed that tax evasion and avoidance of exchange control are strong motivations for migrants to use informal channels. However, this issue can be overcome to a certain extent by using Sri Lanka Post to remit money. According to Sri Lanka Post, their transactions are not subjected to tax. But certain inefficiencies in the systems, as discussed before, may pose a hindrance.

Furthermore, when sending money through informal channels exchange rate fluctuations are not taken into consideration. Also, there is only one rate applied and no buying and selling rate difference affects the amount received by the beneficiary. The unified rate extended by the informal channels have been another attraction of the informal sector to migrants, due to the certainty of the amount received by the beneficiary based in the home country.

Irregular Money Transactions

In addition to the first time migrants and undocumented workers, this study finds that another group of migrants who use informal money transfer systems are irregular money senders. These migrants do not send money regularly to the country as they do not have responsibilities like regular remittance senders. These types of migrants send money to Sri Lanka only when there is an urgent need. They dislike going to financial institutions and opening accounts as they do not use these accounts regularly. They cite convenience as a reason for sending money thorough informal channels.

Table 12.11 provides a summary of the formal and informal channels in terms of speed, transaction cost and outreach. The efficiency of these channels vary depending on the product a migrant would choose to use within these channels. The transaction costs differ based on the products. Also, depending on the urgency and cost requirements, migrants have a variety of products to choose from. Therefore, the best form of product/service suitable for a migrant would depend on his/her needs, requirements, and capacities.

Table 12.11

Summary of the Formal and Informal Channels

Channel	*Products and Services*	*Time Taken*	*Transaction Cost*	*Outreach*
Banks	Bank Drafts Bank Telegraphics Web based	High Low Low	Low Medium-High High	Government banks- high Private banks - moderate Foreign banks- low
MTB		Low	Medium-High	High
Post office network	MO BO	High (2 days-3 weeks) Depends on airmail	Based on Central Bank rate	High
Informal channels	Information not sufficient to reach conclusions	Low	Low	Not an issue as money is transferred to bank accounts

Source: Own compilation.

Measures to Enhance Formal Remittance Channels and the Usage of their Services in Sri Lanka

It is important for countries that measures are taken to attract remittances to the formal channels for reasons discussed previously in the paper. Measures can be undertaken locally as well as in the sending countries to develop the formal channels and to attract money sent through informal channels to the formal channel.

Measures that Can be Undertaken Locally

The government of Sri Lanka has arranged an institutional framework to maximise the development impacts of migration and remittances. Establishment of the MFEPW has been one of the most key steps taken by the government in this regard. The SLFEB and the SLFEA which fall under the Ministry have played a major role in educating migrants about remittance channels through training programmes conducted by them. As a result, even the uneducated have a fairly good knowledge of formal remittance channels and are using these channels to send money. This is a major advantage that Sri Lanka posses. In this background, a majority who use the informal channels maybe those living illegally in other countries. To reduce these inflows through illegal channels many of the measures that can be undertaken locally have to be spearheaded by the government. Many of the following measures/ recommendations have been formulated based on information gathered by stakeholder interviews to, improve the products and services offered by formal channels, lower the cost and improve the speed of using these and to develop the outreach of services in both Sri Lanka and that of the sending country.

Given the size and extent of the informal channels, it is necessary that there is strict enforcement of law in the country with authorities taking measures to minimise the operations of unauthorised agents, who operate openly in many parts of the country. This includes the activity of illegal foreign exchange dealers.

Furthermore, certain government regulations may prevent people from using formal money transfer systems. For example, the recently introduced Know Your Customer (KYC) forms that have to be filled in financial transactions are seen by some as a restriction in attracting inward remittances. The KYC form is a requirement in terms of Financial Transaction Reporting Act No. 6 of 2006. The declaration to be made by the sender (also known as 'Form 2') irrespective of the amount sent. This was by the banking sector as a deterrent in facilitating the remittance of money. It is suggested that this requirement be enforced to only those who remit large amounts of foreign currency.

The government recently established a committee to improve remittance flows to Sri Lanka and this has not been an effective body.

Such committees should be more focused, have a clear agenda and should be constructive. Awareness programmes initiated by the government like street promotions in foreign countries should be carried out to maximise their benefits taking into consideration where they are held, when they are held and the target groups.

The government must facilitate the formal channels to expand their services. Some banks who want to send BPOs to Western countries like Canada, London, UK and Cyprus to facilitate remittances, are facing difficulties in getting visas for these officers. Banks mentioned that it would be helpful if the government could facilitate the process, i.e. by providing a letter to ease the visa process. One bank also suggested the government take the initiative of opening up exchange houses abroad where there is a high concentration of Sri Lankan workers. In Italy, a deposit of about Rs 100 million has to be made with the Italian Central Bank in order to get a licence to open an exchange house. Since a financial commitment of this magnitude is a difficult task to be undertaken by a single bank, the government should take the initiative and then get the local banks to provide services in these exchange houses. This will induce banks to provide services in other countries and it will also attract Sri Lankan workers to send money via formal channels.

The government should provide special incentives like duty free access to goods especially for migrant workers. For example if duty is waived off depending on the money remitted to Sri Lanka and if these duties are waived off to buy equipment needed for self employment, etc., it will encourage workers to remit more money.

The banking network also needs to be integrated in order to promote formal channels and not work in isolation. Better integration will help the banking sector to expand services and reduce their costs.

Measures that Can be Undertaken by Remittance Sending Countries

Policies that can be taken in destination countries to drive remittances to formal channels are as important as policies taken in receiving countries to encourage migrant workers to use formal channels.

Agreements between sending and receiving countries are important in attracting remittances to formal channels. These types of agreements have several benefits. Though the expansion of the Sri Lankan bank network abroad is a good strategy to attract money to formal channels it is also costly. To open up a money exchange center or to assign, a Sri Lankan bank officer abroad as a BDO abroad is very expensive. An agreement between two countries will be a good solution to reduce this cost and thereby increase the amount of remittances which is channelled through formal channels. Bankers should ensure the full discloser of the price to the sender. In addition, this agreement should have an article which ensures the employers debit their workers' salaries into a bank account. Apart from attracting remittance into formal channels, it would ensure the legal conditions of worker remittances. It is important to have a negotiation between financial institutions in both countries to introduce prepaid card systems which allow migrant workers to send money through ATMs. When employers send their workers' earnings to the bank in their country, the bank can issue a card which can be topped up according to each transaction. Migrant workers can use this card to send money to an account in negotiated bank in receiving country and receiver can collect money from an ATM. In addition to these high costly solutions, a simple but important solution can be introduced through these agreements: that is to have orientation programmes. Migration related institutions in destination countries should conduct orientation programmes which educate migrant workers about the services offered/available in these countries.

Formal financial institutions should reduce their charges on remittance transactions by improving infrastructure facilities and by enhancing the competition among service providers. Governments of destination countries should have strict exchange control regulations to reduce the operation of informal channels in their countries. For example, as a result of strict law enforcement and punishment in the Middle East, informal channels are virtually non-existent.

Conclusions and Policy Implications

Sri Lanka has experienced varying forms and intensity of migration in post-independence decades. Temporary migration for the purpose of employment abroad began to be significant only in the late 1970s. This increase was influenced both by domestic policy shifts as well as changes in the international environment. The stock of workers abroad at present is equivalent to 20 per cent of the labour force. With the build up of migrant workers, the migrant remittance flows to the country has risen steadily. In 2007 they amounted to US$ 2.5 billion or nearly eight per cent of GDP. These statistics indicate that the impact of migrant workers and remittances on the economy are large.

The Middle East remains a key destination region for migrant workers. Around 90 per cent of total temporary migrants work in the Middle East, of this around 50 per cent is housemaids. Middle is also the most important source of remittances to the country. North America and Europe were also a significant source of remittances in the late 1980s, however, the significance of North America as a source of remittances has reduced overtime, while that of Europe has increased.

Sri Lanka is struggling to strike a balance between maximising the development benefits of migration, particularly that of remittances, at the same time protecting migrant workers and their families from the adverse impacts of migration. Over the years, the country has introduced a number of programmes to promote labour migrations while protecting the rights of the workers. In an attempt to bring together these various measures and the February 2009 Labour Migration Policy of Sri Lanka was compiled.

Sri Lanka has witnessed a steady increase in remittance inflows over the last two decades, rising from US$ 140 million in 1980 to US$ 2.5 billion by 2007—an increase from less than four per cent of GDP to nearly eight per cent of GDP over the same period. Further, compared to ODA and FDI, remittances have been the most stable as well as the largest source of foreign capital over the period. Remittances have provided significant BoP support to the country by offsetting the adverse impacts of the trade deficit during times of crisis. Further, there are indications that remittance inflows have improved national savings and lifted the level of investment rate of the country. Although high levels of remittance inflows have the potential to cause foreign exchange appreciation, this does not seem to have been a concern in Sri Lanka. These statistics indicate that at least at the macro level remittances have been beneficial to the country.

A large proportion of households (11%) in the country receive remittances. The level of remittances received by migrant households appears to be significant—being equivalent to 48 per cent of mean household income in the country. Households receiving remittances have higher levels of total expenditure, reflecting higher spending on food, non-food, health and education. These households also receive a higher level of income from other sources such as from properties, financial and physical assets. There is some evidence that remittances can help households move to higher income deciles. Remittances also increase the number of sources of incomes of households, thereby improving their ability to cope with adverse shocks. Estimates for expenditure on health and education by migrant, non-migrant households show that on average investments on health and education are indeed higher for migrant households at statistically significant levels. However, school enrollment and morbidity level indicators did not show statistically significant differences between migrant and non-migrant households at the national or the sub-national levels

However, although not discussed in detail in this chapter, there are number of costs associated with foreign employment. The lack of protection and welfare for workers and the social and psychological costs associated with migration has been of concern for policy makers for long. This is of special concern to housemaids and low skilled migrants with low education attainments. There are numerous instances where these workers have been sexually and physically abused and not properly paid for their services. Although the government has taken several steps to improve the rights and freedom of migrant workers and the welfare of families that are left behind, the effective of these measures in improving upon the present conditions is yet to be seen.

Sri Lanka has a well developed financial system with good outreach. The migrant workers too are well informed, through training prorgammes conducted by SLBFE, on the use of formal channels for remitting money and their benefits. However, some are still using informal channels as they do not have necessary documents for using formal channels. To reduce these inflows through informal channels, many of the measures that can be undertaken locally have to be spearheaded by the government. Given the size and extent of the informal channels, it is necessary that there is a strict enforcement of law—authorities should arrest unauthorised agents who operate openly in the country.

References

Amuedo-Dorantes, C. and S. Pozo (2005). "On the Use of Differing Money Transmission Methods by Mexican Immigrants", *International Migration Review* 39(3): 554-76.

Buencamino, L. and S. Gorbunov (2002). "Informal Money Transfer Systems: Opportunities and Challenges for Development Finance", *Discussion Paper* 26. United Nations Department of Economic and Social Affairs.

Central Bank of Sri Lanka (2005). *Annual Report.*

———. (2006). "External Sector Developments and Policies", *Annual Report 2006.*

———. (2008). *Annual Report.*

De, Prabal and Dilip Ratha (2005). "Remittance Income and Household Welfare: Evidence from Sri Lanka Integrated Household Survey". Unpublished paper. Washington, DC: Development Research Group, World Bank.

Dehejia, R. and S. Wahba (1998). "Propensity Score Matching Methods for Non-experimental Causal Studies", *Working Paper* No. 6829. National Bureau of Economic Research (NBER).

DNP (2008). *Public Investment 2008-2011.* Colombo: Department of National Planning, Ministry of Finance and Planning.

F. Pieke, N. Van Hear and Lindley (2005). *Synthesis Study: A Part of the Report on Informal Remittance Systems in Africa, Caribbean and Pacific (ACP) Countries.* C.O.M.P.a.S., University of Oxford.

Foundation for Development Cooperation (2007). *Policy and Regulatory Framework for Remittance: Sri Lanka.* Brisbane, Australia.

Gaggi, P. (2006). "Remittance Services: The Case of Italy". Presentation at *CPSS-WB General Principles for International Remittance Services conference.* May 10-11. Washington, D.C.

Government of Sri Lanka (1994). Act No. 21 of 1985 amended by Act No. 4 of 1994 and The Sri Lanka Bureau of Foreign Employment Regulations (The Gazette of Sri Lanka, 1985-08-28, No. 364/9).

Hernández-Coss, R. (2005). "The U.S.–Mexico Remittance Corridor: Lessons on Shifting from Informal to Formal Transfer Systems", *World Bank Working Paper No.* 47.Washington DC: The World Bank.

———. (2005a). "The U.S.-Mexico Remittance Corridor: Lessons on Shifting from Informal to Formal Transfer Systems", *World Bank Working Paper* 47.

———. (2005b). "The Canada-Vietnam Remittance Corridor: Lessons on Shifting from Informal to Formal Transfer Systems", *World Bank Working Paper* 48.

Hettige, S. (1991) "From Dependent Housewives to Breadwinners", in *CENWOR Women, Poverty and Family Survival.* Colombo: CENWOR.

Higazi, A. (2005). *Ghana Country Study: A Part of the Report on Informal Remittance Systems in Africa, Caribbean and Pacific* (ACP). C. O. M. P. a. S. (COMPAS), University of Oxford. http://www.empro.gov.lk/main.php?pid=About

Institute of Policy Studies (2008). *Sri Lanka-State of the Economy.* Colombo, Sri Lanka: Institute of Policy Studies.

IOM (2000). *Temporary Labour Migration of Women: Case Studies of Bangladesh and Sri Lanka.* International Organization for Migrants.

———. (2008). *World Migration: Managing Labour Mobility in the Evolving Global Economy.* International Organization for Migration. pp.92-93.

Lasagabaster, Esperanza, S.M. Maimbo and S. Hulugalle (2005). *Sri Lanka's Migrant.*

Lasagabaster, Esperanza, Samuel Munzele Maimbo and Sriyani Hulugalle (2005a). "Sri Lanka's Migrant Labor Remittances: Enhancing the Quality and Outreach of Rural Remittance Infrastructure", *Policy Research Working Paper* 3789. Washington, DC: World Bank.

Maimbo, S.M. (2004). Proceedings of the Seminar on *Current Development in Monetory and Financial Low: The Regulation and Supervision of Informal Remittance System*. November.

Ministry of Foreign Employment Promotion & Welfare (2008). *National Labour Migration Policy for Sri Lanka*. Colombo: Ministry of Foreign Employment Promotion & Welfare.

Orozco, M. (2003). "Worker Remittances: A International Comparison", *Working Paper*, Multilateral Investment Fund of the Inter-American Development Bank.

Rosenbaum, P. and D. Rubin (1983). "The Central Role of the Propensity Score in Observational Studies for Causal Effects", *Biometrika* 70: 41-55.

Siegel, M. and M. Lucke (2009). "What Determines the Choice of Transfer Channel for Migrant Remittances: The Case of Moldova", *Kiel Working Paper* No. 1515.

World Bank (2006). *Global Economic Prospects: Economic Implication of Remittances and Migration*. Washington: DC: World Bank.

———. (2008). *Sri Lanka: Addressing the Needs of an Aging Population*. Washington, DC: World Bank.

Appendix A-12.1

Impact Assessment at the Household Level

Unlike in a controlled experiment, where individuals are randomly assigned to treatment and control groups, individuals on their own make the decision to migrate. As a result, comparing indicators of migrant households (households with at least one migrant worker) to those of non-migrant households (households with no migrant workers), as a means of assessing the impact of migration, will result in biased outcomes. This is because, the characteristics of migrant households could be different from those of non-migrant households, and these differences will affect their behaviour patterns. Hence the difference between comparison indicators may be due to other factors that are not related to migration or remittances. Furthermore, remittances are not likely to be an exogenous transfer but rather a substitute for the home earnings that migrants would have had if they had not decided to leave their countries to work abroad. Thus, estimating the impact of migration and remittances on household welfare would require taking into consideration the counterfactual income that the household would have had if the migrant had stayed at home.

One way of estimating causal effect is matching. The idea is to find households that have no migrant workers that is virtually identical to the household based on relevant characteristics that has a migrant worker. This method tries to imitate a randomised experiment by creating a control group that is similar to the migrant households through matching. This study uses propensity score matching to create this control group as described below.

Propensity Score Matching (PSM)

In PSM, the characteristics of each household are summarised by an index variable, the propensity score. This score is then used for match each migrant household with a non-migrant household based on the propensity score (Rosenbaum and Rubin, 1983; Dehejia and Wahba, 1998). The selected non-migrant households are then treated as the control group. It should also be noted that since matching can only be done through observable characteristics, unobservable factors are not controlled for in the analysis.

The use of PSM estimators to correct for self-selection relies on the assumption that there exists a set of observable conditioning variables (X), for which the non-migration outcome (Y) is independent of migration status (M).

In other words, PSM assumes that there is a set of observable conditioning variables that capture all the relevant differences between the treated and the control groups so that the non-treatment outcome is independent of treatment status, conditional on those characteristics.

The PSM[40] methodology applied here consists of the following steps.

1. Migrant and non-migrant households are pooled together. After the pooling, a probit model is estimated to ascertain the probability of migration as given below.
   $P(M=1) = \beta_0 + \beta_1 Z + \varepsilon$
   Where Z is the vector of explanatory variables
   M representing the probability to be a migrant household
2. The parameters of the estimated probit model are used to calculate the propensity score, that is, the predicted probability of being a migrant household, based on the observed characteristics included in the model.
3. Using the estimated propensity score, each migrant household is matched with the nearest non-migrant household, using the 'nearest neighbour' matching procedure with replacement. This method is usually applied with replacement in the control units.[41]
4. Checks for potential biases in the counterfactual income estimates are undertaken by testing for 'balance' and 'common support' after matching.
5. Finally the Average Treatment Effect on the Treated (ATT) is obtained as the average of all these differences.

Data and Empirical Evidence

Consumer Finance Survey (CFS), 2003-04 data, conducted by Central Bank of Sri Lanka was used in the analysis. 11,722 households were surveyed and Table A-12.1 shows the composition of the sample in terms of whether the household has a migrant or not. In total, around 6 % of households have at least one migrant member in their family.

---

40. "psmatch2" procedure in STATA developed by Edwin Leuven and Barbara Sianesi [2003], as a user-supplied routine in STATA.

41. Stata Documentation for the psmatch2 command, *http://fmwww.bc.edu/RePEc/usug2001/psmatch.pdf*

Table A-12.1

Distribution of Households by Household Migrants Status

Household	*Frequency*	*%*
Non-migrant households	11,067	94
Migrant households	655	6
Total	11,722	100

Source: Own calculations.

PSM procedure outlined in methodology section is applied to identify impact of migration on the household welfare of the emigrants. The first step in the empirical exercise is the estimation of the propensity score, that is, the estimation of the propensity to be treated, where the treatment is having a migrant member in family. Therefore, the dependent variable is one if the household has a migrant member and zero otherwise. It also includes the explanatory variables as given in table A-12.2.

Table A-12.2

Description of Explanatory Variables

Variable	*Variable Description*
Location	Dummy variables to represent the location- district of the household
Economic status of the head of the household	Dummy variables to represent regular worker, casual worker, self-employed, unemployed or not in labour force
Ethnicity	Dummy variable to represent head of the household Sinhalese or not
Family structure	Dummy variable to represent extended family or nuclear family
Community unemployment rate	Average community unemployment rate
Community migrant rate	Community variable measuring the average number of migrants from each community household

Source: Own calculations.

Table A-12.3 shows that results of the probit analysis with the relevant significance level for each explanatory variable. Most variables have the expected signs: head of household is not in labour force, extended family structure, and where there is higher community migrant rate, are more likely to have a migrant member than other types of households.

Table A-12.3

Migration Probit Model Results

Variable	*Coeff.*	*Std. Err.*	*P>z*
Economic status of head of the household			
Regular			
Casual	0.340	0.043	0.000
Self employed	0.436	0.042	0.000
Unemployed	0.158	0.122	0.195
Not in LF	0.805	0.042	0.000
Extended family	0.310	0.027	0.000
Sinhalese	-0.303	0.031	0.000
District			
Colombo MC			
Colombo other	0.160	0.075	0.034
Gampaha	0.237	0.072	0.001
Kalutara	0.227	0.076	0.003
Matale	0.178	0.090	0.048
Galle	0.151	0.081	0.064
Kurunegala	0.231	0.072	0.001
Anuradhapura	0.266	0.081	0.001
Ratnapur	-0.266	0.109	0.015
Kegalle	0.142	0.084	0.093
Community unemployment rate	0.001	0.001	0.231
Community migrant rate	0.203	0.004	0.000
Constant	-2.549	0.074	0.000

Note : Insignificant districts are not presented in the table

Source: Own calculations.

The problem of 'imbalance' can occur when assignment of treatment is not random, and large differences in the distribution of characteristics between the treated (migrant) and the control (non-migrant) groups can be expected. An important part of the PSM procedure is to achieve balance in the distribution of observables between the two groups such that the distribution of observable covariates is approximately the same for both groups after matching. 'pstest'[42]

42. Calculates several measures of the balancing of the variables before and after matching.

for equality of means is used for balancing check and mean comparisons are given before and after matching in Table A-12.4.

Table A-12.4

Covariate Statistics Before and After Matching

	Before Matching			*After Matching*		
Variable	*Treated*	*Control*	*p>t*	*Treated*	*Control*	*p>t*
Economic status of head of the household						
Regular	0.06	0.17	0.0	0.06	0.07	0.6
Casual	0.24	0.29	0.0	0.24	0.25	0.3
Self employed	0.32	0.37	0.0	0.32	0.34	0.3
Unemployed	0.01	0.01	0.1	0.01	0.01	0.3
Not in LF	0.37	0.16	0.0	0.37	0.34	0.0
Extended family	0.23	0.14	0.0	0.23	0.23	0.7
Sinhalese	0.63	0.78	0.0	0.63	0.65	0.1
District						
Colombo MC	0.04	0.03	0.0	0.04	0.02	0.0
Colombo other	0.07	0.08	0.1	0.07	0.08	0.1
Gampaha	0.12	0.11	0.0	0.12	0.12	0.8
Kalutara	0.07	0.06	0.1	0.07	0.07	0.3
Kandy	0.06	0.07	0.1	0.06	0.05	0.1
Community unemp rate	9.27	8.66	0.0	9.30	9.60	0.2
Community migrant rate	5.10	1.19	0.0	5.07	5.12	0.5

Source: Own calculations.

Following the PSM procedure the estimated coefficients from the two probit models were used to calculate, for each household, the predicted probability of it being a migrant household, and then each migrant household was matched with the nearest non-migrant household, using the 'nearest neighbour' matching procedure, with replacement. Then to compute the ATT, the counterfactual outcome of the migrant household has been estimated by imputing to it the observed outcome of the nearest non-migrant household. Moreover, in order to make the working sample even more comparable, common support procedure is adopted, that is, the area where there are enough of both, control and treatment observations, to proceed with the comparisons. This also means that treatment or control observations are excluded, that do not have comparable values in the other group.

Table A-12.5

Results

Outcome Variable	*Treated*	*Controls*		*P-value (Difference between Treated and Matched Control Group)*
		Unmatched	*Matched*	
Observations	(2,771)	(47,774)	(2,771)	
Total expenditure	247,664	198,157	209,396	0.00
Food expenditure	95,136	82,805	82,103	0.00
Non-food expenditure	116,566	89,231	87,522	0.00
Durable goods	19,908	13,935	28,890	0.04
Health expenditure	8,901	7,138	6,607	0.00
Education expenditure	7,152	5,048	4,273	0.00
Income from properties	16,642	12,692	12,091	0.00
Household financial assets	7,361	4,001	3,652	0.01
Household physical assets	107,835	25,645	9,220	0.00
Morbidity rate age <=14	0.1	0	0.1	0.69
School enrollment age>=5 & <=14	0.9	1	0.9	0.12

Source: Own calculations.